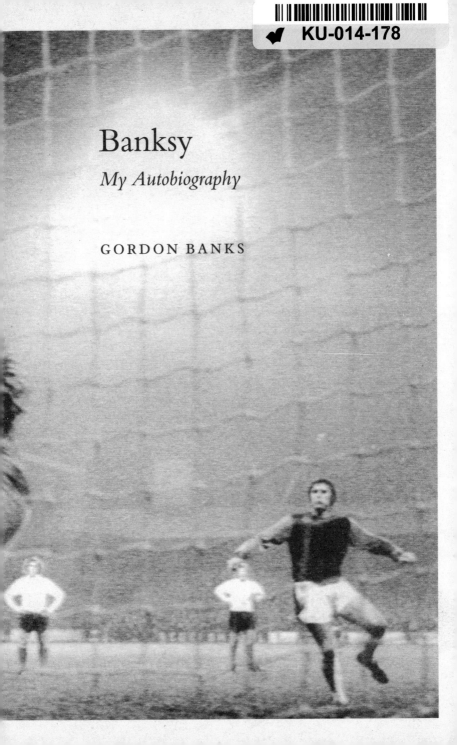

Banksy

My Autobiography

GORDON BANKS

PENGUIN BOOKS

UK | USA | Canada | Ireland | Australia
India | New Zealand | South Africa

Penguin Books is part of the Penguin Random House group of companies
whose addresses can be found at global.penguinrandomhouse.com.

First published by Michael Joseph 2002
Revised edition published in Penguin Books 2003
1

Set in 11/13 pt Monotype Bembo
Typeset by Rowland Phototypesetting Ltd, Bury St Edmunds, Suffolk
Printed and bound in Great Britain by Clays Ltd, Elcograf S.p.A.

ISBN: 978-1-405-94320-8

www.greenpenguin.co.uk

MIX
Paper from
responsible sources
FSC
www.fsc.org   FSC® C018179

Penguin Random House is committed to a
sustainable future for our business, our readers
and our planet. This book is made from Forest
Stewardship Council® certified paper.

PENGUIN BOOKS

BANKSY

Gordon Banks, OBE, was born in Sheffield in 1937. He made a record-breaking seventy-three appearances for England and was a member of the team that won the World Cup in 1966. He passed away in 2019.

My autobiography is dedicated to my family – Ursula my wife and the love of my life; our children Robert, Julia and Wendy; and our grandchildren, Matthew, Edward, Daniel, Eleanor and Elizabeth.

Contents

Illustrations

PICTURE CREDITS

Empics, 12; 15; 22; 23; 27; 28; 35; 40; 41; Colorsport, 14; 17; 24; 26; 34; 36; 37; Getty Images, 16; 25; 43; 44; Popperfoto, 20; 21; 31; 33; J. C. Thompson & Co. Ltd, 29; Chris Morphet, 30; Sporting Pictures, 32; Sentinel Newspapers, 38; H. W. Kokowski, 42; Mirrorpix.com, 45; NI Syndication, 46; Steve Merzer, 48.

Every effort has been made to trace copyright holders and we apologize in advance for any unintentional omission. We would be pleased to insert the appropriate acknowledgement in any subsequent edition.

Acknowledgements

I would like to express my sincere thanks to the following people, all of whom have helped significantly in the production of my autobiography:

Julian Alexander and all at my literary agents Lucas Alexander Whitley; Barclays Bank plc, in particular Janice Hallam at Stafford; George and Alex Best; Ken and Jean Bolam; Chesterfield FC; Terry Conroy; Jimmy Greaves; Trevor Horwood; Roger Hunt; Sir Geoff Hurst; the staff of the *Leicester Mercury*; Leicester City FC, in particular club historians Dave Smith and Paul Taylor, authors of *Of Fossils and Foxes*; Simon Lowe; Manchester United plc, in particular Mike Maxfield; Jackie Marsh; Arthur Montford; Don Mackay; the staff of the Sheffield *Star*; Huston Spratt; Stoke City FC; Martin Taylor; Steve and Deborah Waterall; Rowland White and all at Michael Joseph.

For Sal, Lauren and Ruby.

A Note to Les Scott

My sincere thanks go to Les Scott for his invaluable assistance in writing this book. Les contributes regularly to the Stoke *Sentinel* and the *Bristol Evening Post*, has written extensively for TV and wrote the screenplay for the film *The Rose Of Tralee*.

He collaborated with George Best, Gareth Chilcott and Sir Stanley Matthews on their respective autobiographies, and when I made the decision to write my own I had no hesitation in asking Les to lend a guiding hand.

Thanks, Les. It has been a privilege to work with you and great fun.

1. Family Matters

The mark of a good goalkeeper is how few saves he has to make during a game. A spectacular save is the last resort when all else – positioning, anticipation, defence – have failed. But saves are always what we are remembered for. There is one in my career that people always ask me about, it is seen as my greatest save – though not by me!

It was 1970 and England prepared to play Brazil in the World Cup, 1,500 metres above sea level under the relentless sun of Guadalajara. But the sweltering heat and lack of oxygen at such high altitude were the least of our concerns at the time. One man, bruised from Brazil's defeat four years earlier when they failed even to reach the quarter-finals, and intimating this would be his last World Cup, was determined to make it a swansong to remember. This was a man who could single-handedly affect the outcome of a game at the highest level. He was, of course, Pelé.

In Brazil's opening group match against a talented Czechoslovakian side, Pelé orchestrated the game from start to finish. Brazil won 4–1 and Pelé had been the hub around which every Brazilian move had turned. In that game he displayed a complete mastery of the ball, fantastic powers of acceleration, the cunning to veil his real intentions and the patience to bide his time before making his strike at the optimum moment. He kept the ball flowing, and his unselfishness brought his team mates into the picture time and again.

The England squad attended Brazil's opening game. I watched Pelé with concealed awe: his finely tuned balance, his incredible skill on and off the ball, and his uncanny ability to ghost into the right position at the right time. Once he played the ball it was as if he disappeared into the ether. The Czechs were taken up with trying to close down Jairzinho or Tostao, then, as if springing from a trapdoor, Pelé would suddenly appear in their penalty area to display his predatory skills to the full. The Czechs tried to put two, sometimes three, men on him, but such was his skill and technique that he always found the space to make the telling pass. Knowing Brazil were our next opponents I had sat and watched Pelé closely. By the end of the game I didn't think he was just a great player. I knew he was *the* great player. How could we stop him?

The opening ten minutes of England's match against Brazil are best described as footballing chess, with both sides sounding each other out. Brazil adopted a softly, softly approach. Consummate passers of the ball, they played it around among themselves at walking pace. Such precise passing meant that there was little we could do but watch. In the stifling heat and high altitude, to play a chasing game and try to close them down would have been suicidal. So we bided our time.

Then, just when I thought the game was settling down to a rolling, strolling classic, it suddenly exploded into life. Carlos Alberto played the ball out to Jairzinho on the Brazilian right. Jairzinho was a powerful, direct winger who could go through the gears like Michael Schumacher and cross the ball with Swiss-watch precision. I hit my toes as soon as I saw Jairzinho bearing down our left flank. We were caught on the hop. Bobby Moore had left Tostao free at the near post, Brian Labone was just outside our six-yard box, and Alan Mullery who had been pushing up, was sprinting back, anxiety creasing his face at the sight of Pelé heading towards our penalty box, unmarked.

When I saw Jairzinho arc around the ball, I knew the cross was coming. I moved two feet off my line, expecting him to cross to the penalty spot, in the belief that, since Pelé had now just entered our penalty area, I'd be first to the ball. Only Jairzinho didn't aim for the penalty spot. He whipped the ball across to a point just outside my six-yard box, a yard or so in from my right-hand post.

As I turned my head I saw Pelé again. He'd made ground fast and such was the athleticism of the man, he'd already launched himself into the air. Sidestepping on my toes, I covered the ground to my right and was only two or three paces off the centre of goal when Pelé met that ball with the meat of his head. As an attacking header, it was textbook stuff. He rose above the ball and headed it hard and low towards my right-hand corner. The moment the ball left his head I heard Pelé shout, '*Golo!*'

Faced with a situation like that, your mind becomes clear. All your experience and technique takes over. The skills I had acquired through countless hours of practice and study had become what psychologists call 'overlearned', or, in layman's terms, second nature. I suddenly found myself at a forty-degree angle with my right hand stretching out toward the post, my eyes trained on the quickly descending ball. One thing did flash through my mind: If I do make contact, I'll not hold this. Instinct, over-learning, call it what you will – I knew that if I made contact with the ball, I had to get it up in the air. That way Pelé, following up, would not be afforded a tap-in at my expense. The ball hit the deck two yards in front of me. My immediate concern was how high it would bounce. It left the turf and headed toward my right-hand corner, but I managed to make contact with the finger of my gloved right hand. It was the first time I'd worn these particular gloves. I'd noticed that the Mexican and South American goalkeepers wore gloves that were larger than their British counterparts, with palms covered in dimpled rubber. I'd been so impressed with this innovation that I'd invested in two pairs. Those little rubber dimples did their stuff: the bouncing ball didn't immediately glance off my hand and I was able to scoop it high into the air. But another thought flashed through my mind. In directing the ball upwards, I might only succeed in flicking it up into the roof of the net. So I rolled my right hand slightly, using the third and fourth fingers as leverage.

I landed crumpled against the inner side netting of the goal, and my first reaction was to look out at Pelé. I hadn't a clue where the ball was. He'd ground to a halt, head clasped between his hands, and I knew then all that I needed to know. With the luck of the gods, the angle at which I'd managed to lift that ball was perfect, and it had ballooned in the air and over the bar, out of harm's way for a corner.

As I got to my feet Pelé, ever the great sportsman, came up to me and patted me on the back.

'I thought that was a goal,' he said, smiling.

'You and me both,' I replied.

The TV footage of the game shows me laughing as I turn to take up my position for the corner. I was laughing at what Bobby Moore had just said to me.

'You're getting old, Banksy,' he quipped, 'you used to hold on to them.'

Like hell I did.

When the wind blew in the direction of our terraced house in Ferrars Road, it was the only time you never saw washing hanging out on the line. At the end of our street ran the main Sheffield to Rotherham road, on the opposite side of which stood Peach and Towser's steelworks. The works stretched for nigh on a mile and a half and what I remember most about it was the smell: an acrid mix of fired coal, sulphur-tainted steam and human sweat. Even when the wind wasn't blowing in our direction, the smell was ever present. When it did blow our way the washing was brought indoors because the cosy rows of terraced houses were immediately coated in a film of raven-black soot.

On such days I can recall drawing comic faces in the grime that coated our windowsills. Washing windows and paintwork was a constant job in the Tinsley area of Sheffield where I grew up. My mother seemed to spend half her life with a bucket of water and wash leather in her hands. But it was a thankless and never-ending task, like painting the Forth Bridge.

And when the soot descended it found its way inside every

house no matter how tight the doors and windows were shut, and settled like a blanket over everything. This was part of Sheffield life in the 1940s. No one complained, least of all my mother. No one could remember it being any different. No one worried about the danger to health of this air pollution because we had never been told it was a problem. We lived in ignorant harmony with the smell and the soot, because they were simply the by-products of what everyone aspired to – work. My dad worked in a steel foundry. My mother, or so it appeared to me, divided her time between cooking and washing. I was the youngest of their four sons, the others being David, Michael and John. John was always referred to as Jack, though in truth it was always 'Our Jack', a term of endearment that was always a source of bewilderment to me as a small boy, as I could never fathom why it was needed. 'Our Jack has eaten all his cabbage,' Mam would say, as if to identify which Jack she was talking about.

Dad didn't earn much and, with six mouths to feed, money was always tight for us, as it was for all the other families in our neighbourhood. Tinsley folk may have been poor, but they were proud. I remember one Sunday lunchtime, a man from across the road appearing at his door to sharpen a carving knife on the front step, to try and make the rest of us believe they could afford a Sunday roast. He might have succeeded, too, had it not been for the incongruous smell of fish frying, as out of place on the street on a Sunday lunchtime as we children being allowed to play out. Fish was plentiful and cheap then, and that's all the poorest could afford.

In the forties Tinsley families moved house rarely, if ever. Co-habiting for unmarried couples was unheard of. It was unheard of for couples to set up home together before they were married. That done, the vast majority stayed put until the time came for their children to call the funeral director. There were no nursing homes, no managed flats for the elderly. A house was bought or rented and turned into a home. At various times it was also a nursery (though we didn't use the term 'nursery'), a hospital, a function room and in the vast majority of cases, in the end, a chapel of rest for those who had purchased the house in the first place.

People occupied the same house for such a long time that it seemed to seep into their being, each home, internally and externally, taking on the character of its occupants. From either end of Ferrars Road the terraced houses all looked the same, but I soon learned the subtle individualities of each one. It was the owners' small touches – usually the mother's – that gave them their identities. The highly polished brass letter-box on the front door of the Coopers'; the pristine gold-leaf house number on the fanlight over the front door of the Dobsons' (I had no idea why this number should have survived intact when all the others had become mottled and flaked with age); the net curtains in the front window of the Barbers', gathered rather than hanging straight as in every other home; the red glass vase, no more than four inches high, that balanced precariously on the narrow window ledge in the Archers' front window.

I never saw this vase containing flowers (they would have had to have been very small). Fresh flowers were a rarity in our home as they were in every other house. In the summer Mam would occasionally give me a threepenny bit and send me down to the allotments to ask one of the owners, 'Have you got any chrysanths you don't want?' Chrysanths – that was all the steelmen who worked the allotments seemed to grow in the way of flowers. With their football-like blooms and tall stems these flowers dominated the small living rooms of the houses they fleetingly graced. It was as if, having been denied fresh flowers for the best part of a year, these allotment owners thought, 'What's the point in growing small, delicate flowers that will have little impact in a room? If we're going to have flowers, let's grow them big enough for everyone to see and marvel at.' I only heard their full name, chrysanthemums, when I was in my late teens. True, chrysanths runs off the tongue a lot easier but, looking back, there might have been another reason for our constant use of the shortened version of the name. To have called these flowers by their full and correct name would have invited accusations of trying to get above your station. 'Chrysanthemum' sounds Latin, something only posh kids learned. In Sheffield in the forties such class distinction was as clearly drawn by the working class as it was by the middle and upper classes.

Furniture and the wireless apart, what possessions people did have took the form of such trinkets. The red glass vase in the Archers' front window was typical of the ornaments that used to decorate every conceivable surface in the home, including the walls, where lines of brightly coloured plaster ducks, of decreasing size, seemed to fly up the wall in a desperate bid for freedom. Being plaster ornaments, of course, they never moved. Just like many of the people whose homes they graced.

For a young Tinsley lad, the only escape from a lifetime of work in the steel foundry or pit, was sport, mainly football and boxing. Cricket then was still the domain of the gentleman player and professionals were few and far between. I had three childhood passions, the most important of which was football. In those days it was quite common to watch both the Sheffield teams, Wednesday and United, on alternate Saturdays. With money short, however, I rarely got the chance to see either. In fact, between the age of seven and fifteen, I reckon I saw no more than twenty games at Wednesday or United, though counted myself lucky to have seen that many.

Tinsley County School was only a stone's throw from Tinsley railway shed, where steam trains were housed and serviced. At times there were up to fifty steam engines in there, each belching smoke and steam in competition with that from Peach and Towser's. The phrase 'Go outside and get some fresh air' was never heard from the teachers in my school.

The close proximity of the railway shed was a bonus to me, for my second passion was trainspotting. It's a hobby much ridiculed today, but in the forties, with no television, no computers and few toys, train spotting was a hobby taken up by most of the boys round our way. It cost next to nothing to get started. All you needed was Ian Allan's *ABC Spotters' Book*, a notebook and a pencil. I rarely ventured outside Tinsley and the sight of engines from other towns and cities always filled me with a sense of wonder. They may have come from distant Newcastle or London, or just Wakefield or Bradford. It didn't matter. Just seeing them evoked in me a feeling of travel, a consciousness of places I'd only heard of, or whose names I had only seen on a map. It was as if these faraway places had come to visit me. Though I never moved from my vantage point on that sooty brick wall a short walk from my home, I felt my horizons broaden.

At Tinsley shed my devotion to trains and football combined, for there was a class of locomotive named after famous football teams. I remember it always gave me a great thrill to see these particular engines. Names such as *Bradford City*, *Sunderland*, *Sheffield United* and *Everton* emblazoned above the centre wheel of the engine, with the arced nameplate bearing not only the club's colours but a half caseball made of shining copper. Many of these nameplates now adorn the reception areas of their respective clubs and to see them always brings back memories of my childhood at Tinsley County School.

For quite another reason, the close proximity of the railway shed was a boon to many Tinsley families, mine included. In the shed yard was a coaling stage, under which steam engines stopped to have their tenders replenished with coal. To one side of the coaling stage was a large stockpile of coal, a magnet to the many families on the breadline. Many was the time my mam would send me and one of my brothers down to Tinsley shed to procure coal for our fires in my old pram. We'd fetch the pram from our backyard shed under cover of darkness and push it to a well-known spot in the wooden fence that ran along one side of the shed yard. A number of fence panels had been loosened by countless others keen to put heat in their hearths, and it was simply a matter of my brother raising these panels to allow me and the pram through to the yard. Then my brother and I would walk up and down the sidings near the coaling stage on the look-out for windfall coal. (We never took it from the stockpile; Mam would have considered that to be stealing. Picking up stray lumps of coal that had fallen from a tender or spilled from the coaling stage during refuelling she considered to be no more than helping keep the engine shed yard tidy – a view not shared by the shed foreman.)

The pram was large and navy blue, with highly sprung, spoked wheels. We always had the hood down, because once the carriage of the pram had been filled with good-sized pieces of coal, we could always use the collapsed hood for any amount of smaller lumps. Fully laden, we'd then set off for home, nervously negotiating the rough ground back to the fence. A speedy exit from the shed yard was impossible as the heavy pram would constantly jerk and veer to either side whenever it came into contact with the many stones and bits of iron protruding from the ground. Quite often we had to leave with the pram only half full of coal as we were alerted by the beam of the foreman's torch bearing down on us from a hundred yards away. Once through the loose fence my anxiety lifted and I'd chirp away merrily to my brother, as we pushed our ill-gotten bounty along the smoother pavements back to Ferrars Road, only braving the cobblestones when we had to cross a street.

We'd come in by the backyard door and call to Mam in great triumph like hunters bringing home the kill. Mam, dressed in her 'pinny', would come out to cast an eye over what we had brought home, some pieces the size of a kettle, the small lumps, for making the fire up in the morning, safely stowed in the pram hood. Mam suitably satisfied, my brother and I would then unload the pram into the coalhouse, careful not to break the big lumps. I'd then wash my face and hands in the kitchen sink before changing into my pyjamas and enjoying a supper of toast made on a fork in front of a blazing fire, courtesy of the night's work.

We had no bathroom, the kitchen sink was where matters of personal hygiene were attended to in the form of a twice-daily wash. But Friday night was bath night. A tin bath was taken down from its hook in the shed, placed on newspaper in front of the living-room fire and laboriously filled by Dad with kettles of hot water. First to go was Dad, then Our Jack, then David, Michael and finally, the youngest – me. Being the fifth user of the same bathwater, it's a wonder I didn't get out dirtier than when I went in. The Friday-night bath ritual was not restricted to the Banks household. Everyone I knew had just one bath a week. It was also the only time I changed my vest and underpants. I wince at the thought now, but that's how it was, for me, for every young lad I knew. There were no modern labour-saving appliances such as washing machines to switch on every day. Our clothes were washed every Monday, in the kitchen, with a poss tub and dolly, after which, Mam would hand-rinse everything and then put them all through a hand-operated wringer before hanging them out on the line to dry or, in the event of rain, on wooden clothes horses dotted around the living room. Come Tuesday they would be dry. On Wednesday they were ironed and then put away ready for us to wear again on Friday after our bath, and so the cycle was repeated. This was typical of the many domestic routines adhered to, week in, week out in our house. Mam's life must have been as monotonous as mutton, as regular as a roll on an army drum. That my childhood was always happy, secure and filled with a warm heart, though money was always tight, is all the more to her credit.

In the forties and fifties it was not done for parents and children to show each other outward signs of affection. I had a happy childhood, Mam and Dad were caring and, in their own way, loving, but never tactile or overtly affectionate. My family was not unusual in this. I never came across a family in which the parents hugged and kissed their children, or, devoted any considerable one-to-one time to their offspring. It just wasn't the done thing. Life was hard for the vast majority of families I knew, a matter of daily survival. It was commonly believed that if children were showered with hugs and kisses at every opportunity they would grow up to be 'soft', incapable of coping with the daily grind of working life. By not hugging and kissing at every opportunity, parents believed they were doing their children a favour, instilling in them independence and the ability to cope with the rigours of adult life. Moreover, parents did not have free hours to spend playing with their children even at weekends, or to read to them before bedtime. Because the household chores were so labour intensive, the precious time Mam devoted to my three brothers and I, she did so while undertaking some aspect of housework. Mam would talk to us, acknowledge what we were doing and encourage us in our play while either washing, ironing, preparing a meal or attending to some other daily chore.

Dad, meanwhile, was no different to any other father in that he would come in from work and have his tea. Having satisfied himself that my brothers and I had been up to nothing untoward that day, he'd settle down to read the evening paper. Dad's time immersed in the *Sheffield Star* was sacrosanct. The Victorian notion of the male as head of the family was still very much in evidence and in order for Dad to evaluate and make decisions that affected family well-being, he felt he had to know what was going on in the world. Or, at least our world, which extended as far as the Sheffield boundaries. Gossip apart, his only source of information was the local evening newspaper and woe betide my brothers and I if we ever interrupted his reading of it.

Mam read the *Star* too, though always after Dad and usually when I was getting ready for bed. Mam and Dad reacted in different ways to what they read in the paper. When Dad disapproved of some item of news he would tut and sigh and usually conclude with the statement 'They want locking up,' or, in the case of something appalling such as a serious assault or murder, he would elaborate with 'They should lock them up and throw away the key.' As a small boy I believed that this was a genuine punishment administered by the courts, in which the judge would pronounce the grave sentence that the defendant be locked up and the key thrown away – whereupon the constable would suggest that the canal would be the best place for it. I still think of this when I hear or read this popular phrase.

In contrast, Mam's reading of the paper often appealed to her sentimental side. Such sentiment was invariably applied to the predicaments of people she had no knowledge of, and never would. Her interest in the lives of people entirely remote from her world was like the fascination today for the trials and tribulations of characters from TV soaps. The fact there were other people, rich and poor, enduring emotional upheaval in their lives on a day when she was not, was something of a comfort to her. 'I see the brother of the Earl of Harrogate has died,' Mam would say aloud on reading the piece, no doubt aware only then that there was indeed an Earl of Harrogate with a brother; 'there's always trouble for somebody in this world.' Thus she was confirmed in her belief that life was a sea of troubles.

That I always felt secure in childhood was, I am sure, in no small way due to the small routines of home life. On a Saturday lunchtime, for example, we always had fishcake and chips. Fish may well have been cheap and plentiful, but fishcakes were cheaper still and much more in keeping with a tight budget. It was my job to fetch the fishcake and chips and I did this on a bicycle that had more than a touch of Heath Robinson about it. To buy even a second-hand bicycle was beyond our means but when I was about twelve I cobbled together a contraption from spare parts found discarded on a bomb-site. The front wheel was missing many of its spokes, the brake blocks were worn down to the metal and the hard bakelite seat had a habit of swivelling around whenever I adjusted my position which made for not only an uncomfortable, but often perilous ride. It was on this conveyance that I collected our fishcake and chips on a Saturday.

There were two fish and chip shops in our neighbourhood,

but Dad always insisted I went to the one five streets from where we lived because the chips were fried in dripping. I'd ask for six fishcake 'lots' (i.e. 'with chips'), put them into my mother's string bag and pedal off home. Riding that old bike was a precarious business at the best of times; with a fully laden string bag swinging from the handlebars it was downright dangerous. Once the bag became entangled in what few spokes were in the front wheel. The bike immediately ground to a halt, stood vertically on its front wheel and I was pitched headfirst on to the cobblestones of the street, my hands outstretched in an attempt at breaking my fall. I had skinned the palms of my hands but, far worse, dinner was scattered all over the street. Terrified to go home and ask for more money I simply scooped up the fishcakes and chips off the ground and rewrapped them in the newspaper as best as I could before limping home. I spent that dinner suppressing nervous laughter as I watched Dad bemusedly picking little bits of grit off his chips. My brothers, less particular in their eating habits, simply wolfed their fishcake and chips with all the enthusiasm and relish of lads who seemingly hadn't seen food for a week.

That old bicycle again served me well on Saturday mornings when Mam would give me a shopping list and ask me to cycle to Tinsley Co-op to fetch the groceries. The shop was only in the next street but such was the grocery order, it was better to take the bike than walk as the numerous paper carrier bags full of bulky groceries could be hung from the handlebars and seat. The weekly order rarely varied: a pound of sugar; a pound of butter, not pre-packed but wire-cut from a large block then wrapped in greaseproof paper; plain and self-raising flour; bacon and sausage; three loaves of bread, two white, one brown; a dozen eggs; a drum of salt, either 'Cerebos' or 'Saxa', Co-op marmalade and jam; ginger snaps, rich tea or 'Nice' biscuits; Shippams meat paste for the making of sandwiches; Oxo cubes, Bisto, Echo margarine for baking; tinned fruit; Carnation milk; Heinz (sometimes Armour) baked beans; Ye Olde Oak luncheon meat and the only sort of salmon I knew existed – tinned (the

Co-op's own-brand variety, as John West salmon was out of our budget). There was a lot more, but that was the core of the order every Saturday morning, week in, week out, year after year. The lack of variety was testament to the limited choice available in a country still struggling in the aftermath of rationing. The fact that I was never bored by the food placed before me just goes to show how clever Mam was at using the limited ingredients at her disposal.

It is now a constant source of amazement to me that, with all her chores at home, Mam also had a part-time job as a cleaner-cum-cook up at the Big House, the home of the 'well to do' family of one of Sheffield's lesser steel magnates. I never saw inside the Big House nor glimpsed the family who owned it. The large Victorian house – rumoured to have seven bedrooms and (amazingly) a bathroom – was hidden from sight by a high, soot-blackened wall; the children went to different schools from ours; the parents never patronized the shops in Tinsley.

Mam's job took her into this different world, where she did 'a bit of cleaning and a bit of cooking'. She never talked about her work there or the people she worked for. I suppose she felt it her duty not to gossip, not to 'carry tales' as she called it. The family must have treated her well – she certainly wouldn't have stayed in that house if she hadn't been treated with respect. The only regular time Mam spent away from the daily chores of our house was when she went to do similar work in the Big House. Looking back, Mam's quality of life must have been pretty awful. Dad rarely took her out, even for an hour to the local pub. Our house was where Mam spent most of her adult life. That she made that draughty house a loving home full of warm smiles, is my abiding memory of her.

On Sunday lunchtimes Dad would invariably go off to the pub to meet his mates, leaving me to help Mam cook the Sunday dinner. The preparation of the Sunday roast was always done to the accompaniment of the wireless. I would shell the peas or, if we were having lamb, chop the mint. In those days we would have either lamb or beef – and that piece of meat would be made to last until Tuesday. Chicken then was still an expensive luxury, and we only ate turkey at Christmas.

At noon Mam would switch on the wireless for *Two Way Family Favourites*. On the rare occasion when I heard its title music, 'With a Song in my Heart', nowadays, I can immediately smell a Sunday dinner. The idea of the show was that everyone had a special song in their heart for someone they loved, whether they were in the forces overseas or had relatives who had emigrated. The programme was two way in that it linked a family at home with a loved one abroad. Two presenters in London were linked with colleagues in Cologne and Cyprus (places where our armed forces had a considerable presence) and later, when the programme expanded its remit to include the growing number of people who had emigrated from the UK, Toronto and Sydney.

This being a time of National Service, the show relied heavily on mothers requesting a current hit – usually one of sugary sentimentality sung by the likes of Dickie Valentine, Eddie Fisher, Vera Lynn and Alma Cogan – for their squaddie son. These requests usually ended with a plaintive message, along the lines of, '1954 is not too far away' – the given year usually being two years hence, the duration of National Service. The addresses of the squaddies were always announced as care of their British Forces overseas posting number: BFPO 271 Cologne, BFPO 32 Cyprus, BFPO 453 Gibraltar – code words for faraway places that were a mystery to me, other than that it was where soldiers lived.

This weekly reminder to the nation that Britain still had a military presence abroad, served to maintain the misplaced notion that we were still a major power in world affairs when, in truth, the days of the Empire were long gone.

BBC radio, though changing, still managed to convey a sense of a past in which class distinction was prevalent. This was exemplified by *Family Favourites*, the presenters of which had plummy voices that set them apart from me and everyone I knew. Presenters such as Cliff Michelmore, Muriel Young and Ian Fenner, while sounding sincere and never patronizing, were indicative of a system that didn't allow anyone from Tinsley, Attercliffe or any other area I was familiar with, to work as radio presenters. While some people may have been broadening their horizons through military postings abroad or emigration, the expectations of the Sheffield folk I knew still never extended beyond the steelworks or the pit. No one ever told us there was a world out there waiting for us too.

Family Favourites was followed by an hour of comedy, which I loved. First was the *Billy Cotton Band Show*, a mixture of amiable humour from Alan Breeze and Bill Herbert, novelty songs and danceband tunes from the veteran Billy Cotton Band. Billy always began his introduction to the programme by announcing the week's guests, such as pianist Russ Conway, then, more often than not, making some comic reference to a football match of the previous day. This was especially the case if England had played Scotland, as one of his resident singers was Kathy Kay, a Scottish lass with whom Billy would indulge in playful teasing if England had been triumphant. Billy's opening lines would then be interrupted by a heavenly voice shouting, 'Hey, you down there with the glasses . . . get orn wi' it.' Billy's response would be his catchphrase, 'Wakey! Wakey!' bellowed at the top of his voice, at which his band sprang into action by playing his signature tune, 'Somebody Stole My Girl', popularly known as 'Tan, tanner, rah, rah, rah . . .'

The *Billy Cotton Band Show*'s mix of variety show humour, from Alan Breeze and Bill Herbert, and well sung ballads was universally popular. The band members, seemed to me to be older than God; many of them, I was later to discover, were indeed getting on in years and had been with Billy since he first started his band back in 1925. The show always ended with a spectacular instrumental version of something like 'The Dambusters March' or 'On the Quarter Deck'. Even in variety shows we were constantly reminded of Britain's military past. In so doing, the myth of Britain still being a superpower was perpetuated in the minds of the people.

Billy's show was followed by another half hour of comedy. Series came and went over the years, but one of my favourites was the *Clitheroe Kid*. Jimmy Clitheroe was a man whose height was no more than that of a small boy, which was the character he played in the show. With his piping, precocious voice, Jimmy was full of mischief and a constant source of distress for his grandfather, played by Peter Sinclair, his sister (Diana Day) with whom he had a love-hate relationship, her goonish boyfriend, Alfie Hall (Danny Ross) and his long-suffering mother, played by Mollie Sugden. I loved listening to Jimmy's escapades and antics, and the fact that they took place in a working-class family, in the north of England, helped me to identify much more with this character than the *Just William* books about a mischievous prep-school boy from the Home Counties.

People were nowhere near as sophisticated as nowadays and this was especially true where entertainment was concerned. Our gullibility in believing a man in his forties was actually a 13-year-old schoolboy was as nothing compared to our unquestioning acceptance of the concept of *Educating Archie*, a series that featured Peter Brough and his dummy, Archie Andrews. A ventriloquist on the radio!

When Dad got back from the pub we would all sit down to our first course: a large piece of Yorkshire pudding over which was poured a generous helping of Mam's wonderful gravy. After that Mam would serve the Sunday roast proper. As Dad carved the beef or lamb, Mam would place before me a plate comprising carrots, potatoes, both boiled and roasted, and other vegetables (fresh, never tinned) of the season: in mid-winter, sprouts and turnip, in spring, cabbage and cauliflower, in summer, new potatoes and baby carrots. Autumn would bring parsnips and butterbeans, though there always seemed to be peas, carrots and cabbage of some description. Broccoli I never knew existed, still less mangetout or courgettes. As for spinach, I'd only seen that in Popeye cartoons.

Sunday dinner was the highlight of the week and Mam always followed it with one of her homemade rice puddings for 'sweet' (not dessert). This was served piping hot in a white pudding bowl, the rice topped with a milky skin sprinkled with nutmeg, over which my brothers and I would squabble as we could never agree on whose turn it was to have this treat. Heavy, sweet puddings 'saw you off', in Dad's words. He would not have appreciated a light dessert such as mousse, trifle or ice cream. The alternative to rice would be sago (which my brothers and I used to joke looked like frogspawn but, in keeping with every-thing Mam made, tasted delicious), tapioca or semolina – the latter always accompanied by a large dollop of strawberry jam dropped in the centre which, when stirred in with a spoon, turned the white porridge-like pudding, shocking pink. Dad would then complete his Sunday dinner by eating the rest of the Yorkshire pudding, over which he would spread a spoonful of strawberry jam. I never knew whether our neighbours Mr Cooper or Mr Dobson had similarly quirky eating habits to be indulged in the privacy of their own homes.

Life in Sheffield ground to a halt on a Sunday afternoon, as I suppose it did in every other provincial city and town. I would spend that quiet few hours playing in the street, on the bomb sites, or else listening to the wireless, until teatime, when another ritual arrived at our table. The Sunday salad.

We always had a salad for Sunday tea. After the treat of the roast dinner, tea was a great anticlimax: limp lettuce, totally without flavour, tomatoes, spring onions and cucumber when in season, all accompanying boiled egg cut into slices, luncheon meat or, the perennial favourite, Co-op tinned salmon. This drab meal – a sure sign that Monday was just around the corner – was followed by its only redeeming feature, a dish of tinned pears, peaches or apricots with Carnation milk. Probably in the know-ledge that a salad would hardly fill the stomachs of her four livewire boys, Mam always made us eat a slice of bread and butter to fill us up. It was as if, along with the sinful pleasures of tinned fruit in its glorious syrup and Carnation milk must come the inevitable repentance of sliced white bread and a scrape of butter.

Looking back, while all our meals were home cooked and nourishing, I also ate a lot of things that are now considered unhealthy: bread and dripping, chips, fatty bacon and chops. Yet I never put on weight because I was always playing and running about outside, where the bomb sites were my adventure playgrounds and a piece of cinder-strewn wasteground was Bramall Lane or Hillsborough. I was no different to any other raggy-arsed lad in this respect.

We ate well, but money was tight. Even the purchase of shoes was considered a luxury. Dad was always thinking of ways to make what little money he earned at the steel foundry go further. It may have been an anachronism in 1940s Sheffield, but I wore clogs to school to which my father, in an attempt to extend their life, had fixed steel bars across the soles. You might have thought that going to school in such old-fashioned footwear would make me the butt of childish mockery. Far from it. My clogs made me very popular, since teams of two schoolmates would take me by the hand and drag me across the school playground to see who could make the greatest number of sparks fly. Perhaps my exceptional reach as a goalkeeper was the result of being constantly pulled by the arms about that playground.

Football and train spotting apart, the other great love of my childhood was the cinema. In those days before television, every area of the city had its own cinema and I reckon there must have been more than twenty in Sheffield alone. Our local fleapit, situated next to Tinsley Working Men's Club, rejoiced in the name of the Bug Hut. There I would sit spellbound on a Saturday afternoon, the main feature being either a Gene Autry or Roy Rogers cowboy film, or a comedy starring the likes of Arthur Askey, George Formby or Old Mother Riley. The matinees would be packed with row upon row of grimy kids. In winter the boys wore balaclavas or cub caps on their heads, raincoats buttoned to the collar over short trousers, the girls in pixie hoods, cotton dresses and grey knee-length socks. All pals together.

My oldest brother, Jack, suffered chronic kidney problems and also had a bone-marrow defect that affected his legs. Jack never grew above five feet tall and for much of his childhood was confined to a wheelchair. I used to push him to and from the Bug Hut. When we arrived I would wheel Jack down to the front then take one of the sevenpenny seats some rows back. I remember on one occasion being so engrossed in the film that when it ended I headed straight home without him. When Mam asked me where our Jack was I ran hell for leather back in the direction of the Bug Hut. There he was, only fifty yards from the cinema and all alone, slowly cranking the wheels of his chair towards home. My eyes filled with tears when I saw him, but any sadness for his predicament quickly evaporated when he looked up and caught sight of me.

'Where the bloody hell have you been? You bloody daft ha'p'orth,' he bawled. He had a way with words, our Jack.

When I was about eleven years old, my dad, having had enough of working his fingers to the bone for a pittance, decided to branch out on his own. He left his job in the steel foundry, bought two ramshackle lorries and set up his own haulage business. He worked impossibly long hours but the business never really took off because those old lorries were forever breaking down. After only a few months, during which time Dad had spent more time with his head under the bonnets of those lorries than in the cabs, the business folded. Undaunted, he decided to launch a new business, one he knew plenty about – gambling. For a number of years Dad had supplemented his meagre income running an illegal book on horse racing. Licensed betting shops were still to come, the only legal place to bet in the late forties being the racetracks themselves. Given that most people I knew considered a trip from Tinsley into Sheffield City Centre a major journey, a day out at the races was virtually unheard of. Dad, knowing the steel workers liked a flutter, reckoned he was on to a winner opening up his own betting shop, and he wasn't wrong.

We moved from our Tinsley home to Catcliffe, a mining village on the Sheffield–Rotherham border. Our new house adjoined a series of railway arches. Dad decided one of the arches would be ideal for his 'flapper' betting shop so, by the light of the one dingy bulb, we cleared it out, cleaned it up and helped him install the spartan fittings he needed to get the shop started.

The business did well, but there was a risk in running an unlicensed betting shop. Fortunately, the local policeman who patrolled the village knew everyone and everyone knew him. Should we kids step out of line, he'd clip us around the ear, but we knew better than to run home and complain. To do that would have invited another, much harder clip around the ear from Dad. The local Bobby drank with Dad and the other men of the village, either miners or steel workers, in the working men's club. Many was the time, only a matter of an hour after doing so, he'd be called upon to bring peace to the home of one of his drinking pals as a result of what he would euphemistically call 'a domestic'.

I remember one day being in the betting shop when the Bobby called to inform Dad a raid was imminent.

'Let everyone know, Tom,' he told my dad. 'But make sure there are enough in, so as not to arouse suspicion.'

Such raids would result in a court appearance where Dad would get a ticking-off and a £40 fine. The shop would quickly recoup the money and Dad viewed these occasional court appearances as a small price to pay for our increased standard of living. In return for the tip-off the Bobby would make a Christmas detour to the shop where Dad would hand over a bottle of whisky and a large turkey that naturally had to be handed in as lost property.

The shop that did so well for us as a family, however, also

brought tragedy upon us. One day in the early fifties Dad had left my brother Jack in charge. Having closed up the shop, Jack was heading home with the day's takings when he was set upon by two robbers. In spite of his disability they beat him up badly and made off with the money. As a result of his injuries Jack spent weeks in hospital, his health deteriorated and, tragically, he died. He was a great guy, a loving brother and we were all devastated at his passing. Nothing – home, family, business – was ever the same again. For the first time in my life I experienced the loss of a loved one. I grieved for months, mourned his loss for years and miss him to this day.

That our Jack's assailants were eventually caught by the police and given lengthy jail sentences was no consolation to me for losing a dear brother and a great friend.

My childhood football heroes were always goalkeepers. On my infrequent visits to Hillsborough or Bramall Lane it was always the goalkeepers who captured my imagination. Keepers such as Wednesday's Dave McIntosh, a Girvan-born Scot whose centre parting was old-fashioned even in the early fifties, and United's Ted Burgin, a Sheffield lad like me and my inspiration that one day I too would be good enough to play for one of my local clubs. McIntosh and Burgin apart, there was Manchester City's Bert Trautmann, unique in that he had been a German prisoner of war who had stayed on in Britain to make a career for himself in football. A worthy successor to the great Frank Swift, Bert had been signed from non-league St Helens Town and developed into one of the best goalkeepers of his day. I used to marvel at his anticipation, courage and agility, attributes also of another boyhood hero of mine, Bert Williams of Wolves and England, who proved to me that you didn't necessarily have to be tall to be a good goalkeeper. Another favourite was Blackpool's George Farm. In the fifties, Blackpool, boasting the great Stanley Matthews, Stan Mortensen and Jackie Mudie, were the equivalent of Manchester United today. Their appearance always

ensured a full house. Understandably, most turned up to see
Matthews weave his magic, but the attraction for me was George
Farm with his unorthodox style, catching the ball with one hand
over and the other underneath it. But what interested me was
the way he'd shout instructions to the defenders in front of him.
Farm took it upon himself to organize his defence, which was
very unusual for a goalkeeper at that time.

At the age of fourteen, my appearances in goal for my school
side earned me a call-up for Sheffield Schoolboys. I was thrilled
and honoured to have been chosen to represent my city, but my
memories of playing for Sheffield boys are tainted by the fact that
I was suddenly dropped without explanation after about seven
games. The teacher in charge of the team never told me why or
offered any words of consolation. In fact he never spoke to me
again. It wasn't in me to complain, so I simply accepted my lot
and concentrated on playing for my school until the day came
when I took that big step out into the adult world.

I wasn't a great scholar and on leaving school in December
1952 I got a job as a bagger with a local coal merchant. It was
dirty, hard, physical graft conducted in all weathers. My job
involved shovelling coal into large coarse sacks, swinging them
on my back from where I would heave them on to the back of
a lorry. Though I didn't appreciate it at the time, the work served
to make my upper body and arms muscular, which is a great
advantage for a goalkeeper.

I was fifteen, still developing physically, and the eight-hour
day bagging coal left me tired out by the weekend. I was still in
love with football, but by Saturday I felt too exhausted to do
more than watch the many amateur teams that played in our
area. (I was earning less than three pounds a week, and once I
had paid my mother board and lodging, there was little left for
trips to see United or Wednesday.) One Saturday afternoon I
wandered down to the local rec. to watch a team called
Millspaugh. I was standing on the touchline waiting for the
match to start when the Millspaugh trainer approached me.

'You used to play in goal for Sheffield Boys, didn't you?' he asked.

The Millspaugh goalkeeper hadn't turned up. Would I fancy a game?

My fatigue vanished and I immediately raced home to collect my football boots. The trainer gave me a goalkeeper's jersey, but no shorts or football socks – the players, it seemed, provided their own. It was too late to go back now, so I played in my working trousers and everyday socks. I still recall the bemused looks on the faces of my new team mates as a puff of coal dust shot up from those trousers as I blocked a shot with my legs.

The game ended in a 2–2 draw. I felt pleased with my first taste of open-age football. I was only fifteen and most of the players were in their middle to late twenties. I must have impressed the Millspaugh manager because after the game he asked if I would like to be their regular goalkeeper. Without hesitation I said yes.

After less than a season with Millspaugh, Rawmarsh Welfare invited me to sign for them. Rawmarsh played in the Yorkshire League which was a much higher grade of football. I made my debut in an away game against Stocksbridge Works. Any thought I may have had of making my name in what was then the highest non-league level of football in the county was quickly dispelled when we lost 12–2. Following a second game, a 3–1 home defeat, the Rawmarsh manager let me down gently, saying, 'Don't bother coming again.'

The following Saturday found me back on the touchline watching Millspaugh at the local rec. Once again the trainer approached me.

'Goalkeeper hasn't turned up. Fancy a game?'

Oddly enough, I did.

I had given up coal-bagging and started as an apprentice bricklayer with a local building firm. Much of my time as a rookie was spent hod-carrying for the experienced brickies, which was even harder graft than the coal-bagging. A lot of Sheffield's housing had been destroyed by Hitler's bombs and in the early fifties a massive rebuilding and slum-clearance programme had begun across the city. A lot of the old Victorian terraced houses were little more than slums and many of those that had survived Hitler's bombs, didn't survive the Government's initiative to provide better housing for the nation. Sheffield in the mid-fifties was like one massive building site. There was a shortage of skilled brickies; they were on piece work to keep them to the formidable work-rates required. The more bricks he laid, the more the brickie took home in his pay packet. As a young hod-carrier I had to load the V-shaped hod, lump that on my shoulder and scale two or three sets of ladders up the scaffolding. It was relentless, sweaty work. Having delivered the bricks, no sooner had I descended the ladders and returned to the brick 'fort' to reload, than the brickie would be screaming from up top for more. I was still only fifteen and knew better than to complain. In the run-up to Christmas the brickies, intent on earning more for their families, worked even faster. Health and safety considerations were non-existent. I never wore a hard hat on site. One day a falling brick gave me a mighty whack on the side of my head. I stopped midway down the ladder, blood streaming from a gashed temple. The brickie was very sympathetic. 'Get an effing move on!' he shouted. 'What an effing scene ower nowt. Yon brick was only on yer head for a second!'

They were hard men and hard task masters, those brickies, but they had hearts of gold. Come pay day, many was the time the brickie would slip me a few extra bob out of his own pay packet, as a tip for having serviced him so well and helping him make his piece-work bonus.

Like coal-bagging before it, hod-carrying made my upper body strong and muscular, while constantly running up and down ladders strengthened my legs. I may only have been in my mid-teens, but I was no scrawny, gangly youth.

★

I didn't recognize the man in the overcoat watching Millspaugh from the touchline. After the game he introduced himself as a scout from Chesterfield. He thought I might have some potential as a goalkeeper, and said he would like to give me a try-out in the Chesterfield youth team. There were six games left of the season and if I did well enough in those games, I might be offered terms.

Before that day, the thought of making my living as a professional footballer could not have been further from my mind. But now, this could be my chance.

2. Aspiring Spireite

Chesterfield were in the Third Division North, since at the time the two lower divisions of the Football League were regionalized. This system had been in operation since 1921, when the Football League was expanded to accommodate the growing number of full-time professional clubs. Because the country's infrastructure in the twenties was a network of largely minor roads, travel was both time-consuming and difficult. The Football League, in expanding its remit, decided to form two regionalized Third Divisions with a view to keeping travel time and costs to a minimum. By and large this system worked well, though there were certain clubs, Chesterfield being one, whose geographical position meant they were 'borderline' and often the system did them no favours. It was a long and expensive trip for Chesterfield to Gateshead, Workington or Carlisle; whereas Walsall, Coventry and Northampton, although much nearer, operated in the Third Division South. Likewise, those three clubs had to travel to Plymouth, Torquay, Exeter and Gillingham in the extreme south-west and south-east corners of England.

Chesterfield were considered a small club, but even so enjoyed an average attendance of around 9,000, twice that of today. While they played in the northern section of the then regionalized Third Division, the reserves played in the Central League and the youth team in the Northern Intermediate League. Both these competitions were very strong and invariably, Chesterfield found themselves scrubbing about near the foot of both. The Central League was the premier reserve league for the top teams in the north of England. In this era before substitutes, clubs such as Manchester United, Liverpool, Everton, Blackpool and Newcastle fielded very strong teams week in week out; if a player had not made the first XI at his club, he played in the Central League side. So it was not uncommon to line up against players with a great deal of First Division and even international experience.

In truth, Chesterfield should never have been members of the Central League, the standard of play being way beyond many of the club's second-string players. Chesterfield were the perennial whipping boys, they usually finished bottom of the table and their continued membership of this league was puzzling, especially as the reserve teams of much bigger clubs such as Sunderland and Middlesbrough were forever having their applications to join this league turned down. However, I soon realized why the reserve team were immune from relegation to a lower standard of football: one of the Chesterfield directors was a key member of the Central League Management Committee! Similarly, the Chesterfield youth team played in the highly competitive Northern Intermediate League, alongside the under-nineteen teams from Newcastle United, Sunderland, Middlesbrough, both Sheffield clubs, Leeds and Wolverhampton Wanderers.

My sights were set no higher than a place in the Chesterfield youth team when I first arrived at Saltergate one rainswept evening at the end of March 1953. I'd been told to report to the ground at 6.30 p.m. for training, and found myself getting changed alongside around eighteen young amateurs and part-time professionals.

Chesterfield were one of the few clubs to possess a gymnasium but any thoughts I may have had of working out on wall bars and practising my goalkeeping technique by diving around on crash mats, quickly evaporated.

The 'gym' turned out to be a small cellar-like space underneath the sloping grandstand, no more than twenty-five feet by twelve. Its ceiling was a network of steel girders supporting the grandstand seating above. From one girder hung a plank of wood on a rope. This was for sit-ups. There were two old household mats on which players did press-ups, a short bench and a set of weights. A medicine ball was suspended from a girder above another sloping plank of wood, the purpose of which was never clear to me in all the time I was there. Finally, there was a boxer's punchball, suspended from another girder. It wasn't what Arsenal were used to, but with eighteen players working away in such a confined place, that little gym was a sweatbox. After an hour in there, you would definitely shed a few ounces whether you were working out or just watching.

Pummelling the punchball seemed at first to be an odd sort of football training. However, the trainer set me to work on it and in time I had not only strengthened my wrists, hands and arm muscles, but also improved my sense of timing and co-ordination. In later life, when jumping up above a knot of players to punch a ball clear, I rarely missed, and got good distance. I am sure those early workouts in the Chesterfield gym were the reason.

As I had been promised, I was picked to play in all six Northern Intermediate games left in the season. I must have done something right because I was asked to report back for pre-season training in July 1953. When I did, the manager Ted Davison offered me a contract as a part-time professional player. I was to train at the club on Tuesday and Thursday evenings and play for whichever team I was selected for on the Saturday, for which I would be paid £3 a week. On signing the contract I was ecstatic. I may only have been a part-time player for a Third Division North club, but I couldn't have been happier if I'd been offered full terms with Manchester United. I had been signed by a Football League club and saw this as a first step to a career in football. The day I signed for Chesterfield was the day I allowed myself to dream.

I was so enthusiastic that the thrice-weekly travelling to Chesterfield never bothered me. After a hard day on the building site I would rush home, eat a sandwich, collect my training kit and be out of the door in fifteen minutes flat. I had to be quick because the journey to Saltergate involved a bus from my home in Catcliffe into Sheffield city centre, another bus to Chesterfield, then either catch yet another bus or embark on a brisk walk to the ground. Today many youngsters won't turn up for training or a game at a club unless they are given a lift. The thought of making their own way to training or a match on public transport appears anathema to them. Not to me. As I sat on the bus to Chesterfield, I felt full of anticipation about this new love of my life.

My performances for the Chesterfield youth team earned me a promotion to the A team, then the reserves. I'd allowed myself to dream but the reality of the Central League woke me up with a jolt. Chesterfield Reserves, a team of hopeful young semi-professionals and amateurs, bolstered by two or three full-time professionals who had not been chosen for the first team, were meat and drink to just about every team we came up against. More often than not, Chesterfield Reserves conceded over a hundred goals a season. In 1954–55, for example, we finished bottom with just three wins to our name. I conceded 122 goals in 42 games, an average of three per game; we lost quite often by four or five clear goals, sometimes more. Without putting too fine a point on it, I was a very busy goalkeeper. However, I'd like to think that, for all we conceded one hundred plus goals a season, my efforts prevented it from being even more.

In spite of the constant hammering, my enthusiasm never wavered. I loved playing in goal, especially in the Central League where just about every week I'd come face to face with a hero of mine. Against Leeds United I faced the great John Charles who was having a run out with the reserves on his way back from injury. Known as the Gentle Giant, John was blessed with a magnificent physique and was equally at home at centre half or centre forward. In the air he was peerless and his distribution excellent, his vision enabling him to see openings invisible to others. He had a shot like an Exocet and could shoot from any angle, even when off balance. Above all, he was a great sportsman.

Knowing I was a young lad with only a handful of reserve team games to my name, the awesome figure of John Charles came up to me as the teams took the field.

'Now, don't you worry, son,' he said. 'You do your best out here today. I won't hurt you and I won't go up with you for a ball with my arms flailing. Enjoy yourself and do your best for your club. No one's going to clatter you this afternoon.'

We lost that game 5–0 and I think I'm right in saying John Charles scored three. He was true to his word, however, and never gave me any rough treatment. As a 16-year-old I would have been a pushover for him, but he played it fair and he played it straight. That was Big John, a player whose tremendous sense of sportsmanship was in keeping with his great talent for the game.

On another occasion, following a seven-goal defeat at Wolves, I was soaking my aches and bruises in the Molineux plunge bath when one of the Chesterfield directors emerged through the pall of steam alongside a Wolves official who, to my surprise, wanted a word with me.

'I just had to come and offer my congratulations,' said the Wolves man. 'You let in seven today, but if it weren't for you, it could have been ten. Well done, lad! That was as good a performance in goal as I've seen in many a year. Take heart from that.'

I did.

It was quite common in those days for a top player from a First Division club to see out his career in the lower divisions. Nowadays, even journeymen Premiership players earn so much during their time in the game that few wish to run the gauntlet of sledgehammer tackles from robust young players out to make a name for themselves in the Third Division or non-league. Many of today's Premiership players, even those who have never been awarded star status, use the money they have earned from the game to start businesses, or simply invest it in financial plans and live for the rest of their days off the proceeds. Some may supplement that income with a little media or promotional work.

In the fifties, due to the maximum wage, even well-established players in the First Division did not have that opportunity to earn much from the game, certainly nowhere near the amount of money needed to keep them and their families for the rest of their days. For the vast majority, football was all they knew and when released by a top club, a good number simply dropped down a standard or two in order to carry on earning a living.

Even when players reached their late thirties, such was their desire to carry on earning something from their skills, many were content to play even in the reserves for a Second or Third Division team – a situation you never come across nowadays. There is no room for seasoned professionals in reserve football. Apart from the occasional appearance of a first-team player in need of match practice following injury, the reserve teams of today are the preserve of emerging talent. In these days of rotational squads and multiple substitutes, many seasoned professionals, amazingly, seem happier to sit on the bench, or even in the stand, than play a lower level of football. A footballer's career is relatively short. When your playing days are over, do you want to look back on all that time spent sitting on the bench, or in the stand? You can sit and spectate when you're ninety years old, but you can't stay at the top much past thirty-five. I came across countless seasoned pros who had played top-flight football during my time in the Chesterfield reserves. We even had one or two of our own – most notably, Eddie Shimwell.

Eddie, born in nearby Matlock, had played in three FA Cup finals for Blackpool, including what many consider the greatest ever, that of 1953 when they came back from 3–1 down to beat Bolton Wanderers 4–3. That final was dubbed the Matthews Final because of Stanley Matthews's scintillating play on the wing. It was also the game in which although Blackpool's centre forward Stan Mortensen scored a hat trick, his achievement was not mentioned once in any headline in either the Sunday or Monday newspaper reports of that final. (Can you imagine a player scoring a hat trick in an FA Cup final today and not getting a mention in a single headline?) All the plaudits went to

1. A Coronation street party in Ferrars Road and not a car in sight. Our house was the first one in the third block on the left. You can just make out the steel-works at the end of our road.

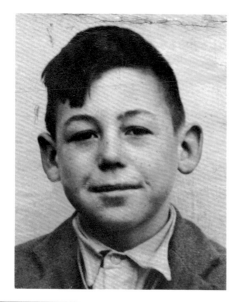

2. Me, aged about nine, during my days as a coal liberator. My idea of bliss was a slice of bread and dripping.

3. Mam and Dad out walking in Sheffield city centre. Needless to say, the car was not theirs!

4. Dad doing a bit of on-course turf accounting at Doncaster. For the steelworkers and coal miners of Sheffield, a trip to Doncaster was a major undertaking.

5. Me at fourteen. The jerkin I am wearing was at the time the height of Sheffield fashion.

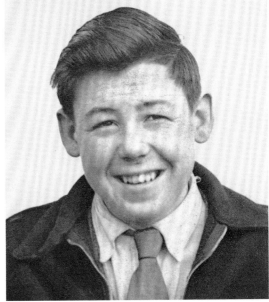

6. On holiday in Scarborough. I was aged about sixteen. Dad is obviously in the holiday mood – he's taken off his jacket and tie.

7. Mam and Our Jack at Scarborough.

8. In goal for Tinsley County Secondary School. Immediately to my left is Bob Pashley, who went on to play for Bolton Wanderers and both the Sheffield clubs. Far right on the back row (next to the teacher) is David 'Bronco' Layne, who became a free-scoring centre forward with Sheffield Wednesday. Centre front with the ball at his feet is Terry Wheighway, who was on the books of Sheffield United. The lad on my immediate left became the only person I've ever known to have a full-length photograph of himself in a passport.

9. Tinsley Rec, where my career as a goalkeeper began. When it rained, it was like a quagmire. When it was cold, the pitch became so icy that the teams had trouble turning round at half time.

10. A dispatch rider with the Royal Signals in Germany. I still have the helmet and wear it if ever I go to Hampden Park for a Scotland–England game.

11. *Below:* My debut for Leicester City reserves against Southend United in 1959. A City supporter ran into the goalmouth and took this photograph. Notice what appears to be a very healthy crowd for a match against Southend reserves!

12. The 1961 FA Cup final. Terry Dyson (out of picture) scored for Spurs. The other players are Bobby Smith (partly obscured by the far post), Colin Appleton, Cliff Jones and Ian King.

Matthews. Being the gentleman and sportsman he was, that never rested easy with Stan, and when he came to write his autobiography in 1999 Matthews insisted the chapter relating to the 1953 final be called 'The Mortensen Final'.

Eddie Shimwell had been a very good right back whose assets were his strength, stamina and timing in the tackle. He signed for Blackpool for £7,000 from Sheffield United in 1946 and became the first full back to score in an FA Cup final when he netted against Manchester United in 1948. In recognition of his services, Blackpool gave him a free transfer in 1957 and he joined Oldham Athletic before arriving at Chesterfield for his swansong.

As any old pro will tell you, you never lose skill – it's the legs that go. Eddie had never been the quickest player and when he arrived at Saltergate it was evident he was slowing up. So much so, he found it difficult to stake a claim in the first team. Eddie was also plagued by a troublesome shoulder injury, but such was his resolve, he kept on playing.

I remember one reserve game when, having received the ball deep in our own half, Eddie took off down the right wing. He hadn't run more than a few yards when his upper body suddenly and violently quivered. At first I couldn't see what the problem was, but on taking a closer look I noticed Eddie's left shoulder jutting through his shirt at an acute angle. Unbelievably, his shoulder had popped out of its socket. I glanced across to the Chesterfield bench and saw our trainer take to his feet, then back to Eddie, who amazingly was still running with the ball. It was then that I saw something even more astounding. Eddie simply carried on running and, with his right hand, reached across and yanked his left shoulder back into place! I'd heard many a story of old pros playing on through injury, but this was the first time I'd witnessed it. I could only marvel at his fortitude and resolve. At the same time, though, I also felt sadness for Eddie. He obviously loved football, but I felt there was no way a seasoned and respected pro should have had to carry on playing with such a debilitating injury just for the money. When later I told him I was concerned about him and that he should put his health first, he just smiled.

'Needs must, Gordon, son,' he said, placing a hand on my shoulder, 'needs must!'

Whenever I see a player go sprawling in the penalty box and writhing around in simulated agony I always wonder what Eddie Shimwell would make of such amateur dramatics, or, if you prefer, outright cheating.

In my time with Chesterfield reserves I became friends with all the players, two of whom became very good friends, Barry Hutchinson and the ex-Sheffield United player Paul Brown. The three of us travelled together from Sheffield for both training and matches. Browny had joined Chesterfield from Sheffield United and I remember the three of us waiting one day on the outskirts of the city for the Chesterfield team coach to pick us up and take us on to a Central League game at Manchester City. I hadn't played that many games for the reserves and, at the time, was still awestruck whenever I came across a player who had been a boyhood hero of mine.

As we waited for the team bus, I looked across the road and was amazed to see the former Sheffield United goalkeeper Ted Burgin, walking by on the opposite side. My eyes were on stalks – Burgin had been a real idol of my youth. On my rare visits to Bramall Lane, I used to marvel at his heroics in goal for United and, though I was now a pro myself, seeing him so close up made me weak at the knees. Browny called his old team mate over. I was amazed at Browny's easy familiarity with someone I had accorded hero status. Browny introduced us and I addressed Ted as 'Mr Burgin', which induced laughter on the part of my team mates and a wry smile from Ted himself. Suddenly, my mouth went dry and I couldn't think of anything sensible to say.

There was little if any coverage of football on television in those days, only marginally more on radio, so consequently you rarely heard a footballer speak. My impression of Burgin was derived solely from watching him from the terraces. Though

Burgin was a Sheffield lad, for some reason I was surprised that he had a local accent. What sort of accent I expected him to have, I don't know. But having thought of him as something of a god, certainly not a south Yorkshire accent like mine. Though still in awe of him, I was struck by the sheer ordinariness of the man. He reminded me of the cheery man from the Pru who called at our house once a week to collect the one-and-six life insurance money Mam and Dad paid, so that, when the time came, they could be given, as Mam would say, 'a decent send off'.

Having met Burgin, he was no less my hero in terms of his expertise as a goalkeeper, but from that moment I saw him in a totally different light – an ordinary bloke on his way to the fish and chip shop.

At that moment, at the side of a road in a village on the outskirts of my home city, it came to me that footballers were mere mortals. I would have no more perfect heroes. It would be an exaggeration to say that my age of innocence was over, though I did sense that something from my childhood had died.

After a while Browny, Hutch and I decided to travel to Chesterfield by train. This was usually more convenient, but on one occasion it put us in hot water with our new manager, Duggie Livingstone. We used a local service that always departed from the same platform, but on the day in question we found it wasn't there. I asked a platform attendant and he directed us to a train on another platform. Browny and Hutch felt uneasy about this departure from the norm, and on seeing the same platform attendant again, to allay their fears, I pulled down the carriage window and asked for confirmation that we were Chesterfield bound. No problem – this was the right one. On the outskirts of Chesterfield the train began to slow down. We gathered our bags only to stand dumbfounded as it started to pick up speed just outside the station. Panic set in as we watched the station flash by.

The train did eventually come to a halt. At Derby. We jumped out as if it were on fire and raced for the nearest telephone. By now it was twenty to three. I rang the club and heard the voice of our trainer, George Milburn, brother of the legendary Newcastle centre forward, Jackie Milburn, uncle of Bobby and Jack Charlton. Not a man to mince his words. When we told him where we were, George told us what we were. He ended the brief conversation by telling us to take a taxi to the ground. It was twenty minutes to three and I knew even if Stirling Moss himself turned out to be the driver, there was no way a taxi would get us to Saltergate in time for us to play against Everton.

We eventually arrived at twenty past three and were told to take a seat in the stand for the rest of the game. Nobody said another word to us about the matter that entire afternoon. Come Tuesday, however, the three of us were pulled out of training and told to report to the manager's office. Duggie Livingstone sat stony faced as he listened to our tale. Then he took to his feet. We would have to drive to Sheffield station and point out to Duggie the platform attendant who put us on the wrong train.

We felt like naughty schoolboys being admonished by the headmaster. Eventually, I spotted the miscreant attendant.

'That's him!' I piped up, like some nine-year-old lad pointing out the school bully.

'You! Come here!' Duggie barked. 'The station master's office. All four of you. Now!'

Once inside the station master's office, we repeated our tale and, luckily for us the platform attendant admitted his mistake.

We sat in silence on the journey back to Chesterfield. Duggie Livingstone never apologized for having doubted us. All he said was that we'd have to come in for training the following night to make up for the session we'd missed, and that he would be docking our wages for missing the match.

No manager today would treat even junior players like that. But that's how it was in those days. More often than not, players had more respect for a manager's position and his seniority of years, than his actual expertise as a football manager. You did what you were told. Irrespective of your character or individual circumstances, if you weren't playing well or if you didn't do as the manager wanted, you got a rollicking. The onus was on the individual player to shape up, not on the manager to assess and address that player's idiosyncrasies or emotions and adapt his methods of management accordingly. Nobody thought anything less of a manager for that. His word was law and there was a democracy of sorts – all players were treated the same, albeit, at times, like naughty schoolboys.

I was later to enjoy revenge at Duggie's expense. The money I earned at Chesterfield enabled me to buy my first car – by which I mean an old Ford van owned by a brickie I knew from my days as a hod carrier. This van had seen better days. The front passenger seat wasn't secured to the floor as the brickie often removed it when loading the van with building materials. The headlights would intermittently cut out and their silver backing had perished so that they provided only a dim glow. The tyres were nigh on bald and the van had the disconcerting habit of jumping out of gear. All of which made even the shortest journey an adventure.

One night, after training, Duggie Livingstone asked if I could give him a lift back into Sheffield as his car was in for repairs. I readily agreed and once out on the country road back to Sheffield, put my foot down. The road home was full of twists and turns and Duggie was forever sliding backwards and forwards on that unsecured passenger seat. When, at fifty miles an hour, the gear stick popped out of its column I thought Duggie's eyes were going to pop out of his head. Then as we were approaching Dronfield the van veered to the right and we were suddenly in the direct path of an oncoming car. It was at this point that the headlights decided to give up on me. I think that was when I heard Duggie utter a muted scream. I swung the van back over to the left. The headlights came back on and in the rear view mirror I saw the tail lights of the other car disappearing down the road. It had been a close thing, too close for Duggie. When I dropped him at his home, I could see his face was ashen.

'Gordon. Don't ever let me ask you for a lift again!' He meant it.

My career with Chesterfield was interrupted when at seventeen I received my call-up papers for National Service. I joined the Royal Signals and after weeks of square-bashing at camps in Catterick and Ripon found myself posted to Germany. Fate had another wonderful stroke of luck in store for me, for it was during my time out there that I met a beautiful young German girl called Ursula. I fell in love with her and I'm even more in love with her now. Ursula and I have been married for over forty years, have three children and five grandchildren. Family life and family values are very important to me, and always have been. When I was a boy in Tinsley we never had much money, but I never felt deprived because there was love in our family and there were frequent little surprises. As a father and grandfather I've always tried to foster such family values.

During my National Service in Germany I managed to play quite a lot of football. When the Army learned that I was a pro I was soon picked to represent first my squad and then my regiment, which I helped to win the Rhine Cup, a very prestigious trophy in Army sport at that time.

Chesterfield must have kept tabs on me because on being demobbed I received a letter inviting me back to Saltergate. The manager, Ted Davison, had a surprise waiting for me: a contract as a full-time professional on £7 a week. I had no agent, no image consultant or PR manager, no lawyer, to pick over the fine print and set up lucrative deals from all manner of ancillary activities. It took me all of five seconds to sign. My dream had come true. I was to be paid for doing the only thing I ever wanted to do in life and, having met Ursula, I'd never been so happy.

★

Many of the reserve team were still young enough to play in the FA Youth Cup and we found to our delight that the experience of playing against seasoned pros and the occasional international in the Central League made us more than a match for lads of our own age.

In 1955–56 I kept goal both for Chesterfield reserves and the youth team in the FA Youth Cup. It wasn't all plain sailing. Playing for the A team against Sheffield Wednesday, I dived at the feet of Wednesday's Keith Ellis and fractured my elbow – a worrying injury for a keeper. But during an operation the surgeon inserted a metal pin to aid the healing process and strengthen my shattered elbow. I have to admit I feared my career as a goalkeeper could be over before it had got off the ground. As luck would have it, and thanks to the expertise of the surgeon, the injury healed so well that within seven weeks I was back between the posts for the reserves and keen to show what I could do in the FA youth team.

The FA Youth Cup was a relatively new competition, inaugurated in 1952–53, and was won in its first five seasons by Manchester United. It was not only an incentive for clubs to develop their own young players but for managers and directors it became a benchmark as to how their club was progressing. Success in the Youth Cup was seen as an indication of a rosy future for a club, the hope being that a generation of players would then progress to first-team football. Many of that extraordinary crop of Manchester United players who monopolized the competition in its first five seasons did make the grade and were of course dubbed the Busby Babes. For other clubs, the reality was often different. In the fifties, as today, if just two players from a triumphant FA Youth Cup team went on to make their mark in the first team, a club's youth policy was considered to have been a success. Of course there have been exceptions. Sometimes no players from a winning FA Youth Cup side proved good enough to make the grade; conversely, there have been occasions when four or five have done so. For example, of the successful youth team of (again) Manchester United of the early 1990s, several went on to win great club and international honours, namely Gary and Phil Neville, Paul Scholes, Nicky Butt and, of course, David Beckham.

We set out on the trail of the FA Youth Cup in 1956 as minnows and surprised not only the Chesterfield supporters but also ourselves by reaching the final. Our opponents were the holders – you've guessed it – Manchester United, who fielded Wilf McGuinness, Alex Dawson, and a blonde-haired lad on the left wing with a humdinger of a shot, Bobby Charlton. Nobody gave us an earthly. We were up against the cream of young English talent. Nearly all the United side were youth internationals, whereas none of the Chesterfield team had ever watched an inter-national youth game, let alone been selected to play in one.

The final was over two legs, the first at Old Trafford. As our coach drew into the car park I was taken aback by the sheer number of supporters milling about. Chesterfield reserves often drew crowds in excess of over 2,000 for home games against First Division reserve teams and at Anfield or Goodison Park the attendance there might be 14,000 scattered around such large stadiums. Seeing thousands of supporters thronging Old Trafford left me in no doubt that this was to be a big occasion.

Match programmes were always issued for Central League games, though to my knowledge they never carried pen portraits of the players, simply the team line-ups. For this game, however, Manchester United produced a special edition of their matchday programme complete with four- or five-line biographies of each player, which I sat and read in the dressing room. The pen portraits detailed how the United players had been spotted playing either for England Schoolboys, or the North of England Schoolboy Representative XI, or even, in some cases, England Youth. My pen portrait said I had been spotted playing for a works team on Tinsley Rec.

As I ran out of the tunnel with my team mates I was dumb-founded to see around 34,000 people in the ground, all but a handful United supporters. From the kick-off they got right behind their team. United forced us on the back foot and within minutes I knew how those Texans must have felt at the Alamo. The United pressure was relentless, shot after shot raining in at my goal. I caught them, parried them, tipped them over the bar and blocked them with any part of my body I could. But for all my efforts and those of my team mates, such constant pressure had to pay off for United and just before half time they scored twice.

After the interval United picked up the same script and soon we found ourselves three goals adrift. There was little we could do to stem the pressure. Inside right Harry Peck and centre forward Bob Mellows, whose goals had been so instrumental in our reaching the final, were playing so deep I thought they'd end up with the bends. With twenty minutes to go United took their foot off the gas and I enjoyed a welcome break from Bobby Charlton's missiles as our forwards went deep into largely uncharted territory. To my delight we managed to pull a goal back and, with five minutes remaining, broke away and nicked a second: 3–2. I couldn't believe it and I doubt if the United players could either. It had been smash-and-grab stuff but with the second leg at home I left Old Trafford in great spirits, feeling we had gained a moral victory.

A crowd of over 14,000 turned up at Saltergate for the return leg, some 5,000 more than the average attendance for a first team game. The second leg was another humdinger. This time we had more of the play but, in spite of our pressure, couldn't claw back the deficit. The game ended 1–1, which gave United a fourth successive FA Youth Cup success. We may have lost, but I gained a great deal of satisfaction from our performances as a team, and was happy with my own efforts. We had taken on the best youth side in English football over two games and had only been beaten by the odd goal in seven. I was looking forward to further progress at Chesterfield.

★

The following season my youth team days were largely behind
me, and along with team mates Harry Peck, Keith Havenhand
and Bob Mellows I was selected for a Northern Intermediate
League Representative squad to play the 1955–56 NIL champions Sunderland, at Roker Park. As it turned out, I didn't play,
and the goalkeeper's jersey went to Alf Ashmore of Sheffield
United. However, just being in the squad had been a boost to
my confidence. It was the first time I had been selected for a
representative team since my days with Sheffield Schoolboys. I
felt my performances in goal were not going unnoticed.

It's interesting now to look at the respective line-ups in the
match programme for that representative game. Only two
members of the Sunderland team who had won the Northern
Intermediate League, Harry Godbold and Clive Bircham went
on to play first team football. Both, however, only played a
handful of games for Sunderland before moving on, in both cases
to Hartlepool. Of the League Representative team, only two
went on to carve out meaningful careers in football: left winger
Kevin McHale of Huddersfield Town and Bill Houghton of
Barnsley. See what I mean about the high fall-out rate of successful youth-team players? The vast majority never fulfil their early
promise, whereas there are others who never make it on to the
books of clubs as youngsters, but prove to be late developers
and enter league football at a relatively older age. The former
Manchester skipper Tony Book is a prime example of the late
developer. Tony didn't sign for his first club, Plymouth Argyle,
until the age of twenty-five. So if you're still kicking a ball
around, remember, it's never too late!

In the 1958–59 season my performance in goal for Chesterfield
reserves saw me pushing the long-serving Ron Powell for a place
in the first team. Ted Davison had been replaced as manager by
Duggie Livingstone and it was he who finally gave me my big
chance in November 1958. Following Friday training I joined
the rest of the players gathered around the noticeboard on which
were pinned the four teams for Saturday. When I looked at the

reserve team my name wasn't included and my first reaction was to check the A team. It still didn't click with me until the regular first team centre half, Dave Blakey, appeared at my side and said, 'Good luck, son.'

I scrutinized the first team line up and nearly choked. Banks was in goal for the Third Division home game against Colchester United!

I thought Duggie Livingstone would take me to one side the following day and tell me what was expected of me, but I should have known better. As with most managers of that era, man-management and tactical analysis were not high on his list of priorities.

The night before my league debut I went to bed early, but couldn't sleep. My mind was racing and I played the forthcoming game over and over in my mind. On the first occasion we won 1–0 and I saved a penalty. Then we won 3–0. At one point I looked at the alarm clock on the bedside table. It was four o'clock. I was angry with myself, certain that by the morning I'd be in no fit state to get out of bed never mind play football. When I arrived at Saltergate the next day the first person to speak to me was our left back, Gerry Sears. 'Big day for you,' said Gerry. 'How'd you sleep last night?'

'Like a log,' I lied.

When a player enters a dressing room before a game, he finds his shirt hanging from a peg with the rest of his strip neatly folded on the bench below. In the fifties, as is often the case today, there would also be a large enamel teapot of steaming tea, next to which would be a dozen or so complimentary matchday programmes.

Like most players I know, I wasn't a great collector of matchday programmes. I have a few, among which are those from my debuts for Chesterfield, Leicester City and England. I wish I'd kept more because with the passing of time, these programmes are a far more revealing read than they were on the day of issue. Today's programmes resemble glossy magazines and many cost what a Chesterfield supporter of the late fifties would have paid for a season ticket. Contemporary programmes carry any amount of photographs and a wealth of statistical information. They are too big to slip into your coat pocket so you have to sit holding them for the whole game.

The typical Chesterfield programme of the fifties was three sheets of A4 matt paper folded to make twelve pages. There was little information other than club news – or 'Saltergate Chatter' – the team line-ups, pen pictures of the visiting team, the league tables and results of the first team and reserves and a key to the board which displayed the half-time scores from other grounds. The rest of the space was taken up by display advertisements. Yet in those days before local radio, Ceefax, and saturation TV coverage of the game, these flimsy programmes were the main source of match information for supporters. The national papers contained little other than the results and goalscorers. Even the local paper, the *Sheffield Star*, never carried more than a few paragraphs of pre-match information.

Barring injury or a late change of plan on the part of the manager, the eleven you saw in the programme was taken to be the team to be fielded that afternoon. (Today's matchday magazines list squads, which might be anything up to thirty-five players.) What's more, a supporter always knew where to find the team line-ups within these programmes: in the centre pages or, failing that, on the inside front cover.

The programme from my debut game against Colchester made much of the fact goalkeeper Ron Powell was set to make his three hundredth consecutive appearance for the club. My selection, of course, denied him that milestone. Although Ron himself was fine about it, I did wonder what sort of reaction I would receive from the Chesterfield faithful when they saw me run out in the goalkeeper's jersey. The very fact that he had been dropped on the eve of his record-breaking game taught me a lesson about football: there is no room for sentiment in the game.

I had been wondering whether my appearance would be a total surprise to supporters, or whether word would have got round the terraces that I was set to make my debut. Near the back of the programme, however, I noticed a small paragraph headed 'Special Note'. It read, 'The opening paragraphs of Saltergate Chatter were printed before team selection. We now welcome and congratulate Gordon Banks as goalkeeper for today's match. Ron Powell will receive congratulations on his 300th appearance soon, on the appropriate occasion.' I took that to mean that they weren't expecting my elevation to the first team to be a lengthy one!

As I look through that programme now, I'm reminded how different football was in 1958. And it's a snapshot of a society that has changed almost beyond recognition. Nowhere is this more evident than in the adverts. There is one for the National Coal Board encouraging people to 'Work in modern mining because it pays', with 'many jobs available in mining, mechanical and electrical for men and boys'. Meanwhile, 'Joyce Mullis ALCM, AIMD (Hons), the gold medallist soprano', offers teaching in singing and piano, obviously appealing to parents whose idea of providing their offspring with opportunities they never had was to hear them play 'The Blackbird Gavotte' on the family heirloom they themselves had never learned to play. Then there is the Dickensian Nathaniel Atrill, 'For all your coal, coke and anthracite needs', and T. P. Wood and Co., with the message, 'Don't get a reputation for always being seen in pubs, order your home supplies of bottled beers from us' – the consumption of beer at home then was ambiguously referred to as 'lace curtain drinking'.

These adverts mirrored football at that time. They were parochial and parsimonious, the organs of small High Street businesses that provided the town with not only commerce but its social glue and identity. Much the same as the football club. The big multinational companies had yet to realize football was a major cultural force and how they could benefit from an association with the game. When they eventually did, in the late seventies, and when television's insatiable appetite for the game further fuelled their interest, it signalled the end of small local businesses associating themselves with their local football club, just as the growth of supermarkets, franchises and chain stores in our High Streets ushered in the demise of many of these mainstays of the local economy.

The decline of not only small businesses but traditional industries gave rise to a shifting population. Now you find Chesterfield supporters in London, Bedford, Truro and Bristol. When I played for the club, the remotest fan I heard of lived in Staveley, some twelve miles away. Clubs received a little money from the eight Football Pools companies, namely Littlewoods, Vernons, Shermans, Zetters, Copes, Empire, Soccer and Trent, while programme and pitch-side advertising amounted to little more than pin money. Therefore match receipts were still the main source of income, but because football was still seen primarily as a cheap form of entertainment for working people, admission prices were low. In 1958 a seat at Chesterfield was as little as 4 shillings (20p), whereas to stand on the terraces cost 1s. 6d. (7½p) – far cheaper in relative terms than the price of admission to a Nationwide League game today. Consequently, like a lot of clubs in the divided Third Division, Chesterfield struggled to make ends meet.

Many football club directors ran local businesses themselves and had neither the wherewithal nor the desire to pump money into the local football club. Many viewed it as a 'private' club at which to enjoy some social recreation on a Saturday afternoon. It would be twenty years or more before football clubs fully realized their commercial potential. In the fifties there were no commercial departments to exploit the club's traditional and corporate identity, basically because no one knew their football club had one.

Next to gate receipts the main source of income for a club came from funds raised by its supporters' club. We were fortunate to have not only the official supporters' club but an organization called the Chesterfield and District Sportsman's Association. Both these bodies regularly contributed substantial sums for the day-to-day running of the club and, on occasions, the acquisition of new players – probably far more than the board of directors ever did, yet without any say in club policy or the running of the club itself.

Also making his debut that day was inside right Arthur Bottom, bought from Newcastle United with money donated by the two supporters' organizations through a series of whist drives, bingo sessions and pie and pea supper nights at which I and other players were invariably in attendance. The demands we make on today's footballers are different. In this era of scientifically planned diet and fitness regimes, we do not expect them to be seen quaffing a few beers, eating steak dinners and socializing until midnight. When I was a player at Chesterfield, it was part and parcel of the job to get out and meet the supporters at their fund-raising nights. It never occurred to you that the end product of such events might be money that the club might use to buy a player to replace you in the team.

From top to bottom everything about a football club had to be conducted on a very small scale because the main body of customers, the supporters, didn't have much money to live on, let alone the disposable income for what today would be called leisure activities.

Back in the fifties there were no corporate boxes, you could get in for one and six and at half time, in the words of a Rochdale programme of March 1959, 'Walk to the tea bar / Straight as a die, / Count out your coppers / And ask for a pie.' Count out your coppers! That's what survival boiled down to, for Rochdale, Chesterfield and many other clubs five decades ago.

In 1958–59 the regionalized Third Division was scrapped and reformed into national Third and Fourth Divisions. Our opponents on my debut, Colchester United, had been members of the Third Division South and so no one at Chesterfield knew anything about them. Or Colchester us. Teams didn't spy on the opposition at the time, especially at this level of football. They played it off the cuff and decided what tactics to use as a game unfolded. The emphasis was on individual rather than collective effort. Anyway, Duggie Livingstone's pre-match team talk comprised a few clichés about 'taking the game to them' and 'playing to our strengths', the latter meaning nothing to me as nobody had told me what our strengths as a team were. I might as well have been away with the reserves because despite making my first team debut, Duggie virtually ignored me. It was only when the bell rang to signal that we should take to the pitch, that my manager directed any conversation to me, and only then, when prompted by Dave Blakey. We stood up and formed a crocodile line in readiness to leave the dressing room. I was a couple of places behind Dave, who, aware that Duggie Livingstone had said nothing about what was expected of me, jerked his head in my direction to indicate he should. At first it didn't click with Duggie, then his face lit up.

'Oh, aye! Gordon?'

'Yes, boss?' I said, eager to hear his words of wisdom.

'Good luck, son,' Duggie said, smiling broadly.

Now well versed in my expected role I sprinted down the tunnel and out in front of the 7,140 fans present to witness my league debut.

The result was a 2–2 draw, with our goals coming from Bryan Frear and Maurice Galley. Despite conceding two goals I came off the field quite satisfied with my own performance, feeling that neither could be put down to goalkeeping error. Back in the dressing room my team mates told me I'd done well, which raised my spirits even more. Even Duggie Livingstone said 'Well done.'

'Played it just like you told me, boss,' I replied.

That night's *Sheffield Green 'Un* reported that, 'Debutant Gordon Banks produced a competent performance in goal.' I slept that night, I can tell you.

I was given another chance to win over the sceptical Chesterfield faithful because I was selected for the following game, a 1–1 home draw against Norwich City, and during the remainder of the season I missed only three matches, through injury.

There were some sizeable attendances in the Third Division in those days. I played in front of over 11,000 at Wrexham, 13,000 at Carlisle United, 15,000 at Notts County, in excess of 17,000 at Plymouth Argyle and 20,505 at Norwich City. Even our home attendances picked up, most noticeably against Hull City and Mansfield Town, against whom we drew crowds of more than 10,000. Chesterfield finished the season a respectable sixteenth – way off the promotion places but well clear of the relegation trapdoor. I was enjoying my football immensely and loved the camaraderie of my team mates, a number of whom are good friends to this day. They were a great bunch of lads and very colourful characters.

Right back Ivor Seemley was a Sheffield lad like me, who had started his career at Sheffield Wednesday. After eight years at Hillsborough he wanted regular first team football and had spent two seasons with Stockport County before joining us. Ivor was a solid player who, following my move to Leicester City, lost his place in the first team only to win it back in the most unusual circumstances when his replacement, Ray De Grucy, was stung in the eye by a wasp during training!

Our other full back, Gerry Sears, was a Chesterfield lad who had been spotted playing for a local youth team. Originally an outside left, Gerry dropped back into defence where he proved himself to be a capable left back. He had one of the sweetest left feet I've ever seen. We used to joke he could have used it to open tin cans.

Our right half, Gerry Clarke, came from Barrow Hill, just outside Chesterfield and was a member of the Chesterfield Boys team which reached the semi-final of the English Schools Shield. Gerry joined Sheffield United from school but, after a couple of seasons in the United youth and reserve teams, signed for Chesterfield. Gerry was a fine wing half and a good leader on the pitch, a quality that eventually saw him become team captain. He went on to give years of loyal service to the club before eventually retiring in the late sixties.

Dave Blakey was a Geordie who had signed for Chesterfield in 1947. When I made my debut in 1958, Dave had already clocked up 350 appearances for the club, which would have been consecutive but for a spell out of the game in 1957 due to a troublesome appendix. He was a huge man who, when the going got tough, remained as immovable as a rock in a raging sea. Like Ron Powell and later Gerry Clarke, Dave was one of those players who spent the vast majority of his career with one club.

My best mate, Barry Hutchinson, vied for the place of left half with Jim Smallwood. Barry had already been at Chesterfield for six years when I made the first team and was to continue playing for the club into the early sixties. He was a creative player, a good passer of the ball with a keen eye for goal and a ready wit. I recall one game, away at Southend United, in which Barry had got the better of the Southend right half, the wonderfully named Mortimer Costello – we won 5–2 and he scored two of our goals. After the game we were enjoying a quick drink and some sandwiches before starting off for home when he was confronted by an indignant Southend supporter who was outraged by what he perceived to be Barry's robust treatment of Costello, though Mortimer himself had just accepted it as part and parcel of the game and given as good as he got.

'I know football is a contact sport,' said the supporter, 'but you overstepped the mark today, young man.'

'Football's not a contact sport,' replied Barry, 'it's a collision sport. Pairs ice skating, that's a contact sport.'

At outside right we had Andy MacCabe, a mercurial Scot who had lived most of his life in Corby. Andy joined Chesterfield from Corby Town, then a Midland League club, and proved himself to be a very tricky winger in the days when it was a common sight to see wingers plying their trade up and down muddy touchlines. Like his counterpart on the left, usually Gwyn Lewis, Andy was a typical winger in that he could be brilliant one game and totally ineffective the next. This inconsistency was a constant source of wonderment to Duggie Livingstone and, at times, much frustration and irritation. In the end I think Duggie just sent them out there and hoped for the best.

Keith Havenhand and I played together in the youth team that had reached the FA Youth Cup Final. As a player Keith had more than just a touch of class about him. He was a scheming inside right and, like most scheming inside forwards of that time, had an intellectual air to his play. He always seemed to be happy with a big smile on his face and he played the game that way too. He wasn't a big lad but he was stocky enough to look after himself in the rough and tumble of Third Division football. Keith scored a lot of goals for Chesterfield and many of them were match winners. Quite often a player wins a reputation for scoring goals though a closer inspection of his record shows that many of his goals are scored when a game is over as a contest. It's all very well scoring a goal when your team is two or three goals up. The true worth of a goalscorer, though, is how many times he puts the ball in the net when you really need him to. In my spell in the Chesterfield first team I can recall at least five occasions when a game was very tight and Keith popped up with the match winner. There may have been more prolific scorers around at that time, but few with a better record than Keith's of notching goals that were crucial to the outcome of a game.

Bryan Frear was an important goalscorer for the club, who could be relied upon for twenty goals a season. Bryan could play equally well in any position in the forward line but to me was always at his best when leading the line. He was one hell of a competitor, as centre forwards had to be in those days. As we prepared to take to the pitch Bryan would be there in the dressing room, right fist clenched, teeth gritted, urging us all to give of our best – though on occasion some of his encouragement had a touch of the Sam Goldwyns about it.

'Let's go out and enjoy ourselves,' said Bryan. 'The result doesn't matter. As long as we win!'

They were a super bunch of lads who played no small part in helping me establish myself in the first team. To a man, they always encouraged me and, when I did make a mistake, told me not to worry and just get on with it. To a young goalkeeper experiencing league football for the first time, this encouragement and support was invaluable, helping my confidence grow with each passing game.

I was learning my trade not in training but out there on the pitch in games. You might think that's a very dangerous way to do it, especially for a goalkeeper, and you'd be right. But in those days there was no different training or specialized coaching for goalkeepers. Certainly in those early years, I was self-taught.

Back in the fifties, unless you were a player destined for a club in a much higher division, there was little to be gained from moving clubs. Players in the Third Division were all paid more or less the same. Marginally more in the Second Division, less in Division Four. Unless a First Division club came in for you, there was little financial incentive to change clubs. A player would only receive a cut of his transfer fee if he had not asked for a move. If he asked for a transfer, he got nothing. Moving to another club of similar size for a couple of pounds extra in wages was only beneficial if you lived within easy travelling distance and didn't have to move home.

At the time most Chesterfield players were on around £9 a week. We heard stories of players at some clubs in the south, such as Brentford, Plymouth and Crystal Palace, being paid more. But the cost of housing and living in general in the south was much more expensive than in the north and midlands. The few pounds gained in wages from such a move would probably be gobbled up by more expensive mortgage payments and so on. Similarly, not many southern players made the reverse move to the lower-paying northern clubs.

In January 1959 *Charles Buchan's Football Monthly*, the most popular football magazine of its day, surveyed the origin of players in the Third and Fourth Divisions. The statistics showed that at the thirteen Third Division clubs from the north and midlands there were only twelve players who had moved from the south of England. In the Fourth Division the situation was even more pronounced: seventeen northern and midland clubs in that division boasted just seven players from the south. As we approached the sixties, clubs in the lower divisions operated in much the same way as they had done in the twenties, thirties and forties. The vast majority of players on their books came from within a twenty-five mile radius and they rarely looked any further afield for emerging young talent. When I was at Chesterfield we had only three players, Dave Blakey, Andy MacCabe and Gwyn Lewis, who had been born outside that radius of the town. The only 'southerner' was the Scot Andy MacCabe who lived most of his life in Corby, Northamptonshire.

Port Vale were also typical of the time. In 1959 they had twenty-three professionals on their books, eighteen of whom were local lads. Likewise Doncaster Rovers, who had nineteen local players on a professional staff of twenty-four.

The very fact that the local team, by and large, comprised local players made the football club a focal point of the community, even for those people who weren't active supporters, and it fostered a deep loyalty and local pride. Everyone in Sheffield was either Wednesday or United, never Manchester United or Spurs. For those who owned a TV set, there was no league football to watch. Consequently, youngsters were never seduced by the glamour and reflected glory of the successful teams. You were never mocked at school for supporting your local team.

Supporters believed the players understood what an important role the local club played in their lives. The majority of players had grown up alongside these fans and, because players were not paid much more than the average working person, continued to live alongside the fans. In my early days at Chesterfield I'd catch the same bus as some of the supporters, who'd chat away to me for the duration of the journey. Whether in the newsagent's, the chip shop or the barber's, wherever I went around the town I would receive praise or criticism depending on how we had done in our previous game. I never viewed such familiarity as an intrusion. I simply saw it as part of my lot as a footballer.

If supporters were loyal so too were most players. It was not unusual for clubs to have several longtime servants like Chesterfield's Ron Powell, Dave Blakey and Gerry Clarke. 'One-club men' were loved by the supporters for that club loyalty. They were loyal, but their devotion presented them with the one opportunity of earning any decent money from football: the testimonial game, awarded to players who had given at least ten years' service to a club. The award was in the gift of the board and usually took the form of a single game against superior opposition, the match receipts from which were given to the beneficiary.

Such loyalty wasn't always a two-way street. Stanley Matthews spent fourteen years at Blackpool during which time the club enjoyed halcyon days. Often Blackpool played money-spinning friendly matches for which the club received a substantial fee, usually payable as a guarantee that Matthews would play. When the time came for Stan to leave the club, the Blackpool board didn't think fit to reward him for his efforts with a testimonial match. The receipts from a testimonial wouldn't keep a player for the rest of his days, but at least it was a way to top up his pension fund. Many people (but not some parsimonious club directors) thought the testimonial game to be a fitting 'thank you' for loyal service, as well as providing a safety net for someone who had to embark upon an entirely different career when in his mid to late thirties.

Today, we have millionaire Premiership players being awarded testimonial games after, in some cases, just six years of service at a club. That rests uneasy with a lot of supporters and I fully understand why. Such players are simply not in need of the money. The decision by Niall Quinn to give to children's charities the proceeds from his testimonial game at Sunderland in 2002 was a gesture as laudable as it was unique.

In total I played in twenty-six league and cup matches. With each game my self-assurance grew and come the final few games I was confident enough not only to shout instructions to team mates, but organize the defence in front of me. I told the full backs when to push on and when to drop back and even started to tell big Dave Blakey when to drop in and pick up. Goalkeeping apart, I felt I was making a positive contribution to the team and took heart from the fact that in the final five matches of the season, I kept three clean sheets, conceding only three goals.

My horizons at this time never extended beyond playing for Chesterfield. I had after all only twenty-three league games to my name, so it came as a big shock during the summer of 1959 when Duggie Livingstone called me into his office one day and introduced me to a dapper man with wavy black hair who he said wanted to sign me – Matt Gillies, the manager of First Division Leicester City, who had offered Chesterfield £7,000 for my services and implied the decision was mine.

'We don't want to sell you,' said Duggie. 'You have outstanding potential and we see your future here at Chesterfield. Whether you sign for Leicester or not is entirely your own decision. Here's a pen.'

Chesterfield were, as ever, strapped for cash and the money was just too good to turn down.

My knowledge of football at the time was hardly comprehensive, but I was unsure what division Leicester played in, let alone where it was. What I did know, however, was that Leicester were a much bigger club than Chesterfield and that they played at a higher level. The very fact that Leicester were willing to pay what was at that time a decent fee for an unknown goalkeeper was an indication of their confidence in my ability and potential. I reached for the pen Duggie Livingstone was jabbing in my direction and signed.

By now Ursula and I were married and living in Treeton, a small mining village just outside Chesterfield. As I arrived home I suddenly realized I had committed my future to another club without consulting her. But I needn't have worried, she was delighted.

'How much are they going to pay you?' asked Ursula.

'You'd better sit down,' I said.

I drew a deep breath. 'Fifteen pounds a week!' I said triumphantly.

Ursula clasped her hands together in joy, took to her feet and we danced around the kitchen together in celebration of our good fortune.

3. Learning My Trade

The summer of 1959 was memorable. BMC launched the Mini,
Fidel Castro became president of Cuba. I was clicking my fingers
to Bobby Darin's 'Dream Lover', tapping my toes to Ricky
Nelson's 'It's Late' and curling my lip to Cliff Richard's 'Living
Doll'. This was the new music of the time and I liked it. Cliff
apart, much of the British chart music took the form of crooners
such as Frankie Vaughan or Anthony Newley, or the skiffle style
pioneered by Lonnie Donegan. That summer the British popular music scene was invaded by the slick rock'n'roll music of
America and we young people took to it in a big way. Popular
music was changing and so too was my life, in particular my
football career.

I was very grateful to Chesterfield for having given me my
chance in League football and was therefore sad to read in the
local press that summer, that my sale to Leicester had caused a
great deal of discontent amongst the supporters, many of whom
were of the mind my fee of £7,000 was too low. I felt flattered.
They had had only half a season in which to judge my worth as
a goalkeeper. Many believed my sale was unnecessary, given that
the Chesterfield Supporters' Club and Sportsman's Association
had donated over £16,000 to the club at the end of the season.
The board, needless to say, disagreed with the supporters' views
on my departure, and snubbed the supporters' association's
suggestion that the financial support they gave the club merited
representation on the board. The Chesterfield chairman, Harold
Shentall, described the idea as 'ridiculous' – when he was asked
by the *Sheffield Star* to say how much he himself had contributed
to the club in the previous year, Mr Shentall declined to comment.

I was further saddened to learn that Dave Blakey, who had

been one of my best pals at the club, had slapped in a transfer request. Dave had given fine service for over a decade and had been granted a testimonial by the board in recognition of his loyalty. The trouble was that Dave had yet to receive the proceeds from his testimonial match – hence his transfer request. Dave eventually received the £1,000 owing to him, and consequently withdrew his transfer request. He continued to give loyal service to the club until his eventual retirement in 1966 after nineteen years with Chesterfield!

That summer Maurice Galley and Ivor Seemley were also put on the transfer list. The money received from my move didn't result in any notable signings. Following my exit Ronnie Powell had come back as first-choice goalkeeper and, in need of cover, Duggie Livingstone signed a lad called Ted Smethurst from non-league Denaby United. Chesterfield's other signing that summer was Brian Frost, a forward from fellow non-league team Oswestry Town. I was pleased to see Brian get his chance in league football because I had been at school with him. We were two of five lads from Tinsley County School who went on to play professional football, an unusually high number from one year at a single school. The others were David 'Bronco' Layne, who became a prolific goalscorer with Sheffield Wednesday until his career was ended through his involvement in the infamous bribery scandal of 1963, Bob Pashley and Terry Leather. In time both Brian and Ted Smethurst made an impact at Chesterfield but initially their signings did little to excite the supporters and detract from the general feeling that the club were lacking ambition and descending into stagnation.

Indicative of Chesterfield chairman Harold Shentall's cur-mudgeonly attitude to fans and reluctance to invest in improving the ground and the squad, was his statement that, 'No one would turn out to watch a mediocre team under floodlights.' As it happens, Chesterfield did eventually install floodlights – in 1965, the last Football League club to do so!

In the fifties floodlights were common on the continent and

had been since before the war. British football, however, had been slow to take them up, due in the main to a negative attitude on the part of the Football Association and the Football League. Floodlights had been first used in English football as long ago as 1878 when an experimental match had taken place at Arsenal. Arsenal's next game under lights, the first to be officially recognized, took place seventy four years later! In 1952 the Gunners entertained Hapoel Tel Aviv and a crowd of 44,000 turned up to sample this novel experience.

The old Arsenal manager, Herbert Chapman, had been lobbying for the introduction of floodlights throughout the thirties, but it was only in the fifties that their true worth was recognized. I readily recall watching a much-anticipated televised match in 1954 between Wolves and Honved that took place under floodlights. In 1954 few people had television sets and televised football was a rarity. Everyone was excited at the prospect of seeing the broadcast, especially as this one was to take place under Wolves' newly installed floodlights. Today such a friendly would create only mild interest in Wolverhampton and pass virtually unnoticed nationwide. Back then the nation awaited this game with bated breath.

Honved, then one of the best club sides in the world, fielded five of the Hungarian team that in 1953 became the first foreign team to beat England at home. That score was 6–3. Earlier in 1954 England's humiliation had been complete when they had travelled to Budapest in May and were hammered 7–1, a record defeat for England. Everyone saw this as an opportunity to restore a semblance of pride to English football.

Those fortunate enough to have a television discovered that they were the most popular family on the street, with friends they never knew they had. Luckily for me I was a friend of Derek Cooper, whose family was the only one in our street with a television set. Even so, Derek at first declined my request to watch the game at his house as his father was in charge of who was to be allowed to watch the match on their TV. It was only after much badgering, pleading and downright grovelling on my part that Derek eventually plucked up the courage to ask if I could watch the game. To my great delight, Mr Cooper said yes.

That evening you couldn't have packed more into their living room if you tried. Naturally the Coopers themselves took the comfy seats. Behind them, two to three deep, stood the men. To the sides, seated on the sideboard and a small table which had been brought through from the kitchen, sat the teenagers, while young boys sat crosslegged on the floor at the front. I was in my mid-teens but was asked to sit down at the front with the small boys, which gave me a great view of the match.

Wolves did not disappoint. Two down inside fifteen minutes they pulled back to 2–2, then, in a finale straight out of *Roy of the Rovers*, scored three times in the last three minutes to win 5–2. It was a fabulous game of football and the excitement generated in the Coopers' lounge was just like being at Molineux itself. Wolves had put the pride back in English football and, just as importantly, had shown floodlights were important to the future of our game.

Following that night, more and more clubs invested in flood-lights to the approval of the football authorities. Though consent for their use in League games was not given until February 1956, when Portsmouth staged the first ever floodlit Football League match against Newcastle United at Fratton Park.

The FA and Football League, however, were less enthusiastic about further games being broadcast on TV. Even in highlight form. The official line was that even televised highlights would have a detrimental effect on attendances. As a consequence, England games and the FA Cup Final apart, television was more or less given the cold shoulder by football's governing bodies until *Match of the Day* was launched on BBC2 ten years later. The football authorities viewed the relatively new though burgeoning medium of television with suspicion. Their belief that supporters would stay at home to watch any team on television rather than attend a game at their local club was an attitude that showed how little those who ran the game understood its paying customers. Football clubs have deep roots and a long tradition. In the fifties every club lay at the centre of its community and there was no evidence that televised football would have a detrimental effect on attendances. On the contrary, over 55,000 paid to watch the Honved game!

The Wolves–Honved encounter was probably the first game in England to be played with a white ball rather than the usual dark orange caseball. It was certainly the first I had ever seen. This novelty caught our imagination and the following day, after school, Derek Cooper and I gathered in our back yard with our pals to whitewash Derek's brown leather ball. We couldn't wait for darkness so that we could play with this new innovation under the gaslight in the street. Of course we were to be disappointed. As soon as we started to kick the ball around the whitewash came off – though, oddly, it managed to stay on our shoes, much to our parents' annoyance.

I arrived for my first day as a Leicester City player in July 1959 full of high hopes and enthusiasm. It was the first day of pre-season training and I immediately knew I'd joined a top club on being told to report to the Leicester training ground on the outskirts of the city. The training ground had been purpose built and had a wooden pavilion with changing rooms, a shower block and a weights room, as well as three full-size pitches. I was impressed; I'd never known such luxury.

I wanted to improve my knowledge of football in general, and other players in particular, which I was sure would assist me greatly in my quest to make my mark as a First Division goalkeeper. My £7,000 fee had instilled in me the idea I would soon be knocking on the door of the Leicester first team. That notion was immediately dispelled when the trainer, Les Dowdells, arrived to tell us there was going to be a press photo call and began to distribute shirts. Les began by handing out six green tops which made me think Leicester played in green! Only when he started to pass round the blue shirts as well did it dawn on me that I was just one of six goalkeepers at the club challenging for the one place in the first team. Being the new boy, I was last in the pecking order!

I soon discovered that Johnny Anderson, who hailed from Arthurlie, and his fellow Scot Dave MacLaren, who had been signed from Dundee, were considered the two main contenders for the first team goalkeeper's jersey. Of the three other keepers I can recall only two: Tony Lines, a promising youngster whose potential had been spotted when playing for the Lockheed works team, and Rodney Slack, a lad from Peterborough who had been scouted playing for a local youth club team.

Chesterfield had given me the chance of playing league football, but Leicester City gave me the opportunity of carving a career at the highest level of the game. I'd worked as a coal-bagger and hod-carrier, often getting up at 5.30 in the morning, and there was no way I wanted to go back to that life. I was determined to give my all at Leicester and buckled down to pre-season training. The fact that I was just one of six goalkeepers on the books concentrated my mind wonderfully. I knew the club couldn't justify six full-time professional goalkeepers indefinitely and I was determined that when Matt Gillies decided who was to stay, I would be one of them.

I did all that was asked of me in training, and in the pre-season friendlies I felt I gave a good account of myself. On the Friday before the first day of the 1959–60 season I trained as usual with my team mates, after which we all headed to the club noticeboard to find out the teams for the opening day of the season.

That's how it was back then. There was no squad rotation system, no horses for courses where a player might be picked because his style was considered suited to a specific game plan, or thought to be problematic to a particular team or opponent. The manager picked his best eleven for the first team. His second best eleven for the reserves and so on. It was black and white and rarely did anyone question the manager's decision. Players had no say in matters.

If the club decided to sell a player, he had to uproot and move home and family to wherever he'd been sold. If a club didn't want the services of a player any more, he was never told in person. He simply received the dreaded 'Not retained' letter at the end of the season – the signal for him to pack his bags and leave. Even if we'd had a voice in matters, no one would have listened. Players were seen by the clubs as commodities, to be hired and fired, bought or sold. There were no agents or personal advisers to look after our interests, no heart-to-heart chats with the manager and certainly no mollycoddling.

As I scanned the team sheets my spirits soared. I was in the reserve team. This was a tremendous boost to my confidence. Having arrived at the club with high hopes I'd been brought back down to earth when I realized I was sixth-choice goal-keeper. Now, after only six weeks and four friendly matches, I was number two. Dave MacLaren had been chosen to keep goal for the first team at West Ham United. The reserves were at home to Southend United. Hardly a classic game in the making, but one I was looking forward to greatly. In the previous season Leicester reserves had been champions of the Football Combination. To make it into that side at the first time of asking was a great boost to my spirits and made me feel I was making headway. However, even I was to be taken aback by how quickly my progress was to gather momentum.

I kept a clean sheet on my debut, a goalless draw against Southend, and also in my second game, a 4–0 victory at West Ham United – my first ever game in London. There followed a 5–2 win against Bristol City and a 0–2 home defeat to Chelsea reserves. Although we lost against Chelsea I came off the pitch feeling I'd had my best game to date. I wasn't the only person to think that.

The Leicester first team were due to play Blackpool at Filbert Street the following Wednesday. The team for that game was pinned up after Tuesday morning training. I was still in the changing room drinking tea and chatting with some of the lads when one of my team mates from the reserves, Richie Norman, sauntered in.

'Seen the team, Gordon?' Richie asked. I told him I hadn't. 'Dave MacLaren's injured. You should go see who Mr Gillies has picked in goal.'

As I walked to the noticeboard I crossly assumed that the experienced Johnny Anderson had been chosen to play. On seeing the team sheet, however, my irritation was immediately replaced by joy. There was my name, in goal against Blackpool the following day. I suddenly felt the whack of Richie Norman's hand on my shoulder.

'Well done, Gordon,' he said, 'well deserved.'

A crowd of 28,089 witnessed my Leicester City debut. It bore certain similarities to my first game for Chesterfield in that the manager said little apart from 'Good luck and do your best'. Matt had obviously waited until the last moment before making a decision about Dave MacLaren's fitness because it was his name that appeared in the match programme. I wasn't mentioned at all. Not that it bothered me – I had other things to occupy my mind, not least a very lively Blackpool forward line that contained Jackie Mudie and Bill Perry, both of whom had played in the 1953 'Matthews Final', and rising stars Ray Charnley, Arthur Kaye and Dave Durie.

I was a little disappointed to learn that the great Stanley Matthews wasn't included in the Blackpool team as I would have loved to have played against the maestro. Stan was forty-four years of age but still eminently capable of playing First Division football. He had, in fact, been a member of the England team only two years previously. But I'd heard that he was at logger-heads with Blackpool boss Ron Suart, who wanted him to play deeper and get more involved in general build-up play rather than simply jink up and down the wing and tease the left back. Football, however, was changing. It was becoming more tactical, teams were becoming better organized and Stan's style obviously didn't suit Suart. Stan was nowhere near as quick as he used to be, but he was still sharp and his talismatic qualities were invaluable to a team. His mere presence in the Blackpool side used to lift the players and would have put up to 7,000 on the gate.

The Leicester crowd gave me their full support that night, as did my new team mates. As a young debutant I couldn't have asked for more from my defence. Len Chalmers, Joe Baillie, John Newman, Tony Knapp and Colin Appleton encouraged me for the duration of the game, saying 'well done' to just about everything I did. Whenever I had the ball in my hands, Len Chalmers and Joe Baillie would run out wide and make themselves available. If I was considering a long kick upfield to our forwards, centre half Tony Knapp told me to take my time. I made a concerted effort to 'command my domain', that is, the penalty box, coming off my line quickly to collect crosses and then telling my defence to push up.

Our inside left, Ken Leek, put us in front, but that wily little predator, Jackie Mudie, pulled a goal back for Blackpool. I think it was Blackpool's Arthur Kaye who played the ball into our penalty box from the right. Mudie latched on to the pass and seeing him free of his marker, I quickly came off my line to close down his vision of goal. Jackie, a shrewd and calculating inside forward, spotted a small gap to my left and simply stroked the ball down that channel and into the corner of the net. There wasn't much power behind his effort; there didn't need to be. Mudie knew I wouldn't reach the ball and went for accuracy rather than venom. The game ended in a 1–1 draw. I was disappointed to concede a goal, but happy that I had managed to get through the game without making a serious error.

I retained my place for the following game, a 2–0 defeat at Newcastle United, but with Dave MacLaren once again fit found myself back in the reserves when Leicester travelled to Blackpool for their return league fixture. My return to the second XI, however, was not to be for long.

While I concentrated my efforts in the Football Combination, the Leicester first team began to leak goals. A 3–3 draw at Blackpool was followed by a 4–3 victory at Birmingham City. Then there came a 1–1 draw with Spurs, a 4–1 defeat at Manchester United and a 3–2 home defeat at the hands of Blackburn Rovers – fourteen goals conceded in five games. Matt Gillies was obviously concerned because for the next game, away at Manchester City, I found myself recalled to the first team. I wish I could say I came back into the team and suddenly Leicester became watertight in defence, but I can't. We lost 3–2 at Manchester City, drew 2–2 at home to Arsenal, then, suffered the ignominy of a 6–1 defeat at Everton. Six! It was like being back with Chesterfield reserves. I was a very busy goalkeeper in that game and for all I conceded half a dozen, I do remember making some telling saves late in the game from efforts by Everton's Bobby Collins, Brian Harris and Alex Parker that could have made the margin of defeat even more comprehensive.

Although my presence in the team hadn't stemmed the tide of goals, I felt that with each game my performance was improving. Following our defeat at Everton I kept my place for the game against Sheffield Wednesday and was to be an ever-present in the team for the remainder of that season. We lost games, of course, but never again were we on the receiving end of a hammering. The emphasis was still very much on attacking football at this time, but in only two games in the new year did we concede more than two goals: a 3–1 defeat against Birmingham City and a 3–3 draw with Everton.

Leicester finished a creditable twelfth in the First Division, not bad considering we had had a poor start with only four victories from our first twenty matches. Our form in the new year gave rise to great optimism and I had taken heart from my own performances. After that disappointing start to our campaign, we only lost six of our remaining twenty-two league games. Since my arrival at the club as sixth-choice goalkeeper it had taken me little over a quarter of a season to establish myself in the first team.

Progress had its price, of course. I was my own sternest critic and I placed great demands upon myself both in physical training and learning goalkeeping technique. I knew I couldn't hope to progress on talent alone. I wanted to continue improving as a goalkeeper and became single-minded in this aim. After my normal training (which, in fact, was the same training every other player at the club did, irrespective of the position he played) I'd ask a couple of the youth team players to stay behind with me at the training ground to practise shooting at me. I was keen to develop, even evolve, the practical side of goalkeeping. Sometimes I'd ask these young lads to ping shots at my goal from a variety of angles. On one occasion, for an hour or so, all I asked them to do was either chip or lob the ball towards goal. I took up a position half way between the penalty spot and the edge of the penalty area. Constantly running backwards to get to the ball, I worked out the best position I could take up relative to the kicker in order to backpedal and still make the save.

Players in training at both Chesterfield and Leicester tended to work to their strengths rather than their weaknesses. To my mind, this was the wrong way to go about things. I made a concerted effort to work on aspects of my game I felt were weak – taking crosses on my left-hand side, for example. I had one of the young lads drive or float crosses into the penalty area for me to collect while under the challenge of two other players. I wasn't always able to make the catch, so I had to work on all the different ways of punching the ball clear when under pressure. Through constant practice I built a repertoire of seven punches, each suited to a particular situation.

Throughout my first season with Leicester I was hell-bent on improving as a goalkeeper and learning as much about goalkeeping as time would allow. A lot of players on establishing themselves in a first team, through a combination of their own satisfaction and sense of achievement, don't work as hard at their own game as they ought to. Many go into a comfort zone, feeling that as a first-team regular they no longer need to work on their technique. On the contrary, that is when the hard work should begin. No doubt you have seen plenty of gifted players who never go on to fulfil what you believe could be their true potential. They rest on their laurels. They work hard in training, they carry out tactical ploys to the letter, but don't apply themselves to greater effect in their own technique, skills and role in the team. In short, they don't push themselves as much as they should. Hence they never fully evolve into players that can contribute that little bit more, or, something special to a team when it is needed. I had no idea how good a goalkeeper I could be, but I was resolved to find out. I worked hard at improving my footwork, my handling, punching, positioning, reflex saves, clearances, both out of my hands and dead ball. I worked at building my stamina and strength, body suppleness and ability to ride a challenge. I studied angles, the flight of the ball and how best to organize my defence in front of me. I worked on taking high balls, low balls, shot-stopping from close range and from every distance and angle. Come the end of the 1959–60 season I knew enough about goalkeeping to realize just how much I still had to learn!

I was ambitious but so too were Leicester City. Unfortunately the club's finances were rather more down to earth. During the season the club had made unsuccessful offers for John White of Falkirk (who eventually opted for Spurs), Hibernian's Joe Baker (who was signed by Italian giants Torino) and a centre forward who had been scoring a lot of goals for Second Division Middlesbrough, Brian Clough. In 1961 Clough made the short move to Sunderland, going on to score 251 goals in 274 games before a bad knee injury curtailed his career at the age of twenty-seven. Leicester simply couldn't compete in the transfer market when the likes of Clough were selling for £45,000, let alone the £73,000 Torino were prepared to pay for Baker. While it showed that Matt Gillies and his new chief scout Bert Johnson were good judges of talent, they could not pay silly prices.

I suppose I was one of Matt's successful signings that season, but I wasn't the only one. In the close season the club had also signed Albert Cheesebrough from Burnley. Albert had gone straight into the first team and only missed one game in 1959–60. The £20,000 fee for Albert, a considerable one for Leicester, proved to be money well spent. He was a fast, skilful, hard-working and versatile forward with a bullet of a shot – but what I remember most about him is his thighs. They were the most enormous thighs of anyone I ever saw, like bags of cement and made even the baggiest shorts appear tight. His bulging calves were no less remarkable, either.

Albert Cheesebrough . . . how the names of the players have changed in the past forty years! Gordon Banks is a straightforward name that would, I am sure, pass without comment in any generation of football. The name Albert Cheesebrough, however, appears now to be exactly what it is: a name from another era of football. We don't have players by the name of Albert Cheesebrough, Arthur Bottom or Mortimer Costello in football in the new millennium. Yet such yeomanesque names were far from unique in football at that time. In the short time I had spent with Chesterfield and Leicester I also came across Grenville Hair (Leeds United), Willie Myerscough (Aston Villa) and Geoffrey Sidebottom (Wolves). There was also Stan Ackerley (Manchester United), Redfern Froggatt (Sheffield Wednesday), Basil Acres (Ipswich Town), Ray Bumstead (Bournemouth), Gerry Cakebread (Brentford), Ralph Gubbins (Hull City), Allenby Cornfield (Shrewsbury Town), Harold Threadgold (Southend), Arthur Longbottom (QPR) and Albert Otheringcroft (Gateshead). Football names to be sure, but ones that seem to have leaped straight from the pages of Dickens or Harold Brighouse's *Hobson's Choice*.

Recalling those players now, I can't help wondering whether, if David Beckham or Michael Owen had been blessed with similarly yeoman surnames, would they now enjoy star status? Can you imagine the snack foods, mobile phone, designer eyewear or soft drinks companies scrambling to secure the endorsement of Albert Cheesebrough or Arthur Bottom if they were the star turns of football today? Moreover, 'Cheesey' and 'Bots' are not nicknames that lend themselves to today's perceived image of a star. Christian names have always been subject to fashion. Subsequent generations of parents rejected Arthur, Albert and Harold as being simply old-fashioned. But surnames you're stuck with. Where are the Cheesebroughs, Bottoms, Cakebreads and Otheringcrofts of today? Curiously, not in professional football, nor have they been for some years. Their absence is a small but poignant reminder of the changing fabric of the game.

Another young player also made his mark during my first season at Leicester – Frank McLintock, a Glaswegian signed from Shawfield Juniors. As a young player he combined the toughness of a Gorbals upbringing with a fine footballing brain to emerge as a stylish wing half whose great vision was the catalyst to many a Leicester attack. At twenty-two he had the guile and nous of a much more experienced player. Frank always made himself available to me for throw-outs with his shrewd positioning in midfield. His skilful repertoire of long and short passes, timed and executed to perfection, probed ceaselessly into opposing defences and were an indication of a great player in the making. When Frank eventually left Leicester for Arsenal in 1964, the £80,000 paid for his services was the highest fee Leicester had ever received for a player. Frank's enthusiasm for football was to play no small part in my development as a goalkeeper, for which I will always be grateful.

Our good form in the new year gave rise to hopes of a good FA Cup run. In the third round we won 2–1 at Wrexham, with goals from Albert Cheesebrough and Ken Leek. (The headline writers were no better then than they are today: 'Cheese and Leek Give Wrexham Food for Thought'; 'Wrexham Leek Early Goal then Are Cheesed Off'.) In round four we beat Fulham 2–1 at Filbert Street to set up a fifth-round home tie against West Bromwich Albion – the first ever all-ticket match at Leicester.

Someone had the bright idea that cup tickets wou[ld]
on the turnstiles at the reserves' Football Combinatio[n]
against Bournemouth. Cup fever had gripped the cit[y]
bumper crowd of 22,890 (obviously a record for a Leiceste. City
reserves match) turned up to see the reserves that day, while I
played in front of fewer than 17,000 in the First Division at Luton
Town. Apparently the atmosphere was terrific and Bournemouth's reserves couldn't believe their luck to be playing in front
of such a large crowd. I still think it's a great way of selling tickets
for a big game.

These days many clubs have a sliding scale of admission prices.
Prices vary according to the perceived attraction of the opposition
or status of a game. Though admission prices are never cheap.
A lot of supporters resent paying more to see their club play
Manchester United or Liverpool in a cup tie. Hiked admission
prices simply annoy a lot of fans who feel their club loyalty is
being exploited. To sell tickets for a big game at a reserve match
or a League match that would normally attract far less than the
ground capacity, seems to me to be a far better way of going
about things. First, the club would enjoy two bumper pay days
instead of one. The extra money taken from the match at which
tickets went on sale would more than equal any price increase
implemented for the big game. Secondly, by doing that, clubs
would not incur the wrath of supporters incensed at having to
pay more than the normal admission price. Even allowing for
the extra costs of policing, gatemen and so on, I am sure clubs
would still benefit both financially and in terms of goodwill.

These days clubs invest heavily in PR departments and community schemes in an attempt to foster better relations with
supporters and the wider public. Yet when they have an opportunity to do just that and make some extra money in the process,
they ignore it. Perhaps this has something to do with people who
work behind the scenes at clubs these days. Many have a proven
track record in marketing and advertising but have never been
football supporters, never mind players. Of course there are chief

executives and commercial directors with a football background, but there are many people in key commercial and administrative positions in clubs today whose first experience of football comes with their taking up the post. They understand marketing but seemingly not football or its supporters. They try to sell the club as they would do any commercial product. But they don't have to, because in the supporters a football club already has inbuilt brand loyalty. What's more, unlike breakfast cereal or toilet tissue, football instils a great level of emotion in its consumers. When such loyalty and emotion is not understood and occasionally ignored, supporters at best feel exploited, at worst antagonized.

If a fan turns up at a home game to hear the stadium announcer pushing the club's own-brand financial services, when on the field the team is crying out for a new striker to avert a decline towards the relegation zone, then he or she is bound to resent his club's scale of priorities. Yet time and again I hear stories of clubs riding roughshod over their supporters' feelings, an attitude that inspires cynicism, not loyalty.

A near-capacity crowd of 38,000 turned up at Filbert Street for the West Brom tie. It became evident that something was wrong during an unusually long half-time interval. After a quarter of an hour we still hadn't heard the buzzer sound in our changing room, the sign for us to go out for the second half. Thinking there may have been a problem outside the ground with ticketless supporters, Matt Gillies told us to take to the field and to keep warm until the match officials appeared. As we filed out in the corridor, our trainer Les Dowdells told us to return to the changing room; the second half was going to be delayed because the referee, Jack Husband, had been taken ill. Then Charles Maley, our club secretary, came with some shocking news. Jack Husband had collapsed in the officials' changing room and died. But it had been decided to continue the game.

When a loudspeaker appeal was made to the crowd for a

suitably qualified official, a former referee came forward to run the line with one of the linesmen taking over as referee. After a lengthy delay we went on to beat West Brom 2–1 with goals from Jimmy Walsh and Albert Cheesebrough, though our celebrations were muted. That the game was allowed to continue speaks volumes about the nation's attitude to death in the aftermath of the Second World War. Nowadays we would all be shocked by such an event, and rightly so, and it would be inconceivable to play on afterwards. But to people with the carnage of war fresh in their minds it seemed hardly to warrant a second thought. The best defence people had erected against six years of destruction and tragedy was, as Mam said, simply to 'get on with it'. So we did.

In the sixth round a crowd of 39,000 saw us bow out of the FA Cup against Wolverhampton Wanderers. It turned out to be a classic quarter-final, full of cut and thrust. Peter Broadbent put Wolves ahead only for Tommy McDonald to equalize. Len Chalmers, two years older than me at twenty-four, had recently been appointed captain. Len played exceptionally well that day but towards the end of the game couldn't get out of the way of a low centre and deflected the ball past me and into the net. In the dressing room after the game Len was inconsolable. I told him, 'It's gone now, Len, so forget it. Next season, luck'll probably be on your side in the Cup.' Nothing could have been further from the truth.

Wolves went on to win the FA Cup that season, beating Blackburn Rovers 3–0, though they were denied a third consecutive League Championship when Burnley pipped them on the very last day – the first time that the Clarets had topped the table all season. Burnley's success was a triumph for the attacking football that was still very much in vogue in 1960 as evidenced by Wolves' goal tally of 100-plus for the third successive season. We played Burnley twice towards the end of the season when they really had their tails up and the league title within their reach. We lost by the only goal at Turf Moor, but dented their progress by winning 2–1 at Filbert Street. Our good form in the second half of the season and the fact that we had beaten the eventual champions at home and had given them a very close game on their own turf, made me believe Leicester could go on to bigger and better things the following season. I wasn't wrong.

As I have said, the emphasis was still very much on scoring goals rather than conceding them. The fact that the best club side in the world, Real Madrid, were an all-out attacking side fuelled the general notion that there was nothing wrong in conceding three or four goals as long as you scored five or six. In the case of Real Madrid, more.

The maximum wage a player in the Football League could earn at this time was £20. On making the first team at Leicester City my wage had been increased from £15 to £17, which on establishing myself in the Leicester team, was increased to £20 less tax. My new found 'wealth' enabled Ursula and I to buy one or two home comforts, one being a television. What televisions there were available in the shops in 1959–60 all seemed to be British made, Bush, Ferguson, Ekco and Ultra. We chose an Ultra, black and white of course with a fourteen-inch screen. For many people, ourselves included, television was still a novelty and the technology nowhere near that of today. When the cathode ray tube blew, as they often did in those days, replacement was so costly that many people when buying a TV set took out insurance to cover the cost.

I watched the 1960 European Cup final on our little black and white Ultra and marvelled at the skill and technique of Real Madrid. All these years on, I still believe Real's performance in that final to be the greatest ever performance, by the greatest ever club side, the world has ever seen. Real beat Eintracht Frankfurt 7–3 and the performances of Alfredo di Stefano and Ferenc Puskas were sublime.

Looking at the margin of Real's victory, one might think Frankfurt were simply a team of journeymen who ran up against a very good side. The truth was that Eintracht Frankfurt were a very good side up against a brilliant one. To put Frankfurt into perspective, Glasgow Rangers were considered to be one of the best teams in Britain at that time. In the two-legged semi-final Frankfurt beat Rangers 6–1 in Germany and 6–3 at Ibrox! For Frankfurt then to concede seven in the final says volumes for how far ahead of every other team Real were. True, Frankfurt scored three, but they were outclassed and outplayed for long periods of the game and the final result was never in doubt from the moment Di Stefano pulled back Richard Kress's opening goal for the Germans.

The European Cup was just starting to take off as a competition. The victory over Frankfurt was Real Madrid's fifth consecutive European Cup success since its inauguration in 1955–56. As a team Real were peerless and their passing, movement off the ball, vision and finishing in and around the penalty box were breathtaking. Everyone else who watched that final was in awe of them.

It was generally felt that Spanish and Italian football was superior to our domestic game. But Real Madrid were streets ahead of any other Spanish team of the day. The football they played seemed to be from another planet. Following that European Cup final I spoke to quite a number of my fellow players and the consensus of opinion was that Real had created a benchmark for us all to aspire to. We knew that, in all probability, we would never reach the sublime level of football displayed by Real that night, either as individuals or as a team, but at least we now knew what was possible. I don't think any club side has ever equalled the performance of Real that night, but many of the great individual and team performances we have seen since, in part, came about through people trying to equal the standard as laid down by Di Stefano, Puskas and company.

Since 1953 when Hungary beat England 6–3 at Wembley, the first foreign team ever to win on English soil, and less than a year later followed up that victory with a 7–1 demolition of England in Budapest, we had known that, in International terms, our football was no longer the best in the world. Real Madrid's domination of European club football merely underlined the point. The success of Real, and the manner of it, woke English football from its long slumber that had been remarkably undisturbed by the watershed defeats at the hands of the Hungarians. Following the 1960 European Cup final, more clubs started to appoint coaches. They realized individual skill and effort was no longer enough, there also had to be collective effort. The FA's coaching school at Lilleshall took on far greater importance and many current and former players attended their courses with a view to learning more about the tactical side of the game and the development of skills and technique.

These coaching schools were under the supervision of Walter Winterbottom, the England manager who also bore the title of Chief of the Football Association's Coaching Staff. Walter was a deep-thinking football man, always more at home with the coaching side of his job than the actual management of teams. The FA and Walter made a great effort to encourage former players, and some current ones, to take up what was then a three-part course leading to full qualification as an FA coach. Following the 1960 European Cup Final, the FA's Coaching Course was fully subscribed and many of those who embarked upon the course would go on to make telling contributions to our game. Jimmy Adamson, Tony Barton, Tommy Docherty, Frank O'Farrell, Bob Paisley and Dave Sexton were all on the same coaching course. They and many others played no small part in changing the way we played the game. Another member of the Class of 1960–61 was Bert Johnson, the chief scout at Leicester City, who Matt Gillies later appointed as first-team coach and whose expertise and enthusiasm was to play a significant part in my development as a goalkeeper.

English football may well have been embarking upon a renaissance but there was still an insular attitude prevalent in a number of people charged with running the game. England, Scotland,

Wales and Northern Ireland had all declined to enter the inaug-ural European Nations Cup, which was won by the USSR. The four respective FAs shunned this new tournament, believing the Home International tournament to be of greater importance. While it is true to say the European Nations Cup had nowhere near the status and kudos of today's European Championship, the fact that we had declined to compete with other European international teams on a competitive basis could only hinder, rather than help, the seeds of progress.

One of the changes that took place in football at this time concerned the strips. Many teams rejected the thick cotton, collared shirts with their buttoned fronts and cuffs in favour of lightweight V-necked shirts with short sleeves. Stanley Matthews, ever the innovator, and Tom Finney had returned from the 1950 World Cup impressed with the lightweight strips worn by South American teams such as Brazil and Uruguay but their suggestions that English clubs should adopt them fell on deaf ears. Three years later Hungary turned up at Wembley wearing similar lightweight shirts, but it took a few more years before English clubs finally saw the benefits to be had from wearing this new type of strip and adopted the style.

The first team to wear these lightweight V-necked shirts in an FA Cup final were Manchester City in 1955 against Newcastle United. In the following year's final against Birmingham City the Mancunians repeated the experiment, this time in their change strip to avoid a colour clash, while Birmingham stuck with the traditional collar and cuff shirts that had been de rigueur for teams since the early thirties.

In 1956 the England team adopted the new style of shirt, though many clubs were slow to take to what was not so much a new fashion as a more practical form of kit. At Chesterfield we had worn the old-style thick cotton collared shirts. Leicester City, however, had made the switch a couple of years before my arrival at the club in 1959.

The significance of this innovation in kit design was that it spearheaded a change of attitude across many aspects of the game at the time. Every aspect of a footballer's kit changed. Shorts became, well, shorter and less restrictive to movement. Not only that, the heavy cotton from which shorts had been made since the Victorian age was superseded by nylon. In keeping with the new style of shirt and shorts, the woollen stockings players had worn for decades were replaced by lightweight cotton designs. Boots also became lighter and lower slung. The reinforced toecap was committed to history as was the steel plate that used to form part of the sole. These changes even affected the way a player laced his boots. The old reinforced boot had a loop at the back of the heel through which the lace was threaded. This was now considered a potential danger to ankles and gradually was dropped by the boot manufacturers. Players now preferred to lace up their boots by wrapping the lace over the upper foot and under the instep rather than bind it around the ankle.

The new lightweight strips were not just symbolic of a game keen to modernize. Nor were they the subject of any commercial or marketing strategy – such things did not exist in football at the time. They were simply more practical athletic solutions, in an era when players were becoming increasingly aware of the need to be more professional and dedicated in every aspect of the game. The fabric of football, quite literally, was changing.

The dawn of the sixties, then, was a time of enormous change in football. Across every aspect of society people's lives were changing. Material comfort and opportunity was increasing. Yet in the north and midlands that I knew, at least, memories were still fresh of depression, war, rationing and shortages. People saved up for things. For instance, when Ursula and I got married, like many young couples of the day we set up home with what bits of furniture we had been given by relatives. Because Ursula had come over from war-shattered Germany, any furniture and other home comforts we acquired had to come from my family and, though we were grateful for what we received, there wasn't a great deal of it.

Today young couples setting up home have considerable aspirations. The vast majority seem to aspire to a middle-class lifestyle from the outset and, if their savings don't run to furnishing their home as they had planned themselves, they think nothing of buying the rest on store or credit cards. Ursula and I set up home in 1959 and, like many other couples, we were petrified at the thought of immersing ourselves in credit. As part of a working-class family in the forties and fifties, I was brought up to look upon credit with a combination of deep mistrust and abhorrence. It was not so much the stigma of taking out credit, more that people felt they would lose face if they were beholden to more people than was absolutely necessary.

People were beholden to the local steelworks or pit for their livelihood; to a building society or rent man for the roof over their heads; for their spiritual fulfilment, people were beholden to God – or else to Sheffield Wednesday or United. To be beholden also to a 'tick book' (a record of hire-purchase payments) to acquire possessions within the home, was considered unbecoming for working folk who saw paying cash as a mark of integrity, honesty and the inbred illusion of financial independence. Tinsley folk would rather make do and mend, rely on hand-me-downs from relatives, or simply go without rather than sign up for what Dad called the 'never-never'. The phrase 'never-never' indicated how we viewed credit: once you succumbed to the temptation of credit, you would never be rid of it. To spend money you didn't have was a fantasy, contrasting with the reality of the daily toil of work, which everyone knew would eventually lead to retirement and days pottering around an allotment. Life was difficult enough with monthly repayments to be found for the building society; to commit oneself to further borrowing was seen as plain madness.

Of course people's expectations were nowhere near as high as they are today. The labour-saving devices of the consumer revolution had yet to sweep Britain and as Mam often said, 'What you never had, you never miss.' Likewise, what others didn't have, you never yearned for. Hence, no credit.

My marriage to Ursula had more or less coincided with my elevation to the Chesterfield first team. We bought a semi-detached house in Treeton for £1,100 but my transfer to Leicester came soon after. In fact, so short a time did we spend in that house that when we sold it we actually owed more to the building society than we had actually borrowed.

Money had been tight during my time with Chesterfield, but in the summer of 1959 we had saved enough for our first holiday. A week at Butlin's in Skegness was hardly the sort of holiday professional footballers opt for these days, but in relative terms, I was lucky. Many of my Chesterfield team mates, like so many other players of the time, were forced to take on a summer job in the close season to supplement their income.

When signing for Leicester City, we moved into a club house formerly occupied by Arthur Rowley, whose career total of 434 league goals remains a record to this day, a record that, I should imagine, will never be beaten.

Our new home was a semi-detached house in Kirkland Road, Braunceston. Ursula and I immediately felt very much at home there, though at times we felt like two peas in a drum. This house was much larger than our first home in Treeton and once we had moved in what furniture we possessed – still the hand-me-downs from my family – we were immediately struck by a feeling of open space. We didn't have a three-piece suite. All we had were two armchairs, one red, one blue, that we had bought when seeing them advertised in the small ads in the *Sheffield Star*. At night we'd watch the television or listen to the wireless, sitting either side of a small marble-tiled fireplace like two bookends. We were gloriously happy. I had found the love of my life. We were ensconced in our own spacious home. I was doing the only thing I wanted to do in life, play football, and was being paid to do so. Life was great. I couldn't believe it could get much better than this.

4. From Number Six to Number 1

Apart from the considerable thrill of having established myself as Leicester's first-choice goalkeeper, the events surrounding my first season at Filbert Street had not been remarkable. All was to change, however. In 1960–61 Leicester embarked upon one of the most notable seasons in their history and football was rarely out of the headlines as a result of events both on and off the pitch.

When I reported back for pre-season training, revolution against the maximum wage was in the air. Fuelled by newsletters from the players' union, the Professional Footballers' Association, many of us debated the rights and wrongs of resorting to strike action in order to free ourselves from contracts that bound us to a club for life and put a ceiling on what we could earn.

Nationwide, supporters too were grumbling. During the close season the Football League had announced that admission prices for adults were to rise to a minimum of 2s. 6d. (12½p). Following the post-war boom when total annual crowds were in excess of 40 million, attendances had been in gradual decline and many supporters believed the increased admission price would only make matters worse. (They were right: 1960–61 saw attendances fall to 28.5 million from 32.5 million the previous season.)

There was discontent in the media, too. While it was widely agreed that English club football had fallen way behind the standard set by the top European sides, a few journalists launched critical attacks on the England team's performances on the international scene. Why, supporters argued, should we be expected to pay more for an inferior product? One particularly stinging attack came from the former Bolton and England centre forward turned football writer, David Jack. Discussing the previous summer's four-game tour during which England managed only a

single win against the USA, Jack called for 'drastic changes' at
the top if we wish to compete with the great football nations of
the world.

Jack was just getting up a head of steam. 'The game we gave
to the world,' he continued, 'is no longer played with skill on
these islands.' Apart from Johnny Haynes who had useful games,
Jimmy Greaves, who was raw but promising, and Bobby Charlton, who could not excel if played out of position, 'not one
forward justified the great honour paid to him as a representative
of his country'.

At the end of the tour FA officials trotted out the usual excuses
for the team's failure, but ignored the most obvious fact: 'The
men at the top chose players who were not the best at England's
disposal. They took poor performers to South America and left
good players at home.' Jack was scathing about having a selection
committee to pick the England team, a view soon echoed by
other commentators. This lobby of opinion soon led to Walter
Winterbottom being placed in sole change of England team
affairs. Not before time – Walter had been England's manager
since 1946!

English football, however, had not so much declined as stood
still in an era when the football of other nations had developed
considerably. When comparing England with Brazil, Italy or
Germany, or Arsenal and Wolves with Real Madrid or Barcelona,
it was easy to conclude the quality of football in England had
declined. It hadn't. For some years our game had been allowed
to stagnate while that of other nations had taken great strides
along new paths of exploration. But in 1960–61 English football
began the process of catching up. The benefits of the FA's
coaching school began to filter through in the early sixties, and
that, combined with the long-overdue introduction of a properly
structured youth policy, played no small part in England winning
the World Cup just a few years later.

One of that summer's innovations was an apprenticeship
system for young players. Previously, a lad of fifteen signed on as

a member of his club's office or groundstaff. While he wanted to concentrate on training and playing for his club's junior teams, the bulk of the apprentice's time was spent either in clerical work or odd maintenance jobs around the ground. Now, while the new two-year apprenticeships would still involve menial tasks such as sweeping the terraces, cleaning the boots of senior professionals and swilling out the changing rooms, there was a commitment that football was to come first.

At the end of his apprenticeship a young player's development would be assessed and, ultimately, the manager would decide whether he was to be offered full-time professional terms, or released. There was (and remains today) a high fall-out rate among young players, but it was believed that having had two years' learning about football in a professional environment, a young player released by a top club could find employment with a club in a lower-division outfit. At worst, he could become a part-time professional or an amateur, but the skills gained in his apprenticeship would benefit football at the grass-roots level.

That summer the Football League announced another innovation to English football, the League Cup. While generally thought to have been the brainchild of Alan Hardaker, the gruff, stoic secretary of the Football League, the original suggestion for a secondary cup competition, for league clubs only, had come from the FA Secretary, later President of FIFA, Sir Stanley Rous. Rous's original idea was for a pre-season competition in which teams would initially compete in groups. He found few supporters among football's hierarchy for his idea but it was refined by Alan Hardaker and the League Cup came into being, to a lukewarm reception.

Arsenal, Tottenham Hotspur, Wolves, Sheffield Wednesday and West Bromwich Albion chose not to compete in the inaugural competition. The imbalance in the number of competing teams meant a number of clubs received byes in the first round in order to form a thirty-two tie second round. Another unpopular feature was that there would be no one-off final at Wembley, but a two-legged final on the finalists' grounds. The League Cup had been devalued in the eyes of the supporters and media before it even got under way.

Alan Hardaker dubbed it the 'People's Cup', meaning presumably a cup free of the pomp and circumstance and bereft of the dignitaries and establishment freeloaders so much in evidence at the FA Cup Final. But it was missing the charm of football tradition, the ivy-covered venerableness of the FA Cup, the romance and drama of a non-league David laying low a Football League Goliath.

Clubs soon found that League Cup attendances were well below what they normally had for league games. In time, however, the League Cup grew in popularity and those clubs that had stood aloof soon joined up when they realized that there was money to be made and that winning afforded entry to European competition. From the start I was all in favour of the League Cup. In time it would repay my enthusiasm with a treasure chest of golden memories.

In the close season Matt Gillies had added two new players to the squad: George Meek, a winger from Leeds United, and George Heyes, an understudy goalkeeper from Rochdale. Both Johnny Anderson and Dave MacLaren had been sold, further boosting my confidence that the boss had every faith in me as first-choice goalkeeper, and, moreover, that I had now truly established myself as the Leicester number one. Johnny and Dave were competent goalkeepers and the fact they had moved elsewhere to find regular first-team football took a little pressure off me. Competition for places concentrates the mind wonderfully, but the fact that I no longer had two able, experienced keepers breathing down my neck lessened my anxiety that one little mistake in a game could cost me my place. I could concentrate totally on my personal game and try to implement some of the goalkeeping techniques I had developed in training.

Once again Matt Gillies was unable to entice top players to

Leicester. He tried and failed to sign the Arsenal centre forward David Herd and Pat Crerand from Celtic, both of whom were to opt for Manchester United, and Dundee's Alan Gilzean, who eventually moved to Spurs. Matt obviously felt that we needed a goalscoring centre forward to replace Derek Hines. Derek was a prolific scorer who joined the club in 1947. He played and scored in the first ever England youth international, a 4–2 win against Scotland in 1947, and in the fifties had formed a terrific front-line partnership at Leicester with the legendary Arthur Rowley. Derek was skilful at running off the ball to create opportunities for team mates, a clinical finisher with a league tally of 116 goals in 299 appearances.

Derek Hines played in the first four games but it soon became apparent that, at nearly thirty, he wasn't going to lead the line in the long term. Indeed, at the beginning of September Derek was replaced from the reserves by the stylish, skilful Ken Leek, whose speed off the mark was breathtaking and who did a terrific job for us up front.

Our opening game of the season bore certain similarities to my debut for the club. It took place at Filbert Street, the opposition were Blackpool and the score was 1–1. We followed that with a fine 3–1 win at Chelsea courtesy of two goals from left winger Gordon Wills and one from Jimmy Walsh, who had taken over from Len Chalmers as captain. On the return train journey the team were in optimistic mood.

But we lost our next game at Everton 3–1 and went down in the following three, two of which were at home to Chelsea and Blackburn Rovers. Things weren't right and Gillies began to ring the changes: Ken Leek came in for Derek Hines, Ian King for Len Chalmers at right back, Frank McLintock for Ian White at right half and Howard Riley replaced George Meek at outside right. By the time we arrived at Old Trafford to take on Manchester United on 10 September the team had a very different look to it from the one that had started the season just a few weeks earlier.

Manchester United were a team in transition. The aftermath of the Munich air disaster still lingered and United were still forced to field young players of promise earlier than their manager, Matt Busby, would probably have liked. We felt we could take advantage of Frank Haydock and Jimmy Nicholson, United's two young wing halves. Our captain, Jimmy Walsh, suggested he and Albert Cheesebrough, as our inside forwards, should push on to Haydock and Nicholson and put them under pressure.

With the likes of goalkeeper Harry Gregg, Maurice Setters, Bill Foulkes, Bobby Charlton, Johnny Giles, Albert Quixall and Dennis Viollet, Manchester United boasted real quality to counterbalance the inexperience. Johnny Giles put United ahead, but Jimmy Walsh proved his point when he equalized for us after forcing Jimmy Nicholson into a mistake in the second half. The game ended 1–1. We had put an end to a sequence of four successive defeats but, more significantly, our performance at Old Trafford was the first indication that the manager's wholesale team changes were beginning to bear fruit.

We lost only four of our next thirteen league games and come December, were handily placed in Division One. That, however, was nowhere near good enough in a season totally dominated by one club. Tottenham Hotspur enjoyed a dream start to the season, winning a record 11 consecutive games, scoring 36 goals in the process. They didn't drop a point until their draw with Manchester City in mid-October, and remained unbeaten until 12 November when their only real rivals to give them a run for the money in the championship, Sheffield Wednesday, beat them 2–1 at Hillsborough. Spurs were magnificent in every respect. Their game plan of all-out attack set several more new records: winning 31 of their 42 league games, registering 16 victories away from home (including eight in a row), and equalling Arsenal's Division One record points haul of 66 set in 1930–31.

We met Spurs at Filbert Street in mid-September and ran

them very close, losing by the odd goal in three. I saw this as another benchmark to our season: Spurs were steamrollering most teams, home and away, but Les Allen and Cliff Jones of Spurs told us after the game that we had given them their most difficult game to date. It is true that professional footballers only say you have played well when they have beaten you. Rarely, if ever, do players compliment opponents when they have lost. However, I felt the comments from Les Allen and Cliff Jones were sincere rather than patronizing. We had indeed given Spurs a good run for their money, which, for all their excellence, was still £20 maximum per man, per week, less tax – the same as the least talented players in the Fourth Division could hope to earn.

When we travelled to White Hart Lane for the return fixture in February, Spurs were top of Division One and well clear of their nearest challengers, Sheffield Wednesday and Burnley. We were sixth, but arrived in London on the back of a six-game unbeaten league and cup run that had seen us beat Everton 4–1 and Manchester United 6–0.

The victories over Everton and Manchester United were ample evidence of how much Leicester were improving as a team. In the previous season I had conceded six against Everton. A year later for us to beat Everton comfortably, then follow that result by hitting Manchester United for six, made me realize just how far we had come. Not only could we compete with the best, we could, on occasion, now beat them handsomely. The acid test for that belief was to be our game against Spurs at White Hart Lane.

We left Leicester station late on Friday morning on the London-bound express. I had long since given up my interest in trainspotting though I have to say, even as a player, I would look out of a carriage window with interest whenever we passed a railway shed or an idling steam engine in a siding. Steam engines appeared to me to have more character and individuality than the diesels that, at the time, were beginning to replace them. I quite enjoyed travelling by train to away games, because I always

associated rail journeys with childhood days out or holiday treats
with the family.

On arriving at the grandest of London termini, St Pancras,
with the adjacent neo-Gothic masterpiece of the Midland Grand
Hotel, the Leicester team were besieged by young, exclusively
male, autograph hunters brandishing either a flip-top autograph
book, each page a different vivid colour, or a sugar-paper scrap-
book containing strange-coloured team line-ups and portraits
clipped from *Football Monthly*, *Soccer Star* and, most garish of all,
Reynold's News. We were only too happy to sign every book
thrust at us by those autograph hunters, who stood in all weathers
hoping to add to their collections of precious signatures. Today,
the autographs of our top players are more difficult to come by.
The stars are protected from fans by security staff and marketing
people anxious to guard the image rights of these highly valued
commodities. Players such as David Beckham, Ryan Giggs and
Michael Owen, while happy to offer their signature for genuine
collectors of autographs, have to be wary of people posing as fans
who seek to sell signed memorabilia for their own gain. Another
sad reflection of the way football has changed its relationship
with its fans. As a member of England's 1966 World Cup team,
I'm often asked to sign match programmes, photographs, replica
shirts and the like. I never refuse, though I try to differentiate
between the genuine fan and the person out to make a quick
buck. I ask to whom I can dedicate the autograph – the 'on the
make' brigade find it difficult to sell on items bearing a dedicated
signature, while genuine fans are only too happy to have autographs personally dedicated.

Thinking back to that match against Spurs reminds me of
the routine we followed on away matches. When in London
Leicester always stayed at the Russell Hotel where we would
be allocated our rooms. I roomed with our left back, Richie
Norman, with whom I got on very well and whose tremendous
sense of humour lightened what could often be the tedious hours
before a game. Once we had unpacked we always went for a

walk to stretch our legs, usually a leisurely stroll around the garden in the centre of Russell Square, then back again to the ornately Victorian hotel. After our evening meal the players chose either to colonize a corner in the wood-panelled King's Bar to play cards – but not drink – or go to the cinema. I always opted for a film. The card school only played for matches, or a maximum stake of tuppence, but it was serious stuff and continued until bedtime at half ten. After breakfast we read the morning newspapers and Matt Gillies would hold a short team meeting in which nothing too tactical or technical was ever discussed, other than a mention of the perceived weaknesses of our opponents and the best way of exploiting them.

At noon we sat down to our pre-match meal. Before our big game against high-flying Tottenham I ate what was then my normal pre-match lunch: a large steak with a side order of toast, followed by a bowl of rice pudding! In 1961 steak was still considered the ideal way for a professional footballer to stoke up with protein. No one knew that the stomach can take up to 36 hours fully to digest a large steak. Far from boosting strength and endurance, it must have sat like lead in the stomach throughout a game. To follow that with a large bowl of rice pudding appears now to be pure recklessness. But that's exactly what we did. It was believed the high sugar content of the rice pudding would boost our energy levels. Looking back, it's a miracle any of us could get up from our chairs, never mind possess the ability to sprint up and down a football pitch for ninety minutes.

Today a footballer's diet is strictly monitored, especially before a game when players will sit down to a selection of easily digestible dishes such as breakfast cereal, scrambled egg, pasta, green salad, boiled fish or chicken. When he arrived at Highbury in 1996, Arsenal manager Arsène Wenger, revolutionized the diets of his players: nothing fried, everything boiled, mainly pasta and definitely no alcohol at any time. I wonder what he would have made of our pre-match meal of steak and rice pudding, followed, in the case of Richie Norman and one or two others, by a fag. I suppose the fact that we were never outrun or overwhelmed by any opponents just goes to show that all the other teams of that era were on a similar dietary regime.

Considering what we were eating, it is amazing to think that football was evolving into a much speedier game. Sharpness and speed off the mark were vital and in Terry Dyson, Les Allen and Cliff Jones, Spurs possessed three of the quickest players around at that time. We set about denying those three possession, believing that if we cut off their supply of the ball, in the main from Danny Blanchflower, John White and Dave Mackay, we stood a good chance of nullifying what the press had dubbed 'the unstoppable force'. That worked, up to a point. Spurs scored twice through Danny Blanchflower (penalty) and Les Allen, but our own forwards, prompted by Frank McLintock and Colin Appleton who teamed up magnificently with Jimmy Walsh in midfield, gave the Spurs defence a torrid time. Jimmy Walsh scored twice and a Ken Leek goal gave us a memorable 3–2 victory. It was only Spurs' third defeat of the season and their first at home. We were ecstatic. We had beaten the best team in Britain in their own back yard. Leicester City had come of age as a team.

We knew we'd never catch Spurs in the League Championship, but our victory fuelled high hopes that we could go on and lift England's other prestigious trophy – the FA Cup. We had already beaten Oxford United, then a non-league side, 3–1, then Bristol City 5–1 in a replayed game that had been abandoned when a torrential downpour swamped the Filbert Street pitch, and were due to face Birmingham City in round five. Between our victory at Spurs and the FA Cup tie with the Blues, we convincingly defeated Newcastle United 5–3 at Filbert Street. Our confidence was sky high, but Birmingham proved difficult opponents. Before a crowd of 54,000 at St Andrews Howard Riley gave us the lead only for me to be beaten by a penalty from Birmingham's centre forward Jimmy Harris. In the replay we squeezed out a 2–1 win in front of a capacity crowd of 41,916.

In the quarter-final we drew Barnsley, who at the time were

a mid-table Third Division outfit. The Barnsley manager, Johnny Steele, had told the press his side 'would not roll over and die'. They certainly didn't.

By now City supporters had Cup fever raging through their veins and 39,000 of them turned up expecting the malady would intensify as we swept lowly Barnsley aside. Ah, the glorious uncertainty of football, especially the FA Cup!

After a great deal of huff and puff on our part, the game at Filbert Street ended goalless. And so to Oakwell for the replay, an equally close affair. Barnsley at this time did not have flood-lights and the game took place on a Wednesday afternoon. There must have been a lot of miners whose grandmothers had passed away earlier that week because a near-record Barnsley crowd of 39,250 packed into Oakwell on a weekday afternoon. They witnessed the Third Division side again belie their humble status by hustling and harassing us and taking the game into extra time. Howard Riley scored for us, Ken Oliver for Barnsley, but a typical piece of opportunism from Ken Leek was finally enough to vanquish the home side.

It had been a typical, gutsy cup tie in which no quarter was asked or given. When a team from a lower division met one from the top flight in the FA Cup, invariably their game plan was to graft and worry away like terriers at their supposed superiors. The pace of the game in the First Division tended not to be fast as in the lower divisions, where the football was very much of the hurly-burly variety, as one would expect, somewhat less skilful than in the top flight and certainly less methodical in the build-up to attack. By hustling and harassing a First Division side, a team from a lower division hoped to disrupt the normal style of their opponents. Barnsley employed this tactic against us and I have to say our normal style of play was indeed thrown out of kilter, though our extra quality did get us through in the end.

Today the pace of the game in the Premiership is such that teams from lower divisions can no longer employ the hustle and harass tactic. If anything, the pace of a game in the Premiership is speedier than in the Nationwide League. You can't harass and hustle the likes of Ryan Giggs, Michael Owen, Harry Kewell or Ray Parlour off the ball if you have trouble keeping up with them! The sheer pace of games in the Premiership has altered the tactics deployed by many teams. When a team from a lower division comes up against a Premiership team, they can no longer hope to pressurize them into making mistakes. They have had to alter their tactics when meeting a top side. For example, they will try to play a containing game while concentrating on their own strengths, on a par or better than those of the side from the higher division. For example, dead-ball situations like free kicks, corners and ultra-long throw-ins (used very effectively by Tranmere in their cup runs of recent years).

Playing against Barnsley was very much like going back to my roots for me. First of all, their right half, Bill Houghton, had been a member of the Northern Intermediate League Select XI for which I was reserve goalkeeper for the game against league champions, Sunderland, in 1956. And then there was the environment of Oakwell. Beyond the open Spion Kop terracing to the left of the main grandstand the winding wheel of a pithead could clearly be seen and the wind that swept the ground was permeated with yeast from a nearby brewery. The smoke and smother of the town was reminiscent of the Sheffield of my childhood. The Barnsley supporters too reminded me of those with whom I had stood cheek by jowl on the terraces of Hillsborough and Bramall Lane: men in flat caps the size of Doulton dinner plates whose dark wool overcoats smelled of Senior Service and lunchtime's best bitter; pale young men with Brylcreemed hair swept into DA quiffs and sporting long sideburns; young and old wearing collar and tie beneath their overcoats befitting the air of what was still seen as a social occasion about a football match; small boys hanging on to the perimeter wall, brandishing wooden rattles painted red and white, their Burberry macs buttoned to the collar, peaked school caps on their heads. No school for them that day. There was no inane chanting, no puerile songs, just cheering and the occasional collective 'aaw' when a shot flashed wide of my goal. A rumbustious tackle from Colin Appleton on Ken Oliver produced a brief but massed hiss, like forty thousand bicycle tyres being simultaneously deflated. Those Barnsley supporters offered constant free advice to the referee throughout the game. Their wholehearted, passionate bias engulfed the ground. Only to end with their silent shuffling off the terraces, in deflation and nervous exhaustion. As the players exchanged muddy handshakes and made for the bath, the suddenly muted supporters disappeared into the murky March evening, heading as I had once done, to welcoming homes with fires roaring up the chimney, the wireless babbling, pots of stew that bubbled like a diver and a wife they called Mother, or a mother they called Mam.

The draw for the FA Cup was made live on radio, on a Monday lunchtime, on what was then the Light Programme. There were only three BBC radio networks in 1961. The Light Programme, as the name suggests, broadcast light entertainment by way of music, comedy and sport. The Home Service provided news, drama and magazine feature programmes and the Third Programme was the home of classical music.

This was our radio drama, especially if we were still involved in the draw. The Light Programme enjoyed a periodic winter boost to its listenership with its broadcast of the FA Cup draw. With each FA Cup draw supporters, players and directors alike would huddle around radios eagerly awaiting the flat voice of a member of the FA to announce their opponents. The draw was one of those small rituals of football that separated the devotees of the game from the passive supporters. Each team was allocated a number, but somehow I could never predict what number Leicester City would be. The Football Association's system for numbering the little wooden balls that were drawn out of a velvet bag defied logic, and was as much a mystery as the workings of the human appendix. The fact that you didn't know what number your team was going to be only added to the sense of drama. The sing-song clunking of the balls when the fickle fingers of fate dipped into the bag to draw one out was somehow comforting. A plummy octogenarian voice (we imagined the wing collars and fob watches) would then announce the number – was this yours? – and a similarly dusty voice interpreted the mysterious number and announced the team. Inwardly (and collectively) you prayed for a home draw, or to avoid the big guns like Spurs or Wolves. When another club was drawn out of the bag to face them, the sense of relief for however brief a time was overwhelming. And all this drama was enacted by people we couldn't see in we didn't know where. Who were these people with your FA Cup fate literally at their fingertips?

The draw for the FA Cup today has been stripped of the strange mystery that surrounded it for decades. They now tell you in advance the numbers of the teams involved. No wooden balls or velvet bag. It is now a mirror image of the officials who administer it, impoverished by way of imagination and as dramatically gripping as last week's National Lottery.

In 1961, unlike now, they didn't bother to broadcast the FA Cup semi-final draw, which took place on the Monday prior to the replay against Barnsley. They simply announced that the winners of our game would meet Second Division Sheffield United at Elland Road, while Spurs were drawn against Burnley.

In choosing the venues for FA Cup semi-finals the Football Association simply allocated a ground they thought to be halfway between the two respective clubs. As both semi-finals were played on a Saturday afternoon when other clubs were fulfilling their normal league programme, the choice of venues depended either on those clubs that were playing away from home that day, or that didn't have a game as they had been scheduled to meet one of the four semi-finalists. This situation resulted in our being sent to meet Sheffield United at Elland Road, Leeds. This wasn't exactly a halfway house in that Elland Road was nearer to Sheffield than Leicester, but the FA announced that should there be a draw, the replay would be allocated to a neutral ground nearer to Leicester by way of compensation.

Over 52,000 fans turned up at Elland Road to witness a tight and taut goalless draw. Both sides were nervous and there were few scoring chances. Sadly, our outside left, Gordon Wills picked up a debilitating injury that was to sideline him for the rest of the season.

The neutral ground nearer to Leicester selected for the replay was the City Ground, the home of Nottingham Forest. Today the City Ground would be a surprising venue for an FA Cup semi-final. At the time, however, all First Division grounds had ample terracing and were capable of holding good-sized crowds. While Villa Park, St Andrews, Hillsborough, Old Trafford and Goodison Park were all capable of housing far bigger crowds than the City Ground's capacity of 43,500, the FA were at pains to be fair to all, rather than simply to maximize revenue by selecting a more distant venue. Therefore it was the case that the distance Leicester fans had to travel to Nottingham was more or less equal to the journey made by Sheffield United fans in getting to Elland Road for the first encounter. Conversely, Leicester to Leeds was a similar distance as Sheffield to Nottingham. So fairness was not only promised but seen to be done on the part of the FA.

For the replay, at the City Ground, Nottingham, Matt Gillies brought in Albert Cheesebrough to replace the injured Gordon Wills. The game turned out to be no better than the first. Being one step away from Wembley both sides were fearful of making a mistake and there was little open, fluid football to be seen. Once again, neither side possessed the temerity or wherewithal to break the deadlock and the blank scoreline sent us to St Andrews for a second replay.

The first twenty minutes of our game at St Andrews provided more drama and excitement than both our previous encounters combined. Within minutes of the start I was diving full length to tip away a stinging drive from the United centre forward

Derek Pace and moments later was happy to see a swerving drive from Len Allchurch clear my crossbar by inches. Down at the other end the United goalkeeper, Alan Hodgkinson, saved well from both Ken Leek and Jimmy Walsh. Both teams had set out their stall, both were going for victory – surely this encounter would not end goalless.

After about ten minutes I thought we were going to make the long-awaited breakthrough when we were awarded a penalty. Unfortunately, our centre half, Ian King, rucked his studs in the turf as he struck the spot kick and the opportunity went begging. Fifteen minutes later, however, we did take the lead. Jimmy Walsh, a player who seemed to hang in the air when he rose to the ball, headed in. Just before half time, I thought we had the game wrapped up when the prolific Ken Leek made it 2–0.

Our plan for the second half was to contain the expected opening onslaught and then hope that, with the clock against them, United would become edgy and make mistakes that we could punish. Just when I thought that plan was working a treat, we gifted United a penalty on 65 minutes. There isn't a lot a goalkeeper can do when facing a penalty other than choose which way to dive. Later in my career I began keeping notes on which side of the goal various players chose to shoot when taking a penalty. At this stage, however, I reacted purely on instinct. Graham Shaw (one of three brothers at the club) stepped up and repaid Ian King's earlier generosity by shooting wide. Though, let it be said, I went the right way!

Maybe some Sheffield players believed, deep down, that their last chance had gone, because we were comfortably in the driving seat until the final whistle, without adding to our two goals. At the end I looked up to the darkened skies above Birmingham and thanked my lucky stars. Two and a half years ago I was thrilled to break into the Chesterfield first team in Division Three. Now I was about to play in an FA Cup final at Wembley. I had never dared dream of such a thing. Wembley was the stage for the best players in the land, the likes of Stanley Matthews, Nat

Lofthouse, Peter Broadbent, Bobby Charlton, Dennis Viollet and Ron Flowers. Internationals to a man. My mind was fogged. Here I was, a player who a little over two years ago had been ecstatic when picked to make his league debut in Division Three. I'd never won a thing, whether it was at a hand of Pontoon on a building site, a game of bingo at the Chesterfield supporters club, a lucky raffle ticket, or waiting for 'Ernie' to pick out the number of one of my few premium bonds. Now I was only ninety minutes away from what every footballer I knew yearned for, an FA Cup winner's medal. Could this really be happening to me? It could and it was.

5. Foxes in the Final

In the space of a year my life had changed dramatically. My performances for Leicester City have come to the attention of the England manager, Walter Winterbottom, and during Leicester's FA Cup run to my delight I was called up for the England Under-23 squad. (In those days the manager of England was responsible not only for the full international team, but also for both the England Under-23 and youth sides as well as being the FA's head coach.)

I played twice for England Under-23s, against Wales and Scotland. Looking back at the teams that turned out in those two games, nearly every player went on to greater things in the game, which shows the importance of having young talent coming through and being given a chance at the highest level. For the game against Wales, England fielded the following team: Gordon Banks (Leicester City); John Angus (Burnley), Gerry Byrne (Liverpool); Bobby Moore (West Ham), Brian Labone (Everton), John Kirkham (Wolves); Peter Brabrook (Chelsea), John Barnwell (Arsenal), Johnny Byrne (Crystal Palace), Les Allen (Spurs), Clive 'Chippy' Clark (West Bromwich Albion), with Alan Mullery (Fulham) in reserve. A line-up that belied the belief held by some at the time that English football was devoid of quality players.

For the game against Scotland, George Cohen (Fulham) came in for John Angus at right back, Mick McNeill (Middlesbrough) at left back for Gerry Byrne, Mick O'Grady (Huddersfield Town) for Peter Brabrook and Peter Dobing (Blackburn Rovers) for John Barnwell. Our opposition for those two games included such stars in the making as the Welshmen Mike England (Blackburn Rovers), Arfon Griffiths (Arsenal), Graham Williams (West

Bromwich Albion) and Barry Jones (Swansea Town), while the young Scots included Pat Crerand and Billy McNeill (Celtic), Alan Gilzean and Ian Ure (both Dundee) and a young blond lad from Huddersfield Town, Denis Law. Crerand, Gilzean, Ure and Law, of course, all went on to make a considerable mark with English clubs, while Billy McNeill became the first British player ever to lift the European Cup when captaining Celtic in their marvellous victory over Inter-Milan in 1967.

Rubbing shoulders with some of the best young players in British football made me even more determined to improve my technique as a goalkeeper. I knew I was still a long way off recognition at full England level, but those two appearances for the Under-23s gave me hope that, one day, with hard work and diligence, I might be good enough. Never for one moment did I think I had 'made it'. On the contrary. The quality of players on show in those matches made me realize how much I had still to learn.

Looking back now at those names, I'm very much reminded of a term used by John Moynihan, a top football writer of the day, who described footballers as being the 'Saturday Men'. In essence, that is what we were. Of course, there were occasionally mid-week games, but Saturday was *the* day for football. With limited coverage of the game on radio and particularly television, and press coverage nowhere near the saturation level it is today, footballers emerged from the relative obscurity of a week of training to ply their trade before the fans on a Saturday afternoon. Saturday was the only time the majority of fans saw players in the flesh. It was the one time when we were in the spotlight, when a week's work on the training ground boiled down to just ninety minutes, the outcome of which would set the mood and emotions of both players and supporters for another seven days. We were very much the 'Saturday Men'.

For now, though, I needed to concentrate on our forthcoming Wembley date. While we had made hard work of defeating Sheffield United in our FA Cup semi-final, Spurs were breezing past Burnley 3–0 in the other tie. The reported ease with which Spurs had beaten Burnley was a little disconcerting. Burnley were the reigning league champions who, along with Sheffield Wednesday and Wolves, had clung on to Tottenham's coat tails in the title race. So magnificent were Spurs, however, that by January the bookies were only accepting bets on the points margin at the end of the season. All championship bets were settled in April, with five matches to go. Nevertheless, Spurs had considered themselves fortunate to beat us at Filbert Street while we, of course, had beaten them at White Hart Lane. Formidable as they were, we had to fancy our chances against them at Wembley.

Spurs were managed by the straight-talking Yorkshireman Bill Nicholson, one of the all-time great soccer bosses. Their captain Danny Blanchflower, also skipper of Northern Ireland, was an articulate and deep-thinking player who not only played a good game, but talked one too (half the night before internationals, apparently). When a player at Aston Villa in the fifties, Danny suggested that the team play to a 3–3–4 system that he had seen on the Continent. This idea was so revolutionary that it was greeted not just with scepticism, but scorn. Pained at such a rebuff, in 1954 he asked for a transfer and eventually signed for Spurs for the then substantial fee of £30,000. The love affair had begun.

When Bill Nicholson took over as Spurs manager in 1958, Danny at last found listening and willing ears for his tactical theories. Without taking anything away from Bill Nicholson and his assistant, Eddie Bayley, Spurs' double success in 1960–61 resulted in no small part from Blanchflower's theories on football and the way it should be played.

Jimmy McIlroy, Burnley's mercurial inside forward, was a Northern Ireland team mate and roomed with Danny. For some reason, McIlroy never produced the sublime form when playing for Northern Ireland he was so renowned for in a Burnley shirt. A reporter from the *Daily Sketch* once asked him why. Jimmy replied, 'It's because Danny keeps me up half the night before a game talking about his theories on football.'

Danny was a beautiful passer of the ball, a midfield player with great vision and one who never knew when he was beaten. He was also football's most quoted player, quite simply because everything he said was so eminently quotable.

The Northern Ireland manager, Peter Doherty, a fabulous player himself in the forties and fifties, was Danny's hero and mentor. Following his hero Peter Doherty's resignation as manager of Northern Ireland, a reporter asked Danny for a comment. 'He was the great North Star,' said Danny, 'that twinkled brightly in the heavens, promising untold glory, beckoning me to follow, and always showing the way.'

I can't for the life of me ever imagine another player, of any era, talking in that way about an outgoing manager. But that was typical Danny Blanchflower. There was a lyrical, poetic quality to the Blanchflower quote that is a far cry from the homogenized blandness of today's media-trained young stars giving their post-match soundbites. Here, for example, is Danny commenting on Northern Ireland's performances in the World Cup of 1958: 'We did not win anything,' he said, 'but in keeping with our reputation as the Cinderella side of international football, we made quite a stir at the ball.'

Along with that Irish lyricism was Danny's ready wit. A journalist quizzed Blanchflower about an alleged secret plan with which to beat England in an international at Windsor Park. Unwilling to reveal his hand, the wily Irishman said, 'Tis true what you have heard. We do have a new plan. We're going to equalize before England score.'

Within a few games of his arrival at White Hart Lane, the then Spurs manager, Jimmy Anderson, offered him the captaincy. Danny told the press, 'I have accepted the captaincy, because I believe we have here the makings of a fine team. I would not want to be captain unless I had something to captain.'

Danny Blanchflower brought to Tottenham and to football

an unorthodoxy that had not been seen, or, permitted for many years. Yet we had out-thought and out-fought both him and Bill Nicholson at White Hart Lane. Could we do so again at Wembley?

Sportsmanship was still very much in evidence in football at this time. The game was very physical, but I cannot recall an instance in any match in which I was involved, where a player took a dive or overreacted to a tackle with a view to getting an opponent in trouble with a referee. It is a commonly held view that the game has always had little place for sentiment. That is not to say sentiment did not exist. During this season Manchester United suffered two heavy defeats against Sheffield Wednesday. In March United lost 5–1 in a First Division fixture at Hillsborough. That day Dave Gaskell was in goal, but their 5–1 defeat was a marginal improvement on their previous encounter. In the fourth round of the FA Cup, once again at Hillsborough, both United's goalkeepers – Harry Gregg and his understudy Dave Gaskell – were unavailable through injury. As the players' loan system was not in operation in 1961, United manager Matt Busby had no choice but to call upon his youth-team goalkeeper, Ronnie Briggs. Briggs let neither his manager nor his team mates down in United's first encounter with Wednesday which ended in a 1–1 draw at Hillsborough. The replay, however, was a totally different story. This game turned out to be an Old Trafford baptism of fire for young Briggs, Sheffield Wednesday winning 7–2. Perhaps a combination of his own adrenalin, the fact Briggs received a late call-up and therefore had little time to become anxious, and an over-protective United defence at Hillsborough, helped Ronnie to acquit himself well in the original tie and concede just the one goal. In the replay I should imagine a degree of self-doubt possessed him and, given his inexperience, he began to worry about whether or not he could produce a similarly sound performance.

What fragile confidence young Briggs may have possessed

must have been shot to pieces when conceding seven goals in front of United's own supporters. Two days later, however, Ronnie Briggs received a letter at Old Trafford. It was written on 2 February 1961 by the Sheffield Wednesday manager Harry Catterick.

Dear Ronnie,

I felt that I must write to you to let you know how highly some of our players, and Ron Springett [Wednesday's goalkeeper] in particular, rate you as a goalkeeper of the future. I should not like to feel that the fact we beat you 7–2 was in any way going to shake your confidence.

All the great goalkeepers have had days when they have been beaten several times, and, of course, being a goalkeeper, when they pass you they are in the back of the net.

You showed sufficient ability at Hillsborough in the first cup tie to convince me and many good judges of the game that you have a bright future. This game is full of ups and downs, and I feel it is part of its fascination to players, managers and spectators, but I am equally sure, Ronnie, that you are going to have far more ups than downs. In addition to which, you are probably with one of the finest clubs in the British Isles and in the very capable hands of Mr Busby and Jimmy Murphy.

Kind regards,
Yours sincerely,
Harry Catterick

Bearing in mind what I previously said about opponents only offering compliments when they have beaten you, it would be crass simply to think this was the case regarding Harry Catterick and his letter. On the contrary, it was a tremendous gesture on his part and I genuinely believe him to have been sincere in his words. Ronnie Briggs was just a teenager and in writing the letter, I think Catterick was hoping his words would lift a young lad whose spirit and confidence must have been laid really low.

In short, what Harry Catterick did not want, was the experience Briggs had suffered at the hands of his own players to have a detrimental effect on his career in the game.

Unfortunately, Ronnie Briggs did not go on to make a name for himself at United, nor in the game in general. Perhaps the shattering experience of conceding seven goals at Old Trafford at such a tender age had something to do with that, though my guess would be that it was simply a case of early potential not being realized. Whatever, I hope he kept that letter from Harry Catterick as a constant reminder to him that the 7–2 scoreline was not solely a reflection on his ability as a young keeper. I have been able to quote Catterick's letter verbatim thanks to a friend who owns a copy – the very fact that a copy exists suggests that Ronnie did, in time, come to derive pride from the letter he received. I would certainly like to think so.

No place for sentiment in football? In 2002, following the death of Glenn Hoddle's father, Derek, a minute's silence was held prior to Tottenham Hotspur's home game against Sunderland. The attendance for that game was 36,062 and the minute's silence was respectfully and flawlessly observed by everyone present that day, including 4,500 Sunderland fans. So appreciative was Hoddle, that he wrote a letter to Sunderland Supporters Association conveying his gratitude for the respect shown in his bereavement.

Hoddle's letter was written in response to very different circumstances from the one penned by Harry Catterick all those years ago. But I make mention of both simply to illustrate that, in certain circumstances, sentiment does play a part in football. It did in 1961 and still does today.

In the week during which Leicester City were preparing for the FA Cup final against Tottenham Hotspur, however, we were to witness behaviour in which not only was sentiment cast aside, but common sense was inexplicably defied. Matt Gillies was to make a decision that made Leicester City headline news in just about every national newspaper. Two days before the final he dropped the player who was our best hope of winning it.

During our last training session before setting off for London the next day, I was doing some ball work with Frank McLintock, Jimmy Walsh, Howard Riley and Ken Leek, when Matt Gillies called Ken over for what I assumed would be a chat about his role against Spurs. After three or four minutes we could see Ken standing head bowed, hands on hips, his shoulders slowly rocking to and fro. Gillies, his back turned to us, was making his way back to the changing rooms. Aware something was amiss, Frank, Jimmy, Howard and I made our way over to Ken. On arriving at his side, Ken looked up and I was astonished to see that he was crying.

'What's up?' I asked.

'He's not playing me. He's dropped me for the final.'

Were it not for his tears, I would have thought Ken was having us on. Ken had scored in every round of the FA Cup and since taking over as centre forward from Derek Hines in September, had scored eighteen goals in the league, a tally second only to that of Jimmy Walsh. To say he was important to the team would be an understatement.

He was inconsolable. Eventually he explained how Matt Gillies had found out that he had gone to a pub the previous night for a couple of pints with some friends. Matt interpreted this as a gross breach of club discipline, a wholly unprofessional act in the week prior to the Cup final. Perhaps it was, but Ken's punishment was severe in the extreme. His replacement was to be our reserve centre forward, 21-year-old Hugh McIlmoyle, a promising player but with only seven league games behind him.

I felt a mixture of shock and disbelief, as did the rest of my team mates. Ken Leek was the best centre forward we had at the club. Even at full strength, with everyone playing to the best of his ability, we knew Spurs would be very difficult opponents. Surely it was a case of Gillies using a guillotine to cure dandruff. Yes, Ken should have known better than to go out in public for a beer three nights before the FA Cup final. But the fact was, that when we didn't have a mid-week match, a Wednesday was one of two nights in a week – the other being Saturday – when players were allowed out for a drink. I thought Matt should have shown some common sense in dealing with the matter. To drop a key member of the team before Leicester City's most important game for years seemed absurd to me. I know his combative play and sharpness made him feared by the Spurs defenders. When we beat them at White Hart Lane, Ken scored one of our goals and won just about every ball against Maurice Norman, who was no mug. Yet this psychological advantage had been thrown away.

There are occasions when a player relishes playing against a certain opponent because, irrespective of the quality of that opponent, he always seems to get the better of him. This has much to do with an individual's style of play. Ken, for example, might find his style as a centre forward bore little fruit when up against, say, Tommy Cummings of Burnley. Though Maurice Norman was no less a defender than Cummings, Ken's style came off to his benefit when faced with that of Norman. Psychology plays its part. When this happens a couple of times, the defender on the receiving end of a run around, starts to think that particular opponent has the Indian sign on him. The defender gets it into his head that no matter how hard he tries, he will never get the better of this particular centre forward. Conversely, such a situation can also work in favour of the defender.

I am sure this 'mind game' was the case with regard to Ken and Maurice Norman. Yet Matt Gillies chose to ignore what I and other Leicester players perceived to be something that would be to our advantage in the final against Spurs.

Football has much to do with fitness, both physically and mentally. Ken's controversial omission from the side – there is no other way to describe it – did not make us any less committed. Nor did it lessen our motivation or our belief that we could beat Spurs and lift the trophy. Subconsciously, however, it must have had an effect on every player. In the build-up to an important game, and an FA Cup final was seen as being the most important game in the domestic calendar, a team must be totally focused. The last thing you want is for the boat to be rocked. In dropping Ken Leek, Matt Gillies had, however unwittingly, blurred our focus and though he had not exactly sabotaged our chances, had certainly disrupted what should have been a tranquil build-up to the final.

It must be said that not one member of the team had anything against Hugh McIlmoyle. Hugh was popular among the Leicester players and, even at twenty-one, no mean player. But Hugh had just seven league matches under his belt. It appeared sheer folly on the part of Matt Gillies to pitch the relatively inexperienced Hugh McIlmoyle into the FA Cup final. The players had no say in the matter. Matt Gillies' word was law. We just hoped Hugh would acquit himself well on the day and that we would not miss Ken Leek's experience and guile as a centre forward too much.

In punishing Ken, Matt was in many ways punishing the team. Standing on a matter of principle is all well and good, but I believe it was a case of Matt Gillies cutting off his nose to spite his face. It wasn't as if Ken Leek had been involved in some Bacchanalian revel until the early hours of the morning. He'd had a couple of pints and, according to Ken, was at home and in bed by eleven – hardly the sort of night out that would impair his performance in the final. Matt Gillies should have given Ken a good ticking off, reminded him of his responsibilities and perhaps, after the final, imposed a fine. That would have been punishment enough and Matt would not have compromised his position and authority as manager. In dropping Ken from the team, Matt Gillies, to my mind, did a lot of harm to our chances of lifting the cup.

Not all players are consummate athletes, one or two have habits out of keeping with our profession, such as drinking and smoking. But if those habits do not impair personal performance or harm the team in any way, as long as they are indulged in moderation, many managers turn a blind eye to them. John Robertson, a key member of Nottingham Forest's League Championship side of 1978 and their European Cup-winning teams of 1979 and 1980, had personal habits not wholly approved of by Forest manager Brian Clough: a very casual dress sense, for instance, and his liking for fags. But Cloughie turned a blind eye to both because neither affected Robertson's performances and contribution to the Forest team. As Cloughie said, 'He thinks I don't know he has a crafty fag when we break off from training. He turns up at the ground in loafers, unshaven and looking like a tramp, but he's the best bloody crosser of a ball in Europe. When John sets off down the left wing, I know he's going to beat his man then float that ball to the far post and on to the head of Trevor Francis or Gary Birtles. That's why I say nowt!'

Don Mackay, manager of Blackburn Rovers between 1987 and 1991, took Rovers to three First Division play-offs in the days before the club benefited from the munificence of Jack Walker. Blackburn's centre forward at that time was Simon Garner, a player not only given to smoking but one who also liked a beer. It was rumoured that, even at home, Garner would drink at least three or four cans of beer a night. Don Mackay, being the good manager he is, was well aware of Garner's liking of cigarettes and beer but let it ride. When asked by a club official why he never brought Garner to task about his smoking and drinking habits, Don said, 'Because he's a twenty-plus goals a season player. Have you any idea how hard it is to find that sort of player these days?'

Brian Clough and Don Mackay were right to adopt a laissez-faire attitude to their players. John Robertson was one of the best, if not the best, wide player in Europe at the time. He created countless goals for Forest. Who can forget the cross he made for Trevor Francis against Malmo in 1979 that won the European Cup for Forest? As for Simon Garner, his 168 goals for Blackburn Rovers remains a club record.

Beer and certainly cigarettes don't help a player where athleticism is concerned, but in certain cases, such as that of Robertson and Garner, they certainly didn't seem to do any harm. Some players never touch alcohol or cigarettes at all and in their preparation for a game like to be tucked up in bed by 9 p.m. However, there are some individuals whose idea of pre-match preparation is a couple of tins of beer in the privacy of their own home. Brian Clough and Don Mackay obviously understood this. For either manager to have laid down the law in an attempt to restrict Robertson or Garner from pursuing their normal lifestyle would in all probability have caused disciplinary problems, which so often lead in turn to a player underperforming on the pitch.

Every player is different. The majority of players find it benefits them to observe a very careful and specific diet and to get to bed early. But there are exceptions. So long as having a beer, a cigarette or a takeaway is done in moderation and such indulgence never impairs personal performance, or gives a poor example to younger, impressionable players, most managers will tolerate it. Players with 'unhealthy' personal habits are not the norm in football. They weren't in the late seventies and eighties and they are even rarer in the football of today. But such personal idiosyncrasies of lifestyle must be weighed against what a player contributes to the team on the pitch. Without doubt the contributions of Robertson and Garner to their respective teams were huge. So too was Ken Leek's to Leicester City. So why Matt Gillies reacted in such a heavy-handed way to a couple of beers, and left Ken out of our Cup final team, I still find baffling. Still, we couldn't change things now. At last we had to turn our eyes to the famous Twin Towers and go and win the Cup for Leicester.

6. The Wembley Hoodoo?

To play in an FA Cup Final is the pinnacle of a player's career. It was certainly my greatest moment at that time. I was twenty-three, had been at Leicester for only two seasons and couldn't believe the good fortune that had befallen me. From Chesterfield reserves to the final of the oldest cup competition in the world in three years.

For such an important game, everything is planned to the last detail. Before setting off for Wembley each player received a meticulous itinerary from club secretary Charles Maley detailing to the minute what time the players had to meet at Filbert Street, the time the coach left the ground for Leicester station and its arrival there. It even stated what time we would be served sandwiches on the train and what the sandwich fillings would be! Everything was planned to a rigorous timetable right up until our arrival on Saturday at Wembley.

Maley's plans took us up until 1 p.m. when the Football Association's player's itinerary known as the 'Programme of Arrangements' took over. This very grand-looking little booklet bears the FA's three lions crest and proudly proclaims that the final will take place in the presence of the Patron of the Football Association, Her Majesty the Queen. Inside everything is clearly set out for players and match officials: which team had which dressing room (Spurs had the North, Leicester the South); how and when we had to leave the dressing room; what we had to do once out on the pitch; what to say and what not to say if addressed by a royal personage. It was all in there. Even the protocol for ascending to the royal box for the presentations is described, with this surreal advice: 'Players and Officials going to the Royal Box are warned to be careful. Do not under any circumstances step back and over-balance on the balcony.' So everything, even not falling off the balcony, is planned to the last detail. (I doubt whether, on the day, we players gave the 'Programme of Arrangements' and the contents therein more than a cursory glance, relying instead on the punctilious Mr Maley to keep us right.) It's a pity that the game itself couldn't have been organized as rigorously, for it took only fifteen minutes for our schemes to go awry.

For people of a certain age, the Spurs team of that day runs off the tongue like a litany: Brown; Baker, Henry; Blanchflower, Norman, Mackay; Jones, White, Smith, Allen, Dyson. We lined up alongside them in readiness to be presented to the Duke of Edinburgh: Gordon Banks; Len Chalmers, Richie Norman; Frank McLintock, Ian King, Colin Appleton; Howard Riley, Jimmy Walsh, Hugh McIlmoyle, Ken Keyworth, Albert Cheesebrough.

Both teams caused a minor sensation by breaking with tradition in wearing tracksuits when taking to the pitch. Ours were pale blue with the club crest, a fox's head, stitched on to the left breast; Tottenham's were white zip-front tracksuit tops, with emblazoned on the back the single word, 'Spurs'.

I remember glancing around the stadium and being impressed by the sheer number of Leicester City fans present, especially in view of the fact that while our average home attendance was over 30,000, Spurs regularly drew crowds in excess of 50,000 to White Hart Lane. Two and a half million people had watched Tottenham home and away in their league and cup games, to this day the greatest number of spectators to watch a team in a single season in the history of British football. Yet each club received a ticket allocation of just 18,000, out of a total of 100,000. It was to the City supporters' credit then that thousands more had managed to track down tickets from whatever source – probably, in the main, from spivs (the term we used for ticket touts in those days) at vastly inflated prices. Each player had received twelve complimentary tickets for family and friends, of whom a Cup finalist suddenly has more than he ever realized!

The Cup final had been given an extra edge by the fact that Spurs were chasing what the newspapers had dubbed 'the impossible double'. No team had won both the League Championship and the FA Cup in the same season throughout the century. Newcastle United in 1905, Sunderland in 1913 and Manchester United in 1957 had each won the League Championship but lost in the FA Cup final. Most people believed the heavy fixture programme and the intense competitiveness of the modern game were such that no team could win both in the same season. I just hoped they would be proved right.

If Spurs felt the pressure placed on them by the press, it certainly didn't show. They were very laid back, taking a trip to the cinema to see *The Guns of Navarone* at the Odeon, Leicester Square, after which they all stayed up till after midnight with a couple of beers back at their hotel. We had all been in bed by ten thirty. When a reporter from the London *Evening News* queried the wisdom of this, it was Danny Blanchflower again who came up with the quotable quote: 'I can only tell you the story of the golfer, Walter Hagen. Hagen was up late before a crucial play-off match, and a reporter told him, "I suppose you know your opponent has been long in his bed?" "Sure," said Hagen, "but do you honestly think he's getting any sleep?"'

Spurs were confident but so too were we. In his pre-match team talk Matt Gillies reminded us of how we had beaten Spurs at White Hart Lane. Our game plan, such as it was, again relied on Jimmy Walsh and Ken Keyworth closing down Danny Blanchflower and Dave Mackay, while Hugh McIlmoyle was to play as a deep-lying centre forward in the hope of dragging the Spurs centre half Maurice Norman out of position and creating space for Jimmy and Ken to exploit.

And that's just how it worked out, for those first fifteen minutes. We set about Spurs with some verve but, after a quarter of an hour, disaster struck. Our right back, Len Chalmers, sustained an injury to his knee ligaments. It wasn't the result of a bad tackle, just bad luck. The damage was so bad that he should have left the field immediately, but there were no substitutes in those days, and he carried on gamely.

I wonder how many players, prior to the introduction of substitutes to English football in 1967, did permanent damage to their bodies through continuing in a game with a bad injury? There are no statistics, but I should imagine it was quite a few. The absence of substitutes apart, the knowledge trainers had of injuries and their effects, was nowhere near as comprehensive then as it is today. When a player was injured he was expected to carry on playing as best he could, no matter how debilitating the injury. Wilf McGuinness, the former Manchester United and England wing half, sustained a bad injury during a United reserve game at Stoke City in 1959–60. The advice from the United bench to Wilf was to 'run it off', which was the advice most benches gave to players who had sustained any type of muscular injury. Wilf bravely carried on but it's hard to run off a stress fracture, which is what he had. Wilf eventually had to have a bone graft, the bone failed to knit and he suffered numerous complications. He did make a return to the United reserve team, for one season, but irreparable damage had been done and Wilf had to retire from playing in his early twenties.

The injury to Len Chalmers was nowhere near as serious, but nonetheless debilitating. He couldn't run, so Matt switched him to the wing, with Howard Riley dropping back. Such was Len's courage that he battled on, wincing every time he limped towards the ball. Len made a positive contribution of a sort, in that a Spurs player still had to mark him in case the ball was played into his feet. But we were effectively playing with ten men.

So many players had sustained serious injuries in cup finals at Wembley in the fifties that the press came up with the line that there was a 'Wembley Hoodoo'. Of course that was nonsense, but players getting seriously injured in Wembley showpiece occasions were becoming an almost annual event.

In 1952 Arsenal were reduced to ten men against Newcastle

United when their full back Wally Barnes badly injured knee ligaments in making a tackle. Typical of Arsenal's spirit, Barnes returned to the fray not once but twice, but so bad was his injury he eventually succumbed to it after half an hour. In 1953 Bolton's left half Eric Bell carried on gamely despite a bad injury to his knee and even managed to score. Two years later Manchester City right back Jimmy Meadows tore knee ligaments and was stretchered off after twenty minutes against Newcastle United.

The following year saw perhaps the most frightening injury of all when the Manchester City goalkeeper Bert Trautmann, a boyhood hero of mine, broke his neck when making a save at the feet of Birmingham's Peter Murphy. As I have intimated, the knowledge trainers had of injuries was very sketchy and Bert carried on playing with his neck broken. It was only after Manchester City's 3–1 success, when Bert complained of severe headaches, that he was taken to a hospital and an X-ray revealed a fracture that could so easily have been fatal.

The 'Wembley Hoodoo' was seen to strike again the following year. On the occasion of Aston Villa meeting Manchester United in the final, the United goalkeeper Ray Wood suffered concussion and a broken cheekbone as the result of a robust challenge (deemed to be a foul) by Villa's Peter McParland. This happened after only six minutes and with Wood off the field, United had to put wing half Jackie Blanchflower, the brother of Danny, in goal. As Jackie was later to say, 'Playing in goal in a Cup final was the moment I realized adrenalin was brown.'

The Cup final of 1958, thankfully, was one in which the 'hoodoo' did not strike. But a much more profound tragedy enveloped this final between Bolton Wanderers and Manchester United. Three months previously Manchester United had been involved in the Munich Air disaster which claimed the lives of over half the forty people on board. Those who lost their lives included the United captain Roger Byrne, reserve left back, Jeff Bent, who was making his first trip abroad (and only because Wilf McGuinness had been injured when playing for United on the previous Saturday), right half Eddie Colman, centre half Mark Jones, left half Duncan Edwards, inside right Billy Whelan, centre forward Tommy Taylor and outside left David Pegg. The United secretary Walter Crickmer also lost his life along with first-team coach Bert Whalley and trainer Tom Curry. Several crew members and journalists also died, including that great goalkeeper of the thirties and forties, Frank Swift, who had been working for the *Sunday People*. In addition to those who died, several United players were so badly injured they never played football again. Having lost so many players, for United to reach the FA Cup final just three months on was a remarkable achievement, testament to their fortitude and courage.

I had heard about the Munich disaster in Germany when serving the final days of my National Service. Like any other compassionate human I feel deeply for those involved in any tragedy, but felt particularly sad when hearing the news of Munich. As with most professions, I suppose, there is a feeling of brotherhood among footballers and I was deeply saddened to learn of the catastrophe that had struck Manchester United. I had made acquaintance with a number of the United players when Chesterfield played them in the FA Youth Cup final, among them Bobby Charlton. Bobby was thrown from the plane still strapped to his seat and miraculously survived. Some of the other lads I knew were not so lucky.

In playing Manchester United in the FA Cup final of 1958, Bolton Wanderers were in a 'no-win' situation. The sympathies of the entire nation were with United that day. Their remarkable resurrection after Munich and their determination to succeed won the hearts of everyone. But Bolton had a cup to win and win it they did.

It was as if fate had spared the Bolton–United Cup final the pain of the 'hoodoo'. It was the only final of the fifties in which no player suffered serious injury. The following year the 'hoodoo' was back to haunt Wembley.

Luton met Nottingham Forest in the final of 1959. Forest

were triumphant but their outside right Roy Dwight, the uncle of Reg (better known as Elton John), was stretchered off with a broken leg. Then in 1960 a similar fate struck the Blackburn Rovers full back Dave Whelan in their defeat by Wolves. Life, however, was to have good fortune in store for Dave. He opened a sports shop in the north west and became so successful that JJB Sports are now nationwide. Dave is still heavily involved with football as chairman of Wigan Athletic and their super stadium at the Robin Park complex in Wigan, which the football club shares with Wigan Warriors Rugby League team, is Dave's legacy to the town. Not for nothing is it called the JJB Stadium.

The plethora of serious injuries to beset FA Cup finals throughout the fifties and early sixties had, of course, nothing to do with a hoodoo. It did, however, have much to do with the pitch and the occasion.

In the fifties and sixties we basically played on three types of pitches. At the beginning of the season pitches would be lush and flat but due to heavy use for the first- and reserve-team games and occasional youth and local representative matches, the inclement weather of winter soon took its toll on the grass. Come January the vast majority of pitches had only grass on the wings, the rest of the pitch resembled a mudheap. Towards the end of a season the winds of March and April dried out pitches, so much so that we often played on surfaces that were as hard as if the ground had been frozen.

Wembley was very different. The pitch was laid with Cumberland turf that was lush but also very spongy. This turf was so pliable that it felt like playing on delicate springs. Only two other football league grounds boasted Cumberland turf, Ayresome Park, the home of Middlesbrough and Doncaster Rover's Belle Vue ground. After a long hard season playing mostly on muddied pitches or bumpy, bone-hard surfaces, the Wembley pitch, with its considerable 'give' and stamina-sapping softness, was not easy to adjust to. Many players when stretching for a ball were caught out by the supple turf and jarred their knee, hence the many ligament injuries to beset FA Cup finals at this time, Len Chalmers included.

The other reason for the injuries was the occasion itself. The FA Cup final was the showpiece of the domestic season, the most important game not only of the year but, in many cases, in the career of a player. Many was the player who made his name in a Wembley final and enjoyed lasting fame through his efforts and accomplishments in this one game alone. Who remembers Mike Trebilcock? Those who do, will remember him for the two goals he scored for Everton when they beat Sheffield Wednesday in the Cup final of 1966. But if I were to ask you to recall anything else about Mike's career, the vast majority of people would struggle. Five years after being Everton's Wembley hero, Mike was playing for Torquay United reserves in the Western League against the likes of Barnstaple Town and St Luke's College. His fame, on the blue half of Merseyside, however, lives on to this day.

Roy Dwight of Nottingham Forest (1959), Norman Deeley of Wolves (1960), Sunderland's Ian Porterfield (1973), Southampton's Bobby Stokes (1976) and Roger Osborne of Ipswich Town (1978) are other examples of players who readily come to mind only for what they achieved in a cup final. The rest of their respective careers has, for the vast majority, been lost to the memory.

In addition to wanting to give everything for their team and club in an attempt to win the FA Cup, players are acutely aware that they may well have just the one opportunity to play in an FA Cup final. Where they might think twice about making a certain tackle in a league game, they have no such reservations at Wembley. They throw caution to the wind and go in where the boots are flying, committing themselves totally. This is especially so where goalkeepers are concerned and may well explain the injuries sustained by Bert Trautmann and Ray Wood. The FA Cup final is do or die for ninety minutes, in which players take risks that they wouldn't normally take in a league match.

This is the other contributing factor to the tally of serious injuries that was dubbed the 'Wembley Hoodoo' in the fifties and early sixties.

That the so-called hoodoo was laid to rest in the sixties came about because players had become increasingly aware of the dangers of playing on the Cumberland turf that had been laid at Wembley in 1949, and compensated for its spring and sponginess underfoot. Also, teams were allowed to practise on Wembley on the day before the final, which helped them get a feel for the pitch. This was not the case when I first played at Wembley. The first time I set foot on Wembley's hallowed turf was when I joined my Leicester team mates when we walked out on to the pitch in our suits to soak up the atmosphere ninety minutes before kick-off.

Although it did not occur to me at the time, looking back now it appears that events had conspired against our winning the Cup in 1961. We were without the spearhead of our attack, Ken Leek, and within fifteen minutes were carrying a passenger in Len Chalmers. With all due respect to Hugh McIlmoyle, who acquitted himself well in this game, had we had Ken to worry the hell out of Maurice Norman and been at our full complement of eleven fit players, I reckon we could have beaten Spurs, though it would still have been difficult. After a quarter of an hour, however, our task had become even harder, though we stuck to it with more than our normal zeal and application, and Spurs found us as hard to break down as we did them.

At half time it was goalless but as the second half progressed the contest of ten men against eleven began to take its toll. We tired a little on the sapping pitch and Bobby Smith put Spurs ahead after sixty-nine minutes. Latching on to a great through-ball from Spurs winger Terry Dyson, Smith controlled the ball, for once beat Ian King and hit a hard drive that was too far to my left for me to get a hand to.

Eight minutes later the game was as good as over when Smith

returned the compliment. Terry Dyson met his cross from the right at the far post to plant a firm header into my net. There was nothing I could have done about either goal, and at 2–0 I knew Spurs had their hands on the Cup and achieved the elusive double.

Spurs had not outplayed us by any stretch of the imagination. For long periods of the game we had been their equal and even, at times, had held the upper hand. Jimmy Walsh and Ken Keyworth did a fine job of containment on Blanchflower and Mackay, neither of whom exerted their normal command on the field. Richie Norman kept their speedy left winger, Cliff Jones, quiet while neither Les Allen nor Bobby Smith got much change out of Colin Appleton and Ian King. We had our moments of promise – Hugh McIlmoyle flashed a shot inches past Bill Brown's left-hand post with the Spurs keeper well beaten, while both Jimmy Walsh and Ken Keyworth had good efforts well saved. But in the cold light of day we were never going to win once Len Chalmers had been injured, though none of us cited that as an excuse for our defeat.

After receiving our medals, in recognition of Spurs' remarkable achievement we stayed at the mouth of the players' tunnel until they had completed their lap of honour (in those days only the victorious side lapped the pitch to receive the acclaim of their travelling support). As the ecstatic Tottenham players made their way back, we lined up either side of the entrance and applauded them on their way to the dressing room. It seemed the sporting thing to do.

To lose a cup final is awful. When Leicester lost a league match I couldn't wait for the next game and the opportunity to rid myself of the general feeling of disappointment. You can't do that after a cup final. The depression lives inside you for weeks. Desire for collective and individual glory aside, we had wanted to win the FA Cup for our supporters who had given us tremendous backing throughout the season. More than once during the traditional post-match banquet at the Dorchester Hotel on Park Lane, I spared a thought for the crestfallen City supporters

travelling home. The banquet is a chance for directors, management, players, club staff and their partners to celebrate, as the
menu of the night said, 'The occasion of the appearance of the
club in the final of the Football Association Cup'. There being
no cup, we didn't do much celebrating.

On returning home I turned to the special Cup final edition
of the *Leicester Evening Mail*'s sports section, commonly referred
to as 'The Green 'Un'. In a piece by Billy King on the front
page, Matt Gillies gave his reason for omitting Ken Leek from
the team. People should be in no doubt: Gillies made the change
for no other reason than the interest of the side, he said, and
'purely and simply because I consider McIlmoyle to be the player
in form and that is all'. Well, that was news to me. Never at any
time was Ken told that he had been dropped because of a dip in
form. In our final league game of the season we had beaten
Birmingham City 3–2, Ken scored one of our goals and had
played so well that two Sunday newspapers gave him the top
mark in their performance assessment of each player. No, it was
all to do with that Wednesday evening drink.

Matt Gillies would have given the true reason for dropping
Ken Leek to the Leicester board. I'm sure that the meticulous
Charles Maley's minutebook would back up my opinion, too,
were it not for the fact that, strangely enough, the pages recording
the minutes of that particular meeting have been ripped out of
the book. Ken was an honest professional who would have
accepted his omission on form grounds. And why would the
manager persist with a below-par player in league games? It just
didn't add up.

Following the Cup final Ken asked for a move. In June he
was transferred to Newcastle United but only spent five months
on Tyneside before moving to Birmingham City. From there
he went to Northampton Town, then Bradford City before
dropping into non-league football, first with Merthyr Tydfil,
then Ton Pentre. He was probably never the same player after
his crushing disappointment in 1961.

As for Hugh McIlmoyle, the unwilling and unwitting partici-
pant in this controversy, the responsibility of leading our line was
too heavy a burden on his young shoulders. Unable to hold
down a regular first-team place, within a year Hugh moved on
to Rotherham United and was to become a football journeyman
in every sense of the word. His subsequent career included three
spells at Carlisle United interspersed with appearances for Wolverhampton Wanderers, Bristol City, Middlesbrough, Preston
North End and Morton. Hugh developed into a fine player and
a prolific goalscorer, particularly in his first spell with Carlisle
when he notched 39 goals in 1963–64, just three short of Carlisle's
all-time goalscoring record set by Jimmy McConnell in 1929.
All in all Hugh scored 200 league and cup goals on his travels.

The 1960–61 season marked a watershed for professional footballers. The Football League agreed to the demands of our union,
the Professional Footballers' Association, that the £20 maximum
wage and the so-called 'slavery contract' (binding players to their
clubs for life) be abolished. The PFA had been engaged in a long
hard battle with the Football League and our victory, which
simply gave us the rights enjoyed by all other workers, was due
largely to the efforts of PFA chairman Jimmy Hill and union
secretary Cliff Lloyd, a former solicitor.

The maximum wage had long been a bone of contention
among footballers. There was no way clubs could pay more for
quality players: the top stars in the First Division, with considerable experience at international level, could not earn any more
than a journeyman Fourth Division player. That, to my mind,
was never right.

According to the Football League, the maximum wage was
designed to save smaller clubs from bankruptcy and give everyone
an equal chance of holding on to their best players. That is why
relatively small clubs often managed to keep a world-class player
for the duration of his career: for example, Preston and Tom
Finney, Blackpool and Stanley Matthews, Bolton Wanderers and

Nat Lofthouse, Middlesbrough and Wilf Mannion. The system may have benefited the clubs, but at the expense of the players.

The maximum wage, it has to be said, enabled clubs in towns of medium size, such as Huddersfield, Bolton, Preston, Blackpool and Blackburn, to do well. In arguing this, the League had a point – one only has to look at the top half of a First Division table in the fifties compared to the Premiership today. This was one of the few positive aspects of the maximum wage.

Football goes in cycles and while the so-called smaller clubs of provincial towns such as Huddersfield and Stoke have been absent from the top flight for quite a number of years, the recent resurgence of clubs such as Burnley, Wolves and Preston is heartening. Indeed, just look at the recent presence in the Premiership of smaller-town clubs such as Coventry City, Ipswich Town, Southampton, Derby County, Swindon Town, Barnsley and, dare I say it, Leicester City. These examples shoot holes in the main argument of the Football League at the time, that should the maximum wage be abolished, it would mean an end to smaller clubs from the provinces gracing top-flight football.

Freedom of contract came about through a test case in the courts when the PFA helped Arsenal's George Eastham, former England Under-23 team mate of mine, to take his former club, Newcastle United, to court on a charge of restraint of trade in refusing him a transfer. George and the PFA won their day in court. Football, and the lot of a footballer, was to change irrevocably.

The highly paid Premiership players of today owe a debt of thanks to the players of 1961 and in particular to Jimmy Hill and Cliff Lloyd who took on the Football League and won the right for footballers to be paid a wage more in keeping with their worth to a club. Jimmy, in his day a fine wing half at Fulham and the manager who began the renaissance of Coventry City, toured the country in his role as chairman of the PFA. He held meetings for players where we aired our grievances about the

maximum wage and discussed how to get it abolished. On both
the abolition of the maximum wage and freedom of contract,
the Football League appeared intransigent. However, by January
1961, facing the prospect of strike action and with their own
lawyers intimating that, legally, they didn't have a case, the
Football League capitulated.

The Football League had been hoping that because the very
nature of a footballer's job involved us being in opposition
with one another, we couldn't form a united front against the
maximum wage and the 'slavery contract'. It was a misplaced
belief. The players encompassed all three of the major political
parties, but, by and large, we soon became united in our opposition to what we believed was a violation of our labour rights.

Arguably the most significant meeting took place in December
1960 in Manchester. The northern-based players, almost exclusively from working-class backgrounds, were well aware of the
hardships endured in the factory or down the pit and the fact
that, in general terms, we earned more than the average working
person. Shouldn't we be content with that? A footballer, however, could do the job of a miner – but could the miner do the
footballer's job?

Then came a crucial contribution from the legendary Stanley
Matthews. Some thought that, because he was better off than the
vast majority of players thanks to his endorsement deals, he
wouldn't commit himself to our cause. They were wrong. Stan
was not the best public speaker, but he was well read and a
known lover of art. When he did speak, he chose his words
carefully and wisely. As he got to his feet that day he commanded
the rapt attention of everyone in the room.

Next to hard, honest, skilful and creative work, is the appreciation of
it, and you, brothers, are not receiving the financial appreciation your
endeavours deserve. I pledge my full support to you all, and, in particular
to Mr Hill and Mr Lloyd. They will guide us to success, because the
winds and the waves are always on the side of the ablest navigators.

That sealed it. It took Stan Matthews but thirty seconds to say his piece, at the end of which every player was united in the cause. And in the end, faced with player solidarity which they hadn't anticipated, the League backed down.

The lifting of the maximum wage had no immediate effect on my earnings, as I was still contracted to Leicester at £20 a week. One player who did immediately benefit was Johnny Haynes, the captain of Fulham and England. The Fulham chairman, the comedian and TV personality Tommy Trinder, had gone on record as saying that, should the maximum wage ever be lifted, he would be happy to pay Johnny £100 a week. Three days after the maximum wage was abolished and with Johnny – advised by Bagenal Harvey, the first football agent in England – ready to negotiate a new contract at Fulham, Haynes reminded Trinder of what he had said. There was no get-out clause. Johnny became Britain's first £100 a week footballer.

Johnny's leap in wages had a knock-on effect at Fulham. Tommy Trinder was forever telling centre forward Maurice Cook that he was only half the player Johnny Haynes was. When his contract was up for renegotiation he was offered £35 a week.

'You're always telling me I'm only half the player Johnny Haynes is,' said Maurice.

'You are,' said Trinder.

'In that case, I deserve fifty quid a week.' He got it.

Not every player saw a huge increase in their wages, even when the time came for a new contract. One of the first Leicester players to renew his contract following the abolition of the maximum wage was Richie Norman. Everyone was eager to know what Richie had managed to negotiate with Matt Gillies.

'Say hello to Leicester's first three-figure-a-week footballer,' said Richie on entering the dressing room.

Everyone was slack jawed. Jimmy Walsh asked Richie what his new wage was to be.

'Thirty pounds, twelve shillings and sixpence,' replied Richie.

Matt Gillies was particularly difficult to negotiate with where wages were concerned and treated the club's money as if it were his own. There were no agents or financial advisers, so we players had to renegotiate our contracts and terms ourselves. I was never comfortable doing this with Matt. Rather than suggest an amount of money, even as a starting point, Matt always asked how much I wanted. I always found it difficult to come up with a sum that would be acceptable to the club, yet would pay me what I believed I was worth. Some players would suggest a sum that was way over the top and when taken to task about it would simply reply along the lines of, 'I'm a top player. My contribution to the team is invaluable, now are you going to pay me what I'm worth, or something like it? Because if you don't, I know plenty of clubs who will.'

I never had it in me to blow my own trumpet. Matt knew this and often took advantage of it. As an improving player, I always asked for more money than my previous contract paid me, but never outrageously more. Whatever I suggested by way of a wage, Matt would pull a face, sigh, then say: 'I'd love to pay you that, Gordon, believe me I would. But the refurbishment of the main stand has cost this club a lot of money. As well you know, we've also spent a lot on the training ground, so that you players can enjoy much better facilities at training. Attendances are up, but so too is the level of entertainment tax the club pays. Travel costs to away games are spiralling and we're even having to cut back on how many apprentices we can afford to take on . . .'

After ten minutes of Matt's excuses I'd feel so bad about asking for a rise I was almost ready to turn out for nothing.

Ultimately I always did receive improved terms at contract time, but never anything like I had hoped for. Johnny Haynes in earning £100 a week in 1961 was an exception, but even First Division players not deemed to be of international standard, such as Maurice Cook, were earning £50 a week. In 1961–62 the Spurs players were earning between £70 and £85 a week. The most I ever earned at Leicester was £60 a week in 1966, when I was England's first-choice goalkeeper. I should imagine England's current number 1 is glad he wasn't born thirty years earlier.

Just about every player today has an agent, even at youth-team level. Johnny Haynes was not only the first £100 a week footballer in England, but also the first in my time as a player to have an agent. Johnny's agent was Bagenal Harvey, an Irishman who was no stranger to the role. Though the role of Johnny's agent was unlike that of many of today's players' representatives.

In the late 1940s Harvey was a pal of the great Denis Compton who played football for Arsenal, was even better known as a cricketer with Middlesex and represented England at both sports. In the immediate post-war years Denis used to receive a considerable amount of fan mail. Being a dual sportsman and a man who, shall I say, led a full social life, Denis simply didn't have the time to reply to all his fan mail and asked his pal, Bagenal Harvey, to help out. When Harvey saw the sheer volume of letters written to Denis he realized straight away that, in addition to his sporting talents, Denis had considerable commercial appeal.

Harvey knew the marketing manager of a company called County Perfumery, based in Stanmore, Middlesex. While the name of this company was not well known, one of its products, Brylcreem, a hairdressing cream for men, was a massive seller nationwide. Men being demobbed from the services were known as the Brylcreem Boys; free from the constraints of service life, men wanted to appear fashionable and smart on civvy street and Brylcreem was seen as the perfect way to maintain their hairstyle throughout the day.

Harvey persuaded County Perfumery that Denis Compton would be the ideal front man for their product – he was stylish, fashionable, a great all-round sportsman and a celebrated 'ladies' man'. In short, the exact image the company wanted for Brylcreem.

Denis was paid handsomely for promoting Brylcreem, though

that was the extent of Bagenal Harvey's involvement as his agent. Denis Compton was soon seen on hoardings across the country and in countless newspaper and magazine advertisements. Interestingly, for someone more famed for his exploits on the cricket field, Compton appeared in football kit, though the strip he wore in the advertisements bore no resemblance to that of either Arsenal or England. The Arsenal directors and the Football Association wouldn't allow their respective strips to be 'degraded for commercial purposes'!

In the late fifties Denis came towards the end of his career as a sportsman so County Perfumery had to look elsewhere for a readily recognizable face to promote Brylcreem. As Johnny Haynes was the rising star of English football Harvey contacted him with a view to becoming the new Brylcreem Boy.

Johnny took over the role from Compton and appointed Bagenal Harvey as his agent, though at no time was Harvey ever involved in discussions with Fulham regarding Johnny's contract and wages. Johnny Haynes, as we have seen, was eminently capable of dealing with that himself.

The issue of players' wages and Johnny Haynes's appointment of an agent to represent him were major topics of debate in 1960. Over forty years on, the subject of players' wages and the role of agents is still high on the debating agenda. There is a body of opinion that the players of today and their representatives wield too much power over clubs. Some feel that while the maximum wage was undoubtedly wrong and an infringement of not only working but human rights, now things have gone too far the other way. That wage demands are crippling many clubs and have a detrimental effect on football in general.

When ITV Digital was placed into receivership in 2002, many smaller clubs, dependent on the money from TV rights, feared for their future. Between 1991 and 2001 the money football clubs received from TV increased sixfold but in that time players' wages rose by the same amount. The collapse of ITV Digital and the subsequent worry that the money promised to clubs would not be forthcoming, signalled the end of football's decade-long financial boom.

The top players will continue to earn fabulous sums of money, basically because the likes of David Beckham, Ryan Giggs and Michael Owen, like Denis Compton in 1947 and Johnny Haynes in the late fifties, have considerable commercial potential. David Beckham wouldn't be at Manchester United and captain of England unless he was a great player and he wouldn't have such great commercial potential unless he was with United and England skipper. His contribution to the United team is considerable, but so too is his importance to the club's commercial arm. Manchester United were reported to have sold over a million replica shirts in 2001 in Japan alone, many of them bearing the name of Beckham on the back. Beckham and other top players today are paid not only for what they contribute to the club on the pitch, but also for what their image means to commercial sales.

Just as the top players and their agents have driven up wages astronomically, so the less exalted players around them have seen their earnings increase proportionately. This has led to a wages spiral throughout the Premiership and on down through the Football League, even into the Vauxhall Conference, as clubs are prepared to pay whatever it cost to attract stars to help get them promotion and concomitant higher TV revenues which were designed to fund the whole operation. It has become a vicious circle because the increased wages were largely financed by money received from TV. Now that television is reassessing the money it pays for the rights to broadcast football, we have gone full circle. Some pundits are now calling for wage restraint, even a cap on how much a player may be allowed to earn from his club – a situation not dissimilar to that which existed in football prior to the abolition of the maximum wage.

Of course, some say football clubs would not be in the situation in which they now find themselves, if the PFA and its members had not succeeded in the campaign against the maximum wage

13. During the big freeze of 1962–63. Displaying all the benefits of Ursula's numerous hot dinners, I collect the ball under pressure from Ray Crawford of Ipswich Town. Braziers filled with burning coke kept the frost at bay, but, as you can see from the pitch, not for long.

14. The 1963 FA Cup semi-final against Liverpool. I manage to punch clear from Liverpool's Ian St John. There was only one team in this game – Liverpool – and they lost 1–0.

15. A very nervous day for me. My first game for England and Alf Ramsey's second game in charge – against the old enemy, Scotland, in 1963. I'm pushing away a low shot from Willie Henderson. Scotland won 2–1, both their goals coming from Jim Baxter.

16. The flying Englishman. A free kick from John White has me at full stretch in my international debut against Scotland. On this occasion I managed to keep the Scots at bay, though that wasn't always the case in this game.

17. Davie Gibson, Ian King, myself and Frank McLintock show our relief at the end of the FA Cup semi-final against Liverpool. This was the moment when I was 'set up' by a photographic editor from a well-known newspaper.

18. Oh dear! In my second game for England I'm mesmerized by the swerve of Pepe's 'banana' free kick. Alf Ramsey was not best pleased. Off to my left in the upper stand at Wembley, one of the few Brazilian supporters present celebrates.

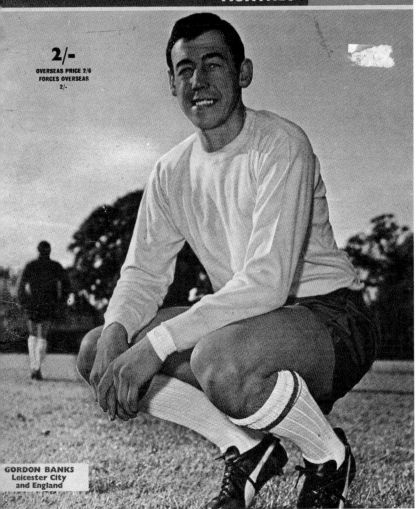

CHARLES BUCHAN'S

FOOTBALL

MONTHLY

The World's Greatest Soccer Magazine

JANUARY, 1964

2/-
OVERSEAS PRICE 2/6
FORCES OVERSEAS
2/-

GORDON BANKS
Leicester City
and England

19. When I was a teenager, *Charles Buchan's Football Monthly* was the football magazine. Unable to afford to attend matches on a regular basis, the only way to see my heroes was in the *Footy Monthly*. When I was featured on the cover of the January 1964 issue, one of my childhood dreams came true.

20. Taking a high cross against West Germany in the 1966 World Cup final, oddly enough under no pressure on this occasion. Looking on, from left to right, are George Cohen, Jack Charlton, Uwe Seeler, Martin Peters, Bobby Moore and Lothar Emmerich.

21. Glory seized from our grasp in the dying seconds of the 1966 World Cup final. Wolfgang Weber's equalizer should not have been allowed. Karl-Heinz Schnellinger handled the ball. You can see Bobby Moore appealing.

22. A golden memory of a truly golden day. I join Martin Peters, Geoff Hurst,
Bobby Moore and Roger Hunt to parade the World Cup around at Wembley.
Notice how we are too exhausted to run.

23. 'Give it here, Banksy.' Winning the World Cup is the most difficult thing a player can do in football. It had been a long hard road and once I got my hands on the trophy I wasn't going to give it up easily – not even to skipper Bobby Moore!

24. The boys of '66. There were no prima donnas, no cliques, no loners. We were a team in every sense of the word. Left to right, back row: Gerry Byrne (reserve), Harold Shepherdson (trainer), Jack Charlton, myself, Roger Hunt, Bobby Moore, Geoff Hurst, George Cohen, Bobby Charlton; front row: Nobby Stiles, Alan Ball, Martin Peters and Ray Wilson. Bobby Charlton looks as though he is about to be taken away as it has all become too much for him!

back in 1961. That, to my mind, is too simplistic a view. My fellow professionals and I were right to take on the Football League over the maximum wage and the so-called 'slavery contract'. That club directors, players and their agents have, in the intervening years, not always exercised common sense in matters of money is hardly the fault of those who successfully campaigned to have the basic labour rights enjoyed by every other profession in Great Britain.

7. Into Europe

How good are football pundits at seeing the future? In the summer of 1961 ten national newspaper journalists were asked to predict who would be among the honours in 1961–62. The consensus of opinion was that Spurs would retain their league title, Aston Villa and Birmingham City would contest the FA Cup final, Everton would land the League Cup, Liverpool and Sunderland gain promotion from Division Two and Queens Park Rangers would be champions of Division Three. Well, at least they got Liverpool's promotion right.

One of the great attractions of football is that the game is so unpredictable. Following our improved league form and our appearance in the FA Cup final the previous season, I was convinced Leicester City would continue to improve this term and that we had a very good chance of winning some silverware. I was so wrong that I could have been writing for the national newspapers.

The close season had seen a flurry of activity on the transfer market and some notable moves. Jimmy Greaves eventually completed his £99,999 record move from AC Milan to Spurs, Brian Clough left Middlesbrough for Sunderland for a fee of £45,000, while at Leicester Ian King followed Ken Leek out of the door when he signed for Southampton for £27,500. Another transfer of note was completed in October when Stanley Matthews left Blackpool and signed for his hometown club Stoke City for the second time in his career. On the managerial front, the former Wolves and England captain, Billy Wright, took over from George Swindin as manager of Arsenal. Matt Gillies, meanwhile, seemed happy with his squad at Leicester because he made just one signing in the close season, Davie Thomson from

Dunfermline, shock winners of the Scottish Cup when, in the replayed final, they had beaten Celtic 2–0. Incidentally, Davie scored one of the Dunfermline goals that day. Unfortunately, Davie found the transition to English football too great a leap and, after being dogged by a troublesome cartilage, eventually returned to Scotland.

As Spurs had won the double they played an FA Select XI in the Charity Shield in the curtain-raiser to the season. Spurs were as formidable as ever, winning 3–2 against what was more or less the current England team before a White Hart Lane crowd of 36,595.

Spurs' double success also benefited Leicester City. As Spurs were involved in the European Champions Cup for the first time, the FA ruled that Leicester, the Cup runners-up, would participate in the European Cup-Winners Cup. It would be my first venture into European football and I was looking forward to the experience with great enthusiasm.

In the close season I had travelled abroad for the first time when Leicester toured South Africa and Rhodesia (now Zimbabwe). I can't remember too much about this trip, other than marvelling at the totally different culture and the natural beauty of those countries. Of the five matches we played we won all but the last, a 1–1 draw in Johannesburg against the Transvaal.

On the day Spurs were winning the Charity Shield, we lost a pre-season friendly at St Mirren 3–1. On the journey home we met the Burnley players who had been playing a combined Hearts and Hibernian XI. In these days of intensive tribal rivalry among some supporters, the notion of two neighbouring clubs fielding a combined team is unthinkable. But this used to happen quite often for a friendly or testimonial match as a way of attracting a larger attendance to a game that had no competitive significance. Indeed, some 21,000 had watched Burnley against the Edinburgh combination.

Pre-season preparation in the sixties regularly featured matches against continental opposition, usually part-timers from

Denmark and Holland who saw English football as the bench-mark they had to aim for in their own development. Today a team of part-timers from the Continent would not be much of an attraction to an English club, or its supporters. In the early sixties, however, any team from the Continent held an attraction. Intercontinental flights were burgeoning, Europe was shrinking and the easy accessibility of England made it a popular destination for teams from across the North Sea.

In the summer of 1961 Danish clubs Odense, Aarhus, AGF Jutland, Aalborg, Holbaek BK and FC Copenhagen all enjoyed fact-finding tours of England as did the Dutch clubs, MVV Maastricht, Ajax, DWS Amsterdam, Sparta Rotterdam, FC Den Haag, Utrecht and FC Zwolle. Many English fans were curious to see what continental football was like, and study the different techniques of foreign players. The English game may well have been developing apace following the defeats of our national team at the hands of Hungary in the mid-fifties, but Danish and Dutch football was coming on in leaps and bounds. The old balance of power in which Italy, Spain, Germany, England and Scotland had been head and shoulders above the rest in Europe, was about to change irrevocably.

Our domestic programme began at Manchester City. Invariably a new football season kicks off under gold-leaf sunshine and our first game at Maine Road was no exception. Unfortunately for us, the opposition was just as hot as the weather, the home side running out 3–1 winners. Then when that was swiftly followed by a 1–0 defeat by Arsenal at Filbert Street on the Wednesday evening, all that pre-season optimism had taken a bit of a jolt. Still, a domestic football season is a long-distance race, not a sprint. We firmly believed that, in time, we would hit a vein of consistent form to put us within reach of the top of the table.

It never happened. Our play throughout 1961–62 was charac-terized by inconsistency. Only once did we string three victories together: against Manchester United, Cardiff and Chelsea in

April, and even that modest little run ended with a considerable bump when we lost 8–3 at Aston Villa. A team scoring three goals away from home should reasonably expect to get something out of the game. But on the day Villa scored from every chance they had. Matt Gillies in fact fielded an unchanged team for our next game at Bolton, which, to my mind, indicates he also saw the Villa match as being 'just one of those games'.

We ended the season in mid-table. Combined with a third-round exit from the FA Cup, this was a considerable let-down after the exciting climax to the previous season and the high hopes that that engendered. I do remember some moments to savour among the dross. For one thing, we exacted a measure of revenge for our Cup final misery by beating Spurs 2–1 at White Hart Lane, with goals from Ken Keyworth and Colin Appleton. We were highly motivated that day and turned on our best display of the season. Another highlight came at the end of August when we drew 4–4 with Arsenal at Highbury. For players and fans alike this was a cracking game of football.

And there's one more memory that stays with me, ironically from that frustrating FA Cup defeat by Stoke City at the Victoria Ground. In the Stoke team was Stanley Matthews, who at forty-seven years of age could still weave his magic, and appeared eminently capable of coping with the pace and rigours of the game. In the first half Stan latched on to the Stoke right half Bobby Howitt's perfectly timed pass, which caught the Leicester defence pushing on. Stan raced on to the ball and was now one-on-one with me. He produced the shimmy he was so famous for, I committed myself to a save to my right, Stan coolly went the other way and calmly stroked the ball into the net.

Years later whenever I met Stan, he would always introduce me by saying, 'This is Gordon Banks. Not many people scored against Gordon – but I did!'

The highlight of a dismal year was our involvement in the European Cup-Winners Cup. None of the Leicester players had any experience of European competition. It was a journey into the unknown.

The first round pitched us against Glenavon from Northern Ireland, a gentle initiation against modest opposition. After our 4−1 victory in the first leg at Windsor Park the return tie at Filbert Street appeared to be a formality, which may have helped restrict the crowd to 10,000, less than half the normal average. We applied ourselves to the task in a professional manner, winning 3−1 (aggregate 7−2) to progress to the next round. Next we drew the plum tie everyone had been hoping for: Atletico Madrid. Everyone connected with the club was licking their lips at the prospect, but on the day of the first leg at Filbert Street, I found myself in a situation that today defies belief.

Two weeks previously I had been training with the rest of my Leicester team mates when I was called over by Matt Gillies.

'Good news, Gordon,' said Matt, 'Walter Winterbottom has included you in the England squad for the Portugal game.'

This came as a huge surprise. I thought I had been playing reasonably well in goal for Leicester, but to be called up for England was a quantum leap in my career. My delight turned to shock when I discovered that England were due to play Portugal on the same day Leicester were playing Atletico Madrid!

I was in a real dilemma. I couldn't let the club, my team mates and the Leicester supporters down, yet to decline Walter Winterbottom's invitation to join the England squad might mean that I would never get another chance at international level.

I talked it over with Ursula, discussed it with my parents and spent much time mulling it over myself. I referred it to Matt Gillies and Bert Johnson, then came to a decision. I would attend both games.

In 1961 the Wembley floodlights afforded insufficient illumination for a football match. Consequently, England games took place on a Wednesday afternoon. With the October kick-off time set at 2.30 p.m. I reasoned that the England game would finish at around 4.30 and, if I got my skates on, I could make it back to Leicester in time for the game against Atletico.

The idea of a player being involved in a World Cup qualifying game, then dashing off to play for his club in a European match on the same day would be unthinkable now, but it did have a precedent. Some years earlier the Arsenal goalkeeper, Jack Kelsey, had played on a Wednesday afternoon in Cardiff for Wales against England, then hurried back to London to play for the Gunners in a prestigious friendly against Juventus. I reasoned that if he could get back from Cardiff to London, I could make it from London to Leicester.

England beat Portugal 2–0, but what was notable about the game was the performance of Portugal's young number 8, Eusebio. Countless times when running from deep, Eusebio posed all manner of problems for England, and gave every indication of being a great player in the making. Twice, from distance, he smacked powerful shots off the post with the first-choice keeper, Ron Springett, floundering on the ground. Ron was a super goalkeeper, but on that day was lucky to keep a clean sheet. At nineteen Eusebio was a totally unknown quantity, but his name was certainly on everyone's lips by the end of the match.

Within twenty minutes of the final whistle I was on my way back to Leicester. Now, you might imagine that as a First Division player on the fringes of the England team, my mode of transport would be a sixties classic like a Ford Zephyr or Consul, the latter with its large bench seat in the front. Or a sporty number like an Austin-Healey Sprite, or perhaps a Vauxhall Victor, with the American-style fly-away wings. How about a Mk. II Jaguar, a Renault Dauphine or even a two-tone Vauxhall Cresta with white-walled wheels? No – what got me from A to B was a small Ford van (though not, I hasten to add, the same one with which I had terrified Duggie Livingstone at Chesterfield). Even driving with my foot flat to the boards for the best part of the journey I cut it fine, arriving at Filbert Street just half an hour before kick-off.

Atletico Madrid, like every other club in Spain – in the world, for that matter – lived in the shadow of Real Madrid. In the first round of the Cup-Winners Cup Atletico had beaten the French side Sedan home and away by 7–2 on aggregate. Though this was Atletico's first time in the Cup-Winners Cup, they had played in the 1958–59 European Cup, having finished runners-up to the holders Real in the Spanish First Division. A storming campaign, in which they brushed aside Irish, Bulgarian and German opposition, eventually ended in a replayed semi-final against, inevitably, Real Madrid. They had also defeated Real in the Spanish cup finals of 1960 and '61. So we had absolutely no illusions about their calibre as a team of quality and fighting spirit.

Despite my mad dash from Wembley I was raring to go, and so were my Leicester team mates. Gillies had not been to see Atletico play, nor sent anyone to spy on them. We knew nothing about their style of play, how they might approach the game and the best way to play against them. Atletico, however, had sent one of their coaching staff to watch our previous game, a 2–0 home defeat by Blackpool.

For the want of a better plan, we set about Atletico as we did any side visiting Filbert Street. We took the game to them from the start and laid siege to their goal. Technically accomplished and comfortable on the ball, Atletico seemed quite happy to soak up the pressure, though they were always looking to catch us on the break. This pattern would prove to be all too familiar in European competition in years to come, but it was a new and puzzling tactic to us then. They were clearly ready to leave with a goalless draw. But they didn't get it.

Ken Keyworth put us ahead and had a second disallowed when the referee ruled that he'd been fouled en route to goal. This baffling decision was European lesson number two for me: referees from other countries interpret the rules differently from British officials.

None the less, it seemed as if Ken's goal was going to be

enough. With less than a minute remaining, however, we were served European lesson number three. In the closing stages of the game we should have played possession football and killed the game off. Instead, we staged one last assault on the Spanish goal in the hope of extending our lead to make life difficult for them in the return leg. Our attack broke down; Atletico's Ramiro brought the ball quickly out of defence and played it up to their number 8, Adelardo, who made ground fast with the Leicester midfield and rearguard struggling to get back and reform; he played the ball inside to Mendoza, who swept the ball into the net. Within seconds of the game restarting the referee blew his whistle for time. Through our inexperience of European football we'd fallen prey to a classic sucker punch.

It was a bitter blow to concede such a late goal. Back in the dressing room Ken Keyworth was still fuming about the goal he had had disallowed but Colin Appleton tempered our disappointment, telling us it was all square, all to play for in Madrid. He was convinced we'd win the return leg.

The return leg was a belter of a game. It wasn't in our nature to sit back, absorb pressure and hope to catch Atletico on the break, so we adopted Matt Gillies's usual game plan: 'Go out there and give it a go.'

In front of over 50,000 vociferous Spaniards in the Vincente Calderón stadium we gave a good account of ourselves, but it was not to be our night. In front of their own fans Atletico were far more positive in their approach and I soon found myself busy. Eventually their pressure bore fruit when Atletico were awarded a penalty following a foul on Mendoza. Fortunately, I anticipated correctly and managed to save Collar's waist-high spot kick to my right. The respite, however, proved only temporary as Atletico were later awarded a second penalty. As Collar stepped up again I found myself with a dilemma on my hands. Would he hit the ball to my right as he had done previously? Or, having failed with his first attempt, choose the other side of the goal? As Collar prepared to take the kick I watched his eyes intently, hoping that they might give an indication as to which side of my goal he was going to choose. In addressing the ball his face was inscrutable, his eyes gave no hint as to which side of my goal he would choose. I quickly made my mind up to dive to my right as I had done before. Collar had hit his first penalty at waist height, which for a goalkeeper is the optimum height at which to execute a penalty save as vital time is not taken up trying to get either down or up to the ball. Yet again Collar hit the ball to my right. This time, however, he fired high. There was no way I could get even a finger to the ball and 50,000 Spaniards roared their approval.

We never relented in our efforts to push them back. Howard Riley and Ken Keyworth both went close to equalizing but when Atletico added to their tally in the second half they were content to play keep-ball, and frustrate all our efforts to get back into the game. Leicester City's first European adventure was over, but there was no disgrace in losing to such a good side, one much more experienced in the ways of European competition than us. Atletico Madrid went on to win the competition, beating Fiorentina of Italy in a replayed final that was held over until September of the following season!

With Jimmy Greaves now in their ranks, everyone expected Tottenham Hotspur to retain their League title in 1961–62. They didn't. The champions were a team widely expected to struggle to maintain their First Division status. Ipswich Town had been promoted from Division Two the previous season and their manager, Alf Ramsey, worked a minor miracle in guiding his unfancied side – largely the same one that had won promotion – to the First Division title.

Ipswich Town may not have had any star players, but they were a proper team. They were a very well-balanced side that possessed creative players, a resolute defence and a pair of rampaging forwards in Ray Crawford and Ted Phillips, who between them notched over sixty goals. But the key to that Ipswich team was the veteran Scot Jimmy Leadbetter. Originally brought in as an orthodox left winger, Alf Ramsey gave Jimmy a new role as a deep-lying, left-of-centre midfield player. Opposing teams were perplexed as to whose job it was to mark him, which left him a lot of space to exploit his vision and superb distribution.

Alf Ramsey proved himself to be a great motivator of his players and a wily strategist, qualities that, in time, would greatly benefit England and yours truly. His method at Ipswich was to get the players to fulfil their potential as individuals, while at the same time devising tactics that blended those players into a formidable unit. After they beat fancied Burnley 6–2 in September, they really hit their stride. Throughout the season Ipswich vied with Spurs, Burnley and Everton for the top spot in Division One. Both Spurs and Burnley were involved in Europe and both enjoyed runs in the FA Cup that eventually saw them meet in the final. Without such distractions Ipswich could concentrate on the League and when Spurs and Burnley both faltered at the wire, Burnley winning only one of their last seven games, Ipswich's fresh and fluent football reaped handsome dividends. They finished three points ahead of Burnley and four ahead of Spurs to be arguably the most surprising Football League champions in the history of the game.

Having won the title, many football writers were still unconvinced about their pedigree, especially as our representatives in the following season's European Cup. The *Daily Sketch* was among the doubters: 'Ipswich, in the end, proved worthy champions. But they still lack sufficient quality in their ranks to make an impact in Europe. One fears that when they do take their bow in the European Cup, their first meeting with continental opposition will prove their undoing.' That writer underestimated Alf Ramsey and his team. In Ipswich's first European tie they beat Floriana Valletta of Malta 10–0 and 4–1!

Of all the clubs I visited as a player the one that provided the best hospitality was Ipswich Town. Whatever the result, a visit to Portman Road was a joy. This had much to do with the board of directors, in particular their chairman John Cobbold and other members of the Cobbold family who were connected with the club. They owned Tolly Cobbold Ales, at the time the premier brewery in Suffolk, and were renowned for their hospitality, sense of humour and liking for a good time. When the Leicester City party arrived at Ipswich station for a game at Portman Road, the Cobbolds, and often other Ipswich directors such as Cyril Catchpole and Sir Charles Bunbury, would be there on the platform to meet us. Their cars would act as an escort for our team bus to Portman Road and once the game was over, the Cobbolds would accompany us back to the station and wave us off.

Never in my time in football did I come across directors like those at Ipswich. When Alf Ramsey was appointed Ipswich manager in 1955, John Cobbold took him into the boardroom and poured a couple of drinks.

'This is the first and last time I'll be serving you a drink in the boardroom, Alf,' said Cobbold, who then threw Alf a key for the drinks cabinet. 'From now on help yourself!'

Alf was never much of a drinker, just the occasional glass of wine with a meal, and I doubt whether he ever took Cobbold up on his offer in his entire time at Ipswich. But that gesture was typical of John Cobbold and, indeed, his fellow directors.

We once played Ipswich Town on Boxing Day and, it being the festive season, the Cobbolds were more than ever in party mood. After the game the Leicester directors were enjoying the considerable hospitality of the Ipswich boardroom when John Cobbald walked in with a pound of frozen sausages on his head. At first no one said anything, but eventually Leicester director Dennis Sharp plucked up the courage to ask Cobbold what he was doing.

'Defrosting my tea, old boy,' replied John Cobbold.

When Ipswich clinched the championship, Peter Wilson of the *Daily Mirror* interviewed the Ipswich chairman.

'Champions! I suppose for the Ipswich board this has been a season of wine, women and song,' Wilson suggested.

'I can't remember us doing much singing,' replied Cobbold.

Immediately following Ipswich's 2–0 victory over us at Filbert Street in March, the Leicester chairman Walter Needham extended the club's hospitality to John Cobbold and his co-directors.

'Would you care to join me in the boardroom for a quiet drink?' asked Needham.

'Yes,' said Cobbold, 'and six very loud ones!'

The Cobbolds' ebullient nature, sense of humour and penchant for a drink and a good time were in sharp contrast to Alf Ramsey, who was, ostensibly, a quiet, sober and serious individual. Yet they got on famously. When Alf left the club to become manager of England in 1963, Ipswich as a team went into sharp decline, but the hospitality of the Ipswich board never faltered. To this day Ipswich Town enjoy a reputation for being a very friendly, family club whose board has continued to make considered rather than impulsive decisions – something exemplified in the fact that the club have only had ten managers since they gained entry to the Football League in 1938.

The next year, 1963, was a remarkable one, both personally and historically. This was the year of the Beatles and the Cuban missile crisis, Concorde and the death of JFK, Dr Beeching and Lady Chatterley, the Profumo affair and the Great Train Robbery, Charles de Gaulle's 'Non' and *Dr No*. (Who could forget the sight of Ursula Andress rising glistening from the sea in that first Bond film?) Before the year was over I was to be in the running for the league and cup double, make my full debut for England in the most important game in our international calendar; and follow that up by facing the best international side in the world.

The summer of 1962 had been a frustrating one for me. When my name was listed in the England–Portugal match programme as being one of only two goalkeepers in Walter Winterbottom's squad for the World Cup in Chile, I had high hopes of making the final squad. But it wasn't to be. Though both World Cup goalkeepers were from Sheffield, I wasn't one of them. Wednesday's Ron Springett and Alan Hodgkinson of United were Walter's choices for the World Cup, while I was put on stand-by. I dutifully kept myself fit, spending countless hours on my own lapping the Filbert Street pitch.

At Leicester Charles Maley retired as secretary and was replaced by Eddie Plumley. While Maley, a highly efficient administrator and stickler for detail, lacked personal warmth, Eddie exuded warmth and friendliness, and his modernizing approach, not least in his handling of the press, was a revelation. His appointment in 1962 was indicative of football's increasing willingness to adapt and take on new ideas as evidenced in a blueprint issued by the Football League Management Committee that summer. That the document was titled 'The Football Revolution' shows the League's seriousness of intent. It contained a number of proposals for the reorganization of football in England:

- The football season to be extended by three weeks into May. The new football season to begin in mid-August with Saturday and mid-week League Cup matches. The Football League programme to commence at the end of the first week of September.
- International matches to be played on fixed dates, with all home nations to play on the same day to minimize disruption to League clubs.
- The Football League to be extended to 100 clubs – divided into three divisions of 20, with a Fourth Division split into Northern and Southern sections each of 20. In the latter, clubs to have the option of being fully professional or part-time.
- Promotion and relegation to be four-up, four-down in every division.
- First round of the FA Cup to take place on 1 December, not early November; third round on 26 January with the final on the last Saturday in May.

- Once the season has commenced, no club to arrange a friendly match until after the third round of the FA Cup.
- The League Cup to be divided into regional zones which would play on a league basis at the start of every season, the winners then going on to a straight knock-out competition with a single final staged in mid-December taking place at a neutral venue. All League clubs to enter.

The clubs, however, gave the blueprint a lukewarm reception. Meeting after meeting took place between Football League officials and club chairmen, working committees were set up. That the enthusiasm of the Football League, and in particular that of their secretary Alan Hardaker, for change was not shared by club chairmen was no surprise to many players. The weeks of debate turned into months and eventually, the League's brave new blueprint for football was shelved – though, in time, one or two of the proposals did come into being.

In 1967 the League Cup final reverted to a single tie and was staged at Wembley, while international matches did eventually take place on fixed dates with the home countries all participating. (It was clearly to the advantage of clubs not to lose their best players for key league games.) The Football League still has ninety-two clubs, with only the top flight being reduced to the prescribed twenty (to facilitate the increasing involvement in European competition). The fear of change was symptomatic of an unwillingness of club chairmen to relax their control over the game. Only much later, with the saturation coverage of football by television, did the fabric of the league programme change. Even then the catalyst to that 'revolution' was money alone, not a genuine desire to make football more appealing to spectators and players, or to retain its advantage over alternative forms of entertainment.

Matt Gillies yet again proved himself to be a wily operator in the transfer market. He brought in Mike Stringfellow, a lithe but speedy winger from Mansfield Town, and a mercurial midfield player, Davie Gibson, who joined us from Hibernian, both for modest fees. And so began a new season with little to suggest it would be very different from the last, still less that we would end it as contenders for the league and cup double.

Every club and every player has a 'bogey team'. There's no logic to it – often they can't remember how or when the superstition began. Mine was Fulham, particularly at Craven Cottage – I never played well there. True to form, I had a nightmare of a game at Fulham on the opening day of the season, not helped by the fact that I broke my nose when diving at the feet of the Fulham winger, Graham Leggat. As I was first to a through ball I expected him to pull out of his challenge. He didn't, and as if to rub salt in my wound, he went on to score both Fulham goals in our 2–1 defeat.

Unlike the previous season, however, we quickly put that opening-day setback behind us. We showed great resolve when we drew 3–3 with much fancied Sheffield Wednesday, then defeated Nottingham Forest 2–1. Mike Stringfellow was proving himself to be a fine player with keen predatory skills. Just seven days after sharing six goals with Wednesday we went up to Hillsborough and won 3–0, Mike taking his goal tally to six in four games.

It was an encouraging start to the new campaign, and our form was to get even better. We lost only one of our next nine games, Leicester's best start to a First Division season since 1925–26. Things were looking up.

Leicester's chief scout, Bert Johnson, having completed his FA coaching course at Lilleshall, was appointed first-team coach. Bert's input had an immediate effect. As a team we became better organized and the individual talents of the players were at last moulded into a cohesive pattern of play. Jimmy Walsh and Davie Gibson were encouraged to track their opposite numbers back to our penalty area to provide extra cover when the opposition were on the attack. The midfield rotated to greater effect, so that more protection was available should our attack break down. Previously it was carte blanche who did this, even as to whether it was done at all. Bert Johnson ensured we had a set pattern of rotation, so that individuals knew who was to move across and supply cover in accordance with which player had pushed on. For example, Graham Cross for Frank McLintock and vice versa, Mike Stringfellow for Davie Gibson and so on.

European lesson number one was implemented, and instead of taking the game to opponents as had always been our policy, we became more patient in our build-up. Confident of our defensive qualities, we were content to soak up pressure and, once possession was regained, use the speed of Mike Stringfellow and Howard Riley to launch a swift counterattack before the opposition had time to fall back and reorganize in defence.

We spent a lot of time with Bert at the training ground working on dead-ball situations, both in defence and attack. Bert introduced a variety of cunning corner kicks and I remember one in particular that proved highly successful. When we were awarded a corner on our right, Howard Riley would take it. As Howard prepared to take the kick, Ian King, Colin Appleton and Jimmy Walsh would gather together on the far side of the penalty box just inside the angle of the area, as if waiting for Howard to deliver. Ken Keyworth, however, would take a position just outside the area, in line with the goalpost nearest to Howard. As Howard stepped back as if about to take the corner, Ken would run to the near post screaming for the ball to be played to him – only Howard would hesitate in taking the corner. Having seemingly made a fruitless run to the near post, Ken would then pretend to berate Howard for not playing the ball in early and trot back out of the penalty area. As Howard once again prepared to take the corner, Ian King, Colin Appleton and Jimmy Walsh would signal that Howard should play the ball to one of them. The opposition, alerted to this, would often forget Ken Keyworth, who having left the penalty area, would then jog to a point just outside the left-hand side of the area, almost parallel to Ian, Colin and Jimmy. Just as Howard was on the point of striking the ball, Ian and Colin would run to the near post and Jimmy to a point just beyond the penalty spot. Howard Riley would then drive the corner kick to the far post into the space Ian, Colin and Jimmy had created, where Ken Keyworth would come charging in to fire a header at goal.

This ploy worked a number of times for us. Ken's late run into space often meant he was unmarked when he connected with the ball. If Ken didn't score and his effort on goal was blocked, there were Jimmy, Colin and Ian to pick up on the rebound. We scored a number of goals from this set piece, though of course, it didn't take long before opposing teams got wise to it. But I cite this as an example of Bert Johnson's input into our play as evidence that, though football was still dominated by individualists, team tactics were assuming greater importance.

'Tactical awareness' was the new big thing on training pitches up and down the country, as coaches thought up ways to counteract the latest game plan. Nowhere was this more the case than at West Ham United. When the Hammers' manager, Ron Greenwood, switched an unpromising wing half, Geoff Hurst, into the attack he also introduced a tactical innovation. Rather than Geoff Hurst taking up an orthodox position at the far post for a cross from the wing, Geoff would play deep, then time his run so that he stayed onside and continue past the advancing defenders to meet the cross which was played into the space between the opposition's goalkeeper and the defence. It worked a treat for West Ham. This produced goals not only for West Ham, but also for England when Geoff and clubmates Bobby Moore and Martin Peters played together in Alf Ramsey's team. Geoff's goal for England in the 1966 World Cup quarter-final against Argentina, and his first in the final against West Germany, were pure Ron Greenwood.

Of course, once the First Division's bright young coaches put their minds to it, they got wise to what West Ham were doing and tried to counteract the danger of Hurst by assigning a player to track him into the box. Geoff, however, was formidable in the air and timed his run so well that the long ball from the flanks was never easy to defend. Especially for goalkeepers who didn't want to come out and be beaten to the ball and leave Hurst with an open goal at which to aim. Leicester tried to stifle this West Ham tactic by closing down quickly on the wide player whose job it was to make the cross. Not only him, but also any West Ham midfielder who was attempting to pass to their wide man, which in 1962–63 was usually Peter Brabrook on the right and Tony Scott on the left.

The evolution of coaching skills was becoming more rapid. Tactics bred tactics as the former students of the FA's coaching school at Lilleshall such as Bert Johnson, Ron Greenwood, Bob Paisley, Tommy Docherty, Dave Sexton, Phil Woosnam and Jimmy Adamson pitted their wits against one another. No sooner had one tactic been seen to work, than another evolved to counteract it. Then another would emerge to overcome the counteracting tactic. The origins of organized football date back to the Victorians, but the origins of the game we know today can be traced back to the work of those Lilleshall graduates of the early sixties.

The first of the winter snows came to the north of England in late November. It was cold in the midlands but we didn't experience snow until December when most of the country rejoiced in a white Christmas. Joy soon turned to frustration as the snow piled up and temperatures plummeted to wreak havoc across the nation. On Boxing Day we enjoyed a 5–1 victory over Leyton Orient in the swirling snow at Filbert Street. That win moved us up to third position in Division One, the title well within our sights.

The snow that had fallen previously was nothing compared to what followed. Blizzard begat blizzard. Snow fell on snow. One morning just after New Year I opened my front door to be confronted with snow that was almost waist high. No one could remember anything like it. Nor was there to be any respite from what the newspapers dubbed the 'Big Freeze' until April. Of course, the football fixture list was decimated, no complete programme of football being possible between 8 December and 16 March. Only three of the thirty-two third-round FA Cup ties were played on the day they were scheduled. Fourteen ties were postponed ten times or more, the match between Lincoln City and Coventry City being postponed a record fifteen times while the tie between Middlesbrough and Blackburn Rovers, originally scheduled for early January, wasn't played until mid-March. Only four Football League games took place on 5 January and five on 2 February. On 9 February six games took place in England but the entire Scottish League programme was post-poned. Bolton Wanderers went the longest period without a match in the history of a football season. Following their 1–0 win over Spurs on 8 December, the Bolton players were not in action again until 16 February. Over 400 matches fell victim to the weather. The final league games of the season were not completed until June.

With this period of enforced inactivity in the winter of 1962–63, some clubs went for weeks without a match and consequently were deprived of their main source of income from home (and a proportion of away) gate receipts. There were increasingly desperate attempts to beat the weather. Queens Park Rangers left their home ground at Loftus Road to play for a time at the aptly named White City in the hope the pitch there would prove more playable. Halifax Town, with their pitch at The Shay covered in a three-inch layer of ice, at one point opened it as a skating rink! Blackpool used army flame-throwers on the pitch at Bloomfield Road while Chelsea employed a high-ways tar burner. Birmingham City rented a snow-shifting tractor from Denmark and Wrexham covered their pitch at the Race-course Ground with 80 tons of sand. They were fighting a losing battle.

At Leicester we managed to avoid too much disruption owing

to a combination of good luck and sheer determination. The previous summer the Filbert Street pitch had been relaid with top soil treated with a combined chemical fertilizer and weed-killer. This generated a little heat that helped keep the frost at bay. The Leicester groundsman augmented this effect by placing oil drums filled with burning coke at various points around the pitch, which raised the air temperature enough to ward off the severest frost. A nightwatchman sat up throughout the Friday night to ensure all was safe. These braziers remained on the pitch until around eleven on a Saturday morning when the groundsman, his assistant and an army of junior players would then remove them. An hour later when the match referee arrived to inspect the pitch it was playable, and the game was given the go-ahead.

In all honesty many of these games should never have been played because, without the braziers, the pitch had partly frozen over again come three o'clock, especially the end that lay in the shadow of the club's towering double-decker stand. Aware that one half of the pitch was just playable, and the other half frozen, I used to run out for games wearing odd boots. On my right foot I would have my normal boot with hammer-in leather studs, while on my left I'd wear a boot with moulded rubber studs that offered better footing on hard surfaces. Under my arm I would carry the other two odd boots. Once I knew which end we were to defend in the first half I would change one boot to make a pair. As the sun began to set the entire pitch would freeze over once again.

Another trick I employed was to file down my leather studs, exposing the nails that attached the studs to the sole of my boots. The exposed nail-heads gripped the freezing ground better. I have to emphasize I was always careful not to expose them in such a way that they would cause injury. Unlike now, match officials never checked the condition of a player's studs before a game, let alone at half time. We would never get away with this dubious ploy today.

Our house in Kirkland Road was typical in that it was uninsulated, had no central heating and coal fires downstairs only. The bedrooms and bathroom would have been ideal refrigerators! To offset the cold, Ursula made more hot dinners than normal and of ever increasing size. That winter I put away countless stews and dumplings, roasts and hotpots. As photographs of the time show, I piled on my own form of insulation.

Though we didn't play a match from Boxing Day to 9 February when the brazier idea was implemented, we then began an unbroken run of matches when other clubs were still struggling to beat the elements. The fact that we were playing regularly when other teams were not must have given us an edge as far as match fitness was concerned. Whatever, we embarked upon an unbeaten run of sixteen league and cup games of which fourteen were won. On 8 April a 1–1 draw at Blackpool saw Leicester City at the top of Division One for the first time since 1927 and with an FA Cup semi-final to come, we had high hopes of achieving the double.

Our excellent run of form ended at Easter, at West Ham, when Bobby Moore's side beat us 2–0 courtesy of two goals from Alan Sealey. But we immediately bounced back to earn a 2–2 draw against Manchester United on Easter Monday, and the following night beat United 4–3 in front of a packed Filbert Street in the return fixture, a result that saw us regain top position in Division One. Following our next game, a 1–1 draw at Wolves, we set off for Hillsborough, the venue for our FA Cup semi-final against Liverpool.

Hillsborough was packed to the rafters, a capacity crowd of 65,000 roaring their approval as both teams took to the pitch. I remember looking up to the alp-like terracing and being amazed at the sight of that heaving and swaying mass of humanity. The noise was deafening, an alarming, volatile collective roar that made me feel the hair on the back of my neck was standing on end. As I took up my position in the goalmouth for the pre-match kickabout, I did so to a backdrop of bedlam. The Leicester fans repeatedly sang 'Cit-eee – Cit-eee' while the Liverpool supporters replied with the recent Beatles hit 'From Me To You'.

When the game got under way the mosaic of red and blue banked up on the terraces once again erupted. It was pandemonium and such a highly charged atmosphere communicated itself to the players. The early exchanges were fast and furious. Liverpool pressed all-out for an early lead and within minutes I found myself called into action time and again. We defended valiantly; we had to, the Liverpool pressure was relentless. There was no opportunity for us to put into practice the free kicks and corners we had rehearsed with Bert Johnson on the training pitch. In order to do that we first of all had to take possession of the ball and move it into the Liverpool half of the field and we just couldn't.

I dived low to my right to collect a shot from Ian Callaghan. Moments later I was at full stretch to save from Ian St John. Then Peter Thompson tried his luck, St John again, then Roger Hunt and Ron Yeats. I felt as if I was performing at the back of a fairground shooting range.

After about twenty minutes of incessant Liverpool attacks we eventually broke out of our own half. Howard Riley and Graham Cross interchanged a series of passes on our right and when the ball was eventually played into the Liverpool penalty area, Mike Stringfellow rose majestically to head the ball into the net. After so much pressure on my goal I couldn't believe we had taken the lead with our first attack. Even more unbelievably, that first attack was also, more or less, our last.

Our goal served only to annoy Liverpool, who then laid siege to my goal in their efforts to equalize. Liverpool's army of supporters roared them on, while the City supporters were no less vociferous in their encouragement of our rearguard action. Liverpool poured forward and my team mates in the Leicester defence went into overdrive to keep the red tide at bay. Legs were outstretched, necks strained, bodies were flung in the way of countless efforts from a seemingly endless procession of

Liverpool players. As the pressure built up, so did the frustration of the Liverpool players. The onslaught on my goal was punctuated by the short sharp flare-up of fraying tempers, a flurry of desperate tackles and the wince-inducing clash of heads as the giant Liverpool centre half, Ron Yeats, fought for aerial supremacy with Ian King. Somehow we survived until half time.

During the break Bert Johnson asked Ken Keyworth, who had been ploughing a lonely furrow for us up front, to drop even deeper to help us contend with what Bert believed would be another relentless onslaught from Liverpool.

'If I go any deeper,' said Ken, 'they'll end up having to carry me off that bloody pitch with the bends!'

In the second half Liverpool redoubled the pressure on my goal. Within minutes I was hurling myself to my right to block a close-range effort from Ian St John. Moments later it was Roger Hunt that I thwarted, then Gerry Byrne, then Hunt again . . . I don't know how many times during the course of the game I was called upon to make a save. All I can say is, never in my entire career did I make so many saves in a match as we stuck to our task of defending the slender lead Mike Stringfellow had given us. The tension was incredible.

In the closing stages time seemed to stand still. Some of the players' wives left their seats in the stands, unable to watch the final minutes. For the umpteenth time I went down at the feet of the marauding St John. With the clock against Liverpool, John Sjoberg put himself in the way of a stinging drive from Ian Callaghan. Frank McLintock denied Roger Hunt with a timely sliding tackle. The ball broke to Callaghan; somehow I managed to get my fingertips to his rasping drive but we still couldn't clear our lines. The ball ricocheted around my penalty area like a pinball. Shots were fired into outstretched Leicester legs. I blocked efforts with any part of the body I could. Still Liverpool came at us as we desperately clung on to the slenderest of slender threads.

Richie Norman put the ball in touch out on the right. The

Liverpool wing half, Gordon Milne, came over to take the throw-in and held the ball above his head for a few seconds as he looked for the best option. Those few seconds were heaven, a momentary respite from constant pressure and a little nearer to full time. In looking across to Milne I saw the linesman signal to the referee that time was up on his watch. Surely there were just seconds left. I inwardly willed Gordon to delay his throw for as long as he liked.

Milne sought out Roger Hunt who, in the space of a hearth-rug, turned Colin Appleton. But Colin wasn't letting Hunt get away; he yanked at his shirt and the referee immediately blew for a free-kick just outside my penalty area. Ian St John ran up to the ball, stepped over it and kept on running while Gordon Milne played the ball into his path. St John angled a shot at goal that, diving across to my right, I managed to deflect up and away. The ball bounced midway between my six-yard box and the penalty spot; red shirts converged, but couldn't control it. Finally a Leicester foot made hefty contact and the ball rocketed away in the general direction of heaven. As far as I know it's still going, because for the first time in ninety minutes, I took my eyes off it. The long drawn-out shrill of the referee's whistle cut the air and I immediately fell to my knees. We'd done it!

The joy of making it to Wembley again was superseded by unbelievable relief. The referee's whistle released my body and mind from ninety minutes of torturous pressure, taut nerves and intense mental concentration. At first this elation cushioned me from both physical and mental exhaustion but, as I embraced Frank McLintock, who was the nearest team mate to me, we almost had to prop one another up or collapse in a tired heap.

According to that Sunday's *News of the World*, Liverpool had thirty-four attempts on goal. We'd had the one. That semi-final performance against Liverpool was, in my opinion, my best ever in a club game, as well as my busiest.

One distasteful footnote to this epic encounter came as we headed for the tunnel. Richie Norman, Ian King and I just burst out laughing in nervous relief as we congratulated each other. Just then a distraught Ian St John passed close by, unable to contain his tears. A press photographer stepped forward to capture his moment of emotion. At the time I never gave it a second thought, but I was soon to learn to my cost that some members of the media can be highly manipulative.

The following day a newspaper printed on its back page the photograph, cruelly cropped to exclude Richie Norman and Ian King so that I appeared to be laughing in the face of a tearful Ian St John. The caption hammered home the point. I couldn't understand it – I was not that callous. The damage, however, had been done. Needless to say, when I next played at Anfield, as I took up my position in front of the Kop, I was pelted with boiled sweets, orange peel and worse. The vitriol directed at me by the Liverpool fans was unbelievable. I simply had to take it because, down there on the pitch, there's nowhere to hide and no way to explain what had really happened. As time went by the incident, thankfully, was forgotten, and as the England goalkeeper I was always to receive a tremendous reception from the Liverpool fans.

The vast majority of people who cover football in the press are good at their job. What they print may not always be true but, by and large, a reporter will not write a story unless he believes it to be true. There are a small minority, however, who have no such scruples. There always has been and, I guess, there always will be. That 'doctored' photograph of Ian St John and I was the work of one of this small minority, but it taught me not to take what I read or saw in the newspapers at face value every time.

For the record, Ian knew I had been set up. On seeing the photograph he kindly contacted me and told me not to worry about it. It's just a shame he didn't tell the Kop!

In light of our previous good form, unbelievably, our semi-final success over Liverpool proved to be the last game Leicester won that season. Our failure was due to a number of factors, not least of which was a crippling injury list. After the Liverpool game we were full of confidence but very much aware that we would have to apply ourselves totally in each of our remaining five matches if we were to achieve our dream of the double. Immediately following our success in the semi-final we played West Bromwich Albion at the Hawthorns. Jimmy Walsh came in for the injured Ken Keyworth, only for me to break a finger diving at the feet of Albion's Ken Foggo. Our trainer, Alex Dowdells, taped up my fingers and I carried on for the final hour of the match but we lost 2–1, Albion's winner coming from a Don Howe penalty.

That broken finger put me out of our three remaining league games, but I wasn't the only player missing in action: Mike Stringfellow, Ian King and Davie Gibson also succumbed to injuries. Their replacements were decent players, but the cohesion and fluidity of the team was affected, and the fact that we had to play three crucial league games in the space of a week didn't help. As Cup finalists and close contenders for the League Championship, we were attempting to fire on all cylinders while being unable to field the same team consecutively in any of our remaining four matches. We contrived to lose each one to finish fourth. Under normal circumstances, to finish fourth in the league and have a Cup final to look forward to would be considered a successful season. But to us it felt like relegation.

The champions were Everton, who clinched the title in front of nearly 70,000 fans at Goodison Park when they beat Fulham 4–1. The newspapers dubbed Everton the 'Cheque Book Champions' because they had spent £180,000 on five players, most notably Tony Kay, who cost £80,000 from Sheffield Wednesday, and Alex Scott, a £40,000 purchase from Glasgow Rangers. Kay and Scott proved more than useful additions to a side managed by Harry Catterick, but for me the key players in that successful Everton team were their young centre half Brian Labone, and Roy Vernon and Alex Young, who between them scored fifty goals that season.

Alex Young was revered at Goodison as the 'Golden Vision' (later the title of a TV play written by the former ITN newsreader and novelist Gordon Honeycombe, that told the story of a group of Evertonians who idolized Alex, and their exploits when they were down in London to watch Everton take on Spurs). Signed from that most romantically named of all British football clubs, Heart of Midlothian, he was wonderful to watch, a darting forward who combined silky, deft skills with great strength, and both made and scored goals with class and style.

Roy Vernon was as sharp as a needle either deep in the midfield or as an out-and-out striker, and was a fine captain. Oddly for such a quick player, he was a heavy smoker, even indulging in a quick one at half time. Later in his career, at Stoke City, Roy would even smoke in the shower – and somehow managed to keep that cigarette completely dry!

The bookies had made us odds-on favourites to win the FA Cup final. We had enjoyed a good, though ultimately disappointing season in the First Division while our opponents, Manchester United, had had a torrid time. On paper United looked a good side; Bobby Charlton, Denis Law, Johnny Giles, Albert Quixall, David Herd, Pat Crerand and Bill Foulkes were all extremely gifted players, as was their captain, Noel Cantwell. Yet United had only just survived relegation to Division Two, finishing three points ahead of their doomed neighbours, Manchester City. In their semi-final United had made hard work of beating Second Division Southampton by a goal to nil. Almost to a man, every sports writer said it was going to be Leicester's year for the Cup. With our strong defence and quick counterattacks we would be too strong for United, who were seen as over-reliant on their brilliant individuals.

On the day, however, just about every Leicester player, myself included, underperformed in what was our worst performance of the season. In contrast to our lacklustre showing, United displayed exemplary teamwork, while also giving full vent to their considerable individual skills. Crerand and Law were out-standing for United, and both Charlton and Giles tackled back tirelessly. We knew what to expect from players like Crerand, Law and Charlton at their best, but we didn't reckon on them being able to build up confidence and get into their stride so quickly.

One of the Leicester strengths was how much we gained from the part contributed by every player both to defence and attack. In the final, however, it was United who gave the perfect example of forwards taking some of the weight off the men behind them. Bobby Charlton dropped back to tackle Howard Riley, and Johnny Giles was always there to help the United right back, Tony Dunne, deal with Mike Stringfellow.

I have to hold my hand up and say United's opening goal was my fault. Twelve minutes into the game the United goalkeeper, Dave Gaskell, threw the ball out to Johnny Giles who swiftly moved it crossfield to Bobby Charlton. I only succeeded in parrying Bobby's low shot and there was the United centre forward, David Herd, to accept the gift.

The result was never in doubt after United's second goal. My intended throw out to the right wing was intercepted by Paddy Crerand, who beat Richie Norman before slipping the ball to Denis Law twelve yards out. Colin Appleton went to tackle him, but Law was far too elusive. He slipped away, swivelled through 180 degrees and fired a low right-foot shot that I had no chance of reaching. It was Law's twenty-ninth goal of the season and his twenty-ninth in all cup competitions.

With ten minutes left a wonderful diving header from Ken Keyworth seemed to put us back in the game. Minutes later, however, Denis Law rose like a Green's cake before planting a firm header to my left. I was beaten, but couldn't believe my luck to see the ball hit the post and rebound straight into my arms. Four minutes from time, my good fortune had run out. I jumped to collect a Johnny Giles cross. As I landed I jarred the heel of my boot and the ball spilled from my hands for David

Herd to poach another goal. At 3–1 there was no way back. United, in the end, deserved to win. For the second time in three seasons I tasted the bitter disappointment of losing a Wembley cup final.

The club's post-match banquet was again at the Dorchester on Park Lane and, as in 1961, was a low-key affair. Our disappointment was, if anything, even greater than our defeat by Spurs. Then we were the valiant losers of an unequal struggle, but this time everyone had expected a Leicester victory. That we had all played so badly on our big day was perplexing to everyone. As our skipper, Colin Appleton, said at that dinner, 'We learned an important lesson today, lads. But for the life of me, I don't know what it is.'

8. England Calls

Since joining Leicester City I'd made a concerted effort to study goalkeeping and its role in the team. Like every other club, Leicester had no goalkeeping coach or specialist training routines. I trained with the rest of the lads and, though I was willing to do all the long-distance running to build my stamina and sprinting to enhance my speed off the mark, I couldn't help but wonder if this type of training was best suited to my role in the team. It seemed silly that I should be doing the same training as the midfield players and wingers. My needs were different, so I took it upon myself to organize my own training regime in addition to my normal work.

In the early sixties both Frank McLintock and Davie Gibson lived in digs. Davie, like Frank, was a Scot who had joined Leicester from Hibernian and was still doing his National Service with the King's Own Scottish Borderers when he arrived at Filbert Street. Davie was a fine ball player, quite the artist and his nimble creativity coupled with granite-like hardness made him formidable on the football field. Opponents feared his extra agility and turning capacity and preferred to stand off and position themselves goalside of him rather than risk a wasted tackle. Davie had an uncanny feel for the ball. Without ever looking down, he could coax the ball on for three or four yards before eloquently hitting a forty-yard through-ball. With his keen all-round vision he could spot Ken Keyworth or Mike Stringfellow making their runs at a distance and calculate his pass almost to the inch.

I liked Davie a lot, both as a player and a friend. When he retired from the game he continued to live in the Leicester area and became a postman before he and his wife opened a residential home for the elderly, which they still run today.

Frank and Davie were very keen to hone their skills and, being single lads, had the time to do it. At my suggestion the three of us got permission from our groundsman, Bill Taylor, to do some extra training on the Filbert Street pitch on a Sunday morning. Players weren't normally allowed to do this, but Bill readily agreed.

On Sunday mornings Bill's job was to redress the pitch following the Saturday game. He'd start by replacing divots in one goalmouth, cut the grass and roll it, gradually working his way down to the other goalmouth. He agreed to allow Frank, Davie and I to practise in the goalmouth he wasn't attending, which suited us fine. First Frank and Davie simply pinged shots at me from all angles to see if they could beat me, after which I had them shoot from a certain position and a given angle. I made a mental note of the angle at which the ball came towards the goal from the given position, and after weeks of this, found I'd learned the best position to take up for making the save.

We practised for ninety minutes every Sunday, week in week out, and it soon began to reap dividends for me. I found I was constantly adjusting my positioning when the opposition were on attack. Whenever an opposing forward was about to shoot, I knew at what angle and height the ball would come and could adjust my position accordingly. I began to anticipate shots on target, moving into position before an opponent actually struck the ball so that when he looked up, the point at which I was standing afforded him a restricted view of goal. Goalkeeping for me was no longer an art. It had become a science.

Of course, it was not exact science. I still conceded goals, but progressively fewer each season. In the five seasons from 1958–59 to 1962–63 Leicester conceded 98, 75, 70, 71, and 53 goals, respectively – and this was at a time when the emphasis was still on scoring goals with five-man forward lines, rather than conceding them. It would be unfair of me to take all the credit – we had a very good team and I had quality defenders in front of me – but I'd like to think I played my part in reducing our goals-against tally.

Throughout the early sixties Frank, Davie and I continued our Sunday morning routine and were occasionally joined by other Leicester players. These sessions were invaluable to my development and with each practice I delved deeper and deeper into goalkeeping. My job was about a lot more than shot-stopping, so I worked on taking crosses under pressure, and practised goal kicks and kicking out of my hands, picking out Frank or Davie at various points across the halfway line.

Having worked on position and angles, I next had to improve my reactions. I'd ask Frank and Davie to half-volley the ball at me from five yards, never telling me which side of the goal it was going. I spent countless hours improving my ability to stop shots from inside the penalty area and discovered that I had to position myself differently and make different types of saves according to exactly where in the area the ball had been struck.

To cope with a shot from the edge of the box I would take up a position a couple of feet inside my six-yard box and expect to hold on to the ball. For a shot from just inside the penalty area, I would move up to my six-yard line to produce a quick-reaction save. A shot from within an imaginary band running from one side of the penalty box to the other and through the penalty spot, required me to position myself just outside my six-yard box to execute a blocking save. Anywhere wide of the six-yard box required that I come out and dive at the feet of the opponent grabbing the ball and gathering into the safety of my midriff. It was all very complicated, but in time it became second nature.

I also spent a lot of time learning to read situations. I often gave the Leicester apprentices a few bob to stay behind with me on a weekday afternoon. I would set up two cones just wide enough apart to enable me to dive and make a save. These cones I would set up behind the touchline on the halfway line. That area was not strictly part of the pitch but the grass was always worn out because that was where the linesman ran up and down in the course of a game. I'd dive about in that area and no one at

the club was aware I'd been training on the pitch because I left
no tell-tale signs. If I had been in the goalmouth, Leicester
officials would have noticed my stud marks on the rolled pitch
straight away. Looking back it's ridiculous to think I had to be
so secretive about learning my trade as a goalkeeper, but that's
how it was. Players weren't allowed on the pitch, except of
course on match days.

I came to realize that a lot of goalkeepers, myself included,
often stood on or near the goal line watching a situation develop
to which they then had suddenly to react. Working after weekday
training with the apprentices, I saw that I could learn to dictate
to opposing forwards rather than have them dictate to me. For
example, having instructed an apprentice to play the ball into the
goal area for a team mate, I started to anticipate a cross or pass by
adjusting my position quickly, causing the opponent to change
his mind. With me off my line, having taken up a position on
the edge of my six-yard box and in front of the intended receiver,
the player feeding the ball into the area was forced to hit a much
wider ball to another team mate in order for his side to retain
possession. Even then I discovered that, being on or around my
six-yard line, I was in the best position to come out and collect
the ball.

These informal sessions with Leicester apprentices took place
almost daily and over the years must have cost me a small fortune
in tips. The best sessions took place on Wednesday and Thursday
afternoons when as many as eight apprentices stayed to help me.
All players were paid every Friday morning. Apprentices were
paid only six quid a week and by Thursday they were skint.

When Matt Gillies appointed Bert Johnson as first-team coach,
I asked Bert if I could have some sessions after normal training.
Bert was all for it and soon had half a dozen or so of the first-team
lads helping me out. One of the things we worked on was
defending corners. Many First Division teams had just two
options where corners were concerned: either hit the ball to the
far post for a towering centre forward, or drive the ball to

the near post where another forward hoped to glance the ball goalwards with his head, or, simply deflect the ball into the net.

The near-post ball always posed problems for goalkeepers because you had to make up ground quickly in order to put yourself between the opponent and the goal. More often than not, in dealing with the near-post corner, goalkeepers found themselves trying to prevent the opposing forward getting a decisive touch while approaching him from behind.

To minimize the danger of a corner driven in at the near post, I asked Bert for extra cover. For example, if the corner was taken from our right, I had right back, John Sjoberg on the near post and right half, Frank McLintock, goalside of the opponent. With my near-post area now adequately covered, I was free to concentrate on the remaining two-thirds of my goal and subsequently better positioned to deal with a long ball to the far post.

With a full back and a wing half covering my near post, I decided I didn't need any other defenders in the six-yard box and two yards beyond it. That zone became a no-go area for Leicester players. I wasn't bothered if two opponents wandered in unmarked, because it was my domain and I considered it was my responsibility and no one else's to win the ball in there.

Bert immediately saw the advantage of this. Leaving opponents in or around our six-yard box at a corner left the likes of Richie Norman, Ian King and Colin Appleton free to pick up anyone running from deep, and Ken Keyworth or Mike Stringfellow available to receive a quick throw-out from me. Then they were away. In short, we found we had a numerical advantage when defending corners, hence Leicester City's reputation as being masters of the counterattack.

We also worked on a procedure for coping with free kicks conceded in midfield. When a team concedes a free kick some forty or fifty yards from goal, it immediately places them under pressure, especially if the kick is to be taken from out on the flanks. Like most Premiership sides today, First Division teams in the sixties would willingly concede territory in midfield and fall back to defend on the edge of their penalty area. When winning a free kick some forty yards from my goal, opponents would invariably aim the kick towards their big target men who the Leicester defence had picked up and marked along the edge of my penalty area. Sometimes the likes of Ian King or Colin Appleton would win the ball in the air, sometimes not. When the ball was won by an opponent his best option was usually to knock the ball down to one of his team mates who would then try and fire in a shot.

Conceding a free kick enabled the opposition to dictate play to us. Should they retain possession of the ball and create a shooting opportunity for themselves, the onus was then on me to make the save. It occurred to me it would be much better for us if we were to cut down the chances of my being placed in that situation. Remember my philosophy: the mark of a good goalkeeper is how few saves he is called on to make.

I also discussed defending free kicks with Bert in some detail and we came up with a number of ways of minimizing the danger. One idea I had was very simple, but proved highly effective for a time. Whenever Leicester conceded a free kick some forty or fifty yards from goal, our defenders would position themselves on the edge of my penalty box as normal where they would jockey for position with their opposite numbers. I would watch the man taking the free kick like a hawk. Just as he was about to strike the free kick I would scream, 'Now!' Immediately they heard this, the Leicester back line would take to their toes and spring a yard or two upfield leaving the opposing attackers in an offside position. The pressure was off us, I was not called upon to make a save and, even though we had conceded a free kick in a dangerous position, we had dictated the play.

Today, all goalkeepers try and dictate situations to opponents. Back in the early sixties, however, this was seen by Bert Johnson as being revolutionary. He liked the idea and encouraged me to do it because he saw the advantages to us as a team. My constant practice, development of goalkeeping technique and specialized self-training helped me enormously. With every day that passed, I learned a little more.

I gave myself a heavy training workload, but I was always careful not to overdo it. I learned that rest was a very important aspect to my training programme; it was vital that my energy levels were at their optimum for the beginning of a match. Overtraining before a game can lead to both physical and mental fatigue in the pressurized environment of a match. Athletes have to tread a fine line between rigorous, beneficial training and too much work. After their pre-season sessions when all the really hard work is done, many footballers have a great start to their campaign. But a long hard programme of fixtures played on heavy pitches takes its toll; a number of players lose form towards the end of the season. I came to the conclusion that this is caused by physical and mental tiredness. Their pre-season training, and the sheer number of games they had played, had caught up with them.

I was determined that this wasn't going to happen to me. I carefully planned my training to ensure I would have as much rest as possible. A day of intense training might be followed by a day of some light running and stretching, and some twisting and turning exercises to improve my agility. This would allow sufficient recovery time for the game on Saturday.

I paid particular attention to stretching exercises. I discovered the value of stretching slowly and gently so as not to induce muscle strain. I realized that my bottom was the part of my body that provided the initial explosive power for a sudden burst of speed and jumping and devised a series of exercises that would increase the power in this area. One such routine involved me sitting down with my legs out in front of me. I'd then bend one knee, pulling the leg closer to my body, then place the foot over my opposite thigh. I would then wrap my arms around the leg I had bent and pull it into my body as close as I could. When I felt the outside of my bottom stretching, I knew that was the time to stop. To complement this, I would also work on exercises that stretched my lower back and the muscles on the outside of my hips, the abductors. These exercises improved my speed off the mark and helped me gain height when jumping up to catch or punch a ball clear. Such exercises helped my continual improvement.

At no time did I consider myself to be anything special as a goalkeeper, but I did believe the role of a goalkeeper in a team to be special. That's why I continually worked at my personal game. It was a journey of self-discovery. There were no books about goalkeeping technique, no specialist coaches and not everything I tried worked. It was, in the main, uncharted territory and there was an element of hit and miss about what I did. If an idea didn't work, I simply ditched it and tried to think of something else.

When it comes to training and practice many players are simply content to work on the things they are good at. I did that, but I also spent much time working on what I perceived to be the weaker aspects of my game. For a time I was never really comfortable when taking crosses from my left. I made myself confront my demons. I spent a lot of time practising taking crosses from the left wing and thinking about how my footwork, body positioning and handling technique could be bettered. I worked at my different techniques for punching the ball clear and which ones to use in any given situation. When I conceded goals, I spent Saturday night and most of Sunday trying to work out why.

I travelled around the midlands with my best pal Richie Norman in my old Ford van, watching as many midweek games as time would allow. I wanted to study the styles of as many other goalkeepers as I could and try to learn from them. I devised my own training schedules that were geared not only to improving my technique, but also to enhancing my agility, strength, reactions and focus. My improvement was constant, but I was never satisfied and kept working at my own game. It paid dividends. In 1963, Alf Ramsey selected me for the full England team.

It is widely believed that when Walter Winterbottom resigned as England manager in 1963, the FA immediately turned to the Ipswich manager, Alf Ramsey and that the rest is history of the most glorious kind. That wasn't exactly how it went. The FA at first offered the England job to Jimmy Adamson, who had been Walter's assistant during the 1962 World Cup finals in Chile. As coach and captain of Burnley, Jimmy was still playing and though he was a key member of Walter's coaching staff at Lilleshall, he turned down the job as England manager as he wanted to carry on playing and saw his future not as a manager, but as a coach. (Jimmy did eventually turn his hand to management, with his beloved Burnley, Sunderland and Leeds United, but his strength was really his coaching.)

So the FA looked to their second-choice candidate, Alf Ramsey. In his time as a right back for England, Alf had seen at first hand the effects of team selection by committee. He was adamant that no official would wield such influence again and became the first England manager to have sole responsibility for team affairs.

For sixteen years Walter Winterbottom had diplomatically negotiated, rather than argued, with the selection committee over who should be included in the England team. During one such meeting five nominees were put forward for the position of goalkeeper. The list was reduced by the voting process until only two names remained, whereby one goalkeeper would be chosen by means of a simple majority vote. When Walter asked how many of the committee had actually seen the two remaining goalkeepers in action he was astonished to discover that the answer was none.

Prior to Alf Ramsey's appointment, selection for the England team was not based purely on ability and form. Much to Walter's frustration, quite often a player was awarded a cap in recognition of his services to the game or, as Walter once said, 'because the committee thought him a decent and deserving chap'. For instance, in 1950 Arsenal's Leslie Compton was selected to play against Wales because, as one of the selection committee said, 'He's a decent fellow, so let's give him a chance.'

Walter was only too aware that the system needed to be changed. He used the Football League representative games as a means of honouring 'the decent chaps' so that he could press for the inclusion in the England team of players who deserved a cap on merit and form.

As the World Cup grew in status and importance in the fifties, Walter wanted to introduce a policy of developing a young England team that would play and mature together and peak within a four-year cycle. In 1959 he persuaded the England selection committee to pick a batch of young hopefuls for a game against Sweden at Wembley. Middlesbrough's Brian Clough and Eddie Holliday, Tony Allen of Stoke City, Trevor Smith of Birmingham City and John Connelly of Burnley were added to a team that also included the youthful Jimmy Greaves and Bobby Charlton. Sweden won 3–2. England had lost only once before on home soil against foreign opposition, the first having been that watershed defeat at the hands of Hungary in 1953. Walter found himself back at square one as the selection committee objected to his policy of introducing youth and reverted to the old regime of panel picking.

When Alf Ramsey succeeded him, all was to change. The Ipswich Town directors had never interfered in the selection of the Ipswich team. Alf had sole control of team affairs at Portman Road, and he knew that if he was to make a success of his new role as manager of the national team, the dinosaur that was the selection committee would have to go. The FA bowed to the inevitable and Alf took the job.

I was happy to be named the reserve goalkeeper when Alf selected the squad for his first game in charge, a European Nations Cup match against France. The Nations Cup was the forerunner of the European Championship and in 1962–63 took the form of two-legged knock-out ties rather than group games. Under Winterbottom England had drawn 1–1 against France at Hillsborough and when the return leg was played in Paris in February 1963, we still had high hopes of progressing past the first round of the tournament.

Alf introduced only one new cap for the game in Paris. Ron Henry of Spurs came in at left back and I once again found myself as second choice to Ron Springett of Sheffield Wednesday. The game turned out to be a nightmare for England, for Alf and for Ron Springett. France won by five goals to two to send England tumbling out of the tournament at the first time of asking and give Alf Ramsey much food for thought. At least he now had some idea of the magnitude of the task ahead of him.

Alf gave debuts to three players in England's next game, at Wembley against the 'auld enemy', Scotland. To my considerable delight I was one of them along with the Liverpool pair Gerry Byrne and Jimmy Melia. It is difficult to imagine the current England manager giving debuts to three players in a game widely considered to be of crucial importance, but Alf did.

The Scotland game was considered the most important match in England's international calendar, of more significance than the European Nations Cup and even, in some quarters, a World Cup qualifying match.

There was a time when every international match, irrespective of the opposition, had real importance and kudos. Bolton's Nat Lofthouse achieved legendary status in English football for his sublime performance against Austria in 1952. Nat's courage in that game earned him the nickname of the 'Lion of Vienna'. It is difficult to imagine a contemporary England player enjoying the pinnacle of his international career and attaining legendary status by virtue of his performance in a friendly international. It just doesn't happen these days.

Managers and coaches use friendly internationals purely for experimentation. The plethora of substitutions deny such games fluidity and continuity and consequently they are not the spectacle they once were. This, and the growing tendency of the media to assign importance only to European Championship and World Cup qualifying games, has served to devalue international friendly matches and I think football is a little poorer for that.

To be picked for England, Scotland, Wales or Northern Ireland was considered the pinnacle of a playing career. Players would give anything to represent their country. Now you have players retiring from international football, often citing 'the growing demands' of the club competitions as their reason. While ever mindful that the pace of football today is much quicker than in the seventies, I would point out that, in 1971–72 when I was a Stoke City player, Stoke played a total of 71 matches that season: 42 League matches, 12 League Cup, 9 FA Cup and 4 each in the Anglo-Scottish Cup and the Anglo-Italian Tournament. Though I didn't play in every game, I played in the vast majority and also managed six games for England. The Stoke City full back, Jackie Marsh, played sixty-nine games for the club that season. As Jackie used to say, 'I'd rather be playing matches. It's much more enjoyable than training!'

The England–Scotland game was not a friendly, but a fixture in the now defunct annual Home International Championship, which also involved Northern Ireland and Wales. Football was rarely seen on television in those days, and the Home Internationals afforded people in Cardiff, Belfast and Glasgow a rare opportunity to see the top players in action. These games were fuelled by strong patriotism and tradition as exemplified by the tunes the military bands played before the games: 'Scotland The Brave', 'The British Grenadiers', 'Scottish Soldier', 'Plymouth Hoe', 'Land of My Fathers' and 'Land of Hope and Glory' set the tone for an occasion of national pride and identity.

The match was the first to be played at Wembley since it had been redeveloped, over £500,000 having been spent on a new roof that swept around the stadium. Whether this new roof rebounded the noise of the fans back into the stadium I don't know, but as the two teams emerged from the tunnel I was taken aback by a deafening noise which was so intimidating it almost brought on palpitations. Wembley was filled to its capacity, and most of the 100,000 crowd seemed to be roaring for Scotland.

As we walked out Jimmy Greaves turned to me. 'I knew they'd rebuilt this place,' said Jimmy, 'but I didn't know they'd shifted it up to bloody Glasgow!'

I was still trying to block out the cacophony of noise and forget my early nerves when there was a horrifying collision between Scottish skipper Eric Caldow and Bobby Smith, England's centre forward. Caldow was carried off with a triple fracture of the leg while Smith hobbled through the rest of the afternoon with what later turned out to be serious ankle and knee ligament damage. In that era before substitutes and the sophisticated medical expertise of today, trainers would gamble with an injured player's ability to struggle on.

After that I recovered my concentration and all seemed to be going well for me until our right back, Jimmy Armfield, uncharacteristically decided to pass the ball across our back line. Heaven knows what Jimmy thought he was doing. Scotland's left half, Rangers' Jim Baxter, thought it was Christmas. Latching on to the gift we had presented him with, he bore down on my goal.

I raced off my line to cut down Baxter's vision of my goal, but he swayed like a bird on a twig. I put all my weight on my left foot and Jim rolled the ball to my right and into the net. Debutant I may have been, but I let the more experienced Jimmy Armfield know exactly what I thought of his crossfield pass. To his credit, Jimmy held his hand up and took full responsibility for his mistake.

Jim Baxter started to run the game and we gave him all the room he needed to display his considerable skills. The England defence was all at sea and, in a moment of desperation, Ron Flowers of Wolves took the legs from under the Rangers winger Willie Henderson and the referee, Leon Horn from Holland, immediately pointed to the penalty spot.

Facing penalties could be like participating in the Leicester City card school. Sometimes you try and bluff your way through even when you know you haven't a strong hand. The cool Jim Baxter, however, called my bluff: he approached the ball as if he was on a leisurely stroll in the park and casually placed it into the left hand corner of my goal as I dived the wrong way. Two–nil. Once again a tidal wave of noise swept down from the terraces and assailed my ears as the Tartan army jigged as one in celebration.

At half time Alf told us to sharpen our passing and get tighter on the troublesome Denis Law, Ian St John and Willie Henderson.

We played better in the second half and enjoyed the lion's share of the play, but could only manage one goal in reply, from Blackburn's Bryan Douglas. During this second period Jim Baxter gave full vent to his swaggering skills. At one point, he received the ball out on our right and, to the amazement of everyone, progressed down the wing juggling the ball up and down on his left foot. The Scottish supporters were in raptures. In the heat of furious combat there was 'Slim Jim' playing 'keepy-uppy' as if frolicking in his own back garden. Baxter, however, reserved his party piece for last. Having juggled the ball down our right wing, he then nudged it forward, swung his left foot over the ball and turned around so that he was now facing down the pitch. Baxter then brought his right leg behind his left and chipped the ball across into my penalty area. Ian St John met Baxter's cheeky centre with his head but I managed to collect the ball underneath my crossbar. The Tartan army went wild and even we England players shook our heads in wonder at Baxter's artful arrogance.

Following the final whistle, as both teams headed towards the tunnel Jim stuck the ball up his shirt and swaggered off the pitch. For all true lovers of football, Baxter's artistry that day was a joy to behold. It was just my luck that he had chosen my England debut as the occasion on which to produce the greatest performance of his career!

Back in the dressing room my spirits were lifted somewhat when Alf Ramsey told me that he was very satisfied with my performance. His encouraging words instilled in me the hope that my England career may only just be beginning.

One month later, in May 1963, Alf Ramsey proved that his words of praise for my debut performance were sincerely meant, when he picked me for England's game against Brazil, despite the finger injury I'd picked up at West Bromwich four days earlier. Having already lost a cup final at Wembley and been on the losing side on my international debut, I was praying for better fortune against the World Cup holders who were, without doubt, the best international team in the world.

Despite being without the world's best player, Pelé, who was injured, Brazil had enough class and quality in their ranks to offer the severest of tests for England in what was Alf's third game in charge. The England team was Gordon Banks (Leicester City); Jimmy Armfield (Blackpool), Ray Wilson (Huddersfield Town); Gordon Milne (Liverpool), Maurice Norman (Spurs), Bobby Moore (West Ham); Bryan Douglas (Blackburn Rovers), Jimmy Greaves, Bobby Smith (both Spurs), George Eastham (Arsenal), Bobby Charlton (Manchester United). The Brazilian line-up was Gilmar; Lima, Edoiardo; Zeuinha, Dias, Rildo; Dorval, Mengalvia, Coutinho, Amarildo, Pepe.

Brazil were unbeaten on their tour of Europe. Alf had watched them in action and had really done his homework. He had noticed Brazil liked to play the ball into the feet of their centre forward, Coutinho, so he told Gordon Milne to take up a position in front of Coutinho when Brazil were in possession to stop this happening.

Alf warned me to be on my toes if ever Brazil were awarded a free kick outside our penalty area. 'They are fantastic strikers of the ball, Gordon,' he told me, 'and can bend and swerve it either way.'

Mindful of Alf's words, I paid particular attention to lining up the wall of defenders in front of me when Brazil were awarded a first-half free kick some seven yards outside our penalty area. I took up a position just to the right of centre and positioned the wall so that it overlapped my left-hand post. I was alert to the danger – but it was all to no avail. The Brazilian outside left, Pepe, sprinted up to the ball and with tremendous power sliced his left foot across it. I'd never seen a ball cut through the air at such a trajectory. It flew over our defensive wall heading for the left side of the goal. Naturally, I moved to my left, only for the ball to veer to my right and bulge the net. I simply couldn't believe that anyone could make a ball move so much in the air. It was a terrific goal and I consoled myself with the thought that there wasn't a goalkeeper in the world who would have got anywhere near it.

At half time, however, Alf was not best pleased. 'I warned you about their free kicks,' he said, 'be on your toes!' I tried to tell him that I had been on my toes, but that the swerve on the ball had duped me. Alf listened to what I had to say, but I could tell from his stern expression that he thought I should have at least got a hand to it.

I made up for it in the opening stages of the second half, though. First I managed to claw away a fierce downward header from Coutinho, then hold on to a long-range effort from Amarildo that was heading for my goal like a snake. Minutes later I saved from both Dorval and Mengalvia. Not conceding another goal during that spell of pressure from the Brazilians turned the game. As the second half progressed we began to assert ourselves and only some desperate defending on the part of the South Americans kept the score at 1–0. England were not to be denied, however. With minutes remaining our concerted pressure on the Brazilian defence paid off. Blackburn's Bryan Douglas latched on to a great through-ball from Bobby Charlton and calmly beat Gilmar.

I felt the draw was no more than we deserved. After a shaky start to both halves, we had grown in confidence and, at times,

more than matched the world champions. On my third appearance at Wembley I finally trooped off the pitch without the taste
of defeat in my mouth and Alf Ramsey, in his third game as
England manager, had gained a highly creditable draw against
the best team in the world. I guess both of us were looking to
the future with some optimism. I know I certainly was.

My performances for Leicester and my inclusion in the England
team led to a number of clubs enquiring as to my availability.
Newcastle United, Wolves and Aston Villa made official
approaches to Leicester regarding a possible transfer but Matt
Gillies and the City board were adamant. I wasn't for sale. Which
suited me fine as I was very happy at the club and with life in
Leicester. Another club seemingly impressed by my performances
was Arsenal. Their manager, the former Wolves and England
captain, Billy Wright, appeared before the Football League
accused of making an illegal approach to me. In Billy's defence,
I can honestly say that I have no recollection of this. I can't
remember Billy 'tapping me up' after any game between Leicester
and Arsenal and he certainly didn't telephone me at home because
Ursula and I didn't have a phone! I have no idea why Billy
Wright was summoned to answer allegations of making an illegal
approach for my services. All I can think of is that a bit of gentle
nudging on the part of Arsenal's George Eastham, who'd often
told me that I'd enjoy life at Highbury, had been blown out of
all proportion. Thankfully, Billy Wright was served with no
more than a warning, though even that was unjustified.

In the long-awaited summer of 1963 I joined the England
squad on their continental tour. The tour was highly successful
and offered concrete proof that, after a disappointing start to his
career as England manager, Alf Ramsey was getting it right. We
began with a terrific 4–2 win in Bratislava over Czechoslovakia,
the beaten World Cup finalists against Brazil just twelve
months previously. We then beat East Germany 2–1 in Leipzig
and rounded off the tour in some style with an 8–1 win over

Switzerland in Basle, Bobby Charlton scoring a hat trick. Alf played me in the first two of those games and his continuing belief in me was a great fillip to my confidence. I felt that now Alf saw me as England's number one goalkeeper, and I was determined to work hard and continue my development in order to prove him right.

9. Down South America Way

We have seen how, in the late fifties, football shirts evolved from the buttoned-collar-and-cuff style into V-necked shirts with short sleeves. Now, in 1963–64, football kit design underwent another major change as it kept pace with the style revolution taking place in British fashion.

Not to be left behind, Leicester dispensed with the V-necked shirts and short sleeves and adopted round-necked, long-sleeved shirts, still in blue, but the collar and cuffs were now white with a blue band circling the middle. Our stockings also changed, from blue with white turnovers to white with two blue hoops at the top.

Round-necked football shirts became de rigueur for just about every club, presumably influenced by the Beatles' circular-collared suits, which themselves derived from the tailoring favoured by the Indian statesman Pandit Nehru. English football, keen to distance itself from the fifties when it had been shown to be second best at both international and club level, was determined to project its modernized image, and imitated this fashion trend. And just as slim jackets, tight trousers and miniskirts could be seen on Carnaby Street and the King's Road, so footballers trotted out at Filbert Street and Stamford Bridge wearing long hair, body-hugging shirt and tiny shorts.

Phrases such as 'With it', 'Fab' and 'It's gear' may appear antiquated now, but were the buzz words of the mid-sixties and on the lips of just about everybody between the ages of sixteen and thirty. There existed a general feeling that the past and anything connected with it had no part to play in this new, vibrant society of equal and ample opportunity. Work was plentiful, wages had improved and, though they were not aware of the term at the time, people found they had 'disposable income' with which to indulge themselves in the latest fashions and advances in consumer technology. The sixties was a time of the biggest, most all-inclusive party that anyone could ever have imagined. Everybody was encouraged to 'do their own thing' and just about everyone under the age of forty came.

London emerged as the epicentre of world fashion, Liverpool as the creative hub of popular music and there, at the centre of everything, were the Beatles. Not only did Paul, John, George and Ringo influence popular music, their influence swept across popular culture. Television's top variety show, *Sunday Night at the London Palladium* was hosted by a young mop-headed Liverpudlian comedian who wore round-collared suits just like the Beatles – Jimmy Tarbuck. For one so young to take over as the host of TV's most popular variety show indicated that the sixties had little time for the old ways. The essence of the sixties was that anybody could play. For the very first time, older generations copied the young, because to be young was 'where it was at'.

The Profumo Affair had shown the Establishment to be no purer than any other stratum of society. Lord Denning's report on the Profumo Affair became a bestseller. The permissive society had arrived and its underpinning was the availability of the contraceptive pill.

Harold Macmillan with his cabinet of earls and aura of the grouse moor and the Athenaeum Club was a gift to the emerging satirists of *That Was The Week That Was*, and a new renegade publication, *Private Eye*. Macmillan gave way to Sir Alec Douglas-Home as prime minister, but the stigma of snobbery and aristocratic values lived on, in sharp contrast to what was happening elsewhere in society. In 1964 when the nation took to the polls, Harold Wilson's Labour Party swept home on his promise of a new, modern society built on the fruits of the 'white heat' of technology.

As the sixties progressed, football strips became more standardized (some would say dull), with the main club colour incorporated in shirts, shorts and stockings. The traditional designs, colour blends and nuances of strips that conferred on a club its own identity were ditched as clubs sought to project an image more in keeping with these revolutionary and radical times. By the late sixties Leicester City took to wearing simply blue shirts, shorts and stockings, appearing indistinguishable from others whose main club colour was blue, such as Chelsea, Ipswich Town and Hartlepool United. Individuality gave way to the formulaic. Liverpool adopted an all-red strip, as did Bristol City, Nottingham Forest, Middlesbrough, Rotherham United, Charlton Athletic and other teams whose primary club colour was red. Many teams chose not to display the club badge on their shirts. Sheffield Wednesday, who as long as I could remember had worn blue and white striped shirts and black shorts, took to wearing plain blue shirts with white sleeves. Similarly, Arsenal, famous for their red shirts with white sleeves, for a time simply wore plain red shirts devoid of their famous 'Gunners' badge, white shorts and red stockings. Even Bristol Rovers, whose blue and white quartered shirt was unique in English football, adopted an all-blue strip – though Blackburn Rovers stuck rigidly to their traditional blue and white halved shirts.

Of the clubs that retained the badge on their shirts, many adopted new designs. Badges based on the traditional town coat of arms, were considered too fussy and redolent of a bygone age, and many were replaced with minimalist designs. It was a case of out with the old and in with the new – a notion totally in keeping with what was happening in society and popular culture at the time. It was only in the nineties, when football clubs became fully aware of their commercial and marketing potential and the value of a branded image, that football strips and club badges reverted to more traditional designs – though, as with any mode of fashion, retro style is never an exact reproduction of the first time around.

★

Leicester City kicked off the 1963–64 season at West Bromwich Albion with the same team that had played against Manchester United in the previous season's Cup final, only the second time in the club's history that a team which had concluded one season had begun the next. With that consistency in team selection it was no surprise that we enjoyed a super start to the season. We began on the traditional glorious summer's day, and we made hard work of our 1–1 draw at West Brom. Our first home game produced a 3–0 win against Birmingham City, and when Arsenal were beaten 7–2 three days later, we once again had high hopes of enjoying a very successful season. But, as so often, our form was to ebb and flow.

Apart from a sparkling spell of form between 21 December and 18 January during which we registered five successive wins in the League, including a fine double over reigning champions Everton, we never realized what I believed to be our true potential. Our wayward form resulted in us losing more games at home (8) than we did on our travels (7), which is not the way to win the championship. However, it was the League Cup that was to occupy our minds during the months ahead.

In the three years since its inception in 1960 the League Cup had come on a bit. It would never possess the ivy-covered venerability of its big brother, the FA Cup, but after three finals it was beginning to grow in importance in the minds of club officials, players and supporters alike. There were still those in the game, however, who believed the competition only added to an already congested fixture programme, and that it was an untidy tournament that lurched through the season from August until the end of April. The League Cup was, in fact, a creature of the night (specifically, midweek evenings). It was rarely played on a Saturday, the only instance being one leg of the previous season's semi-final between Sunderland and Aston Villa, when those clubs found themselves with a free weekend having both been knocked out of the FA Cup.

Having been given a bye in round one, we began our League

Cup campaign modestly enough with a 2–0 win over Fourth Division Aldershot. The club's youth policy was beginning to bear fruit and Matt took this opportunity to blood one of our aspiring youngsters, Bob Newton, who scored our opening goal. (Sadly, that goal proved to be the highlight of Bob's career at Leicester. He never established himself in the first team but later went on to make a name for himself in non-league football.) Newton's appearance against Aldershot showed that Matt was not afraid to call youngsters up for the first team. Moreover, some of these youngsters were to play important roles in our success in the League Cup.

In round three Tranmere Rovers were beaten 2–1, one of our goals coming from Bobby Roberts, for whom Matt had paid a club record fee of £41,000 to Motherwell. Bobby's form when he first arrived at Filbert Street mirrored that of the team itself – inconsistent, probably because Matt couldn't decide his best position. At various times he played Roberts as a defender, a central midfield player, an orthodox winger and even at centre forward, always with wholehearted commitment irrespective of where he was playing. Once he settled into a holding role in midfield, Bobby began to repay his fee with consummate ease and considerable success.

Bobby was a terrific competitor with a cannon-like shot, but his accuracy rarely matched his power and his wayward shooting was often a source of frustration to Bert Johnson: 'One of these days, Bobby, son, you'll knock the hands off the town hall clock.' Shooting high, wide and handsome became such a trait of Bobby that, when he received the ball twenty yards from goal and shaped to strike it, from my end of the pitch I often saw the Leicester supporters anticipate the destiny of that ball and brace themselves behind the goal before Bobby even hit it. Wayward finishing apart, Bobby was a super player and once established in our midfield proved himself to be a player of real class. Today, he is widely regarded by Leicester supporters as one of the club's all-time greats and deservedly so. Bobby kept himself match-fit even when he was manager of Wrexham in the eighties, for whom he played at the age of forty-three. I remember once coming across Bobby when he was a coach at Leicester. I had long since retired from playing, but there was Bobby, training as hard as ever. He is still involved in football, as chief scout for Derby County.

Following our defeat of Tranmere, Gillingham were our next victims, which set up a quarter-final meeting against Norwich City, who had won the League Cup in its second season. A Howard Riley goal cancelled out one from Ron Davies for Norwich and, with a semi-final against West Ham beckoning both teams, we met again in the replay at Filbert Street.

It was Norwich's first visit to Filbert Street for twenty-seven years. The last meeting between the two clubs had taken place in the FA Cup at Norwich in 1954, back in the days when each Leicester player used to take a whiff of oxygen at half time in the hope that it would pep them up. I'm not sure what good this did – nor did anyone else, for this cranky idea was soon dropped. All we had in my time was an interval cup of tea.

Norwich proved to be tough opponents and included in their ranks Tommy Bryceland, a hugely gifted inside forward, Bill Punton, a speedy and tricky left winger, and the Welsh centre forward, Ron Davies, one of the best headers of a ball in the game at the time. This was a typical cup tie, full of blood and thunder and played at breakneck speed. With the score at 1–1 and the game into extra time, Howard Riley settled it to send us through to a meeting with West Ham in a two-legged semi-final.

West Ham's style was in marked contrast to the 'up and at 'em' style of Norwich City. Prompted by Bobby Moore, their build-up from the back was like distant thunder at a picnic. Just when we thought we were having a good time of it, the ominous presence of Moore would gather in midfield and the off-the-ball-running of Johnny Byrne, Geoff Hurst, Ronnie Boyce and John Sissons would soon swamp us. We'd score, only for West Ham to come straight back at us. Their attacks were sophisticated.

When coming out of defence they always did so by passing the ball along the deck with slide-rule precision. Rarely, if ever, did the ball go in the air. When West Ham moved the ball into our half of the field, the darting runs of Hurst, Boyce and Sissons rocked us on our heels. A blend of skill and silky passing was their only arbiter, and the quality of football displayed by both sides gave the game the flavour almost of an idyll. Rarely had the expectation of a football treat been more thoroughly roused as it was on this night, and rarely had it been so completely satisfied. A tremendous game of football ended 4–3 in our favour, but we still had much work to do.

As a football spectacle, the second leg at Upton Park was, if anything, even better. Frank McLintock gave us the lead. Then Bobby Roberts remembered Bert Johnson's instruction and managed to keep his head over the ball when shooting to give us the considerable comfort of a two-goal lead on the night and 6–3 on aggregate. To their credit, West Ham refused to panic or resort to shabby tactics and continued to play the purist football they were so well known for. Their valiant efforts, however, were to no avail and we marched on to a two-legged final against Stoke City, conquerors of Manchester City in the other semi-final.

The first leg was at the Victoria Ground and for my third cup final in four seasons the Leicester team lined up as follows: Gordon Banks; John Sjoberg, Colin Appleton; Graham Cross, Ian King, Max Dougan; Howard Riley, Terry Heath, Ken Keyworth, Davie Gibson, Mike Stringfellow. Stoke, for their part, fielded Lawrie Leslie; Bill Asprey, Tony Allen; Calvin Palmer, George Kinnell, Eric Skeels; Peter Dobing, Dennis Viollet, John Ritchie, Jimmy McIlroy, Keith Bebbington.

Matt Gillies was continuing with his policy of giving promising young City players a chance. Richie Norman was injured and, with Colin Appleton assuming Richie's role at left back, the youngster Max Dougan played on the left side of midfield. Another young prospect, Terry Heath, replaced the injured

Frank McLintock, though with Graham Cross dropping back, Terry enjoyed a more forward role in midfield.

We never really got into our stride against a wily and experienced Stoke side. There had been a lot of rain and the Victoria Ground pitch was very greasy. (We were later told the muddy conditions so suited Stoke that their manager, Tony Waddington, had persuaded the local fire brigade to water the pitch on the morning of the game!) Such greasy conditions always spell trouble for a goalkeeper. When opposing forwards try a speculative shot the ball tends to skid off the wet surface at an alarming speed, which makes judgement difficult. I found myself in such a predicament when going down low to save from the Stoke full back Bill Asprey. I thought I had the ball covered, but it reared up at speed and it was all I could do to claw it away from goal. The Potters' left winger, Keith Bebbington, needed no second invitation and promptly buried the loose ball in the back of the net.

Though we never reproduced the stylish, fluent football of our two semi-finals against West Ham, we were never out of the game and when Terry Heath blocked an attempted clearance by a Stoke defender, there was Davie Gibson to pounce on the loose ball and equalize.

For the return leg, Matt brought in another youngster of promise, Tom Sweeney, in place of Terry Heath. With Richie Norman fit again, Colin Appleton resumed his normal role at the expense of Max Dougan. A crowd of over 25,000 turned up at Filbert Street with great expectations of seeing us win the club's first major trophy.

We didn't disappoint them. Mike Stringfellow scored a cracking goal to give us a half-time lead. Two minutes into the second period, however, Denis Viollet, one of the original Busby Babes, put Stoke level, only for Davie Gibson to restore our lead with a glancing near-post header. When Howard Riley added to our tally, I knew there was only one destination for the League Cup. With only seconds remaining, Stoke City's George Kinnell, a cousin of Jim Baxter, pulled a goal back for Stoke, but by then it was academic. The 3–2 scoreline gave Leicester City their first major trophy since their foundation as Leicester Fosse back in 1884!

It's an odd-looking trophy, the League Cup. For a start it has three handles – I have never discovered why. Unlike the FA Cup, it has neither a lid nor a plinth. The three handles take the form of serpents, though again, I have no idea why. In winning the League Cup, each player received an inscribed tankard rather than a medal, which I found a little disappointing. The tankard resembles any other tankard you might see hanging up at the back of a public bar, only the League Cup tankards were suitably inscribed. That the League Cup had yet fully to capture the imagination of football in general did not detract from our joy at having won it. As a team we were delighted, but even more so for the club and its supporters.

My international career really took off during this season. I became England's regular goalkeeper and received the ultimate honour when I was picked to play for my country against the Rest of the World in a game celebrating the centenary of the Football Association. I'm such a patriot I would have played for my country for nothing; however, for the opportunity of playing against the Rest of the World I would have willingly paid the FA.

Such was the interest in this game that Wembley had sold out six weeks before the match was due to take place. When I walked into the dressing room, picked up one of the complimentary match programmes and looked at the team line-ups, my eyes nearly came out on stalks. Lining up against us were some of the greatest players ever to have graced the game: Eusebio of Portugal, Alfredo di Stefano and Paco Gento of Spain, Denis Law, Jim Baxter, Raymond Kopa of France, West Germany's Uwe Seeler, the magical Magyar, Ferenc Puskas and one of my all-time heroes, the Russian goalkeeper Lev Yashin. I couldn't believe that, after only five games for England, I was about to play against some of the most revered names in football.

Yashin was known throughout the world as the Black Octopus. He invariably wore all black when playing and the assimilation with an octopus came from his superb handling of the ball. No matter how hard a shot, irrespective of the angle, he always seemed to get a hand to the ball. And what hands they were. Lev Yashin had hands like shovels and fingers like bananas; in my entire career in football I don't think I ever saw a goalkeeper with bigger hands. When he jumped to punch the ball clear, he achieved incredible distance. Little wonder: physically he was very strong and when he balled one of his massive hands into a fist, it was like a ham-shank.

Yashin played as a goal-tender for Dynamo, the KGB's ice-hockey team, and it was after watching their sister-team, the mighty Moscow Dynamo, and particularly their goalkeeper Alexei Khomich, that he turned his attention to football. In 1951 he was understudy to his hero and when Khomich was injured playing against Moscow Spartak, Lev, as a substitute, came off the bench and replaced him. Within minutes of coming on, Lev conceded a goal, then another. It was an unpromising start but Lev quickly demonstrated that he had a very special talent for goalkeeping and such were his performances he kept his hero on the bench. By 1956 Lev had established himself in the Russian international side with whom he won a gold medal at the Melbourne Olympics.

He played seventy-eight times for Russia and his performances and great sportsmanship resulted in his being awarded the two highest honours the Soviet government could bestow on a civilian, the Order of Lenin and the Honoured Master of Soviet Sport.

All Russian footballers were supposedly amateurs and Lev's job was nominally that of a police sergeant, though I doubt if he did much policing as he was always playing football for his club or country, for which he must have been in full-time training.

He spent several years of his playing career on tour as the Soviet authorities were keen to use football teams in an ambassadorial or propaganda role – and, quite often, both.

The policy of the Russians was to keep their best players together at one club, such as Moscow Dynamo, and then select them en bloc to play in major international tournaments. He appeared in three World Cups, the last in 1966, when his goal-keeping helped Russia reach the semi-finals. When he eventually retired from football in 1970 his club, Moscow Dynamo, played a Rest of the World XI in his testimonial and a crowd of 120,000 turned up at the Lenin Stadium to see it.

I met him on a number of occasions. Though obviously aware of his world-wide fame, he was a very modest man, quietly spoken and extremely polite. For someone who was supposedly a Russian policeman and played for a club with strong links to the KGB, he had a great sense of humour and would often make light of the harsh realities of Russian life. He spoke a little English but relied on an interpreter, but that didn't stop him telling jokes at the expense of Communism.

Following a visit by the Russian international team to France, I asked Lev what he thought of Paris.

'It's amazing,' he said, 'all those people in Paris and the Government only has one watch tower!'

In 1966 the Cold War was thawing and though there was still much mistrust between western countries and the Soviet bloc, relationships between the two were slowly getting better. According to Lev, life was also beginning to improve for ordinary Russian citizens, though food and the domestic appliances we took for granted in the West were still scarce.

One of Lev Yashin's favourite stories concerned a man in Moscow who went to queue for meat at his local butcher. For four hours the man waited in a long, snaking queue for some meat. When he eventually reached the door of the butcher's shop he was turned away by a KGB officer, who told him that the shop had run out of meat. The man was furious. He waved his fists at the KGB officer and with a volley of expletives told the officer exactly what he thought of the Soviet Government and Communism.

'Go back to your home,' said the KGB officer, 'and think yourself lucky to have a leader such as Comrade Brezhnev. If Stalin was still in power, you would have been taken away and shot for saying such things.'

The man glumly returned home to his wife, who asked him what meat he had managed to buy.

'No meat.'

She got very angry. 'No meat for the family! Nothing has changed. Things are still bad!' said the wife.

'It's worse than you think,' said the man. 'They've run out of bullets!'

I would laugh at his jokes but not as much as Lev himself. Football enabled him to see the world outside Russia. What he made of it, I don't know. Perhaps, having seen life in democratic countries enabled him to put life at home into perspective and making jokes about the harsh realities of life under the Communists helped him cope with it.

In his later years Lev suffered from ill health, which necessitated the amputation of a leg. He died in 1998, but his legend lives on, not only in Russia, but throughout the football world, where his name will for ever be synonymous with great goalkeeping.

The Rest of the World team read like a who's who of football greats of that era. Though they were playing together for the very first time in what was billed as a friendly, I had no doubt whatsoever that the Rest of the World team would provide stern opposition and a severe test of Alf Ramsey's progress at England's helm. Their starting line-up was: Yashin (USSR); Santos (Brazil), Schnellinger (West Germany); Pluskal, Popluhar and Masopust (all Czechoslovakia); Kopa (France), Law (Scotland), Di Stefano (Spain), Eusebio (Portugal), Gento (Spain).

It had been decided that substitutes would be allowed for this game and the Rest of the World bench was formidable in its content: namely, Puskas (Hungary/Spain), Baxter (Scotland), Seeler (West Germany), Soskic (Yugoslavia) and Eyzaguirre (Chile).

The England team comprised Banks (Leicester City); Armfield (Blackpool), Wilson (Huddersfield Town); Milne (Liverpool), Norman (Spurs), Moore (West Ham); Paine (Southampton), Greaves and Smith (both Spurs), Eastham (Arsenal), Charlton (Manchester United). (If evidence were ever needed of how much the English game has changed, it's there in that England line-up, which contained top quality internationals from Blackpool, Huddersfield Town and Southampton.)

The game was in keeping with the occasion. It produced a feast of football and was a personal triumph for Jimmy Greaves, who in such illustrious company showed that he too was a world-class player. All the goals came in the last twenty minutes. Terry Paine gave us the lead, only for Denis Law to combine with Puskas and Di Stefano before sliding the ball under my legs as I came out to cut down the angle. Jimmy Greaves wrapped the game up for England with seven minutes remaining. Milutin Soskic, who had replaced Yashin for the second half, could only parry a thunderbolt from Bobby Charlton and in nipped Jimmy to score a typical poacher's goal. Jimmy had an even better goal disallowed by the referee, who gave us a free kick following a foul on Jimmy rather than play the advantage rule. Jimmy felt that he had the Scottish referee against him as well as the Rest of the World.

It may only have been a friendly to celebrate the centenary of the Football Association, but our victory was a benchmark for England in general and Alf Ramsey in particular. The press saw it as ample evidence that Alf was making good progress in his quest to put England back at the top of world football. It had been ten years since Hungary had arrived at Wembley and put Billy Wright's England team to the sword. Following our victory over the Rest of the World XI, there was a feeling that English football was on the point of being great again.

One swallow doesn't make a summer and one victory over a World XI didn't make England the best in the world, but I had the feeling that we were on our way back.

It was around this time that I had my second experience of how underhand certain members of the press can be at times. Ninety-nine per cent of all the column inches that have been devoted to my career have been honest and objective reporting, sometimes even giving me more credit than I deserved. I was brought up to believe in the importance of honesty and integrity, never to be underhand in my dealings with people. Whenever I took to the pitch, I did so with no other intent than doing my best for club or country, and for the supporters who were paying hard-earned cash to watch the game. Whenever I made a mistake, I held my hand up; I never tried to hoodwink a referee, or cheat a fellow professional. So I found it saddening to be the victim of some misleading and sensationalist reporting, and very cross that it affected my wife.

A journalist from a Sunday redtop approached me regarding a story ostensibly about footballers' diets and how they prepared for a big game, particularly on a Saturday morning. We arranged that he would come to my house and he sat in the kitchen with my wife and I. After a half-hearted interview during which he hardly made a note, he got up to leave.

'I hear you're in dispute with Leicester over money,' he said, apropos of nothing.

I told him that 'dispute' was too strong a word for what was, in fact, simply the renegotiation of my contract. At this time I was on £35 a week. I felt I was giving good service both to Leicester and England and that I was worth a bit more. After all, it was below half what Tottenham Hotspur's players earned, and a good deal less than what just about every other First Division club was paying at the time. I told the reporter that talks were continuing and that I was confident the matter would be resolved quickly to everyone's satisfaction. Then he turned to Ursula and asked if she thought I deserved a bit more money and, of course, she told him yes.

'If Gordon gets a rise, I suppose the extra money will enable you to buy a bit more in the way of food,' said the reporter.

'I suppose it will,' said Ursula as the two of us saw him to the door.

When I saw his article that Sunday, my heart sank: ' "I Can't Live on £35 a Week" Says Gordon Banks' Wife'.

I was furious, not so much because I had been duped but because I knew the trouble and grief his scurrilous piece would cause Ursula. Sure enough, the next time she went to do the weekly shop she ran a gauntlet of angry women who told her, in no uncertain terms, how fortunate we were to have a wage of £35 a week and how they had to manage on much less. Talk was rife at Leicester of Matt Gillies having to spend too much time arguing with me over money, and of how I was opposed to the club's policy of pay parity for every first team player. It was water off a duck's back for me, but it did upset me that Ursula was subjected to some very nasty and wholly unjustified remarks. All I could do was tell her to maintain her dignity and ride it out. With time, the matter would be forgotten, if not forgiven.

The 1963–64 season saw a landmark in the history of Wembley: the first match to be played there under floodlights. No longer would midweek internationals be played at the grand old stadium on Wednesday afternoons when most supporters had difficulty in attending because of their work commitments. I played for England in our 8–3 victory over Northern Ireland. Jimmy Greaves scored four and Southampton's Terry Paine also helped himself to a hat trick.

Another first was achieved when Jim Fryatt of Bradford Park Avenue scored the fastest goal on record. His goal against

Tranmere Rovers was timed by the referee's watch at just four seconds. Jim, a rugged centre forward whose bald head and long pork-chop sideburns made him an instantly recognizable figure, was a journeyman round the lower divisions. Presumably it was this wanderlust that drew him to travel around America when he had retired from football, before eventually becoming a croupier in a Las Vegas casino!

Football was dragged through the gutter in 1963–64 with revelations in the *Sunday People* of a bribery scandal. The paper revealed that a number of players had been paid by a gambling syndicate to fix matches. It was a major news story involving several players, most notably Peter Swan and David 'Bronco' Layne of Sheffield Wednesday and their former team mate, Tony Kay, who had by then joined Everton. The *People* alleged that the trio had taken part in arranging the outcome of a Sheffield Wednesday game at Ipswich Town in December 1962, which Wednesday had lost 2–0. Other players of lesser note were also said to have been involved in match fixing, and all were subsequently arrested and appeared in a much-publicized court case.

The key defendant was Jimmy Gauld, a former Everton, Charlton and Swindon Town player who it was revealed had been the ringleader. The players were charged with conspiracy to defraud. Ten were subsequently jailed and banned from football for life by the FA. Gauld received the heaviest sentence and was jailed for four years and ordered to pay £5,000 costs. The other nine players were jailed for between four and fifteen months.

I was deeply shocked and saddened by this scandal, not only because it besmirched my profession and the game I loved, but also because it involved my old school mate David Layne. His involvement abruptly terminated what I, and many others, believed would have been a very successful career in football.

During the summer of 1964 I was a member of the England party that toured North and South America, and it was during this tour that I lost my place in the England team, albeit only briefly.

The tour began well when we beat the USA 10–0 on a dustbowl of a pitch in New York, a result that went some way to avenging England's humiliating defeat at the hands of the Americans in the 1950 World Cup. The margin of our victory was very pleasing to Alf Ramsey, who had been a member of that defeated England team.

In the dressing room before the game Alf told us how he had never been allowed to forget what had been the most calamitous result in the history of England as an international team. He repeatedly warned us not to be complacent, emphasizing that we had to treat the USA much as we would any top international team. Even as we were leaving the dressing room Alf was still reminding us to be on our mettle. We took to the pitch so wound up we tore into the opposition from the start and could have scored twenty. I hardly touched the ball and spent the vast majority of the game spectating.

Liverpool's Roger Hunt scored four and Blackburn's Fred Pickering scored a hat trick on his England debut. Fred was a very tall and powerful centre forward, not the sharpest or most mobile of strikers but awesome in the air and very difficult to knock off the ball. Fred knew where the goal was and in only three games for England scored five goals. It is indicative of just how many quality forwards were then playing in English football that five goals in three matches wasn't enough to earn Fred a fourth cap following his move to Everton that summer. Today a hat trick on your international debut would mean you are hailed as a superstar and made for life. It contrast, when he retired from football Fred worked as a forklift driver in his home town of Blackburn.

Following our convincing victory over the USA we flew down to Brazil to take part in a four-team tournament with the hosts, Portugal and Argentina. This tournament had been billed as 'Little World Cup' and was seen as a true test of our ability to compete against the very best in world football.

Our opening game was against Brazil, but my dream of playing against the great Pelé was dashed when Alf Ramsey took me to one side after our first training session. Alf told me he thought my form had suffered of late and was going to play Tony Waiters of Blackpool in goal. I was very disappointed, but as a player you must accept and respect a manager's decision. Alf asked me if I was happy with his decision to play Tony. I told him I was far from happy. 'Good,' said Alf, 'because that's the right attitude to have. If you had told me it was OK, I would know you were either lying or that you didn't have the right mental attitude that I'm looking for in my players.'

I watched the game from the sidelines as Brazil gave full vent to their mercurial football powers. For much of the game England were the equal of Brazil, but with twenty minutes remaining the Brazilians stepped up a gear. We conceded three free kicks outside our penalty area and Brazil produced the sort of wizardry that had deceived me at Wembley in the previous season. The final score was 5–1 to Brazil. Back in the dressing room, Alf was not a happy man and I harboured high hopes of a quick recall to the fold.

Two days later Brazil took on Argentina and Alf insisted we all go along to watch and learn from two of the top four FIFA-rated sides in the world (the others being Portugal and West Germany). We sat on benches by one of the touchlines in the cavernous bowl of the Maracanà stadium. Behind us a formidable fence separated us from the massed ranks of volatile Brazilian supporters. We soon discovered English footballers were not the most popular people in the eyes of the Brazilian fans. Even as we walked down the touchline towards the benches we were assailed by non-stop verbal abuse; once we had taken our seats, those fans proceeded to throw the contents of a greengrocer's shop in our general direction. We didn't learn much about either team because our attention was constantly being diverted as we ducked and dived to avoid the oranges, apples, tomatoes, bananas and nuts that rained down from the packed terraces. And, as the old song goes, they've got an awful lot of nuts in Brazil.

Argentina were on fire and raced into a three-goal lead. When the third Argentinian goal went in, Ray Wilson was hit on the shoulder by a tomato. Ray immediately took to his feet, turned to face the Brazilian fans and held up three fingers on one hand and none on the other to remind the Brazilian supporters of the scoreline.

'That's right, Ray,' said Jimmy Greaves, 'you try and appease them.'

That did it. Hundreds of livid Brazilians began pulling at the fencing as if trying to bring it down. Those who couldn't get near to the fence angrily gesticulated at us with fingers or fists, and you didn't have to possess a working knowledge of Portuguese to know what they were insinuating. The atmosphere was turning very, very ugly and Alf Ramsey, a model of self-control, got to his feet.

'Gentlemen, there is no cause for alarm, simply sit and –'

Alf never finished what he had to say. An apple rocketed through the air and hit him square on the back of the head. It was too much, even for Alf. Still exuding calm authority, Alf bent down, picked up the offending apple and carefully placed it on a bench.

'Gentlemen, be so kind as to follow me,' he said.

Follow him we did, and at more than a casual pace as he led us down the touchline to relative safety behind the Brazilian goal, where the distance between us and the supporters was too great for us to be troubled by anything thrown from the terraces.

From our new vantage point I was able to concentrate fully on the game. Pelé was coming in for some really shabby treatment from his Argentinian marker, who stuck to him like a leech. Pelé was hacked and kicked, at times even when he didn't have the ball. In the end it all proved too much for him. With play deep in the Brazilian half of the field, Pelé was coasting about in the middle of the park when an Argentinian defender thought fit to run his studs down the back of one of Pelé's calves. The great man snapped. He turned quickly and landed a 'Glasgow kiss' right on the nose of his tormentor. As head butts go it was a good 'un, the Argentinian defender went to the ground like a parachute with a hole in it, his nose broken.

Today, Pelé enjoys a deserved global reputation for being a gentleman sportsman, a statesman and a fine ambassador of football. But that day against Argentina he showed that he was only human after all. Probably wisely, the referee chose to ignore the assault and, as opposed to the guy with the broken nose, Pelé remained on the pitch. To have dismissed him would in all probability have sparked a full-scale riot. Perhaps fresh in the referee's mind was the fact that less than a fortnight before, 301 people had been killed during a riot at the National Stadium in Lima when Peru's opponents had again been Argentina.

Alf Ramsey recalled me for our next game in the series, a 1–1 draw against Portugal. In our final match we were up against Argentina, who needed a draw to win the competition. This was a very closely contested game between two evenly matched sides, but on the hour, Argentina broke quickly from defence following a prolonged period of England pressure. The ball was played by Silvio Marzolini from our left into the penalty box, where Alfredo Rojas sent a stinging low drive into the right-hand corner of my net. In contrast to the rough-house tactics deployed against Brazil, Argentina had concentrated on playing football against us. In so doing, they showed us what a very good side they were.

Of the three teams we came up against in this competition, Argentina impressed us most. Technically they were our superiors and their level of skill and organization had been very impressive. We were all of the mind that Argentina would be a major force in the 1966 World Cup. We'd been particularly impressed with the skill and general performances of the Argentine captain, who had proved himself to be a world-class player. Alf Ramsey even went as far as to tell our trainer, Harold

Shepherdson, to make a note of him in the dossier they were compiling on possible qualifiers.

'What's his name, again?' asked Harold.

'Antonio Rattin,' replied Alf.

10. Chelsea Blues

Can you imagine the sensational headlines a newly promoted team would make today if they began a season in the Premiership without a manager and with a 15-year-old boy in goal? Yet that is exactly the situation our opponents Sunderland found themselves in when we kicked off the 1964–65 season. After six seasons in the Second Division Sunderland had just returned to the top flight but before a ball had been kicked, the club were in turmoil. On 31 July Alan Brown, the manager who had guided Sunderland to promotion, went off to Sheffield Wednesday, leaving the Roker Park club managerless. Then their first-choice goalkeeper, Jimmy Montgomery, an England Under 23 international, sustained a hand injury in training that ruled him out for two months and reserve keeper Derek Kirby was injured in a pre-season friendly. As the loan system had yet to be introduced, Sunderland had no alternative but to play Derek Forster, their untried youth-team keeper. Forster, an English schoolboy international, had only left school in June. At fifteen years of age he became the youngest goalkeeper to appear in the Football League and, by a matter of days, the second youngest player to play in the First Division.

Before a Roker Park crowd of 45,465 basking in August sunshine, the game proved to be an exciting 3–3 draw full of end-to-end action, and Derek Forster acquitted himself remarkably well for one so young. Sadly, though he was to remain on Sunderland's books until the early seventies, Derek never fulfilled his early potential, making only eighteen league appearances in nine years at Roker Park.

The trip up to Sunderland was one of the longer away trips for Leicester and, like most teams, we undertook most such journeys by train. The only motorway of note was the M1 and rail connections were still the most convenient mode of travel. Manchester City, however, took to the air in 1964–65, chartering a plane to take them to the majority of their away games, which that year involved visits to London, Plymouth, Southampton, Portsmouth, Norwich, Ipswich, Cardiff, Swansea and Newcastle. At the time it was still quite common for a team travelling to the other end of the country to incur not only an overnight stay on Friday, but on Saturday too if there was not a suitable train to get them home. These Sunday morning rail trips were unpopular, not only because they kept players away from their families from Friday morning, but also travelling by train on Sunday was invariably subject to delay caused by track maintenance.

City's chartered plane meant that in many cases the team did not have to leave until the morning of the match and were home the same day. Though it cost Manchester City £140 to charter a plane they made quite a saving in hotel expenses. City players were all in favour of flying because it gave them more Friday and Saturday evenings at home. While this decision to take to the air was taken up by a number of other clubs – primarily Newcastle and Sunderland when making trips to the South Coast, and Plymouth Argyle when travelling up to the North East – the emergence of the motorway network and the consequent cheaper costs of coach travel was to nip this new phenomenon in the bud. Air travel is used only occasionally today, and then primarily as a time-saving rather than cost-saving measure.

Back at Filbert Street the club's wage structure continued to be a major bone of contention. I was still embroiled in talks with the club about wages and I wasn't the only unhappy player: Frank McLintock was so unsettled he put in a transfer request, while Bobby Roberts and Davie Gibson refused to accept the terms on offer. Leicester were offering me £40 a week, a lower basic wage than any other First Division club was paying. To put this in perspective, Southampton of the Second Division were paying their first team players a basic wage of £45, while at Fourth Division Bradford Park Avenue players could earn £40 a week with win bonuses. Frank and I were current internationals; to be on the lowest basic wage in the First Division was out of line with our contribution to Leicester City. Club loyalty is one thing, but downright unfair treatment simply wasn't on.

The uncertainty continued for months, and was not finally resolved until December, when the club offered me £60 a week. I immediately accepted. Why they couldn't have done this in the first place is beyond me. Perhaps the club had been hoping to persuade me to sign for as little as possible. Such a ploy wasn't unknown. Clubs often tried to hoodwink players over their contracts and, without the advice of agents, many signed up for far less money than they should have done.

Bobby Keetch was a tough-tackling wing half with Fulham. Bobby was very much a stylish man about town, in a part of London known for style. Keetch was the original 'Bobby dazzler', a charmer whose swept-back blond hair and suntanned, athletic build made him very popular with the ladies. Bobby spent much of his spare time frequenting the trendy bars dotted along the King's Road and would often appear after matches at Craven Cottage with some young debutante on his arm. Bobby was also a great character who possessed a marvellous sense of humour, but above all he was streetwise.

In 1964 the Fulham manager Vic Buckingham called Bobby into his office to renegotiate his contract. Fulham were in the First Division and though they could boast players of the calibre of Johnny Haynes, George Cohen and Bobby Robson, were almost always near the foot of the table. The football writer John Moynihan aptly and evocatively described Fulham as 'a Saturday afternoon team, offering a feeling of animated recreation rather than solid professionalism'. They were indeed a team whose enjoyment of football, at times, appeared to be more paramount than their desire to win.

As Bobby sat down in front of him, Vic Buckingham placed

two contracts on his desk, indicating it was up to Bobby which one he chose to sign.

'The first contract will pay you £60 a week. Win, lose or draw, that is what you'll be paid,' said Buckingham.

Bobby ummed and ah-ed, then asked what the second contract entailed.

'With this second contract you stand to earn more money than you would if you were at Spurs or Manchester United,' said Buckingham proudly.

Bobby, his enthusiasm aroused, immediately sat bolt upright in his chair. 'Tell me more, boss.'

'This second contract only pays a basic wage of £45 a week,' Buckingham continued, 'but, for every home win, you'll receive an extra £25. For a draw away from home, you get the same bonus, £25, but for every away win, an extra £35. Should we win the League Championship, you'll get a bonus of £500, and £250 if we finish in the top four. If we reach the final of the FA Cup, your bonus will be a one-off payment of £300 and if we win the Cup, you get £600.'

'I'll take the sixty quid!' said Bobby, not giving the matter a second thought.

The contract I negotiated with Leicester City included a bonus of £5 for every home gate in excess of 30,000. If we were to enjoy the successful season I was anticipating, I'd be quids in as the capacity at Filbert Street was up to 40,000. As it turned out, until my departure from the club in 1967 Leicester were only to attract a home crowd of more than 30,000 on seven occasions. In three seasons, then, my total crowd bonus was the princely sum of £35!

Frank McLintock's unhappiness led to his transfer to Arsenal in October 1964 for what was a record fee for a Leicester City player of £80,000. However, Leicester's reputation for paying low wages made it difficult for Matt Gillies in his attempts to bolster the squad. Matt and his scouts were very good at spotting emerging talent, but often lost out to better-paying rivals. In

1964–65 Matt was frustrated in his attempts to sign Colin Bell of Bury (who joined Manchester City), Southampton's Martin Chivers (who signed for Spurs) and Francis Lee of Bolton Wanderers (who joined Bell at Maine Road). What success might we have enjoyed had those players joined Leicester?

After an encouraging start to the season in which we remained unbeaten until our seventh game, our form once again ebbed and flowed. We scored a double over Liverpool (if ever Liverpool had a bogey team it was us), Fulham were beaten 5–1, Spurs 4–2 and there was a thrilling and hard-fought 2–2 draw against Leeds United, a team that had quickly gained a reputation as hard men following their promotion from Division Two. But in the end our final position of eighteenth in Division One was a disappointment to everyone, though we did enjoy good runs in both cup competitions.

Our penultimate game of the season was away at Tottenham Hotspur. It was a meaningless end-of-season fixture for both teams; up at the top of the table Manchester United and Leeds were locked in a battle for the title, which the Reds eventually won on goal average. There were no high stakes to play for in our encounter at White Hart Lane, which was played in a very cavalier manner. Both sets of players were relaxed enough to display their party pieces for the 33,000 spectators.

With ten minutes of the game remaining, we were trailing 5–2 when Spurs were awarded a penalty. The grass at the back of a goal was rarely cut by groundsmen, and as Jimmy Greaves ambled into the penalty area, I stepped back into the goal to rub my hands on the long grass to clean them (I never wore gloves until 1970). As I was bending down with my back to him, Jimmy stepped up to place the ball on the spot. Seeing that I was preoccupied, he dinked the ball with the toe of his boot and sent it bobbling towards the right-hand corner of the goal. I turned just in time to see the ball cross the line. I immediately realized what Jimmy had done and started laughing along with the rest of the players. Party to the joke, the Spurs supporters on the terraces gave an ironic cheer as the ball trickled across the line. With a cheesy grin on his face Jimmy walked up to retrieve the ball so that he could take the penalty properly, only for the referee to blow his whistle, signal a goal and retreat to the halfway line.

I couldn't believe it; nor could anyone who witnessed it. I was furious that Jimmy's joke penalty had been allowed to stand at my expense. I hadn't even been facing play! With the Spurs players doubled up with laughter, I took off after the referee.

'You can't give that!' I said, on catching him up. 'It was a joke of a penalty.'

'Played advantage,' he informed me.

'Played advantage?' I queried. 'From a penalty?'

'Advantage. Best law in football,' he said. 'It lets you ignore all the others for the good of the game.'

I calmed down eventually, if still a little peeved. Over a drink I asked Jimmy if he was ashamed to claim such a bizarre goal.

'Naah,' said Jimmy, 'in years to come when someone is reading the statistics, they'll all look the same.' There speaks a true goalscorer.

Liverpool exacted revenge for our victory over them in the semi-final of 1962–63 by knocking us out of the FA Cup in the sixth round. We had beaten Blackburn Rovers, Plymouth Argyle and Middlesbrough, but for once our Indian sign over the mighty Reds didn't work. Having drawn 0–0 at Filbert Street in front of a crowd of 40,000 – another £5 for me – a Roger Hunt goal put paid to our hopes of another semi-final. At Anfield during the pre-match kickabout four practice balls supplied by Liverpool disappeared into the Kop never to return. No amount of persuasion on my part could induce those Liverpool supporters to return the balls, which had obviously been taken as souvenirs. So we ended up having just one ball to kick about between us. I never brought the matter to the attention of the referee or the Liverpool officials. The Kop had only just forgiven me for the

Ian St John photograph and the last thing I wanted was to get them on my back again.

We fared better in the League Cup, where a terrific run took us to yet another final. Once again we made a modest start, struggling to dispose of Peterborough United, Grimsby Town and Crystal Palace in the early rounds. At the time of the Palace tie, I was harbouring thoughts of a move should my wage negotiations not be resolved. But following our 2–1 victory over Palace, I found the press were batting for me: 'No one could ever accuse transfer-seeking goalkeeper Gordon Banks of playing to get away from Leicester City,' wrote Steve Richards in the *Daily Express*. 'His display for the League Cup holders in last night's fourth-round replay at Selhurst Park was one of his greatest for the club.' Having claimed that it was my 'incredible reflexes' that put us through to the quarter-finals, he said that it was to be hoped that my 'dissatisfaction with the club will be resolved soon'.

As far as I was concerned my dissatisfaction was with Matt Gillies and the board over wages, not the club. Deep down I never wanted to leave Leicester City. I had been very loyal to the club and enjoyed a great relationship with both my team mates and the supporters. Sometimes a player in dispute with his club over wages can feel out on a limb. Press reports can imply he is solely motivated by money and has no club loyalty. Steve Richards's report of our League Cup tie against Palace went some way to dispelling such a notion. However unhappy I was with the terms on offer, I never let it affect my game.

Our lacklustre performances in the early rounds of the League Cup failed to inspire the enthusiasm of the Leicester fans, but that all changed in round five when we were involved in a tie at Coventry City that erupted like a volcano and made up for all the modest football of the previous rounds. A crowd of 28,000 turned up at Highfield Road to witness what turned out to be a sensational night for us. An own goal from the Coventry centre half and skipper, George Curtis, gave us an early lead. Minutes later I bent my thumb backwards in a challenge for the ball with the Coventry centre forward, George Hudson, and spent the following five minutes on the touchline receiving treatment for what was more of a nuisance than a debilitating injury. Luckily the thumb wasn't broken and I returned to the fray. At the other end, almost every shot we had resulted in a goal. Left back Richie Norman helped himself to two, but blotted his copybook when he was put clean through by Mike Stringfellow and, in typical full-back fashion, with only the Coventry goalkeeper Bob Wesson to beat, blazed wide. Richie's miss wasn't costly; both Billy Hodgson and Mike Stringfellow also helped themselves to a couple of goals and a fine effort from Davie Gibson saw us win by an amazing scoreline of 8–1.

We accounted for Plymouth Argyle over two legs in the semi-final which took us through to a final against Chelsea. Although the League Cup final was still a two-legged affair, the competition was given extra kudos in this season when the Football League announced the winners would receive a place in the Fairs Cup (now the UEFA Cup) the following season.

This added incentive gave the final an extra edge and the first leg at Stamford Bridge was hotly contested. Chelsea gained the upper hand courtesy of a 3–2 scoreline, our goals coming from Colin Appleton and Jimmy Goodfellow. Although we had approached the game with every intention of winning it, we weren't too despondent as we were confident we could overturn it in front of our own fans. It wasn't to be. We laid siege to the Chelsea goal for much of the second leg, but their defence held firm and their goalkeeper, Peter Bonetti, was in inspired form. George Graham and Terry Venables were in that Chelsea team but their stars on the night were in defence. Marvin Hinton, Ron Harris, John Hollins, Johnny Boyle and Allan Young, whom Chelsea had signed on a free transfer from Arsenal, all contrived to form an impenetrable back line. For all our concerted efforts to break Chelsea down, the game ended goalless, giving Tommy Docherty's side a 3–2 aggregate win. I was bitterly disappointed,

as was everyone at the club. Not only had we failed to retain
the League Cup, we had missed out on a lucrative place in
Europe.

Leicester City made a profit of £44,000 on the season, and
though we hadn't made it into Europe, the club was presented
with a great opportunity of making extra income and offering
our loyal supporters a football treat when the Football Association
offered us a prestigious friendly against one of the greatest club
sides in the world. Santos of Brazil were on an eight-date tour of
Europe. The opportunity of hosting a match against a team
boasting six of the current Brazil national side, including the
world's greatest player, Pelé, was too good a chance to turn
down. That, however, was exactly what the Leicester City
board did.

The World Club Cup was a two-legged affair played between
the winners of the European Cup and its South American equivalent, the Copa Libertadores. Santos had won the World Club
Cup for the first time in 1962, beating Benfica 3–2 and 5–2.
They had retained it the following year with a 7–6 aggregate
win over AC Milan and were fresh from winning the Brazilian
League Championship and the Copa do Brasil for a record fifth
successive season. Though they boasted Pelé and a string of
top Brazilian internationals, Santos were not a rich club. Their
ground, the imaginatively named Urbano Caldeira Vila Belmiro,
only had a capacity of 25,000 (though major games, such as the
World Club Cup, were invariably switched to the Maracanà,
where 152,000 had seen their game against Milan). The price of
admission to matches in Brazil was very low, so clubs such as
Santos needed to go on tour to generate extra funds. They didn't
come cheap: the fee they wanted for playing at Filbert Street was
£7,500, and that was too much as far as the Leicester board was
concerned.

Santos would have attracted if not a full house of 40,000, then
definitely at least 35,000 to Filbert Street. The profit margin was
considered too small by a Leicester board. What if it was a rainy

night? People might not turn up! Too risky, the directors said. Santos were fixed up with a game at Fulham instead. The crowd at Craven Cottage? 42,000.

The Leicester board were extremely shortsighted in declining this friendly. I am sure there would have been a profit in the end. Money aside, a match against Santos would have been a wonderful gesture of thanks to the Leicester supporters who had stuck by us through what had been an indifferent season in the League. More frustratingly, I was beginning to think I would never get the chance of playing against the great Pelé. After injury had kept him out of the England match against Brazil at Wembley, and Alf Ramsey had left me out of the side that faced the Brazilians in the 'Little World Cup', now the Leicester board had declined an offer of a friendly against his club side. Would fate always keep us apart?

The board also turned down a request from some supporters that the former Leicester city forward, Arthur Rowley, be awarded a testimonial match. Arthur had just hung up his boots following a spell as player-manager with Shrewsbury Town and his career total of 434 goals remains, to this day, an all-time record.

Arthur had played for Leicester before my arrival and his goalscoring record for the club was second only to that of Arthur Chandler, who had played in the 1920s. Arthur's goals-per-game ratio at City was astonishing: between 1950 and 1958, in 321 league and cup appearances, Arthur Rowley scored 265 goals for Leicester City. A record like that demanded nothing but the utmost respect, as did his conduct on the pitch. If Arthur Rowley was not deemed worthy of a 'thank you' testimonial game, I wondered who would be.

In 1998, in a week when Manchester United announced profits in excess of £11 million, Arthur put up his medals for sale. He said at the time, 'I've done it because they're just lying about, so I might just as well enjoy what they are worth.' He's in his seventies now but, in the minds and memories of those

Leicester supporters fortunate enough to have seen Arthur play, he remains eternally young and strong. For ever a hero.

The 1964–65 season ended with Bobby Moore elegantly ascending the steps to the royal box at Wembley to collect yet another cup. A year after West Ham United had beaten Second Division Preston North End to win the FA Cup, Bobby led the Hammers to a 2–0 victory over Munich 1860 to clinch the European Cup Winners Cup. It was one of the best games of football ever to have been played at Wembley and West Ham's success was a tribute to their manager, Ron Greenwood, whose policy of purist football verged on the sublime. The West Ham goals came from Alan Sealey and Brian Dear who were only in the side because of injuries to Peter Brabrook and Johnny Byrne. That Sealey and Dear fitted so seamlessly into the West Ham system was yet another tribute to Greenwood, whose belief in positive, stylish football ran through the East End club from first team to juniors. West Ham became the second English team, after Spurs in 1963, to win a major European competition. Their success fuelled the growing belief that English football was making great strides to being a major force once again in Europe, if not the world. As Bobby said after the final, 'If our game continues to develop the way it has been doing these last three years, next year England will have a team capable of winning the World Cup.' His opinion was later to be echoed by a certain Mr Ramsey.

The season also saw the retirement of Stanley Matthews, who in February, at the age of fifty, had played his last game for Stoke City, against Fulham. Stan enjoyed his final bow on 28 April when a packed Victoria Ground saw a Stan Matthews XI take on an International XI that included the likes of Alfredo di Stefano, Ferenc Puskas and Lev Yashin. It was incredible to think that Stan first signed for Stoke thirty-five years ago and had made his league debut in 1932. For him still to have been playing the equivalent of Premiership football at the age of fifty I still find remarkable, though, according to Stan, 'I made a mistake retiring at fifty. I still had another two good years left in me.'

Tragedy touched football with the death of the Spurs inside forward, John White. I had played against John on numerous occasions for Leicester, and as an England team mate, and considered him a good pal. He was a very skilful player whose wonderful vision enabled him to split an opposing defence wide open with a single pass. He was killed by lightning while sheltering under a tree during a game of golf at the Crews Club in Enfield. John's death shocked and saddened everyone in football who knew him, not only as a great player, but as a great sportsman. His midfield partnership with Danny Blanchflower was the source of Tottenham's double success of 1961, and his tragic and untimely death saddened us all.

I spent a good part of the summer of '65 on tour with England. Having enjoyed a 1–0 success over Hungary at Wembley in May, we set off on a continental tour that was to feature the first appearance of a fiery young red-haired winger from Blackpool, Alan Ball.

The tour began with a 1–1 draw against Yugoslavia in Belgrade. The day before the game we trained in the Belgrade stadium. After the training session Alan Ball couldn't find his trousers. I realized there and then what sort of mettle Alan Ball had, and what kind of character he was. Any other player would have donned a pair of tracksuit bottoms when searching for his trousers. Not Bally. He wandered around behind the scenes and out into the stadium itself wearing nothing but a shirt and underpants, even approaching some bemused Yugoslav officials and in his high-pitched voice asking, 'Excuse me, has anyone seen my trousers? Somebody has nicked them – grey flannels with a brown belt. Have you seen them?'

The culprit turned out to be Nobby Stiles, who eventually took pity on Alan and produced the missing flannels. Bally took it all in good part and Nobby's prank didn't upset or faze him at all. The following day, on his England debut, Alan was our best player, and throughout the tour demonstrated skill and technique that matched his phenomenal energy and enthusiasm on the pitch.

From Yugoslavia we travelled north to Nuremburg, where a Terry Paine goal gave us a 1–0 victory over a West German side ranked number three in the world. That game I consider to have been a benchmark for me, both in my career with England and as a goalkeeper. I felt confident from the first whistle, sure of my positioning, handling, distribution and of the way I organized what was a resolute England back line of George Cohen, Ray Wilson, Jack Charlton and Bobby Moore. Those lads were outstanding and this was the game when I first realized I was becoming comfortable and familiar with their individual styles and idiosyncrasies as defenders. In short, we played as a highly effective unit. The days when England took to the pitch with a team of gifted but disparate individuals were over. Against West Germany we had shown that we had all the makings of a very good team.

We concluded what had been a very happy and successful tour with a 2–1 victory over Sweden in Gothenburg. Alan Ball, with his first goal for England, and John Connelly, were our goalscorers on a mudheap of a pitch that during the long Swedish winter doubled up as an ice rink.

Prior to the game there was a scare about Nobby Stiles. Nobby's poor eyesight was legendary in the game – not to put too fine a point on it, he is half-blind without his contact lenses. As he prepared for the match, he discovered to his horror that though he had remembered to pack his contact lenses, he had forgotten the lens lubricant. It was then that our trainer, Harold Shepherdson, demonstrated just how much attention he paid to detail by producing a small bottle of the vital fluid.

'I leave nothing to chance,' said Harold, accepting Nobby's thanks. 'In case of emergency, I make sure I have everything every player will need.'

'You didn't have a spare pair of pants for Bally though, did you?' replied Nobby.

(Denis Law tells the story of Manchester United's victory banquet after the 1968 European Cup final, which for some reason Stiles attended without his spectacles or contact lenses. When he hadn't returned after fifteen minutes from an excursion to the lavatory, Law and George Best went to look for him. They found Nobby sitting among Rotary Club diners in an adjacent room, oblivious to his mistake!)

Everyone in the England party believed we had had a very successful tour. With the World Cup just a year away, we had made great progress. The team was now beginning to have a settled look about it, and though Alf was still apt to experiment with players, he seemed happy and content with the nucleus of the side. Myself, George Cohen, Ray Wilson, Jack Charlton, Bobby Moore and Alan Ball had figured in all the tour games, while Bobby Charlton and Jimmy Greaves had been absent only owing to injury. Of the players who featured on that tour, only two, Everton's Derek Temple and Mick Jones of Sheffield United, would not be included in Alf's final squad for the 1966 World Cup.

Even without Greaves and Charlton we had remained unbeaten, scoring a memorable victory in Germany, yet surprisingly the press were still finding something to criticize. Our continued development as an international team and our good results were not enough to engender wholehearted support in the papers. Winning wasn't enough, it seemed. We had to win in style. 'Where was the class? Where was the free-flowing, fluent football that English supporters demand of their national team?' One 'old school' writer professed a lack of enthusiasm for international football. Only the domestic club game mattered. Did he keep these views to himself, I wonder, twelve months later at Wembley?

Stuart Shaw, writing in the popular football weekly *Soccer Star*, described our performances on tour as being 'as intellectual as a rocket scientist throwing paper darts'. A lesser man might have been disconcerted by such carping, but Alf Ramsey took no notice of it. On the contrary, the manner of our performances instilled in Alf the belief that his team had the makings of world champions come 1966.

I didn't enjoy the best of starts to the 1965–66 season. While playing for Leicester in a pre-season friendly against Northampton Town I went down at the feet of Town's Joe Kiernan and broke my wrist. It was accidental, but the injury put me in plaster and I missed the first nine games of the season (City's reserve keeper, George Heyes, deputized). Matt Gillies yet again proved himself to be one of the most astute managers in the First Division in signing quality players at bargain prices, when he picked up Jackie Sinclair, a skilful winger from Dunfermline, for just £25,000. Jackie was very quick and, like Mike Stringfellow, liked to come inside and look for goal. Naturally two-footed, he was happy to operate on either flank and did so to good effect during his two years at Leicester. With his boundless energy and ability to make and score goals he was very popular with City fans, but when Leicester's fortunes began to fade, he was snapped up by Newcastle United with whom he went on to win a Fairs Cup winners' medal in the Geordies' victory over Ujpest Dozsa of Hungary.

Jackie Sinclair was a favourite of the City faithful, but the other Matt Gillies signing of the summer of '65 proved even more popular. Derek Dougan is a footballing enigma. Quite simply, there has never been a player like him, nor one so forthright in their views and opinions on the game. After making a name for himself in the late fifties with Portsmouth, Blackburn Rovers and Aston Villa, Derek had dropped into the Third Division with Peterborough United. Like Trevor Ford before him, Derek had no qualms about voicing his opinions on football and its establishment figures. He was a radical and original thinker whose caustic wit and sharp brain made many a manager think twice (at least) about taking him on. The fact that he was playing his football in the Third Division was in all probability due to his reputation as a troublemaker. Managers feared the influence in the dressing room of this radical, offbeat, direct, caustic but above all honest character. Why on earth Matt Gillies signed him, I don't know. What I do know is that Derek was a stylish and formidable player who, in his time at Leicester, channelled his undoubted intelligence on to the field of play to the great benefit of the team and the constant delight of the supporters. Did I say stylish? What with his Zapata-style moustache and one of the first shaven heads in British football – a sensation at Aston Villa in the early sixties – he definitely had a style of his own.

We often hear today about players having 'cult status'. Derek Dougan was one of the originals. Many people thought his best days were behind him when he came to Filbert Street, but he was to prove them wrong. In his two years at Leicester and subsequent eight years at Wolverhampton Wanderers he was to play the best football of his career, maturing into an intelligent and unselfish striker of the highest calibre. He scored 222 League goals in a career that, in the early days certainly, had more than its share of ups and downs. He also represented Northern Ireland on forty-three occasions and would, in my opinion, have been the perfect manager for the national team. As far as I know, he was never offered the post, nor did he ever apply. Perhaps he felt that the people who ran Ulster football at the time wouldn't be comfortable with his brusque, honest style. He was certainly unafraid of confrontation. In his many hard tussles with the era's uncompromising centre halves he would always say, 'I'll see you at the far post' – a phrase that filled them with trepidation and often resulted in yet another headed goal for the Doog.

Dougan made his debut for Leicester in our 3–1 defeat at Liverpool on the opening day of the 1965–66 season, but gave ample evidence of his quality as a player. He was a windmill of a striker whose talent and swirling personality were to leave their mark not only at Leicester City but on football in general. He did a good job for us, though his views were as forthright as ever: 'I was bought cheaply,' he said, 'and in comparison with my contract at Peterborough, paid cheaply.' Not surprisingly, Derek was also a force in the Professional Footballers' Association.

The Doog was never slow when it came to offering advice to his team mates. One Friday morning our centre half Ian King received a message to report to the manager's office. In our previous match we had lost 2–0 at Nottingham Forest, a match in which Ian had not enjoyed the best of games. He was worried Matt Gillies was going to pull one of his manoeuvres, whereby he would talk to a player about his recent performances and work the conversation so that the player talked himself out of a place in the side.

'When he asks me how I played against Forest, I'll have to be honest and say "Not very well",' said Ian, 'then Matt'll say, "If you know you're not playing well, then you're out."'

The Doog told Ian not to worry.

'When the boss asks how you think you've been playing lately, bluff it out,' he advised. 'Say to Matt, "I've been great. Haven't you been watching me, boss? Forest's centre forward Frank Wignall never got a touch. I played him out of the game. I'm playing well, really well. Everybody is saying so. Why are you asking how I've been playing lately?" That way, Matt will be on the defensive. You'll plant seeds of doubt in his mind and he'll not feel justified in leaving you out of the team.'

Ian set off for Matt's office in a very positive mood, determined to bluff it out and maintain his place in the side. Sure enough, during their meeting, Matt asked Ian how he thought he had been playing of late.

'I've been great,' said Ian. 'Haven't you been watching me, boss? Frank Wignall never got a touch. I played him out of the game. I'm playing well. Really well.'

'I know,' said Matt, 'but do you think you can play much better than you have been playing lately?' (Check.)

'Yes,' replied Ian, without thinking.

'Then you're out,' said Matt. (Checkmate.)

Following my injury I returned to the Leicester team in late September for a League Cup tie at Manchester City. It was to be an unhappy return, our 3–1 defeat putting an end to our hopes at the first time of asking. (Manchester City also put an end to our FA Cup hopes that year.) Our league form was once again inconsistent. We enjoyed some memorable results, including a 5–1 win at St James's Park over in-form Newcastle United and five-goal victories over West Ham, also away from home, and Fulham. Having been beaten 5–0 at home by Manchester United, we then went and won 2–1 at Old Trafford, a series of results that summed up perfectly our topsy-turvy season. We played well in fits and starts, but all too often flattered to deceive. In the end our final league placing of seventh was respectable enough, but the overall feeling among the Leicester players was that it should have been better. Matt Gillies had added to our ranks full back Peter Rodrigues, a £45,000 signing from Cardiff City, and the club's youth policy also saw David Nish and Rodney Fern elevated to the first team, but the consistency (both in performance and team selection) was never there.

Against Manchester United we had a strange record over the years, especially at home. We seemed to play really well against United, only to suffer defeat. In 1964–65 we played United off the park at Filbert Street but had to be satisfied with a 2–2 draw. And when the two sides met at Filbert Street in 1965–66, we were the only team in it, yet we lost 5–0. Rarely has a team had so much possession and besieged the opposition's goal for so long only to incur a heavy defeat. Our tally of thirty-six corners and twenty-four shots on goal is an indication of just how much pressure we put on United that day. We hit the woodwork three times without finding the net. United had five efforts at goal and scored from every one! We started the game in much the same way as we were to continue, piling the pressure on the United defence. Yet suddenly we found ourselves 2–0 down; first, from Best's centre, the United centre forward David Herd rose to head the ball past me and into the net. Ten minutes later, following another sustained period of pressure from us, there was a repetition. Best again broke free on the left and Herd raced into the penalty area to meet his cross and plant a firm header past me. I had touched the ball three times in the match and on two of those occasions it was to pick it out of the net. What United gave us, of course, was a lesson in finishing. Our mistakes were severely punished, but we didn't capitalize on theirs.

The margin of error in top-flight football is very small and nowhere more so than in goalkeeping. Unlike outfield players, a single error of judgement on a goalkeeper's part almost invariably leads to a goal conceded. That is why I worked constantly at my game. I had established myself as a First Division goalkeeper and as England's number one, but I never stopped practising and developing my craft as a goalkeeper, particularly my positional sense and anticipation.

While on international duty I had noticed a marked difference between British and foreign goalkeeping styles. The British keepers tended to be physically strong and dominated the whole of their penalty box. As I have described earlier, I had become very technically minded, whereas the continental goalkeepers I came across tended to stay on their own line more and rely on agility and reflexes. My style was to organize my defence so that I didn't have to make a save at all. When a shot did come in I hoped that my positioning would make it easy to save, thus minimizing the chance of a mistake.

Yet crowds love the spectacular save while quietly taking for granted the efficient work that results from correct positioning. A prime example of this came in the England–Poland game played at Goodison Park in January 1966. During the first half Roger Hunt turned his marker, then hit a dipping shot towards the centre of goal. The Polish goalkeeper, Szeja, jumped up and with one hand tipped the ball over the bar. The Goodison Park crowd, appreciative of Szeja's acrobatic effort, gave him generous applause. Minutes later I was involved in a similar situation when the Polish forward, Sadek, tried his luck from similar distance. Having anticipated Sadek's effort and got into position, I simply jumped and plucked the ball from under the crossbar. With the ball safely clutched to my chest there was almost silence throughout the ground. The Pole, in his flamboyance, had conceded a corner, whereas I had made what looked like a routine save – and retained possession.

Yes, goalkeeping can be a thankless task. But the fact that at times the fans might not have appreciated what I was trying to do never bothered me. Thankfully, though, one man did: Alf Ramsey.

I was relieved to finish the 1965–66 league season without picking up an injury. I gave nothing less than 100 per cent effort and application during the run-in, but the impending World Cup was always at the back of my mind. Leicester finished the season on a high note, beating West Ham United 2–1 in a highly entertaining game at Filbert Street. In the West Ham team that day was Bobby Moore, whom I was expecting to play alongside in the World Cup. Geoff Hurst and Martin Peters were also in that Hammers team. Geoff then had only a handful of England caps and Martin was thought of as a squad player, albeit one with considerable potential. Little did I realize the crucial roles both were about to play in the destiny of the World Cup.

In April of that year Geoff had won only his second cap, against Scotland in a cracking Home International match. We'd prepared for the Scotland match by training at Somerset Park, home of Ayr United, while staying at a nearby hotel. On the morning of the match I was given a foretaste of what was to come when bidding farewell to one of the hotel porters. He had been attentive and helpful throughout our stay and good value for the five-bob tip I'd given him.

'Thanks for everything. Enjoy the game,' I said.

'Awa'n boil ye heid! I hope we pulverize ye!' he replied, adding in the most polite of voices, 'Oh, 'n' thank ye for the gratuity, Mr Banks.'

Though there was still an hour and a half to go before kick-off, the roads leading to Hampden Park were a seething mass of tartan-clad humanity. As the England team bus made its painfully slow progress towards the ground, some just leered at us, many jeered but a good proportion hurled insults and crashed their fists against the side of the bus. John Connelly was beginning to feel very uneasy but Bobby Moore allayed his fears.

'Don't worry about it,' Bobby told him, 'it's just the traditional Clydeside shipbuilders' welcome for the England team.'

In the sixties shipbuilding still dominated life in Glasgow. The shipyards, open to the sky, began at Greenock, from where they embraced the Clyde for miles. I can still hear the evocative sound of the Clyde at full tempo: an army of hammers echoing in the empty bellies of hulls, the fiendish chatter of riveters at work, the sudden squeal of metal tortured in a spray of bonfire-night sparks that died of cold as they fell. Ships could be seen lolling in cradles from Greenock to the very heart of Glasgow. Some were just keels, like whale skeletons; others, gaunt hulls of rusty red smeared with rectangles of airforce-blue paint. I saw vast oil tankers, seemingly miles long, almost ready for the bottle of champagne and then years in the Persian Gulf ahead of them. These were the shipyards of Billy Connolly and the labour activist Jimmy Reid, boiler-suit blue and testosterone driven. Come half five of an afternoon, out would spew the cloth-capped sprinters racing for the idling crocodile of Corporation buses.

As we probed our way towards Hampden it appeared as if all those Clydeside shipyard workers were on their way to the match, as well as a good many from Glasgow's other artisans. They numbered in excess of 135,000 and at no time did I spot the friendly face of an England supporter.

Few grounds in the world could match Hampden for atmosphere and fanatical support on the day of a big game. The din of fists on the side of our bus matched the din of those shipyards – hammer, hammer, thump, an incessant racket that could unnerve even the strongest of constitutions. As the faces jumped up at the windows the invective continued.

'We'll dee ye sassenachs the day! We'll have ye heids!'

Anglo-Scottish encounters would be eagerly anticipated by the players, too. With a Scots manager, there tended to be six or seven exiles in the Leicester first team squad at one time. For

England to lose would doom me to a whole season of merciless chaffing and ribbing from these exultant Scots. It wasn't always friendly banter, either. On one occasion, during a five-a-side match Jimmy Walsh and I riled each other so much that we actually squared up; Ian King and Davie Gibson had to step in and separate us. Our behaviour was out of character, but it shows just how high emotions ran among English and Scottish players prior to a meeting of the 'auld enemies'.

The players were fervent, but the supporters verged on the rabid. As we disembarked from our team bus, fists were brandished and cans and bottles touted as we ran a gauntlet of abuse to the players' entrance.

'Ganna de ye lot the day, no mistakin', ye shandy-swiggin' southern bigheids!'

And that was from the commissionaire on the door.

'Are they always like this?' Geoff Hurst asked.

'No,' I told him, 'come kick off, they get all worked up.'

When the teams walked out on to the pitch at Hampden, the noise descending from the heaving terraces was deafening: 135,000 tartan-clad souls not only made the welkin ring with one collective tumultuous roar, they appeared to crack it from east to west. After the official presentations I took off, cap in hand, to one of the goals for the pre-match kickabout. It was like being greeted by tens of thousands of irate geese, such was the incessant hissing resounding all around me. When the game kicked off the din somehow became louder than ever. Denis Law played the ball back to Billy Bremner. Billy played it forward to Jimmy Johnstone and when Jimmy made a darting run deep into the England half of the field, approval thundered down from the terraces like some Alpine avalanche.

Alf Ramsey had opted for a 4–3–3 formation for this game, though he would later modify this to 4–4–2 for the World Cup. In front of me was a back line of George Cohen, Jack Charlton, Bobby Moore and Keith Newton. The three-man midfield comprised Nobby Stiles, Bobby Charlton and John Connelly with Alan Ball, Roger Hunt and Geoff Hurst in attack.

Once we had repelled the Scots' initial onslaught the game settled down. Liverpool's Roger Hunt worked tirelessly, making angled runs that pulled the Scottish defence all over the park and created space for Bobby Charlton and John Connelly to exploit.

The Hampden pitch was pretty devoid of grass after a season of constant use (unlike Wembley). Hampden was the home of Queen's Park, who had the twin distinctions of being the only senior club in the UK to retain pure amateur status as well as being Scotland's oldest football club, founded in 1867. I often used to wonder who on earth they played against? (That sort of question has always intrigued me. I once read that Baker Street was the first ever station on the London Underground. I thought, What was the point of opening just one? Where could you go?) In fact, during their formative years Queen's Park played against English teams and actually competed in the FA Cup, reaching the final twice, in 1884 and 1885, losing to Blackburn Rovers on both occasions. Queen's Park's average gate at Hampden Park in the sixties was around 1,000. Hampden Park on the occasion of a Scotland–England game was a sight to behold, but I often wondered what it was like to play for Queen's Park in that cavernous stadium with its Alp-like terracing when it was all but empty. The voices of the players must have echoed eerily around the fine old stadium. There must have been more atmosphere on the moon. Now it was packed to the gunwales with 130 times that number.

Hampden roared as Jim Baxter fed the ball to Willie Wallace some twenty yards from my goal. The Hearts centre forward took the ball on for a few yards before hitting a thunderous low drive, the sheer pace of which took me by surprise. Having thrown myself to the ground, I managed to gather the ball into my chest at the second attempt. As I lay there spitting the dust and grime from my mouth I noticed a pair of boots and blue stockinged legs inches from my face. I looked up to see Denis Law, his hands grasping the white cuffs of his shirtsleeves and a menacing smile on his face.

'And I'll be here every time. Be sure of that Gordon, son,' he said, displaying his Cheshire Cat grin to the full. I knew Denis was playing mind games in the hope of putting a bit more pressure on me, but I also knew he would be true to his word. Should I ever slip up and spill the ball, he would be there to plant it in the back of the net.

Pressure never affected me, only helped me concentrate. The bigger the occasion, the more at stake, the more I liked it and, it seemed, the better I played. As Alf Ramsey once told me, 'Thrive on pressure, Gordon. You get no juice out of an orange until you squeeze it.'

Though playing only his second game for England, Geoff Hurst was already showing the prowess he would go on to achieve in international football. He exuded confidence. Whenever Bobby Charlton was on the ball, Geoff was screaming for it to be played to him. Any striker wants the ball played in early – the earlier the better. Bobby was just the man for the job. After about fifteen minutes of frantic play Bobby played the ball into Geoff some twenty-five yards from the Scottish goal. Before the Scots could close him down, Geoff let fly and the ball sailed past the flailing arms of the Scottish keeper Bobby Ferguson. When the ball ballooned the net I had a good idea what it would be like to play at Hampden for Queen's Park. There was almost total silence. Though some eighty yards from Bobby Charlton, I heard him scream, 'It's there!' His voice was as piercing as that of a pub singer in Westminster Abbey.

Roger Hunt scored a second to put us in the driving seat, but this was Scotland against England and even though two goals adrift, the Scots would fight to the death. Roger added to his tally but Denis Law made good his promise, opening the account from the home side. Bobby Charlton once again put some daylight between the two sides when scoring with a typical guided missile, but still the Scots wouldn't roll over. Celtic's Jimmy Johnstone put them right back on track with a fine opportunist goal and in the final stages reduced the Scottish deficit even further. I thought I had all my angles and my positioning correct as Jimmy corkscrewed his way past Keith Newton and Jack Charlton, but Jimmy simply glanced up, saw where I was and with great deliberation sliced across the ball with the top of his boot. The ball curled away from me only to return to its original line of trajectory and into the far corner of the net. I wouldn't have thought it possible for any player under such pressure, running at speed and with only a marginal view of the goal, if any, to have scored like that. Yet Jimmy Johnstone did. It was a great goal from a player blessed with an abundance of natural skill.

With the deficit reduced to 4–3 and roared on by the massed ranks of their supporters, Scotland laid siege. With only a minute of the game remaining my heart skipped a beat when Jimmy Johnstone, who had given Keith Newton a torrid afternoon with his jinking runs, turned Keith yet again and set up Willie Wallace, whose forehead smacked the ball wide of my left arm and goal-ward. The sardine-packed terracing took to its toes. I feared the worst but there was the diminutive form of Nobby Stiles stretching up into the air as far as his limbs would allow to head the ball off the line.

'Goa-ohhhhhhhhhh!' moaned 135,000 voices in unison.

Nobby saved the day for England. What's more, his last-minute clearance off the line had saved every English player from a year of merciless ribbing from Scottish club mates. I could have hugged him for that alone.

The shrill of the referee's whistle sounded the end of hostilities. It was my first senior success at international level over the Scots in four attempts, as it was Alf Ramsey's. The Scottish bubble had been pricked and the Hampden bogey, where England had not won since 1958, had been laid. The close understanding between Bobby Charlton and Geoff Hurst was remarkable in what was

only their second game together. Jimmy Greaves had missed
the game through injury, and his return could only strengthen
our hand.

The victory also demonstrated to Alf Ramsey that England
had strength in depth and good, workable options. The character
and application we had shown in winning against what was a
very good Scotland team, galvanized the squad and reinforced
our conviction that we would be a force to reckon with in
the World Cup. Alf liked his players to show mettle and to
demonstrate that they would not be intimidated by even the
most hostile of receptions. Scotland in full cry in that atmosphere
at Hampden was a severe test of our credentials as an international
side, and we had passed it, if not quite with flying colours, then
certainly with distinction.

There were two things that Alf would not tolerate in his players:
indiscipline and complacency. Anyone who didn't toe the line
found himself out on his ear. I'd hardly call myself a rebel – in
fact I was always totally committed – but even I was to receive a
disciplinary warning shot across the bows on occasion in 1964.

It was just before the party left England for a game against
Portugal in Lisbon. The game was scheduled for 17 May, little
over a week after a long and strenuous domestic programme.
The England team had assembled immediately after the last
league game of the season at our usual hotel in Lancaster Gate.
We had a couple of days to kill before leaving for Portugal, and
many of us were champing at the bit, but Alf's rules didn't permit
us to step out of the hotel of an evening. I had resigned myself
to another night cooped up in my room reading newspapers or
a book, when Jimmy Greaves and Bobby Moore knocked on
my door. Jimmy said that he and Bobby and a few of the other
lads were going for a quick pint. Did I fancy joining them? I
didn't need asking twice.

Our little group consisted of Jimmy, Bobby, Johnny Byrne,
George Eastham, Ray Wilson, Bobby Charlton and me. Jimmy

had convinced us that there'd be no harm in going out for just a couple of pints. He knew a quiet pub just along the road and that's where we headed. Of course we were recognized immediately we walked through the door, but no one ever bothered us, nor thought to tip off the press. In those days the press didn't camp on our doorsteps round the clock (they only sent a single reporter to cover matches), so we felt confident our little jaunt would go unreported. Besides, no one thought the sight of England players out for a quiet drink was anything out of the ordinary, or newsworthy.

Last orders were called, by which time we'd had a couple of pints, with Bobby Moore and I each buying a round. Jimmy G, however, was adamant that he couldn't go out for drink and not do the honours. He knew 'a little club just down the road'. We fell into line behind Jimmy and soon found ourselves in a quiet corner of a cosy little den where we could continue our evening in conviviality. So enjoyable was it, in fact, that we lost track of the time. It was past one in the morning when the seven of us sheepishly slipped away to our respective rooms, thinking we'd got away with it.

On entering my room I switched on the light and immediately knew I was in trouble with the boss. There, on my pillow, was my passport. (When he joined the England squad every player handed his passport to Alf for safe keeping.) He'd obviously found out about our little escapade and the passport on the pillow was a message to me that my place on the trip to Portugal was far from assured. I was still gathering my thoughts when the door opened and in walked the others, all with passports in hand.

The following morning at breakfast, Alf said nothing about the incident. In fact he didn't mention it until after our final training session in Lisbon. As the session came to an end Alf said, 'I believe there are seven among you who would like to remain behind for a chat with me. Is there not?

'If I had enough players here with me, not one of you would be getting a shirt against Portugal,' Alf said sternly. 'Consider this a warning shot across the bows. I will not tolerate the sort of thing that happened in London before we left. You are here to do a job – for your country – and so am I. Thank you gentlemen. I look forward to the game against Portugal in the knowledge that what happened the other night will never be repeated.'

We needed no further warning. It was quite clear that our international careers would be finished should we overstep the mark again. Happily, we achieved a notable 4–3 win against the Portuguese, with a hat trick from Johnny Byrne and a goal from Bobby Charlton. Though I had conceded three goals, I saved what to my mind would have been another two and came off the pitch feeling satisfied with my performance. Perhaps I had gone some way to redeeming myself? Alf, however, thought differently. He dropped me for the next game against the Republic of Ireland.

Along with ill-discipline, Alf Ramsey's great bugbear was players who took their place in the side for granted. I was never that complacent, yet Alf never missed an opportunity to ensure that it stayed that way. Following one game I was leaving our hotel to start my journey home to Leicester when I saw him in the car park. 'See you Alf,' I said, waving goodbye. Alf nailed me with a cold piercing stare. 'Will you?' he said.

It is well known that Alf had taken elocution lessons. I don't know why. Perhaps he felt that a plummy accent would help his cause when his name was being bandied about for the England job among the many Old Etonians on the FA. Alf was the sort of manager who knew he could never be 'one of the lads', and his accent helped to distance himself from the players. He had a brilliant footballing mind, though, was totally dedicated, occasionally taciturn, yet often witty and warm. His record as England manager speaks for itself. Of the 113 games he took charge of, England lost only 17. At times he appeared cold and distant, yet I know of no one who played under him who doesn't have great affection for Alf Ramsey, the quintessential 'player's man'.

At times Alf appeared to be at pains to play down his humble background, although he wasn't ashamed of his roots, and certainly no snob. Perhaps he felt the need to be on his guard in the company of FA officials who might look down their noses at his Essex upbringing. His father had a smallholding in Dagenham in the 1920s from which he sold hay and straw to dairies and the various companies which still delivered by horse and cart. Alf's first job was as a delivery boy for Dagenham Co-op in 1935, a job he held until he was called up for National Service.

It was during his time in the army that he first played for Southampton, the club he joined as a full back when his service days were over. In 1949 he was transferred to Spurs for what was then a record fee for a full back of £21,000. He won thirty-two caps for England and was a key member of the Spurs 'push-and-run' side that won the League Championship in 1952 under Arthur Rowe. Though he had only an elementary education at school, he was intelligent and an avid reader. Though his attempts to appear better read than he actually was sometimes misfired.

Jimmy Greaves came from a similar east London background, but enjoyed a more fruitful education and was, in fact, the head boy of his school. On leaving school Jimmy worked for the *Sunday Times* only for Chelsea to step in and give him his chance in football.

Following an England training session prior to a game against Hungary at Wembley, the players were discussing with Alf who was the best club chairman. Jimmy hadn't said much, so Alf asked him if he had any thoughts on the matter.

'Not really,' said Jimmy, 'there's small choice in rotten apples.'

'I'm surprised that you, of all people, Jimmy, haven't anything more worthwhile to say on the subject,' said Alf. 'The English language is the most descriptive of all. Surely you can think of something more imaginative than, "There's small choice in rotten apples." English is the language of Shakespeare.'

'That is Shakespeare,' said Jimmy, much to Alf's embarrassment.

Alf was proud to be English, as we all were. He had an enormous influence on me as a player and as a man, and I can pay him no higher compliment than that. When he died of a stroke in 1999, Lady Ramsey went in person to the Ipswich Registry of Births, Marriages and Deaths to complete the solemn task of officialdom. The death certificate gave his occupation as, 'Knight of the Realm, England Football Manager (Retired)'. To that I would have added, 'Gentleman, friend to all his players, and the only England manager to have won the World Cup.'

Prior to the World Cup commencing in July 1966, England set off on a short tour of northern Europe. We began in Helsinki with a 3–0 victory over Finland, a scoreline that did not reflect the degree to which we outclassed the Finns. Alf used this game to give a run-out to a number of squad players, such as the experienced Jimmy Armfield, Leeds United's Norman Hunter, Ian Callaghan of Liverpool and a young, lithe, left-sided midfield player from West Ham, Martin Peters.

Alf saw the tour as a means of fine-tuning the side and giving every player in the twenty-two-man squad a final opportunity to show what he was capable of at international level. Alf rested me for the next two matches – a 6–1 victory over Norway in which Jimmy Greaves scored four, followed by a hard-fought 2–0 win over Denmark – opting for first Ron Springett of Sheffield Wednesday, then Chelsea's Peter Bonetti. I returned for our final game in Katowice against Poland. When we disembarked from our plane we saw at first hand what life was like behind the Iron Curtain. Even in the month of July Katowice appeared grey and foreboding, the city skyline was drab in the extreme, a mishmash of charcoal grey blocks of flats, chemical works and coalmine winding gear. The people looked very poor and what few cars we saw seemed to belong to another age. Jimmy Greaves surveyed the sight, turned to Alf and said, 'OK, Alf, you've made your point. Now let's get back on the plane and bugger off home.'

Alf continued with Martin Peters for the game against Poland, but his inclusion was the only one that surprised the press. The team that took to the pitch against the Poles, Peters apart, was the one the media expected to open our World Cup campaign. Once again, Martin Peters gave Alf much food for thought. Playing in a 4–3–3 formation, Martin ghosted about the pitch creating space not only for others, but for himself. Martin impressed me with his great sense of positioning and vision, the more so since he was only twenty-two years of age. A well-drilled shot from Roger Hunt gave us a 1–0 victory over Poland and brought the curtain down on a tour in which we had remained unbeaten. Since our participation in the 'Little World Cup' in Brazil, we had now played twenty-one internationals and lost only one (against Austria, a match I had missed through injury). The spirit and confidence in the England camp were sky high, prompting Alf to repeat to the press a statement he had expressed some months earlier – that England would win the World Cup.

Our World Cup preparations had gone extremely well, but the build-up to the tournament in England began with sensation, then farce. The World Cup itself, the Jules Rimet Trophy, had been on display at, of all places, a Stanley Gibbons stamp exhibition at the Central Hall in Westminster. One morning security staff approached the glass case in which the trophy was displayed and were dumbstruck to find it had been stolen. Shock waves reverberated around not only England, but the world. The theft of the World Cup was a huge embarrassment to the Football Association and to the whole country. The police immediately launched a nationwide investigation. Ports and air-ports were closed for a time as the search for the World Cup began. The story was headline news every day and, despite apparently leaving no stone unturned, the police could uncover neither clue nor motive.

A week after the event a Londoner named Dave Corbett was walking his dog, Pickles, around Norwood in south London when the dog disappeared into the front garden of a house and began digging at the base of a hedge. Pickles uncovered a newspaper-wrapped parcel and when his owner went to investigate he was astounded to find the parcel contained the stolen World Cup.

I can only imagine the relief that swept through the corridors of the Football Association and, indeed, Scotland Yard. The recovery of the Jules Rimet Trophy made even bigger headlines and the cartoonists of the time had a field day – especially in the *News of the World*, the newspaper in which the stolen World Cup had been wrapped. Not surprisingly, one of their cartoons featured Pickles unearthing the package with a caption that read, 'The dog that knows which newspaper sniffs out the top story.'

A man was subsequently arrested and charged with the theft of the gold statuette. Apparently he had demanded a ransom from the FA for its safe return. He was given a custodial sentence, though many people believed there were others involved who had not been brought to book. To this day the affair remains a mystery. It was not to be the last time that the Jules Rimet Trophy was to find its way into the hands of someone other than the captain of a victorious international team, but that's a story for later.

The '66 Tournament was the first World Cup fully to exploit its commercial potential. It was also the first to enjoy blanket live TV coverage worldwide, and this played a key role in the unprecedented commercial success of the competition. The tournament adopted a corporate logo: World Cup Willie, a cartoon lion kitted out in a Union Jack shirt and white shorts. Willie appeared on every conceivable product from badges, sports bags, T-shirts and pennants to cereal boxes, ashtrays, soft-drink cans and cuddly toys. He even released a singalong novelty record (helped by Lonnie Donegan), the opening lines being, 'Dressed in red and white and blue, it's World Cup Willie, we all know he's true, World Cup Willie'. The 'World Cup Willie' record received a lot of radio airplay but was only a minor hit, although, curiously, it sold very well in Japan – for the simple reason, according to Jimmy Greaves, that the disc itself fitted Tokyo's parking meters.

The choice of Lonnie Donegan to sing the first official World Cup song was, at the time, an odd one. Lonnie Donegan had been a big star in the late fifties, enjoying a string of top-ten hits in his skiffle style. Lonnie, however, hadn't had a hit since 1962 and in 1966 his style of music seemed to belong to another era. In pop music the Beatles ruled supreme, and the charts were dominated by groups such as the Rolling Stones, Troggs, Yard-birds, Animals, Kinks, Small Faces and Hollies, from Britain alone. The only UK solo performers to chart regularly were Cilla Black, Tom Jones and Georgie Fame and I couldn't imagine any of them singing 'World Cup Willie'. So the official World Cup song, aimed at young teenagers, was sung by someone youngsters perceived to be of their parents' generation. So while everyone could sing the song, it wasn't hip to buy the record.

The marketing people learned an important lesson from the 'Willie' experience. In future, if they couldn't get a current top pop star to record a football song, they went for the team, a ploy that was effected with some success until 1990, when New Order bit the bullet and recorded 'World In Motion' as England's official World Cup song for Italia '90.

In many ways the marketing of the 1966 World Cup set the scene for what was to come. The days of people counting out their coppers and asking for a pie would soon be committed to history as supporters dug deep to buy anything and everything from World Cup Willie duffel bags to jumpers and jerkins. The strangest souvenir I can recall was marketed by Daniel Schuster's Football Souvenirs of Sutton, Surrey. Schuster's produced a glass wellington boot with World Cup Willie on the front, marketed as 'a real souvenir for your mantelshelf'. This five-inch-high glass wellie was supposedly a liqueur glass. It appeared that the imagination of those who made and sold World Cup souvenirs under licence knew no bounds.

The very phrase 'for your mantelshelf' is suggestive of another era, seemingly an anachronism in this period of 'G' plan furniture, central heating and the emergence of Terence Conran's Habitat. While we rightly see the sixties as a decade of radical innovation, we tend to forget that, for every person swept along by the tidal wave of change in popular culture and new social opportunity, there were many who lived lives of modest expectation, whose lifestyle and homes had changed little since the fifties. In an era when domestic consumerism really took off, the material desires of many people were held in check by low wages and, as such, didn't extend much beyond a real souvenir for their mantelshelf – still the centrepiece of their living rooms.

In 2002 some thirty-two nations contested the World Cup finals in South Korea and Japan. In 1966 there were just sixteen, divided into four groups of four. The group winners and runners-up proceeded to the quarter-finals, which were played, as now, on a straight knock-out basis, followed by the semi-finals, the play-off for third and fourth place and then the final itself. England kicked off the tournament on 11 July and in less than three weeks, on 30 July, it was all over. They didn't drag it out in those days: thirty-two matches concentrated into twenty days around which television had to fit their schedules. Television was playing an increasingly important role in spreading the gospel of football, but football's governing bodies were still very much in charge of the game and beholden to no one.

The tournament took place in four zones throughout the country and eight grounds were used. The south-east zone used Wembley and, for just one game, France versus Uruguay, White City. The White City stadium was a strange choice as a World Cup venue, given that London boasted White Hart Lane and Highbury, two of the best stadiums in England at the time, as well as the cavernous Stamford Bridge.

White City was known more as a greyhound stadium than a football ground, but its inclusion had much to do with its ability to offer covered accommodation for 50,000 in a capacity of 60,000. Much of Highbury's ample terracing was open to the elements, as were the paddocks on the lower tiers of the East and West stands at White Hart Lane. Today, alongside the A40 Westway flyover where the White City Stadium once stood, there are now houses and offices offering covered accommodation for all.

The Group Two matches took place at Hillsborough and Villa Park, Group Three at Goodison Park and Old Trafford, while Group Four was staged at Roker Park, Sunderland, and Ayresome Park, Middlesbrough.

Few grounds met FIFA's minimum requirements for seating, so clubs such as Sunderland, Middlesbrough and Aston Villa had to install temporary grandstands, though grand is hardly the right word for what was actually put in. At Roker Park and Ayresome Park, for example, low rows of benches were placed on the terracing where the crush barriers that were already in place restricted the view of the pitch for many supporters.

England matches, prime games such as the semi-finals and those involving Brazil apart, attendances for the 1966 World Cup were decent rather than staggering. Many matches were played in front of crowds that were well below capacity, for two basic reasons. First, the price of admission was nearly three times that of Football League games. For example, the minimum admission price for children was 7s. 6d. (37½p), whereas they were used to paying only 2s. 6d. (12½p) to follow their clubs. This prevented many from attending games, or made them selective about which matches they did attend. The second reason was that many games took place at the same time. If an attractive game was on television, what was the point of going along to their local ground and pay to see a less interesting match? For example, only 24,000 turned up at Old Trafford to see Hungary against Bulgaria when England's game against France was broadcast live on TV. Attendances at Old Trafford in particular suffered from this conflict of interest, the highest attendance of the three games staged there being 29,886 for the game between much-fancied Portugal and dark horses, Hungary.

Disappointing attendances occurred especially when England played. On the afternoon of our quarter-final against Argentina, West Germany played Uruguay at Hillsborough, Portugal, North Korea at Goodison Park and Russia took on Hungary at Roker Park. Whereas we played in front of a full house at Wembley, 40,000 turned up at Hillsborough and 42,000 at Goodison Park. Healthy crowds in themselves, but below capacity for both those two stadiums. The telling difference was at Roker Park where only 22,103 turned up to see Russia dispense with Hungary. The English public loved the World Cup but, for a good proportion, their love of cosmopolitan football did not outweigh their love of watching England.

The draw of the host nation live on television, and its adverse effect on the attendances at other games, was a lesson FIFA learned during 1966. In subsequent World Cups, not only did matches involving the host nation not clash with other group games, all group matches were to be given staggered kick-off times. The structure of the World Cup finals would never be the same after '66 when the power of television was seen for the first time.

England not only had home advantage, but had been drawn in Group One and all our games were to be played at Wembley. Alf had originally picked a squad of forty players that, three weeks prior to the tournament, had been pared down to twenty-two. The eighteen players unlucky to miss out on the finals were goalkeepers Tony Waiters (Blackpool) and Gordon West (Everton); full backs Chris Lawler (Liverpool), Paul Reaney (Leeds United) and Keith Newton (Blackburn Rovers); half backs Marvin Hinton and John Hollins (both Chelsea) and Gordon Milne (Liverpool); forwards Joe Baker (Nottingham Forest), Barry Bridges (Chelsea), Gordon Harris (Burnley), John Kaye (West Bromwich Albion), Peter Osgood (Chelsea), Fred Pickering (Everton), Peter Thompson and Tommy Smith (Liverpool

– yes, Tommy was a forward in those days), Derek Temple (Everton) and Terry Venables (Chelsea).

The final twenty-two comprised myself and two other goal-keepers, Ron Springett (Sheffield Wednesday) and Peter Bonetti (Chelsea); full backs Jimmy Armfield (Blackpool), Gerry Byrne (Liverpool), George Cohen (Fulham) and Ray Wilson (Everton); half backs Jack Charlton and Norman Hunter (both Leeds United), Ron Flowers (Wolverhampton Wanderers), Bobby Moore and Martin Peters (both West Ham United) and Nobby Stiles (Manchester United); forwards Alan Ball (Blackpool), Ian Callaghan (Liverpool), Bobby Charlton and John Connelly (both Manchester United), George Eastham (Arsenal), Jimmy Greaves (Tottenham Hotspur), Roger Hunt (Liverpool), Geoff Hurst (West Ham United) and Terry Paine (Southampton).

Alf's backroom staff was tiny compared with that in attendance for England games today. Apart from Alf himself, it comprised trainer Harold Shepherdson (Middlesbrough), the assistant trainer, Les Cocker (Leeds United), who also acted as our physio, and Wilf McGuinness (Manchester United), who helped Alf with the coaching. That was it, four people in total, though we did enjoy the services of a doctor for the duration of the tournament. (Don't knock the doc – he managed to get himself on the official photograph of the final squad, and not on the end of the back row either. Dr Bass was pictured wearing an England tracksuit and seated left of centre, between Alf and Jimmy Arm-field, with Alan Ball, Ian Callaghan and Nobby Stiles sitting on the ground at his feet!)

I felt Alf's final twenty-two was as strong as it could be. With all due respect to those players who had just missed out, I don't think there was anyone missing from the squad that could have added greatly to it. Alf got it right and not for the first or last time.

Alf was confident we could go on and win the World Cup, though doubts were expressed not only by certain members of the press, but a number of people in football. The Scotland manager of the time, John Prentice was on record as saying, 'England won't win'. The Leeds manager, Don Revie, sat on the fence: 'England can take the trophy, but I would not say they will win it.' Matt Busby of Manchester United was similarly non-committal: 'Certainly Alf Ramsey knows what he is aiming for and England could do well . . . but unless England find that attacking flair, I am afraid they will have to struggle to get through to the final and win.'

The Celtic manager, Jock Stein, was a little more positive in his assessment of our chances, saying, 'So much depends on . . . luck and the run of the ball. Given both these things, England could do really well.' But one of my boyhood heroes, the former Manchester City goalkeeper Bert Trautmann, who was then general manager at Stockport County, gave us little chance. Some thought we lacked sufficient players of world class to go all the way to the final and win it.

The press were no more encouraging. The *Daily Sketch* was typical, saying, 'We wish Alf and the boys all the luck in the world. If we are to even reach the heady heights of the semi-finals, they will need it,' while Robert Page writing in the *Soccer Star* said, 'England for the quarter-finals, the semi-finals at a pinch. But no further I'm afraid. It will be a Brazil–West Germany final.'

Alf Ramsey believed we could win it and had publicly said so, as had Bobby Charlton and Jimmy Greaves. I certainly believed we could win the World Cup, as did all twenty-two members of the squad. As a nation, though, England certainly did not expect.

No opening ceremony of any great sporting occasion could have been better stage-managed than the opening of the World Cup at Wembley on 11 July 1966. The weather was perfect: blue skies and a warm sunny evening. A cosmopolitan crowd packed the stadium and Her Majesty the Queen was in attendance along with the Duke of Edinburgh. The football world waited with bated breath for the commencement of what had been dubbed the first modern World Cup tournament. There was a great sense of anticipation and hopes were high for a feast of cavalier football. The opening ceremony began at 6.30 p.m. as Wembley thrilled to the massed bands of the Guards. Across the planet, 500 million people, the world's largest television audience, watched. In the wake of the massed bands of the Guards, youngsters paraded the flags of all the competing nations. Twenty-two boys – no girls, note – represented each nation and wore the strip of their designated country.

Once the parade massed on the pitch, the Queen, accompanied by the Duke of Edinburgh, emerged to be greeted by a roar audible from inside the England dressing room. Sir Stanley Rous, president of FIFA, welcomed Her Majesty and called upon her officially to open the tournament. That duty done, there was a fanfare of trumpets, the signal for us to emerge from the tunnel alongside our opponents, Uruguay. We walked out into the warm air of a July evening to be greeted by a tempestuous roar from the terraces.

We were fit and raring to go. Never had our spirit been higher, but the first ten minutes after Bobby Charlton had got the game under way were nightmarish. I stood unemployed in my penalty box watching players flitting eerily about the pitch. When Bobby kicked off, the atmosphere had been electric, but after only fifteen minutes I sensed that the game was going to be a damp squib and prove almost too much for the nerves of my team mates.

I think it's fair to say that, man for man, the Uruguayan players possessed superior technique. They had an outstanding striker in Penarol's Pedro Rocha, but the negative tactics they employed sent the carnival atmosphere of the opening ceremony evaporating fast into the cooling London night. The Uruguayans were setting the pattern some of us feared might dominate the tournament. They became a cloying cobweb of shifting pale blue shirts, hell-bent on suffocation rather than inspiration. I reckon that throughout the first half I must have touched the ball no more than half a dozen times, more often than not, simply to field a wayward through ball. Riveting stuff it was not.

We tried – Lord knows how we tried – but we just couldn't find a way through Uruguay's blanket defence. Jimmy Greaves fizzed a shot inches wide of the post. Bobby Charlton hit a sumptuous volley into a thicket of legs, but that was about as near as we came to breaking the stalemate. During the last ten minutes the crowd that had roared us on to the pitch began to boo Uruguay for their delaying tactics. Their goalkeeper, Ladislao Makurkievicz, at one point actually threw the ball off the pitch when a ball boy was trying to throw it on!

When the final whistle sounded, the Hungarian referee Istvan Zsolt signalled an end to play with an almost apologetic spread of his hands. On hearing the whistle blow, Jack Charlton, Alan Ball and George Cohen simply turned and ran towards the tunnel as if wanting to put it all behind them as quickly as possible. At least we hadn't lost, and I had kept a clean sheet (no great achievement, given that I'd been a virtual spectator throughout), but I left the pitch feeling very deflated. The Uruguayans on the other hand were ecstatic and ran around hugging each other as if the World Cup had already been won. The Wembley crowd let them know what they thought of their spoiling tactics, however, and I walked up the tunnel back into our dressing room with the sound of jeers ringing in my ears. What a start!

Elsewhere in the first round of group matches, the goals everyone had been hoping for flowed. West Germany posted their intent with a 5–0 victory over Switzerland. Two of Germany's goals were scored by a 19-year-old who stole all the headlines that day for his assured performance against the Swiss. It was the first time that the vast majority of us had ever heard the name Franz Beckenbauer. Brazil too got off to a flyer. Goals from Pelé and Garrincha gave them a 2–0 victory over Bulgaria in front of a crowd of over 47,000 at Goodison Park. Both

Brazilian goals came from trademark 'banana' free kicks but a superb match was marred by the rough treatment meted out to Pelé. He was man-marked, at times ruthlessly, by Bulgaria's Peter Zhechev and picked up an injury that put him out of Brazil's next game against Hungary. In Group Four Russia gave ample evidence that they too would be a force to be reckoned with, beating North Korea 3–0 at Ayresome Park. After such a disappointing and turgid start, the goals flowed and the '66 World Cup began to take on a life and identity of its own.

Following our game against Uruguay, we returned to our base in the Hendon Hall Hotel where, between training sessions at the Bank of England ground in Roehampton, we watched the tournament unfold on TV. Much of our pre-tournament preparation had taken place at the FA's coaching school at Lilleshall in Shropshire, but as all our group games were at Wembley it had been decided we would be London based. Hendon is hardly a backwater, but quite often I would join other players for a stroll down the high street and at no time were we pestered by the press, or even unduly bothered by over-enthusiastic fans.

Not having our every move scrutinized by the media, our base at the Hendon Hall Hotel took on a very relaxed atmosphere. What spare time I had was spent reading newspapers or watching television in the TV lounge – hotels in those days didn't have sets in every bedroom. At 10.30 every night Alf would join us in the lounge. So regular was he, you could set your watch by him. He'd simply say, 'Goodnight gentlemen,' and that was our signal to go up to bed.

After a day on the training pitch I was ready for bed then anyway. Not that television offered much incentive to stay awake. There were only three channels: BBC1, BBC2 and ITV. There was little daytime television other than *Watch With Mother* and some specialist schools programmes. Programmes for grown-ups began on BBC1 at 5.55 p.m. with a ten-minute news bulletin followed by regional news programmes. Those of a certain age might remember the BBC's early and disastrous football soap called *United!*. This saga followed the on- and off-field antics of a fictitious team called Brentwich United. *United!* was certainly not from the hard-hitting school of soaps such as *EastEnders* and *Brookside* and its early-evening slot ensured that whatever drama unfolded was strictly family viewing. The Brentwich United players all had comic-book names, such as Jimmy Stokes (played by George Layton), Curly Parker (Ben Howard) and Vic 'Hotshot' Clay (Warwick Sims). It was the brainchild of the writer, Brian Hayles, and the technical adviser was Jimmy Hill!

United! had a curiosity value though it never took off as a soap. Scenes portraying Brentwich in action were shot at actual league matches. Brentwich – or so it appeared, as this was black and white television – played in red and white stripes and white shorts. For added realism, footage of Sunderland or Stoke City in action (both these teams wore the same strip as Brentwich) were cut into the matchday scenes. Such editing was rarely convincing and led to some odd and unintentionally humorous moments, such as when George Layton as Jimmy Stokes would be seen leading the Brentwich team out of their dressing room, only to cut to footage of Sunderland's Charlie Hurley running down the tunnel. These surreal images didn't help the credibility of the series at all and together with storylines that portrayed the mundane side of life at a football club – 'Holiday time is over, so it's back to work for the players of Brentwich United', and 'Deirdre (Beverley Jones) runs short of envelopes in the club office and Gregg Harris (Graham Weston) is worried about being fit for Saturday' – saw the series disappear after little over a year.

BBC1 closed down at 11.40 p.m. with the *Epilogue*, a five-minute sermon given by a guest broadcaster from one of the faiths. BBC2 also ceased transmitting at around that time with *Late Night Line-Up*, a series which looked at the world of the arts and popular culture featuring the analysis of such worthies as Denis Tuohy, Joan Bakewell and Tony Bilbow. ITV also ceased transmitting programmes at around 11.30, so even if Alf had allowed us to stay up to watch television, there was nothing to watch. And of course there wasn't the all-night social life that you find in cities today. Last orders in the pubs was 10.30, ten o'clock on Sundays, while nightclubs were an innovation barely heard of by young working folk. The routine of people's lives had still to change: most went to bed at around 11 p.m. and the streets were safe at night, simply because few people were out and about by then.

As we sat in our rooms whiling away the hours until we could get out there and show that the Uruguay match was not our true form, Alf was analysing his strategic options. Blackburn's John Connolly had played on the left against the South Americans, in a more or less orthodox wing role. Now, when he announced his team for our second match against Mexico, Alf revealed his new thinking. There was to be an important change to our formation – and our personnel.

Against Mexico, Alf Ramsey brought Martin Peters into the team on the left side of midfield in place of John Connelly. Alan Ball was also replaced, his position on the right being taken by Southampton's wide man Terry Paine.

Martin Peters was a midfield player rather than an orthodox winger like John Connelly. Replacing midfielder Alan Ball with winger Terry Paine was a balancing move: in dropping one winger, Alf had brought another one in on the other flank. The selection of Terry Paine indicated to me that, even at this stage of the proceedings, Alf obviously still thought there was a need for an orthodox winger in the team. Perhaps he believed such a player would stretch opposing defences, creating space and opportunities for Bobby Charlton. Though the side was more or less settled, it was obvious that Alf was still not one hundred per cent certain about his best eleven, or even what the preferred formation should be.

Prior to the Mexico game we enjoyed a day out at Pinewood film studios. Being a big movie fan, this was a cracking treat for me as well as a good ploy on the part of Alf. He had noticed how down we were after the Uruguay game; we needed something to brighten our spirits and bring some fun back into the general mood of the camp. As Alf said when announcing the trip, 'Laughter is contagious.'

Before we went down to Pinewood we had a training session at Highbury during which Jack Charlton and Alf exchanged words, and I was dragged in to their disagreement. With the training over, all the players were keen to get away, have some lunch and relax. Jack, however, had a point to make to Alf and was adamant it would be made. We had all watched Brazil beat

Bulgaria, with both goals coming from free kicks. Jack took Alf to task about what we would do to counteract free kicks should we come up against the Brazilians. Jack believed the best way was for one of our defenders to stand between me and my goal line. Alf asked me what I thought of this and I immediately said I was against it.

'A player in front of me? That'll obstruct my line of vision,' I complained, 'which is the last thing I want.'

Jack couldn't see this at all. The debate raged on and on with Jack becoming more belligerent as it progressed. The more we debated the issue, the more it annoyed and exasperated the other players. After forty-five minutes of this, Bobby Moore stepped in.

'Alf, you told us earlier that laughter is contagious. Well, let me tell you, the three of you have just found the cure.' Bobby's intervention immediately prompted Alf to wrap things up.

'Gordon is in charge of his own penalty area,' Alf said sternly. 'Gentlemen, the matter is closed.'

The trip to the Pinewood studios was highly enjoyable. They were filming the new James Bond movie, *You Only Live Twice*, and we all met Mr Bond himself, Sean Connery. The Bond movies had taken cinemas by storm. Though there had been a thaw in the Cold War, spies and espionage were still very much a part of the news. The space race between the USA and the Soviet Union was continuing apace as both countries strove to be the first to land a man on the moon. The reality of real-life spies such as Kim Philby, the 'Third Man' (after Burgess and Maclean) who defected to the Russians in 1963, was one of a dreary, alcohol-fuelled paranoia, a far cry from the speedboats, careless violence and sex without guilt of James Bond.

The James Bond films purveyed the fantasy that government took a laissez-faire attitude to Bond's penchant for bedding any amount of delectable women. His promiscuity mirrored the increasingly liberal attitude to sex among young people who were the first generation to have the contraceptive pill. The sophistication of the James Bond character, not only with regard to gadgets, but also food and drink, because something to which the masses could aspire. All of which made the Bond films a highly popular product of their time.

The stunts 007 pulled off in his films, however, were nothing compared to the one Ray Wilson managed during our visit to Pinewood, where a buffet lunch was supplemented by a copious amount of bottled beer. As soon as Alf saw the beer on offer, he immediately restricted everyone to one bottle each. Ray Wilson somehow managed surreptitiously to consume about eight during the lunchbreak. As the afternoon wore on, Ray became more and more outrageous and loud. We managed to keep him out of trouble, though it was touch-and-go at times. Ray didn't help his cause, especially when we met Yul Brynner, who told us that he was soon to appear in the theatre in Newcastle reprising his role in the musical *The King And I*.

'What're they calling it up there, then?' asked Ray, much to the amusement of himself. 'The King and Why Aye?'

We spent the afternoon trying to keep Ray as far away from Alf as possible. If Alf had ever discovered what state Ray was in, he would be in big trouble and may even have been dropped from the squad.

Mexico and France had played out a 1–1 draw in their opening game, which was a good result for us. It meant that we went into our game against Mexico with every team in the group level on points.

Mexico were not right out of the top drawer of international football, but were a useful side whose main strength was their very organized and effective defence. Against England they opted for a sweeper, Jesus del Muro, who played his club football for Cruz Azul. Del Muro started the game playing behind a back four with 22-year-old Ignacio Calderón of Guadalajara in goal. For nearly forty minutes we floundered on Mexico's resolute back line. I remember thinking that it was going to take something special for us to breach their defence. No sooner had I thought this, than Bobby Charlton conjured up a piece of football magic that was very special indeed.

Bobby received the ball deep in our half of the field and, like a thoroughbred racehorse, glided down the pitch with the Mexicans conceding midfield and falling back around their penalty area. Bobby kept the ball under immaculate control and, when looking up some thirty-five yards from goal, saw his way barred by a blanket of olive shirts. He took the ball on another five yards, no more, then, without breaking stride and with hardly any backlift, hit a thunderbolt of a shot with his right foot. The ball cut through the air like a bullet and was still rising as it ballooned the back of Calderón's net. Wembley erupted and I dare say millions of people across England leapt from their armchairs. It was a tremendous goal in the true Bobby Charlton tradition. We were off the mark, and how!

All these years later, Bobby's thunderbolt against Mexico is still considered to be among football's all-time greatest goals, and rightly so. In the dressing room after the game we heaped praise on Bobby for his marvellous effort only for Bobby's brother, Jack, to intervene impishly.

'You're full of compliments for our kid,' laughed Jack, 'but what you're all forgetting is, it was me who made the two-yard pass that set him on his way!'

Ominously, in Group Two, Argentina were involved in a bad-tempered match with West Germany. Over 47,000 turned up at Villa Park expecting to see a vibrant encounter between two fancied teams. What they saw was a dull, defensive battle littered with fouls. Argentina's Jorge Albrecht received his marching orders following a very reckless challenge, though many thought that several of his countrymen should have followed him. Argentina had beaten Spain 2–1 and knew a draw against the Germans would be enough to see them progress to the quarter-finals. West Germany, whose attack had ravaged Switzerland, were choked by a ten-man Argentine defence well marshalled by their skipper, Antonio Rattin. The behaviour of the Argentinian players left much to be desired and their dirty tactics and petulance resulted in a warning from FIFA about their future conduct. As we were to find out, it went unheeded.

In Group Three Portugal coasted to a 3–0 victory over Bulgaria, which ended the Bulgarians' hopes of further progression, while at Roker Park one blinding flash of genius from Igor Chislenko of Moscow Dynamo gave Russia a 1–0 win over Italy. Against Russia, Italy left out their 'golden boy' Giovanni Rivera of AC Milan, and their leading goalscorer, Paolo Barison of Roma. The casual approach of the Italians suggested they believed they had some divine right of qualification. The Italians believed their defeat against Russia to be of little consequence, as their remaining tie was against North Korea, a team the star-studded Italians expected to beat easily. Such optimism would prove to be misplaced for one of the greatest World Cup upsets of all time was in the offing.

The day before our victory over Mexico I joined my England team mates to watch what was without doubt one of the best games of the qualifying stage. That night, to the accompaniment of 52,000 wildly cheering fans at Goodison Park, I witnessed the demise of Brazil. Their conquerors were Hungary by three goals to one, and the Hungarian victory was well deserved.

The Brazilian team was a mixture of youth and experience, welded together by the great Pelé. Pelé, however, was injured and watched from the stands as his team mates were torn apart by a rampant Hungary who, in Ferenc Bene and Florian Albert, possessed players of lightning speed whose direct running caused Brazil all manner of problems.

It was an exhilarating game, the speed and tempo of which laid bare the defects of the Brazilians. Sadly, old hands such as Bellini, Djalma Santos and even the great Garrincha, had no answer to the pace of the Hungarians, while the younger members of the side – Jairzinho, Tostao and Alcindo – lacked the necessary experience.

When Portugal finally put paid to Brazil by the same scoreline in their next game, it came as no surprise. The press hailed it as the end of an era. With the benefit of hindsight, it wasn't. Brazil were merely a team in transition. They had too many players over the age of thirty and too many youngsters. The notable exception was Pelé, who at twenty-five, though yet to reach his prime, had already won two World Cup winners' medals. Though substitutes were still not allowed, teams could name a non-playing reserve. For their games against Hungary and Portugal, the Brazilian reserve was Edu, who at sixteen was the youngest player in this World Cup. His inclusion was indicative of a Brazilian team in the throes of major change and whose sights were set on the future.

Pelé didn't fail in the '66 World Cup, he was kicked out of the competition. The great man returned against Portugal, but the treatment meted out to him by Oporto's João Morais was more brutal than that which had resulted in his injury against Bulgaria.

Pelé's injury after half an hour put an end to what the press said would be 'a contest to decide the world's greatest player' between him and Eusebio. Everywhere he went Pelé was surrounded by three Portuguese defenders who were none too subtle in dealing with him. The leniency with which referees viewed physical and robust play in this era was evidenced by a scything tackle from Morais that made no contact with the ball and took Pelé out at the knee. The referee, George McCabe of England, simply awarded a free kick, as probably most referees of the time would have done. Football was considered to be primarily a physical game. When a foul was committed, a free kick was given and that was usually the only action deemed necessary. The players accepted this lenient view as did those who watched the game. Only in exceptional circumstances was a player sent off. When a player did receive his marching orders it was usually for persistent foul play, or for one tackle that was considered by the referee to be career-threatening to the victim.

The tackle from behind was an accepted part of the game, certainly by Europeans, and body-checking was part of the football culture of South America. Football may have been emerging as the beautiful game, but it still followed a very hard and sometimes cynical script.

The players who fouled Pelé received at most a ticking-off from the referee, to which the common response was a knowing smile. That foul was nothing personal, the smiler implied, I'm just doing my job.

Pelé was kicked out of the World Cup, but even if he had been fully fit and firing on all cylinders, Brazil would have had little chance of winning the World Cup. They were simply not good enough for that. The supporters, however, had paid good money to see the world's greatest footballer in action and they should not have been robbed of that sight by such cynicism. Portugal's approach against Brazil baffled me, quite simply because they had no need to resort to such shabby tactics – they were good enough to beat Brazil with their sheer footballing craft. In Eusebio they possessed the one player who could come anywhere near Pelé's brilliance.

The 1966 World Cup produced many memorable images of great, golden moments. In contrast to that is the haunting photograph of Pelé's exit from the tournament. With a coat draped round him, he looks sadly over his right shoulder as he limps from the Goodison Park pitch. His expression seems to be asking, 'Why?' At the same time there is something in his eyes that suggests he was also thinking, 'I'll be back.'

While everyone was digesting the fact of Brazil's elimination, the unbelievable news came that North Korea had beaten Italy 1–0 at Ayresome Park. The Italians were out, undone earlier by their swaggering overconfidence against the Russians. The scale of the upset was comparable to the United States' defeat of England at Belo Horizonte in 1950.

The Italians had, on the night, looked a strangely dispirited bunch and the unknown Koreans seized their chance. The goal that clinched it was scored by Pak Doo Ik, who, as a result, found himself immortalized in football folklore. The Koreans had played as if they meant to win, the Italians as if they were in a dream. North Korea's victory set Teesside alight. Middlesbrough had not produced the biggest crowds for the World Cup, but it had produced fantastic support for the Koreans, whom the Teessiders adopted as their second team.

North Korea joined Russia in qualifying for the quarter-finals from Group Four and were to be far from finished as far as shock scorelines were concerned. The Italians flew home with their tails between their legs. When they landed at Genoa airport they were pelted with tomatoes and eggs, and their manager, Edmundo Fabbri, was immediately dismissed. Like Brazil, they too had to rebuild for the future.

In our final group game two poacher's goals from Liverpool's Roger Hunt gave us a 2–0 victory over France. The win saw us top our group with two wins and one draw to our name. Most satisfactorily from my point of view, we were yet to concede a goal.

Our success was somewhat tempered by two problems. Nobby Stiles picked up a booking following a foul on Jacques Simon of Nantes, which meant that should Nobby pick up another caution, he would be out of the tournament. Nobby was very worried about this. His fiercely competitive, robust style of play had been described in some quarters as 'dirty' and the general consensus of opinion among the press was that Alf Ramsey should check Nobby's robustness, or simply leave him out of the side. Nobby was a tigerish tackler, but I knew him well enough to know that he never deliberately hurt an opponent. Every team needed a hard-man ball-winner and Nobby fulfilled that role for us. They didn't come much smaller in stature or bigger in heart than Nobby. He was a bubbling, bouncing dynamo of football industry, permanently hungry for the ball, and took it as a personal affront that he might be denied it.

There was only ten stone of Nobby, but many opponents

recoiled from engaging with him in the tackle as if they had been confronted by ten tons. There was nothing subtle about his tackling and once he won the ball he was not a fluent distributor of it, rarely passing it more than a few yards. But that was all he was supposed to do. Both Nobby Stiles and Alan Ball accomplished this task with great success, as Alf had perfectly summed it up during one of our training sessions. Alf had emphasized that he wanted Nobby and Alan to go out and win the ball.

'What do you want us to do with the ball when we get it?' asked Nobby.

'Do you both have dogs?' asked Alf. Nobby and Alan both nodded. 'And do you ever take your dogs on to a public park?' asked Alf. 'Throw a rubber ball about and tell the dog to run after it, bring it back, and lay it at your feet?'

'Yes,' replied Nobby and Alan together.

'That is what I want you to do for Bobby Charlton,' said Alf. Get the ball, give it to Bobby. Simple, but crucial to England's effectiveness.

Alf was under pressure not only from some quarters of the press but from certain FA officials to drop Nobby, but once again he showed that he was his own man and that team selection was entirely his domain and no one else's. 'Just play your usual fair but hard game, Nobby,' Alf said, 'and leave me to do the worrying.'

Our second problem to arise from the game against France was more serious. Jimmy Greaves was on the end of a very late challenge from Jean Bonnel that resulted in an ugly gash on his left shin requiring fourteen stitches. With our quarter-final against Argentina only three days away, we all knew that there was no way Jimmy was going to be fit.

Having finished top of our group, we had qualified for the quarter-finals along with second-placed Uruguay. West Germany and Argentina went through from Group Two. Portugal and Hungary from Group Three, with Russia and the surprise package, North Korea, from Group Four.

Against France, Alf had once again opted for one orthodox winger by playing Ian Callaghan from Liverpool. With Jimmy Greaves injured, I knew Alf had to make a change for the team against Argentina, but had no idea he would alter things so dramatically. We had used three different line-ups in our three group matches. For the Argentina game Alf made a monumental decision. He decided to ditch wingers completely and play two midfield players in wide positions – Alan Ball on the right and Martin Peters on the left. Alf also introduced Geoff Hurst as a replacement for the injured Jimmy G.

The 4–4–2 formation we had adhered to for some time went out the window. We were now to play 4–4–3. I thought at the time that the decision to dispense with wingers was a good one. Alan Ball and Martin Peters were highly intelligent players. They worked tirelessly, dropped back and helped out in defence, were good when going forward and, particularly in the case of Martin Peters, could make quality crosses into the opposition's penalty area. More importantly, those crosses were made early, before opponents had time to get organized in defence.

The pressure on Alf to leave Nobby Stiles out of the side for the Argentina game gathered momentum. Some FA officials thought Nobby's robust style would only serve further to inflame the team that had already received a warning from FIFA about their conduct. Alf, however, resisted all calls to drop Nobby. 'If Stiles has to go, then so do I,' Alf told the FA, and meant it. The last thing the FA wanted was the England manager walking out before a World Cup quarter-final. Needless to say, the anti-Stiles brigade quickly backed off. Once again, Alf had shown that, irrespective of the outcome of the Argentina game, he would not be dictated to regarding team selection.

'Alf's gone out on a limb over you,' our assistant trainer, Les Cocker, told Nobby. 'Don't let him down!'

The idea that 4–3–3 was a new formation that revolutionized British football and sounded the death knell for wingers is only partly true. In fact, 4–3–3 was nothing new, though it was new to England as an international team. The 4–3–3 formation, with midfield players, or half backs, fulfilling roles in both defence and attack as well as the middle of the park in preference to orthodox wingers, whose prime job was one of attack, had been applied with some success in Italy. 4–3–3 was a variation of both the old 'W' formation, in which a team played with two full backs, three half backs and five forwards, and the 4–4–2 system Alf had preferred in previous England matches.

In Italy the 4–3–3 formation had been deployed with considerable success by both AC Milan and Internazionale. The Italians referred to 4–3–3 as *catenaccio*, which in English means 'door bolt' or 'chain'. The Italians played 4–3–3 as a very defensive and cautious system, with which teams denied opponents scoring opportunities by defending the 'scoring space' and adopting man-to-man marking, supported by a sweeper. Italian teams such as Inter-Milan, under the coaching of Helenio Herrera, relied heavily on counterattacks spearheaded by speedy strikers. 4–3–3 paid handsome dividends for Inter when they won the European Cup in 1964 and 1965. Though 4–3–3 brought success, the way Inter played resulted in some very sterile football. Once one of their counterattacks had produced a goal, irrespective of how early in the game their goal had been scored, Inter shut up shop, fell back into defence, and relied on their *catenaccio* system to stifle all the efforts of their opponents to equalize.

The origins of 4–3–3 can be traced way back to the 1930s when Switzerland, managed by the Austrian Karl Rappan, used the *verrou* system (*verrou* also means 'door bolt'). The pre-war Swiss side adopted a rudimentary sweeper in defence and relied on breakaway attacks to score goals. This system was truly innovatory back then. Though bereft of world-class players, Switzerland made an impact in the 1938 World Cup in France, beating a powerful German team 4–2, only to go out at the hands of the beaten finalists, Hungary. Before that tournament in 1938 Switzerland had employed the *verrou* system in their 2–1 victory over England in Zurich. As Stanley Matthews, who played in that match, recalled in his autobiography, *The Way It Was*:

The Swiss were content to fall back and rely on defence, where they played a roaming defender between their back line and their goalkeeper ... I had never come across such a system before. We tore into the Swiss, but they were up to everything we threw at them. They beat England 2–1, with both the Swiss goals coming from swift counter-attacks, one of which resulted in a very dubious penalty. We camped out in and around the Swiss penalty area but try as we did, the equalizing goal remained elusive. Switzerland's football hadn't been pretty, but from their point of view, their new style of play proved highly effective.

The Italian sides of the early sixties perfected the Swiss *verrou* system and Alf was to develop 4–3–3 even further. He wanted us to be more adventurous than the Italians. Rather than simply falling back to defend a one-goal lead and remain in our shell, Alf wanted us to play the ball quickly out of defence to Alan Ball or Martin Peters, who in turn would hit early balls in for Geoff Hurst.

'We shall not rely on defence. We will still take the game to the opposition,' said Alf.

The work rate of Bally and Martin Peters was to play a vital role in the success of the 4–3–3 system. Both worked immensely hard to help out in defence and fulfil their role as wide midfield players. If Alan played the ball in from the right, Martin would be there to support Geoff Hurst and Roger Hunt in attack. Conversely, when Martin crossed the ball from the left, Alan would be buzzing about the penalty area looking to pick up any pieces. As I have said, both Martin Peters and Alan Ball were very intelligent players. Martin had great vision and a very cultured left foot while Alan was blessed with electrifying speed and great tenacity. Possibly their most valuable assets were their lungs, which must have been like sides of beef, so much ground did they cover.

Alf didn't need to spend countless hours with a blackboard explaining the 4-3-3 system to the players. Although we hadn't played it as a team, we all had a good grasp of how it worked, for we had all come across 4-3-3 in some form or other when playing against continental teams. Alf only had to talk us through the system to convey the finer points of how we would deploy it.

Alf conducted his team talks in the afternoon. At the Bank of England training ground at Roehampton we would train in the morning, break for lunch, then gather in the conference room for one of Alf's talks. After a hard training session, lunch was very welcome.

The first day we had lunch at Roehampton, everyone was delighted with the quality of food on offer. The menu consisted of tomato soup as a starter, a main course of a sumptuous side of beef, enormous Yorkshire puddings (as Ray Wilson remarked, 'This chef's idea of a balanced meal is Yorkshire pudding on your dinner plate, and one on your side plate') and all the trimmings, followed by a pudding, or sweet (as I still called it) of a delicious homemade apple pie with creamy custard. Everyone was in agreement that this was first-class cuisine. The only problem was, this menu never changed. By the seventh consecutive day our appetite for this sumptuous carvery was wearing thin and we would have given a king's ransom for beans on toast or a salad. I can only assume that roast beef and apple pie was the only meal that the chef at the Bank of England training ground could make. For chef's special, read chef's only.

After lunch Alf allowed us half an hour to relax before calling us to a team meeting in the conference room. On those July days the sun streamed through the large plate-glass windows and, following such a large lunch, a number of players struggled to keep awake. Jimmy Greaves introduced an added element of excitement to Alf's team talks by running a book on how long Jack Charlton could stay awake. The stopwatch was started as soon as Alf began to speak, and stopped the moment big Jack's eyes closed and his chin dropped on to his chest.

Alf's words of wisdom fell upon deaf ears as the attention of half the squad focused on big Jack. I won a few bob, as did Bobby Moore, Ray Wilson, George Eastham and, of course, Jimmy himself. On one occasion Alf was midway through a long talk about Portugal when Jack momentarily nodded off, only to sit bolt upright again when startled by one of his snores. Jimmy Greaves immediately blurted out, 'All bets are off!' much to the bewilderment of the boss. Needless to say, Alf soon twigged, and Jimmy's involuntary interruption of Alf's team talk put the kybosh on that little entertainment.

On 23 July, the day of the quarter-finals, the sun shone, the attendances were good and the explosions came.

The first excitement came at Goodison Park, where North Korea rocked world football on its heels by racing into a three-goal lead against Portugal. Goodison giggled in disbelief. The waves of incredulity wafted back to every television and radio as the nation struggled to come to terms with what was the most amazing scoreline of the World Cup. Surely North Korea couldn't maintain this sort of form, especially against the much-fancied Portuguese? They couldn't. Eusebio took the game by the scruff of the neck and, slowly but surely, Portugal eroded North Korea's early advantage. At half time it was 3–2, and in the second half the doughty North Koreans felt the full force of the brilliance of Eusebio. Bent on absolute destruction he tore into the North Korean defence. Come the final whistle, Portugal were winners by five goals to three. Eusebio helped himself to four goals, with the fifth coming from Augusto.

Just by reaching the quarter-finals and giving Portugal one almighty shock, North Korea had achieved more than they could have ever hoped for when setting out from their homeland. In coming back to win the game from three goals down, Portugal

had shown themselves to be as sound in character and tempera-
ment as in technique. As for Eusebio, his virtuoso performance
saw him elevate himself to a status in world football that hitherto
had been the sole preserve of Pelé.

While the drama of Goodison was unfolding, we were
involved in drama of a very different kind in our game against
Argentina. It was an afternoon when the passions, the ruthlessness
and the national pride that had been grafted on to the pursuit
of the World Cup surfaced in both majestic and disgraceful
ostentation.

The game was only minutes old when Alan Ball was cynically
felled by Silvio Marzolini. The referee, Rudolf Kreitlein of West
Germany, took no action except to award a free kick. The tone
of the match had been set.

We took the game to Argentina, a signal for the body-
checking and cynical fouls to gather momentum as the Argentines
resorted to all manner of thuggery to keep us at bay. We had
what I thought were legitimate appeals for penalties turned down
following fouls on Alan Ball and Geoff Hurst as we continued
our onslaught on the Argentine goal. Herr Kreitlein was rapidly
filling his notebook with Argentinian names and ten minutes
before half time decided that the 'unofficial referee', the Argentine skipper, Antonio Rattin, who had disputed every booking,
had to go.

Herr Kreitlein was a small and dapper man whose somewhat
irritatingly authoritative manner served only to further the dis-
pleasure of the Argentinians, and of Rattin in particular. Every
time the referee penalized the South Americans, the volatile
Rattin ran up to him, pointing imperiously, his gestures indicating sheer contempt for the official. Having committed a series of
fouls Rattin was called over by Kreitlein. The Argentinian skipper
gazed down at the referee as if he had a bad smell under his nose.
Herr Kreitlein spoke only a few words before Rattin spat forth a
volley of invective at his face. It was the last straw for the German,

who turned to the team benches and raised his right arm to indicate that Rattin had to go.

That's when the real trouble started. Rattin refused to accept this decision. Kreitlein repeated his arm movement. Rattin shrugged his shoulders, gesticulated with his hands to indicate he didn't understand why he had been sent off and stood his ground. The game was held up for seven minutes as chaos reigned. I stood dumbfounded on the edge of my penalty box as I watched a heated argument develop between the match officials, the players, the Argentinian management and FIFA delegates. At one point the South American players left the pitch en masse, as if to suggest that it was a case of 'one off, all off'.

The Argentinians furiously argued with the referee's liaison officer, Ken Aston, and Harry Cavan, the FIFA match delegate. At one point two police officers came on to the scene, probably worried that should matters escalate even further, they might have a problem of public order to deal with. Indeed, by this time the Wembley crowd were getting very agitated, catcalls and boos raining down from the terraces. On the touchline there was much pushing and shoving as the police officers struggled to keep the tempestuous Argentinians and the beleaguered FIFA officials apart. Eventually Ken Aston and Harry Cavan managed to convince the Argentina manager, Juan Carlos Lorenzo, and his delegation of fellow countrymen that Herr Kreitlein's decision was irreversible. Rattin was off.

Well, off the pitch at any rate. The match resumed with Rattin hurling insults from the sidelines. At this point drama degenerated into farce as Argentine players fell to the ground like bags of hammers every time one of our players came near them. Once on the ground they writhed around like electrocuted earthworms. It was pantomime stuff but no one was laughing. Least of all Bobby Moore, who resisted the temptation to restore parity of numbers by not retaliating to a slap in the face from Alberto Gonzalez. Bobby's composure in the face of such extreme provocation was

exemplary, but no more than we had come to expect from our
captain.

The breakthrough we had been labouring for eventually happened thirteen minutes from time. From wide on the left wing,
Martin Peters crossed the ball into a space between the Argentine
goalkeeper Antonio Roma and his defence. Geoff Hurst timed
his run to perfection. He ghosted into the space, leapt like a stag
and, with a deft flick of his head, guided the ball past the static
Roma and into the net. The Wembley terraces exploded into a
heaving mass of colour and noise. Hats were hurled, arms held
aloft, as 90,000 people celebrated what was to be the winning
goal.

Geoff's goal had its origins more at Upton Park than the
England training pitches at Roehampton. I had seen the West
Ham wingers cross the ball like that many times. Martin Peters
was very adept at floating the ball into the danger area between
a goalkeeper and his back line, and there was no one better than
Geoff at getting on the end of such a cross. So a tactic that
evolved on the Hammers' training ground won the game for
England. In such a tight game we needed players capable of
producing a moment of true inspiration to catch the opposition
off guard. Fortunately, on this day, England had such players in
Martin and Geoff.

Our joy at winning a place in the semi-finals was tempered
by Argentinian bitterness. When the final whistle blew, all the
tempestuous emotion of a team who believed they could have
won the World Cup was once again unleashed on the referee,
who had to be escorted from the pitch by Ken Aston and a small
posse of the Metropolitan's finest.

At this point Alf Ramsey did something that was very
uncharacteristic. In the time-honoured tradition of international
matches, George Cohen offered to exchange shirts with the
Argentinian number eleven, Oscar Mas. The two players were
in the process of doing just that when Alf intervened and put a
stop to it. He was so obviously angered by the conduct of the

Argentinians that he would allow no gesture of friendship or fraternization from his team.

The photograph of Alf tugging at George Cohen's arm to prevent him swapping shirts with Mas appeared worldwide in the press on the following day. As far as South American countries were concerned, of course, the photograph portrayed Alf as the bad guy. But even worse damage to his reputation was to follow.

Let me explode another myth. Legend has it that, when talking to the press after the game, Alf Ramsey described the Argentinian players as 'animals'. He didn't. What Alf actually said was, 'The behaviour of some players in the competition reminds me of animals.' While the inference was clear enough from the context, he never directly referred to the Argentinians as being animals. Alf was making a general remark about some of the dirty players in the World Cup – he could equally have been referring to those who cynically and crudely kicked Pelé out of the tournament. But the damage was done. The South American press, in particular that of Argentina, widely reported that Alf had specifically described the Argentinian players as 'animals'. The British papers picked up on this and took a similar line. Thus a myth was created and Alf Ramsey, to my mind, very badly maligned.

For years to come this misinterpretation of Alf's ill-advised post-match comment was to hang like a millstone around his neck whenever England came up against a South American team. Moreover, I believe the hostility aimed towards Alf and the England team in the 1970 World Cup in Mexico, was prompted by the reverberations of those notorious words, transmitted and distorted by sections of the world's press.

Alf took it all on the chin. Two aspects of his character that I admired were his grace and dignity. Alf must have known he had been misquoted, but he steadfastly refused to involve himself in what would have been a slanging match with the press in order to clear his name. I am only glad that this book has allowed me the opportunity to put the record straight on his behalf.

As for the match itself, in particular the dismissal of Antonio

Rattin, the whole affair was highly regrettable and, with firmer refereeing, seemingly avoidable. Herr Kreitlein must shoulder some of the blame for the way it degenerated. He was quick to punish minor infringements while allowing more serious misdemeanours to go unpunished. When players feel they are not being protected by an official, they invariably take matters into their own hands and trouble escalates. Having said that, the Argentinian players were the main culprits. Their whole attitude to the game, and the competition in general, left much to be desired. The tragedy of it all was that the Argentinians were very good footballers. Their tactics were negative because their strength was their defence, but in players such as Rattin, Oscar Mas, Ermindo Onega and Luis Artime, Argentina possessed footballers of real class. Their Achilles heel, however, was their lack of discipline.

Following the game FIFA suspended Antonio Rattin for four international matches, and both Ermindo Onega and Roberto Ferreiro for three. The Argentinian FA was fined £83. 8s. 6d. (£88.42½p), this paltry and curious amount being the equivalent of 1,000 Swiss francs which, at the time, was the maximum fine FIFA could impose in such circumstances.

Ermindo Onega received his ban for ungentlemanly conduct (spitting in the face of an official), and Rattin for bringing the game into disrepute. Luis Artime and Jorge Solari were both cautioned during the game. As were the Charlton brothers, Jackie and Bobby, the first and only time that ever happened. Argentina were also warned that unless they could guarantee the good behaviour of their players and officials, they could face a ban from the 1970 World Cup, although that would have been of no consequence as they didn't qualify.

Why did the Argentinians behave as they did? While their actions were inexcusable, they may perhaps be explicable. It may be claimed that Antonio Rattin laboured under a misunderstanding. He had been booked for a foul on Bobby Charlton and was later to claim that at the time of his dismissal he had merely wanted to complain to Herr Kreitlein about some of our tackling. The referee spoke no Spanish, so Rattin needed an interpreter. According to him, he was in the process of asking for one when the referee gave him his marching orders.

Unlike in Europe, in South America it was quite acceptable for a team captain to speak to a referee, and even question his decisions. Rattin said he simply couldn't understand why Herr Kreitlein took exception to this. Herr Kreitlein presumably felt that as a European he should adhere to European standards of conduct on the field.

I believe that the meeting of two differing footballing cultures was at the root of the trouble that day. Both football cultures played to the same set of rules, but it was the way those rules were interpreted that sparked the trouble and controversy.

There remains to this day a noticeable difference between European and South American football, despite television's global coverage and the fact that many of South America's top players now ply their trade in Europe, although it is far less marked today than it was during that notorious semi-final.

The pressure on us eased somewhat with our having reached the semi-finals. The expectations of the media and the supporters had been high, but we felt we had achieved something by making it to the last four. Should the worst happen, and we were to lose, at least we would derive a modicum of satisfaction from being the first England team to have reached a World Cup semi-final and, in so doing, be ranked by FIFA among the top four sides in the world. It had been a good many years since England had been rated so highly and was indicative of the progress we had made under Alf's management.

If someone were to ask me which of all the games I played for England was the one I considered to be the best in terms of pure football, I would have no hesitation in saying it was our semi-final against Portugal. Portugal were the bookies' favourites and understandably so. They had a number of world-class players at the peak of their powers, no one more so than Eusebio, a player who combined exquisite grace with explosive power. The game took place the day after the other semi-final, in which West Germany had secured their place in the final by beating Russia 2–1 at Goodison Park. The last time the Germans had reached the World Cup final had been in 1954, when Jules Rimet himself handed them the trophy that bore his name following their shock 3–2 defeat of Hungary. With their sights on a second World Cup success, the word coming back from the German camp was that they hoped England would beat Portugal because they felt they stood a better chance of beating us in the final than the Portuguese.

The West Germans may have wanted England to reach the final but, incredibly, this view wasn't shared by the entire nation. Following our victory over Argentina, Lord Lovat wrote a letter to *The Times* in which he described Argentina as a 'small but friendly nation'. I have no qualms about that, but the noble lord then went on to say that 'Argentinian players had been left jerking in agony on the pitch by English footballers'. His letter also said that 'The Argentine were the better players and England have got through to the last four by a lucky disqualification and by crippling two Frenchmen earlier in the tournament.' I didn't have a clue who Lord Lovat was, or with what authority he was speaking, but I quickly came to the conclusion that he knew precious little about football. What he had written was not true and, quite frankly, his unpatriotic stance I found galling. Happily, however, the unknowledgeable peer's view was not shared by the rest of the country, who firmly got behind England for a match that the *Daily Mail* believed 'had all the ingredients for a classic game of football'.

Alf Ramsey decided to field an unchanged team against a Portuguese side that had already earned a £1,000 bonus per man for reaching the semi-final. (Oddly, the Portuguese players would have received less – a £500 bonus each – for reaching the final, though a Lisbon bank had promised each player £750 if they won the tournament in addition to the £500 promised by the Portuguese FA.) Like my England team mates, I was simply on a £60 fee per match, though the team had been promised a £22,000 bonus should we win the World Cup.

Portugal were, to my mind, the most complete footballing side in the World Cup. In Eusebio, the 'Black Panther', they had the star of the tournament. He was an exceptionally gifted player who was one of the best strikers of the ball I have ever come across. The name Eusebio equalled goals, and not of the bread and butter variety. His were invariably dramatic, always memorable and tended to overshadow the magnificent work he did in midfield.

For Eusebio was not just a goalscorer. In the mid-sixties his peerless skills kept Benfica among Europe's foremost clubs and Portugal, who prior to his emergence had been no menace to anyone, among the most feared teams on the international stage. Eusebio had dominated the tournament and had almost single-handedly taken Portugal into the last four. Like many great players he wasn't tall, but he had very broad shoulders, exceptional upper-body strength and powerful legs that pumped him all over the pitch at remarkable speed. At full throttle he must have seemed like a blur to defenders. Of course that didn't bother Nobby Stiles, who had been assigned by Alf to mark him – without his glasses, everybody was a blur to Nobby.

At the time I didn't wear goalkeeping gloves unless the conditions were very wet. Prior to leaving the dressing room I'd chew on two or three pieces of sugar-coated Beechnut gum and then smear some saliva into the palms of my hands. This tacky goo gave me a better grip when handling the ball, and also a degree of traction when palming it away during a diving save, so that I gained better direction. Chewing gum also helped my concentration immensely. When the dressing room buzzer signalled that we should make our way out to the Wembley tunnel, I went up to Harold Shepherdson, and asked him for some gum as usual. His slack-jawed expression told me all I needed to know: he didn't have any. I began to panic.

'I've got to have it, Harold,' I told him. 'You know how greasy a ball gets out there at night.'

The Wembley pitch consisted of lush, springy Cumberland turf that, when damp with evening dew, gave goalkeepers all manner of problems. The ball would literally shoot off the surface and even posed problems when volleyed, because moisture clung to it, making it slip and slither in your hands like a bar of soap.

Alf Ramsey asked why I was all dithery. 'Harold, go and get some Beechnut. Now!'

'Where the hell am I going to get it from?' queried Harold, now sharing my panic.

'I'm a football manager,' said Alf, 'not a bloody owner of a sweetshop!'

It was then that one of the lads, I think it was Jack Charlton, remembered there was a little newsagent's at the end of Wembley Way, opposite what is now the Hilton Hotel, that stayed open late at night.

'Gordon simply has to have it. Move it!' barked Alf, to poor Harold. He tore off his boots, donned his ordinary shoes and shot out of our dressing room like a track-suited rat out of a drainpipe.

As the teams lined up shoulder to shoulder in the tunnel awaiting the referee's signal to take to the pitch, I wasn't in line. At one end of the Wembley tunnel are two very imposing wooden gates and set into one of the gates, is a small door. With the teams on the point of filing out of the tunnel, there was I standing peering out of the open door, anxiously awaiting Harold's return.

'Delay the referee!' I heard Alf tell Bobby Moore who, as captain, was at the head of the line.

As luck would have it, the band that had provided the pre-match entertainment hadn't cleared the pitch yet, anyway. I stomped my boots on the ground in frustration, wrung my hands anxiously and willed Harold to appear. Riddled with anxiety I peered through the open door where hundreds of supporters who had been unable to find a last-minute ticket were milling about outside. In the distance I saw Harold, running for all he was worth across the Wembley car park, an arm raised in triumph. Those supporters must have wondered what on earth was going on and who I was looking for. Looking back, I often imagine the face of the newsagent as the England trainer appeared in his shop desperate for chewing gum only minutes before the World Cup semi-final!

M. Schwinte, our French referee, blew his whistle and the teams began to walk up the tunnel just as a breathless Harold arrived at the gate. He was so out of breath that he couldn't speak. He just thrust the gum into my hand and collapsed against one of the gates. I ripped open the waxy wrapping and threw three pieces into my mouth as I ran up the tunnel to take my place in line. The TV footage of the teams taking to the pitch shows me chomping away like mad, the commentator saying, 'And there is Gordon Banks, chewing his gum and looking very relaxed.' He didn't know the half of it.

Everybody made a telling contribution to what was a great game of football and a memorable night, though I must make special mention of Nobby Stiles, who stuck to Eusebio like bark to a tree, and Bobby Charlton, whose performance in midfield was sublime. The 90,000 crowd were solidly behind us and Wembley's circular roof was almost lifted by the continuous chant of 'Eng-land! Eng-land!'

The players warmed to the atmosphere. Alf Ramsey had told us that, when we came up against a team willing to come out and play fluent football, we would hit our true form. This was just such an occasion. The result was ninety minutes of pulsating football. The game came alive right from the kick-off with Nobby Stiles remaining deep to counteract the considerable threat of Eusebio. Nobby, ably supported by Bobby Moore and Alan Ball, denied Eusebio the room to display his talent and the great man was never able to tear us apart as he had so many other teams.

After thirty-one minutes the Portuguese goalkeeper, José Pereira, blocked a shot from Roger Hunt. The ball rebounded into the path of Bobby Charlton, who calmly stroked it across the lush turf and into the net. The Wembley terracing turned into a sea of Union Jacks; we had taken a mighty step towards the final.

During the second half Portugal asserted themselves and for a time our slender advantage looked very shaky. We defended manfully, however, none more so than Jack Charlton, who was embroiled in a titanic struggle for aerial superiority with the giant Portuguese striker José Torres. With only twelve minutes remaining, a gloriously fluent move produced a second goal. The ball moved from Bobby Moore to George Cohen, who hit a long pass down the right wing. Geoff Hurst and José Carlos battled for possession, with Geoff seizing control. He pulled the ball back across the edge of the penalty area and Bobby Charlton, racing in, hit one of his trademark thunderbolts.

Pereira had no chance. We had made a goal out of nothing, and the Portuguese players were the first to acknowledge it. A number of them even shook Bobby's hand as he ran back to the halfway line for the restart.

I thought we were home and dry, but I was mistaken. Portugal staged a grandstand finish and eight minutes from time were awarded a penalty. A cross from Antonio Simoes was met by the towering José Torres and, with our back line on the wrong foot, Jack Charlton handled the ball. I knew nobody saved Eusebio penalty kicks, but I was determined to give it a try.

I had discussed Eusebio and his penalty taking in some detail with Alf during training. I'd made a mental note that he always seemed to hit the ball to the goalkeeper's right and made my mind up to go that way. As I prepared to face the penalty, however, I caught sight of Alan Ball who was repeatedly pointing to my right with some agitation. When Eusebio placed the ball on the spot, Portugal's captain, Mario Coluna, clocked what Bally was up to, ran up to Eusebio and whispered something in his ear. Eusebio nodded.

This threw me into a quandary. Initially I'd had no doubt in my mind about which way to dive. On seeing Coluna whispering to Eusebio, however, I was convinced the Portuguese skipper had told Eusebio to change the direction of his penalty. I decided to double bluff them, and dive to my left.

Eusebio hit the ball to my right. It was the first goal I had conceded in 443 minutes of World Cup football. I could have strangled Bally. But for him 'giving the show away' I might still have had a clean sheet. After the game, Alf took me to task about the penalty. He was furious with me for diving 'the wrong way', seemingly forgetting what we had discussed in training. I tried to explain that it was Alan Ball's action and Coluna's subsequent reaction that had made me change my mind, but that cut no ice with Alf.

Portugal now had their tails up. Minutes from the end, Coluna latched on to a crossfield ball and hit a rasping drive that was heading for the roof of my net. Instinctively I took to the air. I only managed to get the fingertips of one hand to the ball, but that was enough to deflect it over the bar.

At the final whistle the Portuguese players were devastated but, to their eternal credit, highly sporting in defeat. Eusebio was inconsolable and wept unashamedly. It had been a classic game which the Portuguese coach, Otto Gloria, summed up perfectly when asked which team he thought would win the final. 'Surely,' said Gloria, 'this was the final tonight.'

Football may have been the winner that night. But it was England who were in the final of the World Cup.

13. Alf's Final Word

People say there is no room for sentiment in football. By and large they're right, but sometimes you just can't avoid it. Jimmy Greaves and the World Cup final was a case in point. Jimmy had been a key member of the England team for seven years, during which time he had been his country's most prolific goalscorer, but Alf Ramsey – ever the pragmatist – decided to play the same team that had done so well against Argentina and Portugal. Obviously I was delighted for Geoff Hurst, but I couldn't help feeling desperately sorry for Jimmy.

Of course, Alf's decision was the correct one and, deep down, I think Jimmy knew from the moment he was injured against France that his chance of playing in the World Cup final had effectively gone. The Argentina game had been just three days after Jimmy picked up his debilitating shin injury against France, and he also realized that with the semi-final scheduled only three days after that, he wouldn't make it for that match either. Jimmy was of the opinion that should we reach the final without him, Alf wouldn't change a winning team. Though I'm sure that he did cling on to a secret slender hope. Characteristically, when Alf announced an unchanged team Jimmy immediately wished Geoff Hurst the best of luck.

The myth about English people being quiet and reserved went out the window on 30 July 1966. The England team were carried on an unprecedented tidal wave of enthusiasm to victory in the World Cup, but it was far from plain sailing.

On the morning of the match, I joined half a dozen of the lads on a walk down Hendon High Street, both to stretch our legs and kill some time. We'd all got up early and had long hours to fill until going off to Wembley. Even at 8.30 a.m. the streets were buzzing and countless people came up to us to wish us luck.

I bought a paper, but back at the Hendon Hall Hotel my mind was so concentrated on the game ahead that I kept rereading the same paragraph without taking it in. Finally I cast the paper aside. When the time came at last for the squad to leave for the stadium, I was taken aback. I had been told that there were a few wellwishers outside waiting to wave us off, but on leaving the hotel I was staggered to see a crowd well in excess of two thousand people gathered around the forecourt. 'The whole country's behind you,' someone called as I made my way to the team coach.

I hoped against hope we wouldn't let everyone down.

We were confident, but Alf Ramsey had ensured we weren't complacent. Alf had the knack of putting everything in perspective. He'd done his homework on West Germany and had made us aware of their strengths without making us fearful of them. Since 1965 England had played twenty-two internationals and lost only once. As a team we were on a roll and really believed we could go on and become world champions, as Alf had always maintained.

All those little dressing-room rituals take on extra significance when you're killing time before a big game. And they don't come any bigger than the World Cup final. I must have tied my boot laces at least three times before I was happy that the knot was comfortably secured at the side of the boot and not across the lace holes, where I might be aware of its presence when kicking the ball. The strips of bandage that served as tie-ups also came in for undue attention: in binding them around my stocking tops they must lie flat, not twisted. I paid more attention than usual to making sure that my goalkeeper's top was tucked smoothly down into my shorts: not crumpled, not bunched so that the base of my back felt exposed. I could have no distractions, even of the most minor sort. No irritations. No excuses for myself.

I warmed up with a series of stretching and bending exercises. Then pummelled a ball against the wall of the warm-up room, repeatedly catching it on the rebound until my hands were accustomed to the feel of it. That done, I repeated the ritual preparation of my strip and boots.

Nobby Stiles traipsed across the dressing room and into the toilet for the umpteenth time. Jack Charlton stood in front of a mirror applying Vaseline to his eyebrows. Ray Wilson dipped into Les Cocker's kit bag, found a little jar of Vicks VapoRub, smeared some around his nostrils, then applied a dollop to the front of his red shirt. Bobby Moore sat impassively, his socks rolled to his ankles as Harold Shepherdson rubbed copious amounts of liniment into his legs. Bobby Charlton and Geoff Hurst held a conversation as both made last-minute adjustments to their boots, Bobby seated on the bench, bending down, Geoff checking the tie-ups on his casually crossed legs. Nobby, back from the loo, sat with his arms folded and legs outstretched. Martin Peters sipped tea from a white china cup, the sort you used to see in British Rail buffets. George Cohen, ready and willing, sat leafing through the special-edition matchday programme. He paused at a page listing details of past finals, and started to read. How could he, at a time like this? How could he take anything in? Why would he want to? Roger Hunt leaned forward, elbows resting on his knees, hands clasped, his eyes focused on the floor. Suddenly he sat upright, clapped his hands together and sniffed, then resumed his leaning posture, elbows on his knees, hands clasped and found something else of interest in the concrete floor. Nobby passed me on his way to the loo again.

I intermittently took deep breaths, trying to stay calm, as Alf said his piece, but my mind was roller-coasting. Much of what he wanted to say he had said in the days before, particularly during the Friday team meeting. So he didn't say much now. He didn't have to.

'Jack, be hard and competitive . . . Nobby, get a foot in . . . *Is*

that stud longer than the others? No. It's the floor. It's not flush . . .
Alan, work and work and work up and down that line. Always
be looking to play the ball in early . . . *That left tie-up seems a bit
tight. If I just extend that leg . . . that's better* . . . Long ball, short
ball, it doesn't matter, Martin, as long as it's the right ball . . .
Bobby, control the middle . . . *Must look for Bobby for an early
throw out* . . . Bobby, be aware of Seeler; he can get up high for a
little fellow . . . *Not in my bloody box he won't* . . . George and
Raymond . . . *Raymond??? I've never called him Raymond. Suppose
that's his proper name though* . . . When Gordon has the ball, go
wide, give him the option . . . *Yes, be looking for them* . . . And –'

Burrrrrrrrrrrr!

That's it. We're off!

'Good luck to you all.'

And you, Alf.

'Best of luck . . . Best of luck . . . Best of luck . . . Good luck
. . . Good luck . . . Come on. Come on! *Let's go!*'

Even though I had planned to wear gloves, Harold Shepherdson
still gave me chewing gum. It tasted really good in my dry and
caked mouth. I spat into the palms of my hands anyway as I
followed Alan Ball out of the liniment-scented warmth of the
dressing room into the cool Wembley tunnel. The West German
players were already in line, bobbing up and down, jiggling arms,
keeping leg muscles loose. Their studs on the concrete floor
chattered away like eleven Volkswagens having tappet trouble.
The German goalkeeper Hans Tilkowski extended a hand. I
wiped my hands down the front of my jersey, tentatively shook
his hand, then chewed way like mad on the Beechnut again to
conjure up a good gob of goo.

Standing in line, I noticed just how tidy Alan Ball's hair was.
How red it was. How much shorter than me he was. I could
gaze down on his scalp, which had tiny freckles on it. I wondered
if he knew they were there.

Somewhere away in the distance I heard a band playing. Then

no band. From the head of the line came the shrill blast of a whistle. The lads in front of me began to walk up the slight incline towards the rectangle of light I could see at the mouth of the tunnel. What a tunnel. I never realized it was so long. My legs kept walking but the light at the end of the tunnel didn't seem to come any closer. It was like a dream in which I'd walk or run, but get nowhere. A sudden and deafening roar swept down the tunnel and assailed my ears. The rectangle of light grew bigger. Bigger still. I walked out into sunshine so bright that I had to squint. A cacophony of noise avalanched down from the undulating masses on the terraces. The volatile sound of Wembley in full cry.

I glanced up to where I thought my parents, my brothers, my wife Ursula and our son Robert might be and raised an arm in that direction. They would think I had seen them. I imagined Ursula saying to Robert, 'There, Daddy has seen us. Picked us out from all these people. I told you he would.'

Flanked by Alan Ball and Roger Hunt I stood guardsmanlike as the bands played the national anthems. I didn't normally sing out with gusto, but I did on this occasion, happy to have some release from the nervous tension that had built up inside me.

Then a hurricane of hurrahs from the terraces. A sea of Union Jacks. The constant collective chant of 'Eng-land! Eng-land!'

Both sides fidgeted nervously as the long wait neared its end. The presentations seemed to take an age as the dignitaries passed along the teams. In red shirt, white shorts, red stockings, the England team: Gordon Banks; George Cohen, Bobby Moore, Jack Charlton, Ray Wilson; Alan Ball, Nobby Stiles, Bobby Charlton, Martin Peters; Roger Hunt, Geoff Hurst. And the West Germans, in white shirts, black shorts, white stockings: Hans Tilkowski; Horst Hottges, Willi Schulz, Wolfgang Weber, Karl-Heinz Schnellinger; Helmut Haller, Franz Beckenbauer, Wolfgang Overath, Siggy Held; Lothar Emmerich, Uwe Seeler.

★

We kicked off under gold-leaf sunshine, though previous heavy rainfall had made the pitch soft and greasy. In such conditions errors of judgement were inevitable, especially where the pace of the ball was a factor. But an error of a different kind gave West Germany the lead.

One of our prime strengths was our resolute back line, but it was an uncharacteristic mistake in defence that allowed West Germany to open the scoring after just thirteen minutes. Ray Wilson went up to meet a centre but his header lacked power and length. The ball fell to Helmut Haller who, from my left, shot across the face of goal.

Although Haller's shot lacked pace, Jack Charlton's defensive position between Haller and myself momentarily unsighted me. I saw the ball late. Before I could adjust my positioning it had passed me and crept into the right-hand corner of my net.

I was devastated. Having been on the losing side in two FA Cup finals at Wembley, for a split second I could see it happening all over again. My disappointment at conceding an early goal, however, was quickly replaced by resolve and determination. The game was still young and I knew we had plenty of time to assert ourselves. What's more, I was convinced we would do just that.

West Germany could have put up the shutters then and defended their lead. To their credit, they instead continued to play with purpose and poise and it was clear to me that they were hunting a second goal.

Five minutes later we caught them napping. Wolfgang Overath committed a foul on Bobby Moore on our left-hand side. Bobby quickly got to his feet, looked up to see where Geoff Hurst was, then floated the free kick into the West Germany penalty area. Before the Germans had sensed the danger, Geoff ghosted into their penalty box and, free from a white shirt, headed the equalizer. It was almost a carbon copy of Geoff's goal against Argentina. Wembley filled with noise and I skipped up and down in my penalty box punching the air with my fist at the joy of it all.

Level once again, both teams settled down to play competitive but entertaining football, much to the appreciation of the packed terraces. Nobody pulled out of a tackle, yet no one opted for brute force and ignorance, each team matching the other in technique and intelligence.

As the game proceeded neither team was able to get on top. Prompted by Bobby Moore, we took the game to the Germans only for them to come straight back at us. Alan Ball seemed to be the epitome of perpetual motion. Unflaggingly buzzing up and down our right channel he was having the game of his life and causing the German left back Schnellinger all manner of problems.

Deep into the second half it was Alan who won the corner that led to our second goal. Schnellinger looked glad of the rest but there was no respite for Alan, who raced over to take the corner himself. He swung the ball over for Geoff Hurst to hammer it towards Tilkowski's goal. Schulz lunged at the ball but didn't strike it cleanly. The ball ballooned into the air. As it dropped, Martin Peters stepped forward to rifle it into the net. There was a pleasing symmetry about the timing of the goal – having fallen behind after thirteen minutes, we were now in the lead with thirteen minutes left.

Those minutes ticked away, each one seeming like an hour. But we were going to win – I could sense it. Then, with the game in its dying embers, the Swiss referee Herr Dienst penalized Jack Charlton for a foul on Siggy Held.

It looked like a harsh decision to me and big Jack wasn't happy about it either. In his view the foul should have been given the other way for backing in. Lothar Emmerich drove the free kick into my penalty box, which was a sea of red and white shirts. I thought I saw Schnellinger help the ball on with his hand. (Although I was too busy to notice it at the time, the linesman must have thought so too because he raised his flag briefly, then inexplicably lowered it again.) The ball bounded across the face of goal towards my left-hand post with me in hot pursuit. Wolfgang Weber came sliding in. I saw that Ray Wilson had extended a leg in an attempt to block the ball should it come low, so I threw myself towards the post, with my outstretched arms above Ray's leg. One of us was bound to block Weber's effort.

Wolfgang Weber was a highly intelligent footballer. He was quick off the mark, but his mind was even quicker. As Weber slid in to meet the ball he glanced up, assessed the situation immediately and lifted the ball with the toe of his boot. Ray tackled fresh air, I grasped at nothing and the ball shot over both of us and into the net. The disappointment I felt was matched only by my disbelief.

For all Weber's skill, however, the goal should never have been allowed to stand. Although the referee failed to spot it in the goalmouth mêlée, I am quite certain that the ball was handled. As soon as Schnellinger's hand touched the ball both Bobby Moore and Martin Peters appealed, but Herr Dienst would have none of it. The goal stood. Seconds later, Herr Dienst did blow his whistle – to send us into extra time.

I felt as if the bottom had dropped out of my world. Glory had been snatched away when I practically had it in my hand. All manner of emotions swept through me. In a matter of moments I felt deep disappointment, only for that to be displaced by anger, then self-pity and, last of all, gritty determination. I reminded myself that we hadn't lost. That game and the World Cup were still ours for the taking. I told myself that I must apply myself totally, both mentally and physically, for another thirty minutes. That was all. I knew I could do that. I convinced myself that on this day, of all days, I could do anything. I would do whatever it takes and hang the consequences. If the boots were flying, I'd dive in. This was the World Cup final and I wasn't about to start calculating the risk of injury. Wounds heal, but do you ever get over disappointment and failure?

During the interval Alf took to the pitch and issued to us all, the challenge of our lives: 'You have won the World Cup once,' he said, 'now you must go out and win it again.'

I looked across to Bobby Charlton, Nobby Stiles and Alan Ball. Their heads were nodding, their faces a mixture of strain and determination. Bobby Moore clapped his hands together.

'We're gonna do it, come on. We're gonna do it,' he urged us.

After a gruelling ninety minutes on a stamina-sapping pitch such as Wembley's, the pace of a game usually drops in extra time. Not in this game. I looked on in amazement, wondering how anyone could maintain such a tempo. Alan Ball was every-where, his appetite for the ball as greedy as the jaws of a lion. Bobby Charlton glided as if the match were only ten minutes old. Nobby Stiles made his previous performances in midfield look like a warm-up run. Roger Hunt criss-crossed Wembley like a pinball. Big Jack was imperious in defence and Bobby Moore . . . Well, Bobby was Bobby. In the frenetic pace of the game he remained as cool as a bank of snow, elegantly and seemingly effortlessly controlling our back line, though his sweat had stained his shirt as red as a Kansas school house.

Luckily I managed to hold on to everything the Germans threw at me – and Held, Seeler and Haller threw a lot. With ten minutes of extra time on the clock, Nobby Stiles played a long ball down our right wing. Who chased it? Alan Ball, of course. Alan hit a low ball into Geoff Hurst, who was some ten yards from Tilkowski's left-hand post but facing the touchline. Geoff swivelled and hit a rising drive. The ball cracked on to the underside of the crossbar and bounced almost vertically down-wards before being headed away by Wolfgang Weber.

I didn't realize it at the time, but I was watching football history in the making. Roger Hunt, following up Geoff's effort, was in no doubt that the ball had crossed the line. The West German players were equally convinced that it had not. Encour-aged by the Germans to take a second opinion, Herr Dienst walked over to the Russian linesman, Tofik Bakhramov. For what seemed like an age, the two conferred as an anxious silence descended on Wembley. German players stood hands on hips, Geoff Hurst was on tenterhooks and the crowd was treated to the rare sight of Alan Ball standing still. Eventually Herr Dienst turned away from his linesman and pointed to the centre spot. Wembley erupted once more. It was a goal.

And it *was* a goal. I am convinced. True, I was standing at the other end of the pitch, but Roger Hunt's reaction and subsequent testimony have left me in no doubt as to the legitimacy of Geoff's effort. Roger was a prolific goalscorer, he alone was right there when the ball crashed down from the crossbar into the goal-mouth. Believe me, if Roger Hunt had thought for one moment that the ball had not crossed the line, he would have knocked it in himself. He didn't, because he knew it was a goal.

Not only that, but the linesman, Bakhramov, was up with play and looking along the goal line. So the two people best positioned to judge whether the ball had crossed the line said that it had. That there were some whose position did not afford them such a privileged view, who swore that the ball had not crossed the line, is of little consequence. And that was the view taken at the time by the referee.

None the less, the debate concerning the legitimacy of England's third goal continues to this day. I can understand the Germans wanting to continue their efforts to prove the ball did not cross the line (though no concrete proof has ever emerged), but I cannot for the life of me fathom what motivates the many English people who assist them in their campaign. Professors and boffins from the Institute of Rear-End Speech have wasted countless hours of computer time trying to show that the ball never crossed the line. It galls me that some of my countrymen should spend so much effort trying to prove that the goal, which to all intents and purposes won the World Cup for England, should have been disallowed. What is the point? And where's their patriotism? To the best of my knowledge, no Argentine has protested with such vehemence against Maradona's 'hand-of-God' goal against England in the 1984 World Cup, or tried to prove that Sol Campbell's disallowed effort for England against them in France '98 should have stood.

The devastating blow we had received seconds from the end of normal time was almost repeated in the final minutes of the extra period. Not once, but twice. With little over a minute of the game remaining, Siggy Held latched on to a pass from Emmerich and dispatched a fiery shot towards the left-hand corner of my net. Fortunately I'd taken up a good position and my angle was spot on. I hit the ground as though felled by a sniper's bullet and gratefully clutched the ball to my chest. Moments later West Germany were back. Held nodded the ball across the face of goal and caught me wrong-footed. As I quickly attempted to readjust my balance I watched helpless as Uwe Seeler's lunge was only the width of a bootlace from making contact with the ball. That, however, was only a prelude to the climax of what had been a cliffhanger of a game.

Once again the ball was delivered into my penalty area only for the imperious frame of Bobby Moore to chest it down and move upfield with seemingly effortless authority. Bobby momentarily looked up, spotted Geoff Hurst some ten yards inside the German half of the field and chipped the most exquisite pass in his direction. Bobby's limbs must have been experiencing crippling weariness, but you'd never have known it from the way he played that ball downfield. To this day I find it hard to believe that, so late in the game, Bobby could emerge from defence with such élan and have the vision to execute such a deft pass over such a distance – in the last minute of extra time in the World Cup final. Who else could have done that?

Geoff took the ball on his chest. At first I thought he was going to saunter towards the corner flag to kill time, but suddenly his legs began to pump and, unimpeded by flagging German defenders, he took off towards Tilkowski's goal.

Famously, three supporters came on to the pitch thinking that the referee had blown for time. Where are they now? Who were those lads who took to the pitch thinking it was all over? Their anonymous presence has seeped into the fabric of history.

Hans Tilkowski did what he had to do. He came out to narrow the angle, but Geoff summoned what dregs of strength remained in his body and blasted the ball goalwards. The roof of the net bulged and what followed was unforgettable.

I ran to the edge of my penalty area and punched the air in a display of complete and utter joy. Bobby Charlton dropped to his knees. Nobby Stiles and George Cohen unashamedly hugged one another. Alan Ball ran five paces before doing a cartwheel across the pitted emerald turf. Jack Charlton looked up to the heavens and appeared to say 'Thank you'. Roger Hunt leapt in the air, both hands outstretched above his head.

Seconds later, it was indeed, all over. When the whistle blew, Bobby Charlton cried like an innocent man suddenly released from jail. Nobby danced his famous toothless jig. Alan Ball ran and whooped around the pitch like a Comanche. Martin Peters saluted the crowd. Me? I felt as Christopher Columbus must have felt when realizing he hadn't sailed over the edge of the world. Jimmy Greaves came on to the pitch and hugged Nobby Stiles. Ron Flowers grasped me to his chest. Meanwhile, Alf Ramsey remained a model of dignity and grace, refusing to be drawn into what he obviously regarded as the greatest moment in the lives of his players, although the success was as much his as ours.

Bobby Moore eventually led us up the thirty-nine steps to the royal box and the World Cup. Before shaking the hand of Her Majesty the Queen and receiving the trophy, Bobby had the good grace to wipe the palms of his hands on his shorts. A captain in every sense of the word.

England's dream of winning the World Cup had been realized and so too had mine. As I descended the steps from the royal box clutching the medal every player in the world yearns for, I couldn't believe the journey I had made. The road from Tinsley Rec to a World Cup final had been long and winding, but the difficulties I had encountered along the way suddenly evaporated as my whole being was engulfed with euphoria.

The England post-match banquet was held at the Royal Garden Hotel in Kensington Gardens. The Prime Minister, Harold Wilson, called in to see us, then joined in the singing with the crowds outside. The speeches were made, wine and champagne flowed. Cars flying Union Jacks honked around London until the small hours of the morning. Alf Ramsey, the architect of our success, took the arm of his wife Vickie and travelled back to their home in Ipswich to 'make ourselves a decent cup of tea'. It was all over, like the man said, but the memories will reside with me for ever.

Alf, later and deservedly Sir Alf Ramsey, was sheer class. He was in a class of his own. Some managers are tactically aware. Some excel in coaching. Others are good at motivation and man management. Alf's strength was that he was strong in all depart-ments. That's what made him so special. That's what made him the manager who won the World Cup for England.

Always fair in his dealings with players, always scrupulously honest, he was a man of unyielding integrity and absolute loyalty. Alf put his job on the line for Nobby Stiles when some people had called for Nobby to be dropped. Alf remained steadfast in supporting Nobby, and he was to all his players, and his loyalty was reciprocated. He was devoted to the team ethic, yet at pains to point out that no one was indispensable. He bore no grudges and he had no favourites. Alf's unrivalled knowledge of the game and the opposition were complemented by superb tactical acumen, yet his instructions to us as a team were always clear and simple.

How best to sum him up? At the post-match banquet, the Secretary of the Football Association, Dennis Follows, intro-duced Alf as 'a great man'. When Alf took to his feet, he was at pains to correct that statement: 'With all due respect to the Secretary of the Football Association, there are no great men,' said Alf, 'only men.' Alf Ramsey may have been just a man, but there is no doubt that he was one possessed of an extraordinary talent.

I have never felt that Alf received the recognition he truly deserved for having planned and guided us to victory in the World Cup. Why did the Football Association never think fit to have an extra winner's medal struck and presented to him? Why no statue in his honour outside Wembley? Whatever the reason, it's a shame, it really is, for had it not been for Alf Ramsey we would never have won the World Cup.

The team received the promised bonus of £22,000 from the Football Association. We all agreed that the team's success should be shared by the whole squad. So we decided to divide the bonus equally among all twenty-two members. That meant we received £1,000 each; in practice, after the deduction of 40 per cent income tax, we were richer to the tune of £600 each for winning the World Cup. Still, we didn't play just for the money.

By contrast, it's interesting to note that during the official pre-tournament photocall, a London street vendor blagged his way past security and joined the press in taking photographs of the England players. He then had those photographs screen-printed on to T-shirts and sold them outside Wembley before our games. He told us he made over £1,500.

The late Kenneth Wolstenholme, the commentator who during his BBC broadcast famously said, 'Some people are on the pitch; they think it's all over. It is now!' had the good sense to copyright those words. Ken told me that over the years he made more money from the royalties than the entire team earned for winning the World Cup.

But this is just a footnote; a comment. It certainly isn't sour grapes. I and every other member of the team would have played for nothing. Money was of no importance to us. The glory of winning for England was paramount, and the joy we felt and still feel from knowing we had brought so much happiness to so many people is something money could never buy.

14. The Leaving of Leicester

Winning the World Cup in 1966 was a watershed for English football. Things were never to be the same again. But although winning the World Cup certainly had a profound effect on our domestic game, other factors unrelated to football also played their part.

The consensus of opinion is that the success of Alf's 4–4–2 formation in the final brought to an end, almost overnight, the use of orthodox wingers in English football. The truth is somewhat different.

Prior to the '66 World Cup, many coaches (including those early graduates of the FA's coaching school at Lilleshall discussed earlier) had been asking wingers to adapt to a new pattern. While still operating on the flanks, wingers had increasingly been asked to play deeper. The success of Alf Ramsey's 4–4–2 and 4–4–3 systems served to make the four-man midfield more common. The difference after 1966 was that 4–3–3 and 4–4–2, variations of which had previously been common in the professional game, filtered down through semi-professional football to park teams.

If anything, our success in the World Cup served as a convenient benchmark for the myriad changes that were affecting not only football, but the whole of society at that time. Following England's historic 6–3 home defeat against Hungary in 1953 and the subsequent success of Real Madrid in the 1960 European Cup final, it had taken some time for English football to get its house back in order. The changes undertaken in the late fifties gathered momentum following Real's sublime performance at Hampden, and finally bore fruit in the mid-sixties. Our success in the World Cup final was not so much a new beginning as a grand finale to ten years of gradual modernization and change.

Though I had no idea at the time, change was to be very much in prospect for me when the 1966–67 season got under way. Winning the World Cup had spawned a sharp rise in league attendances. A crowd of nearly 50,000 saw Leicester City's opening-day defeat at Liverpool, and the healthy gates were to continue throughout the season. In 1965–66 just over 12 million people had passed through the turnstiles at First Division grounds. In 1966–67 that figure increased by 2 million. The knock-on effect of our success in the World Cup was that English football was once again rated the best in Europe, if not the world, and the growth in attendances reflected that.

Manchester United, Tottenham Hotspur, Nottingham Forest, Leeds United and Liverpool were locked in a battle for the Championship, though Leicester were never far behind. For much of the season we fluctuated between fifth and eighth, a performance that considering the size of the club and its financial resources, was no mean achievement.

I was also on the top of my form in goal. My development continued apace and at twenty-nine I was looking forward to at least six more years of top-flight football. So it came as something of a bombshell to me when the Leicester manager, Matt Gillies, told me he believed my best days as a goalkeeper were behind me.

The portents had been there in March 1967 when Gillies suddenly – and in the eyes of the City supporters, controversially – sold Derek Dougan to Wolves for £50,000. The Doog was a cult figure at Filbert Street, as he would later become at Molyneux. His contribution to the team had been significant and he was enjoying playing First Division football again. Wolves were in the Second Division, though on course for promotion. Derek wasn't keen to move, but when your club would rather have the money you can generate in the transfer market rather than your contribution to the team, you might as well move on. And that's how Derek saw it. As it was to turn out, the move proved to be to his advantage. The Doog enjoyed the best days of his playing career with Wolves, forming a prolific scoring partnership up front with John Richards.

With the benefit of hindsight I suppose the signs were plain enough. The Leicester board had lost little sleep when they let one icon go, and I was only too aware that in Peter Shilton the club possessed a reserve goalkeeper of considerable promise. Peter was only eighteen, but I had seen enough of him on the training ground and in reserve matches to know he had all the makings of a great goalkeeper.

I never feared for my place. Why would I? After all, I was England's number one and we had just won the World Cup. The French sports paper, *L'Équipe* had ranked me as the number one goalkeeper in the world. What's more, FIFA had published their best eleven from the '66 World Cup and I had secured the goalkeeping position. I firmly believed that my best days as a goalkeeper were ahead of me. History was to prove that I wasn't wrong. My mistake was to believe that Matt Gillies and the Leicester board were possessed of similar foresight.

It was a Tuesday morning in April. In our previous match we had fought a hard earned goalless draw with a Leeds United side that needed points for their championship challenge. I felt I had played well in that game, so after training when Matt Gillies called me over for a 'wee chat', I had no idea what was to come.

'Gordon, the directors and I have been talking,' said Matt. 'Not to put too fine a point on it, we think your best days are behind you, and you should move on.'

I was speechless. Dumbfounded. Shell-shocked. It took a few moments for me to gather my thoughts. Even then all I could think of was to ask Matt to expand on his statement.

'What are you saying, gaffer? That I'm finished here?'

'I think it's best for all concerned,' he said.

I drove home in a dream. I felt rejected, unwanted. I had that dreadful feeling one has with the realization that though you believed yourself to be popular, others had been talking with a view to undermining your position. My anxiety sprang not only from this sudden rejection, but also the total surprise. In two sentences my world had been turned upside down.

When I told Ursula what had happened she couldn't make sense of it either. The following day at training, I told my Leicester team mates; though it was news to them, I gained the impression that they were not shocked or surprised. Later in the day, things became clearer. Richie Norman told me that Peter Shilton had issued an ultimatum to the board: unless he played in the first team, he would leave the club. Richie was my best pal and I didn't doubt his word. Indeed, other team mates I spoke to that day backed up Richie's version.

I would like to go on record as saying that I hold nothing against Peter for approaching the board and stating his own case in such explicit terms. From the moment I became aware of his potential, I believed he would eventually succeed me in the first team – I just didn't think it would be so soon. Even at eighteen, Peter had tremendous confidence in his own ability. He did what he had to do to further his career. I wasn't surprised by his ultimatum to the board. What surprised me was the board's eagerness to comply.

Matt's 'wee chat' signalled the end of the road for me at Leicester City. I was placed on the transfer list at the behest of the club with the fee set at £50,000 (the same as for Derek Dougan), and I awaited developments.

A number of clubs showed interest. West Bromwich Albion, Manchester United, Liverpool and West Ham United all made enquiries. For reasons unknown to me, both West Brom and Manchester United never followed up their initial approach. I quite fancied Liverpool and for a time I thought a move to Anfield might be on. The Liverpool manager, Bill Shankly, had told me on a number of occasions that, should Leicester ever wish to sell me, he would be in for me like a shot, but when push came to shove, Shanks didn't take up the option. The lack of interest on the part of Manchester United and particularly Liverpool had, I believe, much to do with the fact that many managers still didn't fully appreciate the worth of a good goal-keeper to their team. Some years later, after I had played a game at Anfield, I asked Bill Shankly why he hadn't signed me.

'I wanted to sign you, Gordon, son,' Bill told me, 'but the board here wouldn't let me. They said it was too much money for a goalkeeper. Jesus Christ, son, what do directors know, eh?'

I never knew whether to believe Bill or not. Even in 1967 he was a legend at Anfield, a patriarch who ran the club his way – the Liverpool board had a reputation for never interfering in team affairs. I think that if he had really wanted to sign me, he would have won round his sceptical directors.

For years the top clubs like Manchester United and Liverpool, thought little of paying big fees for outfield players, but never for a goalkeeper. Manchester United had been happy to shell out big money for players such as Gordon McQueen, Martin Buchan and Joe Jordan, but in the late seventies and early eighties when Peter Shilton and Pat Jennings were seeking moves, United never came in for them, seeming to be content with Gary Bailey in goal. Now Gary, like his successors at United, Jim Leighton and Les Sealey, was a fine keeper, but in all truthfulness not in the same class as Shilton, Jennings, or Ray Clemence. For years Manchester United tried and failed to repeat their League Championship success of 1967. I firmly believe if they had invested in a top-class goalkeeper it would have paid handsome dividends and they wouldn't have had to wait twenty-six years between Championships. The fact that when Manchester United did eventually win the Premiership in 1992–93, they had the excellent Peter Schmeichel in goal, only reinforces my point. Sir Alex Ferguson, like many other managers now, fully realized what a difference a top-class goalkeeper could make to a team.

With Liverpool's interest cooling, West Ham United seized the initiative. The West Ham manager, Ron Greenwood, was keen to do business and from my point of view the prospect of linking up with my England colleagues, Bobby Moore, Geoff

Hurst and Martin Peters was very appealing. West Ham were only a marginally bigger club than Leicester, but I liked their football philosophy and their purist approach to how the game should be played. Ron Greenwood struck me as an honest, decent guy who was a man of his word. He was, and it was Ron's desire to keep his word that scuppered my proposed move to Upton Park.

Earlier in the season Greenwood had enquired about the Kilmarnock goalkeeper, Bobby Ferguson, only to be told that he was not for sale. Kilmarnock, however, had told Ron that should they ever want to sell Ferguson, they would ring him first. Ron promised the Kilmarnock officials that should they ever do that, he would buy Bobby Ferguson at the drop of a hat. Now I had been speaking to Ron Greenwood and we got on well. But just as we were about to agree terms, someone dropped the metaphorical hat: Kilmarnock rang him to say they were ready and willing to sell Bobby Ferguson. Greenwood got in touch and told me that he couldn't go back on his word, and West Ham couldn't afford to have both Ferguson and me at the club at the same time. So I was back on the market.

Initially I was disappointed. It would have been great to play in the same club team as Bobby, Martin and Geoff every week, but I have always shared Mr Micawber's belief that 'something will turn up'. Two days later, it did.

Matt Gillies called me into his office one morning in April 1967 to tell me he had received a firm offer for me, and that, as I had not asked for a transfer, he and the board would discuss the payment of a loyalty bonus in recognition of my seven years' service at the club.

This was great news. Who had made this 'firm offer'?

He told me it was Stoke.

Stoke City, a mid-table First Division side, were hardly the most fashionable club of the day, but I'd played against them often enough to know they were a good side with the potential to be even better. Having discussed the matter with Ursula, I told Matt that I was interested and he immediately arranged for the Stoke manager Tony Waddington to come over to Filbert Street to discuss terms. I had no idea what wages Stoke City were offering, but as Leicester were known for the lowest pay in the First Division, I didn't think I was going to take a drop.

Prior to meeting Tony Waddington, I had another meeting with Matt to discuss the proposed loyalty payment. It didn't go well.

'Have you and the board reached a decision?' I asked.

'We have.'

I settled back in my chair to await the good news.

'We've decided not to pay you a penny,' he said.

I was flabbergasted and furious. I told him exactly what I thought of him and the directors, but he wouldn't be swayed.

'There's to be no compensation payment and that's final,' Matt said firmly.

'Then the deal's off,' I told him. 'If it means me staying here and playing in the reserves, then so be it. You and the board can sing for that fifty grand.'

I left Matt's office in a dark mood and found Tony Waddington sitting in the main foyer.

'I'm sorry, Mr Waddington, but the deal's off,' I said with a shrug, and proceeded to tell him why.

His face betrayed no emotion whatsoever and he didn't say much. He simply stood up and said, 'Leave this to me,' before sweeping into Matt's office without knocking.

Five minutes later he marched out. 'Two grand all right?'

I told him that would be fine by me.

'Good!' he said. 'Then let's do the deal and get out of here.'

We did the deal and I became a Stoke City player there and then.

A couple of years later, I was on Stoke City's pre-season tour of Holland, and one night in our hotel I got talking with Doc Crowe, a Stoke City director. I told him how happy I was at Stoke and the story of how my transfer would have fallen through if Tony Waddington hadn't persuaded Leicester to come up with the compensation payment.

'Did they hell,' said Doc, 'we paid you that!'

He went on to relate how Tony Waddington had found Matt Gillies as awkward and intransigent as I had. Having got nowhere with him, and afraid that the deal would fall through, Tony had simply walked out of Matt's office and plucked the £2,000 figure out of the air, knowing that his own directors would back his judgement and that the Stoke board, already committed to paying Leicester £50,000, Tony knew, wouldn't baulk at parting with another couple of grand if that's what it would take to sign the current England goalkeeper.

For two years I'd had no inkling that it had been the Stoke board who had paid the compensation – the money had simply been credited to my bank account. It was typical of Tony Waddington; he was a great guy and one of the most underrated managers in football. Tony realized the importance of a good goalkeeper to a team and I'd like to think he believed that his board's money was well spent. Later he said my efforts in goal saved Stoke City twenty goals a season. Whether that was truth or flattery, it was nice of him to say it.

Some say that Tony was ahead of his time in recognizing the value of a good goalkeeper to a team. To my mind it was more a case of other managers being behind the times. Whatever, I loved the man. He was a manager who always set out to sign gifted players to entertain the supporters; a manager who always believed that football at its most inspirational and creative has a place in the best of all possible worlds.

His first priority was to his players, his second to the supporters who paid their hard-earned cash to watch us. He never forgot how important the role of football was in the lives of working people, as evidenced by his marvellous description of football as 'the working man's ballet'.

★

Ursula had lavished so much love and attention on our home in Kirkwood Road that it sold almost straight away. We found a house about ten miles from Stoke, just over the Cheshire border in an area known as Madeley Heath. The house, which had a mock Tudor frontage, was larger than our Leicester home and, though the area was known as a heath, there was a substantial amount of woodland close by, evoking a feeling of country living. We settled in straight away, and on my first day at Stoke City, the warm reception I was given made me feel equally at home there too.

I made my Stoke City debut at Chelsea on 22 April 1967 (just twelve days after my final Leicester appearance against Leeds – though it seemed much longer). Chelsea won by the only goal of the game and, though disappointed not to have begun a new chapter in my career with a victory, I came off the Stamford Bridge pitch happy in the knowledge I hadn't let myself or my new team down. Tony Waddington seemingly thought so too because he patted me on the back, said he was pleased with me and raised my spirits no end by telling me, 'Your best is yet to come, and it'll coincide with the best days this club has ever known.'

Fate decreed that I was to make my home debut for Stoke against Leicester City. Needless to say, I was really on my mettle that day. Goals from Peter Dobing, Harry Burrows and young John Mahoney gave us a 3–1 win over my old team mates, who I have to say were generous in defeat.

Only two games of the season remained, against Arsenal and Manchester United. United had clinched the League Championship the previous Wednesday evening by beating West Ham 6–1 at Upton Park (that might have been me conceding six, had my move to East London gone through!) and over 60,000 packed Old Trafford to see them crowned as champions. Though they were missing Denis Law through injury, United were still formidable with Bobby Charlton, George Best and Nobby Stiles at the top of their form. The pressure from United was virtually ceaseless, but I learned in this game that Stoke City had a resolute defence. Despite all that pressure we held on for a goalless draw and what my new team mates believed was a moral victory.

I could never have believed when I kept goal for Leicester City at Liverpool on the opening day, that by the end of the season I would be playing for another midlands club. You never know what life has in store, and that's very true of football. England were the world champions, but in April 1967 in a European Championship qualifying match, we slipped up in sensational style at Wembley, much to the joy and delight of our friends north of the border.

Following the World Cup, England had drawn with Czechoslovakia and beaten both Northern Ireland and Wales. It was evident from those games that, as world champions, England were now the prize scalp on the international scene. All three teams had raised their game and pulled out all the stops in an effort to beat us. In addition to this greater team effort there was an undercurrent of resentment on the part of some nations towards our success in the World Cup. A number of people in South America even believed the tournament had been rigged to enable England to win it. This, of course, was absolute tosh. I know FIFA have done some strange things, but to think they would (or could) manipulate a World Cup in favour of a chosen team is utter nonsense.

I suppose that behind this accusation lay the fact that we had played all our games in London, at Wembley. All I can say is that that is how we came out of the draw for the qualifying group. As far as World Cups were concerned, the team from the host nation usually played their matches at the national stadium. In the 1958 World Cup in Sweden the hosts played in Stockholm, and Chile in Santiago in 1962. Mexico played all their matches of the 1970 World Cup at the Azteca stadium in Mexico City. To the best of my knowledge, no one has ever implied that those host nations had been favoured. However, the pattern in more recent tournaments has been that the hosts play at least some group and second-round matches outside the capital – France visited Lyon, Marseille and Lens in 1998, and may even have benefited from a slightly less intense atmosphere than the pressure-cooker of their national stadium. So the home-town effect cuts both ways.

In '66 the winners of Group One had been designated to play their quarter-final tie at Wembley, the runners-up at Hillsborough in Sheffield. It so happened that we won Group One, so we played Argentina at Wembley. If we'd finished as runners-up – and that was entirely possible after we drew our first match against Uruguay – we would have happily headed north.

Whether out of jealousy or resentment, it appeared some people had it in for England and there were all manner of outlandish theories as to why we had won the World Cup. I'd like to think we won it because we were the best side in the tournament and the world. The final against West Germany was our forty-fourth match under Alf Ramsey and we had lost only six times. Over the same period of time, that record was unmatched by any other international team.

Conspiracy theorists apart, those teams who knew we had been worthy winners spared no effort when facing us. England were there to be shot at, and in April 1967 Scotland came up with the firepower.

Neither players nor supporters need to be motivated for a clash between England and Scotland. It is the oldest fixture in the international calendar, one steeped in history, permeated by patriotism, fuelled by fervour and fanaticism and completely nerve-racking to play in. As if there weren't enough at stake, the game was given additional importance because it was both part of the Home International Championship and a European Championship qualifier.

England did not get off to the best of starts. Jack Charlton broke a toe in the early stages and, as he could not be substituted, he had no alternative but to play on. Alf switched Jack up front, which affected the balance of the team. Minutes after Alf had dealt with that change, we suffered another setback. Scotland's Billy Bremner caught Ray Wilson with a tackle that was later than a privatized train. Despite damaged ankle ligaments, Ray too carried on valiantly. Jimmy Greaves, back in the England team, also picked up a knock and though Jimmy's injury was not as serious as Jack's or Ray's, it definitely took the edge off his performance.

With England effectively down to nine men, I think we did well to give what was a very good Scotland team such a close game. No doubt any Scot reading this will say that I'm making excuses for our defeat, so let me say that, on the day, Scotland were the sharper and more incisive team and deserved their victory. In fact, they would have beaten any nine-man team in the world!

Seriously, though, the Scots were up for it from the start. They took to the pitch hyped-up but in control of their emotions. They exuded gritty determination and their will to win was there for all to see. As both teams walked out on to the pitch, I knew we were in for an almighty battle because of one astonishing sight – *Denis Law was wearing shinpads!* In all the games I had played against Denis, I'd never seen him wearing the protectors. I remember thinking, If he's tooled up for battle, what can we expect from Billy Bremner, Tommy Gemmell, Eddie McCreadie and John Grieg?

As far as the Scottish lads were concerned, this was their World Cup final and in no time at all we were made to realize just how much that meant to them. Fiery and combative from the start, Scotland took the lead through Denis Law. Receiving the ball from Jim Baxter, Denis turned in the space of a hearthrug and fired a shot to my right. I managed to parry the ball, but in a flash Denis was there to lash the rebound into the net. It was like Hogmanay, Burns Night and the resurrection of Harry Lauder all rolled into one as thousands of Scottish supporters wildly celebrated.

The game then developed a pattern of attack and counter-attack. Bremner, McCreadie and Gemmell snapped away at the heels of anyone in a white shirt. Bobby Charlton probed and prodded but found the Scottish defence as uncompromising as the truncheon of a Glasgow polis. Twelve minutes from time, Celtic's Bobby Lennox outwitted George Cohen on the byline, cut inside and crashed the ball past me and into the net.

Almost from the restart a limping Jack Charlton pulled a goal back. I was hopeful we could get something out of the game, but fate had other ideas. Having evaded two tackles, Jim McCalliog bore down on my goal at an angle and I quickly came out to narrow his vision of the goal. I should have given more cover to my near post to force McCalliog across the penalty area. Instead McCalliog glanced up, saw the gap I'd left and struck the ball with venom. The ball flashed by on my near side and I was left to curse what I knew had been a silly mistake on my part while I picked the ball out of the net.

We were far from done for, however. Geoff Hurst put us back in the game with a fine piece of opportunist finishing and in the closing minutes we laid siege to Ronnie Simpson's goal. At one point I thought we had scored the equalizer but Jimmy Greaves's effort was hacked off the line. The seconds ticked away, the Scottish players dug in, and their supporters got behind them in no uncertain terms. Scotland defended like demons in and around their penalty area. They denied us space in the approaches to goal and began to frustrate us to the point of desperation. There was conflict, there was drama and in the end, when Herr Schulenburg from (of all countries) West Germany sounded his whistle, there was defeat for England.

It was bedlam. Scottish supporters poured on to the pitch, many producing penknives. They were no threat to us, however. Those Scottish lads had only one thing in mind – to take a chunk of the Wembley pitch back home with them as a souvenir turf of their famous victory over the world champions. The famous turf was left pitted and scarred as dozens of ecstatic Scotsmen carved it to pieces. Legend now has it that there is a house in Bonny-bridge that has a Wembley penalty spot in the centre of the lawn in the back garden. I believe it!

The despondency felt by the England players was in marked contrast to the euphoria of the Scottish team. Any thoughts I had of the Scottish players being gracious in victory and appreciative of our efforts were immediately dispelled by Denis Law at the post-match buffet.

'Gordon, come here, son. We need your help over here,' said Denis Law as I entered the room. 'Can you provide the answer to a question that has stumped us?' asked Denis, looking from me to his pals Jim McCalliog, Jim Baxter, Billy Bremner and Ron McKinnon.

I told him I'd try.

'England are world champions,' said Denis, as if butter wouldn't melt, 'but we've just beaten you. So does that mean we are the world champions now?'

Denis and his team mates roared with laughter. To the side of him was a large bowl of mayonnaise, but I resisted the temptation.

I took all the ribbing from the Scottish lads in good heart. They were worthy winners on the day and deserved to savour their moment of triumph. It was a great time to be a Scottish football supporter, for while their victory over England did not make them the official world champions, two months later Celtic became the first British team to be crowned European champions following their superb victory over Internazionale in Lisbon. The balance of power in the football world seemed firmly to lie in Great Britain.

As the England team coach left Wembley, our police motor-cycle escort had to pull up at a crossroads. There was a pub on one corner and outside were hundreds of Scottish supporters toasting their team's victory. They saw our coach and, perhaps befuddled by copious amounts of alcohol, at first took us for the Scotland team. Glasses were raised and bonnets thrown into the air. There were cries of 'Well done!' and 'Great performance!'

Alan Ball stood up to acknowledge their good wishes and suddenly it dawned on them who we were. I'd never seen Alan Ball move so quickly. Pint glasses, pies and bottles crashed against the side of the coach. Our driver, throwing caution to the wind, put his foot down and shot across those crossroads with a bevy of tartan-clad supporters in hot pursuit. I was left trying not to think about their reaction if England had won.

Between 1968 and 1970 Tony Waddington slowly but surely turned Stoke City from a middling First Division side into one capable of challenging for silverware.

Tony had taken over as manager in 1960 when Stoke were poorly placed in the Second Division and pulling crowds of around 9,000. His success was built on a strategy of blending youth and experience, a philosophy he adhered to throughout his seventeen-year spell as manager of the club.

The Stoke City side of the late sixties was very much in the Waddington mould. Players such as Jackie Marsh, Alan Bloor, Eric Skeels, Tony Allen, Mike Pejic, Bill Bentley and Denis Smith were all products of Stoke's successful youth policy. The experience of the home-grown players was backed by a number of seasoned professionals of quality whom Tony had signed for modest fees.

Tony Waddington had the knack of persuading good players who were coming to the end of their careers that they had two or three more years at the top when their respective clubs thought otherwise. By and large he was right. Grateful for a few more years in top-flight football, the experienced pros Tony signed rarely let him down. He wasn't the most technically minded of managers, nor the most adept at tactics, but he didn't have to be. Good, experienced players don't need to be told what to do in a game. They know.

Full back Alex Elder had won a Championship medal and played in an FA Cup final for Burnley as well as winning forty caps for Northern Ireland. Willie Stevenson had won both the

League Championship and FA Cup with Liverpool. I had been in the same England Under-23 team as Peter Dobing who, in addition to a spell at Manchester City, had played for Blackburn Rovers in the 1960 FA Cup final. Both Maurice Setters and David Herd had bags of First Division experience under their belts and had been in the Manchester United side that had beaten Leicester City in the 1963 Cup final. Roy Vernon (Blackburn and Everton) and Harry Burrows (Aston Villa) were also seasoned First Division players.

And then there was George Eastham. George was an exceptionally gifted player from the traditional school of inside forwards. He scored a lot of goals and also created a lot for his colleagues. George was what we used to call a 'schemer', a highly creative player with superb vision who was able to pass the ball inch-perfectly. His first club had been Newcastle United. From there he moved on to Arsenal, doing exceptionally well at Highbury where his performances won him a place in the England team. (He was, of course, a member of the England squad of '66.)

To fine-tune the team, and provide balance between youth and experience, Stoke had Terry Conroy. Terry was a Republic of Ireland international. Naturally two-footed, he possessed incredible stamina, lightning pace and one of the best body swerves I ever saw. As Jackie Marsh once remarked after seeing Terry execute a sublime dummy on Arsenal's Ian Ure, 'TC, you not only sent Urey the wrong way, the crowd on that side of the ground had to pay again to get back in.'

The camaraderie in the Stoke dressing room was fantastic and with so many players who 'knew their way around', hardly a day went by without me splitting my sides with laughter at the antics and comments of my team mates. Sometimes the joke was well and truly on me.

When Stoke were in London once for a game against Chelsea, Terry Conroy, Jackie Marsh, George Eastham and I decided to kill time on the morning of the match by going for a walk around the streets near our hotel. Before long Terry spotted a pavement artist and we strolled over to view his work, which turned out to be an amazing series of chalk drawings of the heads of the England team that had won the World Cup. We gazed down at a drawing of a bald head over which a few lines of yellow chalk had been scratched to indicate strands of hair.

'It's Bobby Charlton,' said Terry, convulsing with laughter.

Another paving stone showed another balding head, this time with black chalk hair. The mouth was a black circle with two white rectangles on either side of the circle to indicate teeth. Above the mouth were two large white circles of chalk, each boasting a brown dot in the middle for eyes.

'Nobby Stiles. Brilliant!' said Terry, warming to this artwork of the most primitive type.

We shuffled along the line of crude drawings with Terry, Jackie and George howling with laughter at each one. Eventually we came to a paving stone that showed a face with a crooked nose and a gormless expression surmounted by a manic scribble of black hair.

'Who's this supposed to be?' I asked.

'Gordon Banks,' said the artist proudly.

That did it for Terry. He collapsed to his knees. Tears streamed from his eyes and he beat the pavement with his fists and howled. Jackie Marsh and George Eastham clutched their stomachs with their hands in a vain attempt to calm themselves, and slid down the wrought-iron railings they had been leaning on for support.

When I saw them there, helpless with laughter, I had no choice but to join in.

One of the prerequisites of being a good team player is the ability to take a joke. If you can't have a good laugh at yourself, you're in trouble. A football changing room is a testosterone-driven man's world. Out there on the pitch you have to know how to dish it out and how to take it. The same is true of the dressing room. If a team mate cracks a joke at your expense, or plays a prank on you, the worst thing you can do is take it seriously. A petulant reaction only invites more gibes and jokes at your expense. The best way to deal with it is to see it as a test of character. If you're the sort of player who takes exception to jokes at your expense, team mates will see that as a flaw in your character. The way footballers see it, if you're too sensitive to take a bit of playful ribbing, you're not the sort of player they can depend on to roll your sleeves up and battle when the going gets tough on the pitch. Wallflowers are biennials, but their life expectancy in a football dressing room is much shorter.

You have to take the stick from your team mates and the knocks from the opposition. As a goalkeeper, I experienced plenty of the latter. In the sixties every First Division club seemed to have a barnstorming centre forward whose first job would be to test the mettle of the opposing goalkeeper. With their first attack, the opposition would cross the ball into the penalty box and their number 9 would try to clatter me. You had to be up for that; it was part and parcel of the job at the time. Only if you gave as good as you got, or simply demonstrated that you were able to cope with such robust challenges, could you win the mind games.

There was a game in 1969 against Sunderland, however, when I definitely came off second best, though the injury I received was accidental and came late in the game. Terry Conroy had given us the lead at Roker Park and we looked comfortable for both points. There were only fifteen minutes of the game remaining when Sunderland's Gordon Harris split our defence with a through ball. Sunderland's young centre forward, Malcolm Moore, gave chase and I came quickly off my line. It was touch and go who would reach the ball first, but I was determined that it would be me.

As Moore advanced into the penalty area I came out and dived at his feet to collect the ball. Unfortunately Moore's momentum carried him on. As he slid forward in a last-ditch attempt to get a toe to the ball, his knee whacked against my forehead and everything went black.

The next thing I remember is being prostrate on the ground with a knot of players watching as the Stoke trainer Frank Mountford wafted smelling salts under my nose. I momentarily regained consciousness and told him I was going to be all right, but Frank wasn't so sure. He called for a stretcher and I lay there listening to my team mates debating what best to do. Then Peter Dobing asked who could play in goal.

David Herd immediately rallied to the call. 'Me. I can play in goal,' said Herdy, with not a little confidence.

'Are you sure?' asked Peter. 'There's a quarter of an hour left –'

'Give me Gordon's top,' said Herdy. 'I tell you, this lot won't put a single goal past me.' Peter looked at Jackie Marsh and Alex Elder who shrugged their shoulders to indicate it was worth a try.

I vaguely remember Frank Mountford asking Eric Skeels to help him remove my goalkeeping jersey, then everything went black again.

I woke up in Sunderland General Hospital. The first person I saw was a nurse who said I was suffering from acute concussion. It took some time to gather full consciousness and when I did, I noticed Frank Mountford sitting at the end of my bed. He asked me how I was feeling. I told him I just wanted to go home.

'How'd we get on?' I asked. 'Herdy said they wouldn't put a single goal past him. Was he as good as his word?'

'He was,' said Frank as he gathered my clothes together. 'They didn't score a single goal. They scored four!'

Goalkeeping. It isn't as easy as it looks.

In addition to physical strength you need mental toughness to be a goalkeeper. It's no good performing heroics for eighty-nine minutes to keep the opposition at bay, only to lose concentration for a moment and let in a soft goal. Luck is part of the goalkeeper's lot and you have to be strong enough in character to accept it and override the bitter disappointment you feel when you are the victim of bad luck and poor decisions.

Every time I took to the pitch I hoped that all my hard work would not be ruined by a bad decision on the part of an official, or some bad luck. Of course, these things do happen many times over the years and often either of these factors cost me a goal and thus my team the points. I even remember one match when a controversial decision and bad luck combined.

In 1973 Stoke City were riding high when we went to Anfield. Liverpool were in a great run of form and no team relished playing them on their home turf where they rarely lost. The game was a thriller. We worked hard for each other and deserved the lead Jimmy Greenhoff gave us with a well-timed header just after the half hour. Roared on by the Kop, Liverpool laid siege to my goal, but for all their dominance had only an equalizer from Emlyn Hughes to show for their efforts.

The Liverpool players had been taken to the very limits of their skill and stamina by a Stoke City side whose commitment was absolute. A draw at Anfield in those days was considered a great achievement for a visiting team and I thought we deserved nothing less, but events in injury time conspired to deny us what was rightfully ours.

With only seconds remaining Jackie Marsh clipped the heels of Liverpool's Ian Callaghan. Callaghan, though off balance, carried on with the ball at his feet for a couple of yards. The referee Roger Kirkpatrick waved play on, but when Callaghan stumbled and went to ground, he brought the play back and gave Liverpool a free kick just outside our penalty area on my right-hand side.

We thought it was a bad decision but didn't protest. Callaghan hammered the free kick into a very congested penalty area. The ball was deflected by Eric Skeels and I quickly adjusted my positioning to get in line with the flight of the ball, only for it to take another slight deflection off the calf of Kevin Keegan and into the net. This was more like pinball than football. At the restart Jimmy Greenhoff only tapped the ball to Geoff Hurst when Mr Kirkpatrick blew for time.

After pulling out all the stops for the best part of the game, a highly controversial refereeing decision and two cruel deflections all in the last thirty seconds meant I came off that pitch on the losing side.

Football can be a very cruel game, especially for a goalkeeper. When a week of hard work and preparation goes down the pan in a moment entirely beyond your control, it's devastating. But I found it best not to think too much about it. To dwell on bad luck and poor refereeing has a detrimental effect on your mental attitude. If you're not careful, you think fate has it in for you and wallow in self pity. Far better to simply accept such things as part and parcel of the game, and find consolation in the fact that over time these things tend to be cancelled out by an equal number of favourable events. All you can do is not dwell on the last game, but look forward to the next one. Stay assertive and positive and you won't go far wrong.

Having been at the club for a number of years, the products of Stoke City's youth policy such as Alan Bloor, Eric Skeels and Denis Smith brought continuity and stability to the team. On the other hand, Tony Waddington's policy of signing experienced pros capable of playing two more years at the top, also saw a gradual but steady turnover of players.

This curious mixture of stability and transience enabled Stoke to survive quite comfortably in Division One without ever threatening the elite band of clubs challenging for honours. But all that was to change in 1970.

At the start of the new decade the Stoke team had a much more settled look about it. The home-grown talent had matured in experience and blossomed; many of the ageing players had moved on, and though George Eastham and Harry Burrows were both in their thirties, they were still good for a few years yet. Tony was still signing experienced pros, but in Jimmy Greenhoff and John Ritchie there was a crucial difference. They were both experienced First Division players but, unlike David

Herd and Roy Vernon, they were not near the end of their careers. They were in their prime.

John Ritchie was in his second spell at Stoke and Tony Waddington had signed him on both occasions. The first time had been in 1961, when John was a part-time professional at Kettering Town. (He actually took a drop in pay to play league football because the money he earned from his job in a shoe factory and his Kettering wages were more than Stoke were offering.) John quickly adapted to life as a full-time professional and his goals for Stoke led to a £80,000 move to Sheffield Wednesday in 1966. When Danny Williams took over as manager at Hillsborough, John found himself out of favour and Tony Waddington had no hesitation in paying just £28,000 to bring him back to Stoke. What a bargain he turned out to be. John scored 176 goals for Stoke in 343 appearances. He played alongside Jimmy Greenhoff, signed from Birmingham City in 1968 for £100,000, to form a striking force that was to figure significantly in the renaissance of Stoke City that would see us challenging for the League Championship, FA Cup and League Cup.

The turning point for Stoke City came in 1970–71 and it followed another important stage of my own career, for in the summer of 1970 I played in another World Cup for England. It turned out to be a highly memorable tournament, one in which Brazil more than made amends for their lacklustre showing in 1966 by producing the greatest team performance in the history of international football. A World Cup in which I was, at last, given the opportunity to pit my wits against the man I believed to be the greatest footballer in the world – Pelé.

25. England – World Champions. Need I say more?

26. I spent countless hours after normal training working hard to improve my technique as a goalkeeper. Here I am on duty with the England squad. The glove I'm wearing seems to be the sort you often see lying forlorn in a road.

27. Training with England. It looks as if I've been caught out by the speed of a break from the opposition – it must have been Alan Ball.

28. Alf Ramsey was the greatest manager I ever played for. His knowledge of the game, tactics and opponents was second to none. Here Alf offers his England charges the benefit of his profound knowledge and, as always, we are attentive listeners.

29. Leicester City's four home internationals. From left: Derek Dougan (Northern Ireland), myself, Davie Gibson (Scotland) and Peter Rodrigues (Wales).

30. Welcoming a young Peter Shilton to Filbert Street. Little did I know that my days at Leicester were numbered. Notice our training tops: Graham Cross reckoned they'd been knitted by Matt Gillies' mother.

31. It was difficult to adjust to the speed and flight of the ball in the high altitude of Mexico '70. Here I appear to be just about coping. In the background is Norman Hunter, who for all his fearsome reputation was booked only four times in his career (which, of course, may say much for the tolerance of referees in those days!).

32. The save that brought me global fame. As soon as the ball left Pelé's head I heard him shout 'Golo!' But I had other ideas.

33. The ball balloons over the bar to safety. Bobby Moore said, 'You're getting old, Banksy. You used to hold on to them!'

34. The mark of a good goalkeeper is how few saves he is called on to make. Organizing your defence is the key to good goalkeeping. Here I'm telling Bobby Moore, no less, who he should be marking.

35. In action for England against Scotland in 1971. Also in the picture are Martin Chivers (number 10), Roy McFarland, Billy Bremner and Bobby Moore. England won 3–1.

36. George Best about to pounce and flick the ball away from me during the game at Windsor Park in 1971. To this day, George still insists his goal should have been allowed. I'm with the referee on this one.

15. Pelé and Me

It always gives me great pleasure to tell my grandchildren that I had a number one hit. The England squad recorded 'Back Home' (with another catchy little number on the B-side, 'Cinnamon Stick') prior to leaving for the 1970 World Cup in Mexico and the record-buying public liked it in sufficient numbers to make it number one in May of that year. 'Back Home' spent a total of sixteen weeks in the charts and was replaced at number one by a band called Christie with 'Yellow River'.

Also in May, on the day the England squad left for Mexico, there was news of another kind from a more exalted level of the pop world. To general disappointment and great sadness it was announced by their record company that the Beatles were splitting up. It was, said one radio DJ, 'the end of a glorious era'. Little did I realize, that statement would soon also be applied to English football.

England's pre-tournament match schedule began with a game against Colombia in Bogotá. We had spent the previous two weeks in Mexico, gradually building up our training programme to acclimatize us to the searing heat and condition us to the thin air of high altitude. The heat was stifling but initially it was the altitude I found particularly difficult to cope with.

We stayed at a hotel in Guadalajara with a lift that wasn't working. I carried my suitcase and bags up two flights of stairs and by the time I reached my room, my lungs were heaving like forge bellows. The altitude also had an effect on the ball itself. It took me some time to grow accustomed to the quicker pace and swerve of the ball in the rarefied atmosphere. As a goalkeeper my problems were compounded by the sublime quality of the light. It was so bright I often lost sight of the ball as it came towards me through the shadows cast by the stadium, or even by players. I was left in little doubt that the conditions in which this World Cup was to be played would have a huge bearing on my individual performance and that of the England team. I was happy that I had addressed every possible eventuality regarding weather and conditions, but there was one aspect of Mexican life that I had overlooked, an oversight that was to have a crucial bearing not only on my World Cup but also England's hopes of winning it.

The Mexico acclimatization fortnight was tough graft. Alf and Harold Shepherdson pushed me to the limit in training and, along with some of my team mates, gave me numerous rigorous shot-stopping sessions. I felt that I was on top form and playing the best football of my career. During one of these sessions, Bobby Charlton turned to me after I had saved yet another of his thunderbolts and said, 'Gordon, I've run out of ideas of how to beat you.' Coming from a player of Bobby's prowess and stature, that was praise indeed. I felt really great. The confidence I had in my own ability was sky high and, looking back, my performances in 1970 were, I think, my best ever. As a goal-keeper, I could get no better.

After one shot-stopping session I went into the dressing room for my daily medical and weight check, and discovered I had lost seven pounds in weight that day alone. By the end of the fortnight I weighed twelve and a half stone, the lightest I'd been since I was seventeen.

Alf Ramsey had organized two warm-up matches against Colombia and Ecuador, as he believed teams used to playing at sea level would be disadvantaged in Mexico unless they had experience of playing at high altitude. Oddly, his opinion was seemingly not shared by the West Germans, who, notwithstanding their reputation for wonderful organization on the pitch and off it, did not arrive in Mexico until eighteen days before the tournament began. I believe Alf was right to organize the trips to Colombia and Ecuador, despite subsequent events. It wasn't his fault that our presence in Colombia turned into a nightmare.

From the moment I set eyes on it I didn't like Bogotá. We had been booked into El Tequendama Hotel which, I'd been told, was the best in Colombia and on a par with any top hotel in any principal city in the world.

On the drive from the airport, however, rather than looking forward to five-star hotel service, I found myself struggling with my conscience. I hadn't just seen poverty as a child, I'd experienced it. But the poverty I had known was nothing compared to what I saw on the streets of Bogotá. On the outskirts of the city we passed cardboard shanty towns where exhausted mothers clutched babies with distended stomachs and stick-like limbs. Knots of ragamuffin children stood about here and there at the side of the road to watch us pass by. Their faces shocked me: children of around seven or eight years of age who looked like old men and women. They were dressed in grime-ridden shirts and filthy trousers or shorts, and many of the younger children were shoeless. As our team coach flashed by we looked down into rows of vacant, expressionless eyes staring back at us.

The coach probed deeper into the city. I was appalled by the filth on the streets. At one point we passed a dead horse lying at the side of the road. Three days later when we returned to the airport, it was still there. To us the place looked like a living hell. Unlike the wretches clinging to existence in the shanty towns, we could at least comfort ourselves with the thought that we could catch a plane out. But there was a point when we began to wonder if we would ever see the back of Bogotá.

Alf Ramsey had warned us of the possible pitfalls of life in this city. Under no circumstances were we to eat anything that hadn't been prepared by the chef who had been appointed to cook for the England party. Alf told us to drink bottled water only, and to ensure that the bottle was opened in our presence so we could see that the contents hadn't been topped up with tap water. We were banned from going on our customary leg-stretching walks that were a favourite way of passing the time in a foreign city before a match. We were warned of the perils of Bogotá sub-culture. To minimize the chances of getting into trouble, Alf told us to stay within the confines of El Tequendama. Little did he know, there was plenty of trouble lying in wait for us behind the hotel's opulent façade.

Our friendly against Colombia proved to be a useful workout. Bogotá is 8,500 feet above sea level, some 1,500 feet higher than Mexico City, and though the rarefied atmosphere did pose problems, we coped. Every one of us was on the top of our game and fitter than we had ever been in our lives. I made an encouraging start to the match when I came off my line and saved at the feet of García, arguably Colombia's one truly world-class player. Five minutes later I foiled García again, diving low to my right to gather a snap drive after he had turned Keith Newton. Having coped with Colombia's initial pressure, we took the game by the scruff of the neck and began to control it. In the end we ran out comfortable winners courtesy of two goals from the ever improving Martin Peters, and one each from Bobby Charlton and Alan Ball.

On the same day Alf gave the rest of the squad a run-out under the guise of England 'B' against a team comprising Colombian squad members to ensure that every member of the squad had a game under their belts at altitude. In a competent and professional performance all round, a goal from Jeff Astle of West Bromwich Albion gave victory to a team that contained the likes of Peter Bonetti, Norman Hunter, Nobby Stiles, Colin Bell, Jack Charlton and Allan Clarke. Every player had been keen to do well, irrespective of which team he played in, because at this juncture the squad comprised twenty-eight players and Alf would have to trim it down to twenty-two for Mexico. Press speculation was rife as to the names of the six players Alf would send home. As it was to turn out, speculation about the 'unlucky six' put a strain on Alf's relationship with the British press, yet the atmosphere between manager and journalists was to be even more sorely tested by his handling of a major crisis.

During our stay at El Tequendama a curious incident took place. Bobby Moore visited the Green Fire jewellery shop in the hotel lobby to look for a present for his wife Tina. Bobby was accompanied by Bobby Charlton, shopping for a gift for his wife Norma, together with Nobby Stiles and Liverpool's Peter Thompson.

Minutes after leaving the jewellery shop, the manageress, Clara Padilla, approached Bobby Moore asking him to explain the disappearance of a $600 bracelet. The Colombian police were summoned. After a prolonged discussion involving both Bobby Moore and Bobby Charlton, Clara Padilla, Alf Ramsey and two FA officials Moore and Charlton put their signatures to formal statements and the matter seemed to be closed.

It was an odd incident, news of which quickly spread among the members of the squad, though none of us thought it anything more than a simple misunderstanding, which had been quickly cleared up. Alf impressed upon us all that we should not breathe a word of it to anyone, especially the press. As Alf told us, 'This sort of incident tends to get blown out of all proportion.'

Following our game against Colombia we travelled to Quito where goals from Francis Lee and Brian Kidd gave us a 2–0 victory over Ecuador. Quito is over 9,000 feet above sea level and the air is so thin that even a modicum of physical effort leaves you panting for breath. During the game the ball deviated through the air like a cricket ball delivered by a top-class swing bowler. By now I was getting used to the increased speed and swerve of the ball and felt pleased with the fact that I managed to hang on to every shot that came my way.

Again Alf organized a 'B' international for the remainder of the squad, this time against the Ecuadorian champions, Liga. The in-form Jeff Astle helped himself to a hat trick in this game and a goal from Emlyn Hughes gave our second string a handsome 4–1 victory.

The favourable results were secondary to the experience gained from playing at such a high altitude. We were all becoming acclimatized by now and when we left what had been a very successful and convivial trip to Ecuador, our confidence was as high as the altitude.

The day after our game against Ecuador we set off for Mexico City and the World Cup. Our flight involved a long stopover at Bogotá where we had to change flights. Rather than having us hang around the transit lounge for the best part of a day, Alf had arranged for us to return to El Tequendama for some relaxation.

Back at the hotel Alf had arranged a film show for us in the TV lounge. I'll never forget that film. It was *Shenandoah*, starring James Stewart and Doug McClure, a 1965 saga about the American Civil War and how it affected one family in Virginia. I'd seen the film twice before but, like most of the lads, I sat down to watch it again as it provided a welcome change from endless hands of three-card brag.

About halfway through the film, two suited Colombians came into the room for a quiet word with Bobby Moore, who left in their company. At the time, I never thought anything of this. In his role as captain of England Bobby was often called away to give interviews to the local press, or meet visiting officials from the British Embassy. Even when Bobby didn't come back, we still had no reason to think there was any cause for concern.

My suspicions were still not aroused when we assembled at Bogotá airport for our connecting flight to Mexico City and I noticed that Bobby wasn't with us. Alf Ramsey didn't say anything about Bobby's absence. None of the press corps questioned it, and as two FA officials were also absent, I simply believed Bobby had agreed to do some interviews for South American TV companies and that he would follow us on a later flight.

That journey to Mexico City was the most eventful and chaotic flight I have ever undertaken in my life. For a start, we ran into an electrical storm when nearing Panama City where we were scheduled to stop for refuelling. The plane rolled and dipped, and at one point dropped like a stone when we entered an air pocket. It was harrowing even for the most seasoned air travellers, of which Jeff Astle was not one.

Jeff was a nervous flyer at the best of times, and this was far from being the best of times. Jeff was riddled with anxiety and though Nobby Stiles and I were of a stronger disposition and did our best to allay his fears, poor Jeff couldn't help himself and went into a panic attack.

'He needs a drink to calm his nerves,' said Nobby.

Alf had banned the drinking of alcohol, but a couple of the lads managed to procure a few miniature bottles of vodka from a stewardess. We surreptitiously mixed the vodka with lemonade and administered the 'medicine' to Jeff, two or three doses of which calmed him down somewhat, though he was still far from being relaxed and happy. Fifteen minutes later, the electrical storm was behind us, and it seemed a mere trifle compared to the earthquake Alf Ramsey had just triggered.

Alf took to his feet to address the players and the accompanying press corps. I found what he said completely unbelievable. Bobby Moore had been arrested in Bogotá accused of stealing a bracelet from the Green Fire jewellery shop. The accusation had been made by the manageress of the shop, Clara Padilla. Furthermore, Padilla alleged that Bobby Charlton had covered for Bobby Moore while he stole the item.

Bobby Moore a thief and Bobby Charlton his accomplice? He might as well have been told Mother Teresa had been arrested for cruelty to children, it was that outlandish and unbelievable.

Of course, our concern was for the welfare of Bobby Moore, in custody in Bogotá. It was a disturbing thought that someone, out to disrupt our preparations for the World Cup, may have stolen the bracelet and planted it on Bobby. We in the squad were aware of the allegations against the two Bobbys, but this was a bombshell to the press corps. On hearing Alf's statement the journalists flapped like chickens in a hen house with a fox in residence. They were now privy to the biggest and most sensational story of the World Cup but, such was the technology of the day, being en route to Mexico City, they had no means of contacting their editors back in London.

By the time we touched down in Panama City for an hour-long refuelling stop, Jeff Astle's 'medicine' had gone to his head. We tried to keep him out of Alf's way, and did our best to smarten up his shirt and tie and make him look a bit more presentable, reasoning that it would be most unwise to provoke Alf's ire at a time like this. But we needn't have bothered. Alf Ramsey was like a man possessed. He paced around like a caged lion, his face inscrutable but his mind obviously preoccupied by the plight of his captain.

As soon as we entered the airport building the press boys ran to the telephones, just like in a courtroom drama when they scramble to file their reports of a sensational trial. The press found themselves in a cleft stick. Here they were, stuck in Panama en route to Mexico City when their editors wanted them back in Bogotá to cover the breaking news of Bobby Moore, no less, being accused of shoplifting. Some were told by their editors to hire a car to take them back, obviously unaware that the Colombian capital was some 2,000 miles away. By coincidence, many newspapers had assigned reporters to cover the RAC London to Mexico Rally (which can you believe it, Jimmy Greaves had entered), so several motor-racing correspondents suddenly and unexpectedly found themselves taken off the rally story and re-routed to Botogá.

When we eventually arrived in Mexico City the media were lying in ambush. The Bobby Moore story was now global news and a veritable army of TV, radio and press journalists jostled for position alongside photographers whose cameras flashed and whirred away at anyone and everyone. Jeff Astle, having been administered a little more nerve tonic, was by now unsteady on his legs and the photographers captured him looking as if he had

not changed his clothes from the moment we left Heathrow over
three weeks ago. Dozens of microphones were thrust in front of
Alf Ramsey. Alf realized that he had to say something, so he
issued a complete denial of the allegations that had been brought
against Bobby Moore. I'd never seen Alf appear so uncomfortable. On all the previous occasions he had been confronted with
a barrage of questions from the press, he had remained cool, calm
and collected. Now his speech came in gusts, like linnets in the
pauses of the wind. Alf was rattled and he wasn't the only one.

The local newspapers had a field day. If anything, they were
worse than the British press. The Mexican newspaper *Esto* had
managed to find out that a midlands brewery had sent a case of
beer to Jeff Astle. Apparently, prior to leaving England, Jeff had
given an interview for a magazine in which he mentioned that
this particular beer was his favourite drink. On reading this, the
marketing department of the brewery dispatched a case of their
product to Jeff care of our hotel in Mexico, simply as a goodwill
gesture for the World Cup. *Esto* had been tipped off about the
case of beer by a hotel worker and ran the story along with the
photograph of a dishevelled Jeff (who was in truth a very moder-
ate drinker) passing through arrivals at Mexico City airport. The
brewery got more free publicity than even they had dreamed
possible.

Esto linked this story to that of Bobby Moore and when Alf
Ramsey was shown the headline, 'England Arrive – a Team of
Thieves and Drunks', he nearly had a coronary. To his credit,
Alf quickly regained his composure. Holding the newspaper in
his hand, he walked up to Jeff who was sitting in the lounge of
our hotel and uttered the words every England player dreaded:
'Jeffrey, a word please . . .'

The one person to keep his cool throughout this whole sorry
affair was Bobby Moore himself. Bobby refused to be rattled
because his character and psychological make-up wouldn't allow
it. When the heat was on, when the game was frenetic and
fraught, Bobby was immune to the pressure. Throughout this

whole affair he was to remain a model of probity, and conducted himself at all times with grace and dignity.

I have no doubt in my mind that Bobby was stitched up by someone out to disrupt our preparations for Mexico, or someone out to make monetary gain from involving him in a trumped-up charge. They definitely chose the wrong man when they picked out Bobby Moore. Bobby was unflappable. He took everything in his stride and never ever lost his head. His personality and character were very strong and his unruffled self-belief enabled him to survive the attentions of the Colombian authorities. They found no chink in his armour and eventually dropped the ridiculous charges that had been brought against him.

I shudder to think what might have happened if the allegations had been made against any other member of our squad. I doubt that anyone but Bobby could have emerged psychologically unscathed from an experience like that, facing an inexplicable charge in a foreign jurisdiction thousands of miles from home. And then to go out and play arguably the best football of his career – that was the measure of the man.

The case against Bobby began to look more and more ludicrous as the investigation conducted by the Colombian police progressed. Bobby was in danger of being imprisoned by the police for the course of the investigation, but the President of the Colombian Football Association, Alfonso Senior, intervened and suggested Bobby be placed under 'house arrest' at his home. That was the first positive point. The FA tour party officials then received a telephone call from the Prime Minister, Harold Wilson, who said he was willing to speak to the President of Colombia himself in an attempt to clear Bobby's name. Ultimately Mr Wilson's proposed call was unnecessary because the case against Bobby fell apart by itself.

The Green Fire manageress, Clara Padilla, told the police that she had seen Bobby Moore slip, what now had evolved into a $3,000 bracelet sporting a large diamond, into the left-hand pocket of his England blazer. (You will recall that the bracelet was worth $600 a few pages back. Well, that's South American inflation for you!) The problem with this tale was that our blazers didn't have a left-hand pocket, as the Colombian police discovered when looking at Bobby's. Padilla then changed her story, saying she had not actually seen Bobby pocket the bracelet, but had acted on the word of another customer in the shop, one Alvaro Suarez. Señor Suarez said he had seen Bobby slip what was now a $6,000 bracelet studded with diamonds and emeralds, into 'a pocket somewhere on his person'. The Colombian police stated that, 'having subjected Suarez to further and more intense questioning' – one can only imagine what that may have entailed – he too changed his story. Now he 'thought he might have seen the England captain put something in his pocket'.

Clara Padilla tried to wash her hands of the whole affair, saying that she had in fact seen nothing and had been put up to it by Suarez. Then the police discovered that, rather than being a prospective customer, Suarez was a close friend and business associate of the owner of the jewellery shop, Danilo Rojas. It seems that the Green Fire was in financial difficulties as were its owner, Rojas, and Alvaro Suarez.

When Bobby appeared in court and the so-called evidence against him was presented by the prosecution, the judge, Pedro Durado, threw the case out. Bobby was free to go and rejoin us in Mexico. Bobby was mightily relieved, though he at no time betrayed the anxiety he must have felt. He left the court displaying the same dignity and grace he had maintained ever since his arrest.

'I have nothing against the Colombian police and authorities,' Bobby told the waiting reporters. 'Charges were brought against me, they simply acted on them and they did their job. Their job was to establish the truth and they achieved this. I was totally innocent of the charges brought against me and that has been established. All I want to do now is join up with my fellow England players in Mexico and give my undivided attention to helping England retain the World Cup. Thank you, gentlemen.'

What a man!

Had dark forces been at work? Had there been a conspiracy to prey on visiting celebrities by desperate people in deep money trouble? You decide. Suffice to say, very soon after Bobby's release Alvaro Suarez disappeared off the radar. Perhaps, following his exposure in the media, he simply lay low. As for Clara Padilla, she took off for the USA and, to the best of my knowledge, like me, never returned to Bogotá.

When Bobby Moore arrived at our hotel, the entire England squad lined up outside the entrance to applaud him. He hadn't had a change of clothing for nearly a week, yet he looked as smart as if he were stepping out of a tailor's shop after a complete makeover. His blazer, shirt and trousers were completely unruffled, as was the man himself.

As a postscript to this affair, I later found out that some eighteen months earlier a well-known Hollywood film star, a guest at El Tequendama, had been accused of shoplifting by the Green Fire jewellery store. Allegedly, a sizeable amount of money was paid by the star's 'people' to hush the matter up. Bobby Moore and Alf Ramsey provided less easy pickings.

The unlucky six players that Alf omitted from the squad were Ralph Coates (Burnley), Brian Kidd and David Sadler (Manchester United), Bob McNab (Arsenal), Peter Shilton (Leicester City) and Peter Thompson (Liverpool). Alf gave permission for Thompson and Sadler to remain with us under the strict instruction that neither should 'abuse their freedom'.

The twenty-two-man squad tasked with retaining the World Cup for England was, to my mind, a stronger selection than the one that had won it in 1966. We had greater quality in depth and more players at the peak of their powers. We all knew we had a huge task ahead of us, but to a man we firmly believed we could lift the World Cup again, and so too did Alf Ramsey.

That we were not the most popular side in the tournament was brought home to me when we watched the opening ceremony at the Azteca stadium on television. As in 1966, each country was represented by twenty-two children. When the poor Mexican children representing England entered the Azteca, they were roundly booed and jeered by the home crowd. As Alan Mullery remarked at the time, 'If that's their response to children in England shirts, what sort of reception will the Mexican supporters give the England team?'

We were soon to find out.

We were drawn in arguably the toughest group of the lot, Group C. We were up against Romania, Czechoslovakia and, of all teams, Brazil, who were coming into the World Cup on the back of an unbeaten run that stretched back over two years. Brazil had won all six of their qualification matches, scoring twenty-three goals in the process and conceding just two. The Brazilians were a major threat to us, but as two teams were to qualify from each group, we were very confident of progressing in the tournament. In fact, for all the prowess and power of Brazil, Pelé et al., we believed we were good enough to beat them.

Our first match was on 2 June, in Guadalajara against Romania. The hostile reception the Mexican supporters gave us when we took to the pitch was no surprise to anyone. The Mexican press had done their utmost to blacken our name and had even exhumed Alf's misquote of 1966 when he had supposedly described the Argentinians as animals. The fact that Alf had insisted we bring our own food, chef, even our own team bus and driver to Mexico seemed to antagonize the Latin American press. They accused us of being pompous, aloof, rude, unfriendly and anti-social. In fact, all Alf had done was to set a sensible trend. In subsequent World Cups just about every team in the world would take along their own chef who prepared meals to the strict dietary requirements laid down by the squad dietician.

Alf ignored his bad press, but such was the hostility towards him, his indifference was interpreted as aloofness. In truth his mind was too occupied with matters of football to be bothered by such peripheral matters as what the press were saying about him. Here our FA learned a valuable lesson. It was to be twelve years before England were to participate in the finals of another World Cup. That was in Spain in 1982 when Ron Greenwood was manager of England. Mindful of the bad press Alf had been given, the FA made sure Ron Greenwood had an official PR officer by his side to help him deal with questions from the world's media.

We failed to sparkle in our opening match against a physical and defensively minded Romanian team. Quite honestly, the game was a poor advert for international football, but we achieved our aim. We won, thanks to Geoff Hurst who latched on to a super pass from Francis Lee to score the only goal of the game with a shot that passed through the legs of their goalkeeper Adamache. Romania had been tough and difficult opponents, but we knew, and had known ever since the draw had put us in the same group, that our second game, against Brazil, would be harder still.

The match was scheduled for 7 June, five days after our victory over Romania. The day before the game Alf made me tremble at the knees when he approached me and said, 'Gordon, a word please.'

A year earlier, almost to the day, Alf had beckoned me in similar fashion. That had been before the first game of our tour of Central and South America, against Mexico. The news Alf gave me that day was devastating. He quietly and sympathetically told me that he had just received a telephone call from England informing him that my father had died. Dad had been very ill for some months. As a family we had tried to prepare ourselves for the worst, but Alf's words still came as a great shock to me. I was grief stricken. Alf offered words of comfort and condolence. The Mexico game was the furthest thing from my mind and he knew it. He told me there was no question about my returning home for the funeral.

I caught the next available flight home and on the journey steeled myself for saying one last farewell to Dad. He had always been a tremendous source of strength and inspiration to me, not only in my career, but throughout my life. His passing hit me hard and by the time I eventually touched down at Heathrow I was emotionally drained. But I knew that I had made the correct decision to return home to be with my family, and Dad for one last time.

A year later I was on tenterhooks, anxious to hear what Alf had to tell me. I hoped against hope it wasn't to be bad news concerning a member of my family. However, from his body language I got a hint that the news he was about to impart wasn't of the tragic kind.

'Gordon, a gentleman is on the telephone for you,' said Alf. 'It is a call I think you should take.'

I took the call and was astonished to hear a plummy voice on the other end of the line informing me that he was an equerry from Buckingham Palace.

'Mr Banks, I have the considerable pleasure and duty to inform you that you have been provisionally proposed to receive the Order of the British Empire in the forthcoming honours list to be awarded by Her Majesty the Queen,' said the voice. 'The purpose of my telephone call is to establish if you are willing to accept the said award, and to determine if you are in a position to accept it personally at Buckingham Palace. The occasion will be most auspicious.'

For a split second I thought it must be a wind-up. Alan Ball, Nobby Stiles, Jack Charlton and Alan Mullery were forever playing pranks and winding up other members of the team. But the fact that Alf Ramsey himself had summoned me to the telephone, convinced me the call was genuine. They wouldn't dream of involving Alf in one of their practical jokes. Besides, I could never imagine Nobby or big Jack coming up with a word like 'auspicious'.

I was floating on air. I wasn't just pleased, I was euphoric. I informed Mr Equerry that I would be delighted to receive such an honour and thanked him profusely. He swore me to secrecy, so I couldn't share my pleasure and pride with my team mates. I couldn't think why I had been chosen for an OBE and simply assumed the award was in recognition of my services as a goal-keeper to British football and, in particular, England. As is my way, in the end I decided not to question it too deeply and simply enjoy the moment. My joy was tinged with one sad regret: that Dad hadn't lived to hear of my OBE. Though in all probability he would not have shown it, I know Dad would have been as proud of me as I have been to be his son.

A couple of days before our game against Brazil, Alf Ramsey made an uncharacteristic faux pas. Following a training session he gathered us all together and told us that the eleven who had finished the game against Romania would start against Brazil. Full back Keith Newton had not recovered from the injury he had picked up against the Romanians, which meant his Everton team mate, Tommy Wright, was to continue at right back. Chelsea's Peter Osgood had replaced Francis Lee and Ossy could not contain his joy at having been selected to face Brazil.

Later that day we had a team meeting and Alf began talking about the roles of Francis Lee and Bobby Charlton, only for a perplexed Franny to point out that he hadn't been selected.

'But you are in the side, Francis,' said Alf.

For some reason Alf had completely forgotten that Peter Osgood had come on for Franny Lee against Romania. Alf was very embarrassed and Peter very disappointed. But not half as disappointed as he was going to be. Towards the end of the team meeting, Alf named our five substitutes and Peter Osgood wasn't even among them. Ossy, needless to say, was most upset about what had been a genuine oversight by the manager.

We were staying at the Hilton Hotel in Guadalajara and hardly got a wink of sleep on the night preceding our game against Brazil. Hundreds of Mexican supporters held an all-night anti-

England vigil in the street outside. They constantly chanted 'Bra-zil', honked car horns and bashed dustbin lids together. The England party had taken up the entire twelfth floor of the Hilton but the constant noise kept us awake all night. I was sharing a room with Alex Stepney of Manchester United. At one point a group of Mexican supporters gained access to the floor and banged on our door.

I jumped out of bed and swung the door open just in time to see half a dozen Mexicans in their late teens and early twenties being chased down the corridor by a furious Jack Charlton.

The hotel security staff and the local police hitherto had maintained a heavy presence at the hotel. Oddly, on this night they were conspicuous by their absence. The most anyone managed was two hours' sleep.

The following morning at breakfast, Everton's Brian Labone told Alf, 'I could sleep for England.'

'That's as may be,' said Alf, 'but what the nation wishes to know is, are you in a fit state to play football for them?'

Brian said he was. We all were. We had snatched only a couple of hours of fitful sleep, but such was our motivation and state of mind, we couldn't wait to get out there and face the Brazilians.

In Brazil's opening match against a technically accomplished Czechoslovakian team, Pelé had illuminated the proceedings from start to finish. Brazil won 4–1 and Pelé had been the focal point of every Brazilian move. I was left in no doubt. Pelé was the greatest footballer in the world. He combined effectiveness, vision and power with grace, beauty and style. Just to see him taking the ball on his chest was to witness athleticism of the highest order. When Pelé met the ball in the air, his first touch was wonderfully deft, on a par with the perfection he displayed when taking the ball on the ground. His shooting was both powerful and accurate and it was obvious he didn't give a jot which foot he used since both were equally deadly. Physically he was very strong. His speed off the mark was like lightning. Even when running at full gallop, Pelé's co-ordination made him appear to be marvellously relaxed. I believed him to be *the* great player. For years I had been looking forward to the chance of playing against him in a major competition. Now the moment had come. He was at the peak of his powers and, to be honest, such was his brilliance I didn't know how we would be able to contain him.

The teams filed out on to that emerald rectangle in Guadalajara. England, all in white, were Gordon Banks (Stoke City); Tommy Wright (Everton), Bobby Moore (West Ham), Brian Labone (Everton), Terry Cooper (Leeds United); Alan Ball (Everton), Alan Mullery (Spurs), Bobby Charlton (Manchester United); Martin Peters (Spurs), Geoff Hurst (West Ham), Francis Lee (Manchester City). Brazil were in their famous yellow shirts and blue shorts. This was their starting eleven: Felix; Carlos Alberto, Brito, Piazza, Everaldo, Paulo Cesar, Clodoaldo, Rivelino, Jairzinho, Tostao, Pelé. On the bench for England were Peter Bonetti (Chelsea), Emlyn Hughes (Liverpool), Jeff Astle (West Bromwich Albion), Nobby Stiles (Manchester United) and Colin Bell (Manchester City).

When Alf received the Brazilian team sheet he noticed that the influential midfield player, Gerson, wasn't playing. He was out with a thigh injury and had been replaced by Paulo Cesar. 'That's like replacing a Jaguar with a Mercedes,' Alan Mullery remarked on hearing the news.

Alf had reverted to 4–4–2, a system the players liked and which was more suitable to us as a squad because it allowed squad players to slot in comfortably. Colin Bell for Bobby Charlton, big Jack for Brian Labone, Nobby for Alan Mullery and so on.

At the team meeting Alf had emphasized the roles everyone was to play. In the centre of defence Brian Labone was to pick up and mark Tostao, while Bobby Moore would sweep around the back and pick up the bits. Alan Mullery had one of the most difficult tasks. Mullers was to 'sit in' just in front of the back four and push up when we were on the attack. Hard work, especially as the temperature in the stadium was over 100°F. (Absurdly, the match was set to kick off at noon, to suit television schedules back in Europe. You can safely say that World Cup football was by now organized to suit the TV companies, not the fans in the stadiums – still less the players.) Bobby Charlton was going to anchor the midfield and be our playmaker, pushing on with Mullers when we were taking the game to Brazil. Alan Ball and Martin Peters were going to work up and down the flanks, with Franny Lee playing off Geoff Hurst up front, with Geoff being our target man.

The onus was on our full backs, Tommy Wright and Terry Cooper, to overlap Bally and Martin Peters, receive the ball from our midfield and provide the crosses for Geoff. That was the plan, anyway. By and large, it was to work very well.

A crowd of over 72,000 packed into the Guadalajara stadium. During the national anthems I scrutinized the Brazilian line. They looked awesome, as physically strong as they were technically adept. The heat was so withering I was sweating buckets just standing in line. This was unreal. What did the man say about mad dogs and Englishmen going out in the midday sun? I remember wondering how Alan Mullery could possibly fulfil the role Alf had assigned him for a full ninety minutes.

The opening ten minutes were spent prodding and probing at walking pace in an attempt to sound one another out. The ball was allowed to roll unhindered by the side not in possession. Each side watched the opposition pass it in triangles, waiting for a mistake, keeping possession. Tackles were few and not full blooded. Short passes, safe angles, guiding the ball with care from our box to theirs. Wright to Mullery to Charlton to Ball to Lee. Strolling players in the searing heat. It was absorbing stuff.

Franny Lee tried to find Hurst but Brito extended a leg and Brazil leisurely wandered upfield. Brito to Paulo Cesar to Clodoaldo to Pelé. Whack! Alan Mullery dumped the great man on the ground. Mullers held up the palms of his hands to the referee in recognition of his cumbersome tackle and kept on the right side of the official by extending a hand to Pelé, offering to help him to his feet. Pelé ignored it. Mullers smiled and rubbed the top of Pelé's head with his hand.

'You OK mate?' enquired Mullers.

'I am not . . . your . . . "mate",' replied Pelé.

'It's best that you are,' said Mullers, 'believe me, yer don't wanna make an enemy of me.'

Pelé simply shook his head and smiled to himself.

I watched from my privileged vantage point as the game unfolded and the Brazilians treated me to a sight I thought I would never see on a football pitch. A walking midfield. With the instep of his right boot, Carlos Alberto leisurely pushed the ball into the path of Tostao. Tostao to Rivelino to Pelé. I took to my toes, arms hanging at my sides like a gunslinger ready for a high-noon shootout. Pelé turned, hit the ball out wide to the left only for Peters to spring forward and intercept. Peters to Ball to Charlton to the overlapping Wright.

'Go on, Tommy, son.'

Wright to Lee who played the ball back. Bobby Charlton arrived from deep and at some speed. Thump! Bobby hammered the ball at head height to Hurst who had taken up a position on our right. It was as if Geoff was nodding 'good morning'. His head dropped, the ball smacked against his forehead and it bounced once before reaching Franny Lee. Lee to Ball to Wright and back to Lee again. The Brazilians appeared to me to be overcome by a complete lack of concern. They simply watched and waited. Not one man in a yellow shirt ran towards any England player who had the ball.

Geoff Hurst had drifted into the Brazilian penalty box, Piazza shadowing him. Franny Lee waved his foot over the ball then poked it two yards forward with his left boot before smacking it goalwards with his right. The ball covered twenty yards in no time at all. Felix in the Brazilian goal had his angles spot on and didn't have to move an inch. He put his hands out in front of his head and gathered Franny's effort as if someone had thrown him a practice ball in training. He threw the ball out to Carlos Alberto who stroked it down the wing to Jairzinho.

Suddenly, the game exploded into life as Jairzinho took off like a rocket. We had been caught off guard by his sudden burst of speed. Jairzinho raced towards Terry Cooper and jinked as if about to cut inside. Terry put all his weight on his right foot and Jairzinho flashed past on his left-hand side. I took my eyes off Jairzinho for a split second to glance around my penalty area. What I saw spelled trouble.

The rest is history, which I have described in Chapter 1: Tostao free at my near post, Alan Mullery trying in vain to close down Pelé, Jairzinho's textbook centre and Pelé's perfect header.

Ninety-nine times out of a hundred Pelé's shout of '*Golo!*' would have been justified, but on that day I was equal to the task. Although I've tried to analyse that save as best I can in the opening pages of this book, it was really just about being in the right place at the right time – one of those rare occasions when years of hard work and practice combine in one perfect moment.

As Pelé positioned himself for the resulting corner he turned to me and smiled. He told me he thought that he'd scored. So did I – and I told him as much.

'Great save . . . mate!' he said.

The tremendous spirit of mutual respect between the teams demonstrated during that incident was to prevail throughout the rest of the match. It was a fantastic game of football. We knew we could match Brazil in the possession stakes, and our passing was as good as theirs. We held the ball up well, which is essential in such heat. We adapted our style to the slower, more methodical pace of international football, which was very much the opposite of the hell-for-leather tempo of our domestic game. On entering the dressing room at half time I was surprised to see non-playing members of the squad such as Jack Charlton and Peter Osgood, along with Peter Thompson and Brian Kidd, hacking at large chunks of ice with knives and chisels. Alf had instructed them to place broken ice in towels, which we were then told to drape around our necks to cool us down. It felt great so I asked Peter Thompson to hack off some more ice and place it in a polythene bag for me. I intended to take the bag of ice out with me on to the pitch, place it behind one of the goalposts and, when play was down in the Brazilian half of the field, use it to cool myself down.

And so we returned for the second half. We waited and we waited. We hung about on the pitch under the pitiless sun for nigh on seven minutes, waiting for Brazil to take to the field. The delay was never explained, but I was pretty sure that the Brazilians were employing an old tactic of theirs.

My mind flashed back to a friendly we had played against Brazil in Rio de Janeiro in June 1969. On that occasion they had employed delaying tactics before the game. Following the signal from the referee, we had been ready to take to the pitch only for an official from the Brazilian FA to tell Alf Ramsey that his team were not ready. We hung about kicking our heels for five minutes before Alf asked the Brazilian official what was going on.

'The Brazilian team are almost ready, Mr Ramsey.'

Another ten minutes elapsed before Alf summoned the official once more.

'The Brazilian team are almost –'

Alf cut him short.

'If the Brazilian team are not out in this corridor, ready to take to the field in thirty seconds,' said Alf tersely, 'I will order my players to change back into their clothes and we will return to our hotel.'

The official burst into the Brazilian dressing room, slammed the door behind him and within twenty seconds their team emerged.

On this occasion, however, there was little we could do but endure the burning sun and wait.

Less than ten minutes into the second half we were on the attack so I went over to the polythene bag anticipating a brief but welcome dip into my store of ice. I couldn't believe it. All I found was a bag of tepid water. In little over ten minutes, every chunk of ice had melted.

As if it weren't hot enough, Brazil contrived to turn up the heat still further. Bobby Moore, who was having the game of his life, came across to challenge Tostao. That left a gap in the centre of our defence which Alan Mullery filled. Brian Labone was marking Pelé, but now without the back-up of Mullers. Martin Peters arrived to support Brian, but as he did so Pelé jinked one way, then the other, and found the space to roll the ball into the path of Jairzinho. Terry Cooper was on to Jairzinho in a flash but in his eagerness lost his footing on the lush turf. Jairzinho sidestepped to his right and I came quickly off my line to cut down his view of the goal. I was just beyond the left-hand angle of my six-yard box when Jairzinho stubbed the toe of his boot at the base of the ball. It lifted over my spreadeagled body and into the opposite corner of my net.

'Yeaaaaaaaah, *Go-olo!*' Jairzinho screamed.

He whirled away and all I could do was watch disconsolately as he jumped so high in the air it looked as if he were attempting to touch the roof of one of the stands.

We gave it everything we had. Bobby Moore was imperious. Alan Mullery indefatigable. Alan Ball unlucky when he cut in from our left and saw his shot cannon off the Brazilian crossbar with Felix well beaten.

Towards the end, I thought we would deservedly equalize. Jeff Astle had only just come on as a substitute when he found Felix in no man's land and the Brazilian goal at his mercy. Everaldo and Piazza had collided when going for the ball. Everaldo recovered first but played the ball across the face of the Brazilian goal and Jeff was on to it in a flash. Jeff had finished the season as the leading goalscorer in the First Division and he had been presented with the sort of chance that was normally meat and drink to him. Whether it was because he had only just arrived on the pitch and was yet to be properly adjusted to the pace and intensity of the game, I don't know. Whatever the reason, he missed the sort of chance he normally gobbled up. With Felix stranded, Jeff scuffed his effort wide. The chance was gone, as was our chance of taking something from an even and exhilarating game.

Following the final whistle, after shaking hands with Brian Labone, Pelé went across to Bobby Moore, grabbed his face with both hands and gave it an affectionate squeeze. They then hugged one another and exchanged shirts. I think that gesture on the part of Pelé summed up the entire game, and in particular, the performance of Bobby Moore. It was, I am sure, Bobby's intention to go up to Pelé and congratulate him. But the Brazilian beat him to it. The victor saw fit to lavish praise upon the vanquished, because Pelé knew Bobby had been outstanding, and that Brazil had been as fortunate to win, as we had been unlucky to lose.

There had been little to choose between the two teams, but there had been one telling difference. Finishing. Brazil had taken their best chance and we had missed ours. At that level of football the consequences of missing a chance can be catastrophic. To be fair to Jeff Astle, although he missed our best chance, we did have other good opportunities to score. That we didn't proved to be our own downfall. None the less, we emerged proud in defeat. Brazil took both points, but the real winner that day was football.

That save from Pelé is considered by many to be the greatest I ever made. It is certainly a save I am very proud of, one that gave me a lot of satisfaction. As for being my best ever? Such opinions are always subjective. I believe the reason my save against Pelé has received so many accolades is largely due to the fact that it was made in a very high profile match in front of a global TV audience. The following day I made newspaper headlines across the world and my name as a 'world class' goalkeeper was made. That's really something for others to judge, but immediately following the Brazil match, Alf Ramsey put it into a broader context, and got it about right. When asked to comment on my performance, Alf told the football writer, Bryon Butler, 'His performance today was a continuation, rather than the culmination, of the standards he set himself over the years.'

It's hard to judge, but a save I made in 1971, during a match between Stoke City and Manchester City at the Victoria Ground, is one that I consider to be better than the one I made in Guadalajara.

Wyn Davies was a superb header of the ball, a centre forward who leapt to a phenomenal height. The Stoke defenders Denis Smith and Alan Bloor had unwittingly blocked my line of sight. When the ball was crossed from the wing to the far post I thought it had been overhit and would carry on and run out of play. Suddenly, there was Wyn towering above the ball some eight yards from my goal line. The ball cannoned off his forehead and headed for the left-hand side of my goal at head height. In such circumstances, with ground to make up, a goalkeeper has to think himself into the space. I took off immediately I saw Wyn about to make contact with the ball and somehow made up the ground. I not only got my hands to the ball but managed to hold it while soaring through the air.

Ask any Stoke City player and they will tell you that was my best ever save. Ask Rodney Marsh, though, and he'll say it was a save I made at the foot of my right-hand post from a Francis Lee header at Maine Road in 1972. Jimmy Greaves believes it was eclipsed by one I made at White Hart Lane, when, from six yards, I was suddenly confronted with a sumptuous volley on the turn from Alan Gilzean. Diving to my left, I managed to hold the ball in my left hand before gathering into my chest as I came back down to earth. The way Jimmy tells the story, on seeing me produce that save he turned to Alan Gilzean and said, 'If I were you, Gilly, I'd give up now. I've long since given up thinking of ways to try and beat him.'

My greatest ever save? From Pelé, Francis Lee, Wyn Davies

or Alan Gilzean? That's the beauty of football. It's all about different opinions, as the guy standing next to you in the pub would no doubt disagree!

Following the Brazil match Alf gave us permission to attend a cocktail party at our hotel to which our families were also invited. Ursula was back in Cheshire with the children, but it was great to see Mam and Aunty Dorothy. We caught up on the family news and, of course, I had some news of my own to tell them – my impending OBE. Mam was, naturally, absolutely delighted. She also told me how proud she was of the performance I had given against Brazil. It was all beginning to sink in, especially when one of the lads produced a copy of the Mexican newspaper *El Heraldo*. The Mexican press had been very anti-England, but *El Heraldo* carried a photograph of my save from Pelé under the heading 'El Magnifico'.

Bobby Moore saw me grinning at the headline and came over to me. 'I think they're referring to the header,' he said with a straight face.

This is family reading, so I won't tell you what my reply to that was.

The Mexican press may have warmed to us a little, but the Mexican public were still very hostile when we took to the pitch for our final group game against Czechoslovakia. I had more trouble with the crowd during this game than the Czech forward line. They pelted me with orange peel, apple cores and coins throughout the first half. I complained to the referee, who drew the matter to the attention of the FIFA officials present. They in turn asked the Mexican police to stand behind my goal and that changed things drastically: about five times the amount of orange peel and coins then rained down. I wouldn't be short of change for the telephone after this game. We dominated proceedings against the Czechs, but it was no classic. An Allan Clarke penalty gave us a 1–0 victory, but that was enough to see us qualify from our group, along with Brazil, who in their final group match beat Romania 3–2.

Jack Charlton replaced Brian Labone in the centre of defence against the Czechs. Towards the end of the match, the Czech full back Dobias tried his luck from twenty-five yards. The ball swerved through the thin air and what should have been a comfortable save for me, suddenly became a problem. I managed to get the fingertips of my right hand to the deviating ball and push upwards. I immediately spun around and was astonished to see the ball return from the crossbar and straight into my waiting hands.

'Brilliant!' said Jack, 'and what yor ganna dee for yor next trick against them Jormans?'

Little did I realize at that moment, but my next trick was to be a disappearing act.

16. Message in a Bottle

To this day I'm at a loss to explain what happened, exactly. All manner of wild and crazy theories have been put forward, the most common being, that I was nobbled. All I knew was that I was going to miss a match crucial to our prospects of retaining the World Cup. A game that, with hindsight, was a watershed for English football at international level.

Everything was going to plan. We had qualified for the quarter-finals and the spirit and confidence of the players was very good. There were even wonderful moments of light relief, courtesy of our police motorcycle escort.

We travelled from our hotel to the training ground in the coach Alf had had brought over from England, and on every trip we were escorted by the same motorcycle outrider from Mexico's Finest. In his pristine khaki uniform, mirror shades and knee-high black leather boots he was an imposing figure. We dubbed him Alfredo.

The first time Alfredo accompanied us, he rode diligently ahead of the bus, taking his duty seriously, ever on the lookout for anyone who might want to disrupt our journey. After a few trips, however, Alfredo must have become bored with the routine of it all and began to demonstrate just how confident and competent he could be on two wheels.

We were driving to the training ground on a country road that passed through the occasional small village when I happened to glance up.

'Hey-up, look at this fella!' I said, alerting the rest of the lads.

Alfredo was standing up on his motorcycle with both arms outstretched. We all stood up to watch his antics and gave him a round of applause. Alfredo looked over his shoulder, acknowledged our appreciation with a nod of his head, then showed us what he was really capable of.

With his motorbike doing about thirty-five miles an hour, Alfredo turned around to face us, sat down on the handlebars and once again stretched out his arms like a circus tightrope walker. I couldn't believe what I was seeing and neither could the rest of the lads. A highway patrolman riding backwards? We all fell about laughing before giving him another round of applause. I think our appreciation only spurred Alfredo to be even more adventurous.

I stood slack-jawed as Alfredo turned around to face the same way as the bike and momentarily sat on the pillion before easing himself back. He then leaned forward, gripped the handlebars with either hand and executed an amazing handstand – still speeding along at thirty-five miles an hour, remember.

We all started to whoop with delight at his extrovert show-manship. I'd been a dispatch rider in my time with the Royal Signals, but I'd never seen anyone perform stunts like this.

Every day after that Alfredo entertained us with the sort of tricks you'd expect from Evel Knievel. But although he seemed to be a terrific bloke, eventually we realized he was a mixture of showman and bully. We saw the ugly side to him one day on our way to the training ground. Alfredo had just treated us to another round of his trickery when he entered a small village. The road was so narrow there was only room for one vehicle to pass. Up ahead, an old pick-up truck was parked outside a store, blocking our path. Seeing the truck, Alfredo waved one arm up and down to indicate that our coach driver should slow down and stop. Alfredo parked his motorcycle behind the pick-up and was about to enter the village store when the owner of the truck appeared.

Alfredo's demeanour suddenly changed. From being jocular and clownlike, he turned very nasty and aggressive. He shouted angrily at the owner of the truck and with wild gesticulations tore a strip off him for parking his truck on the road. He probably wasn't anticipating an enormous luxury coach on that dusty little road.

It looked to me as if the driver was going to move his truck to allow us to squeeze through and that would be the end of the matter. As he walked towards the cab, however, he suddenly turned and seemingly said something disparaging to Alfredo. That did it. Alfredo turned on the man and began to slap him about the face. He then produced his baton and gave the truck owner one almighty blow across the thighs.

Concerned for the wellbeing of the truck driver, Alan Ball, Bobby Moore and I started for the door of the coach, but Alf prudently intervened.

'Do not become involved, gentlemen,' said Alf, barring our way with an outstretched arm.

The chastened truck driver jumped into his cab and made room for us to get by. Alfredo walked up to our coach and saw that he needed to explain his behaviour.

'Is no problem,' said Alfredo. 'He should no park here. I want let him go, but he show no respect for this uniform. You are not in England now, my friends, and I am not your London Bobbies. I deal him my way. He no do it again.'

'I bet he don't,' said Bobby Moore.

Moments later we were on our way again. Needless to say, we saw no more of Alfredo's stunt riding.

Alf had been meticulous about our healthcare: food, drink and even sunbathing. He did allow us to soak up some sun, but only for twenty minutes a day and in strict rotation. The only players to get a really good tan were David Sadler and Peter Thompson, who, having stayed on with our party after being released from the squad, were at liberty to spend as much time around the pool as they liked. Curiously, there was one squad player to get a good bronzing even though subject to these strict sunbathing limits, and that was Bobby Moore. For a time this perplexed me, until David and Peter told me that they'd gone up on to the roof of the hotel to take in the view of the surrounding area and found Bobby up there, doing some illicit sun-worshipping in a pair of skimpy shorts.

The quarter-final against West Germany was scheduled for Sunday 14 June in León. On the preceding Friday Alf allowed us to have a beer with our evening meal. After all these years I can't remember if the bottle I was served was opened in my presence or not, but I do know that half an hour after drinking that beer I felt very ill indeed.

I reported to Neil Phillips, our team doctor, who diagnosed a simple stomach upset and expected me to be as right as rain the next morning. At this juncture I had no reason to be particularly concerned: Peter Osgood had had an upset stomach but had recovered within twenty-four hours and I thought I would do likewise.

I passed an uncomfortable night at the hotel, most of it being spent in the loo. On Saturday morning I felt well enough to make the 150-mile trip to León. The plan was for us to train on the pitch at the Guanajuato stadium in the afternoon, but on that journey, I began to feel decidedly the worse for wear.

The lads were very chirpy. Some played cards, others read newspapers or books, a few just sat and chatted among themselves or watched the scenery pass by. I sat at the back of the coach praying for the journey to end. I was suffering from terrible stomach cramps and felt in imminent danger of being violently sick or something even more embarrassing, or both. I was sweating profusely yet shivering with cold, despite the 100°F temperature outside.

Dr Phillips checked me over and administered some anti-nausea pills. 'Give it half an hour,' he said, 'you'll feel a lot better.'

But I didn't.

The journey to our hotel in León seemed to take an age. When we eventually arrived I went straight to the room I was sharing with Alex Stepney and crawled into bed. In less than five minutes I was up again, rushing to the loo, which was where I stayed – I was glad that the wash basin was situated conveniently close to the toilet.

Alf Ramsey and the backroom staff held a meeting among themselves to discuss my situation. They decided to wait until the Sunday morning before making any decision about my fitness. The press boys guessed something was amiss, but Alf played down my situation: 'There is no cause for concern. Gordon Banks is just feeling a little off colour. We've had players like this before and normally they recover after a few hours' rest.'

The trouble was, I was being sick (or worse) so often that I was getting no rest. This was no 'normal' tummy upset. I felt as weak as a kitten. My limbs ached; my stomach cramped. I continued to sweat and shiver as if I'd been pushed outside on a winter's day wearing nothing but a pair of shorts. That night I spent more time shut in the loo than I did lying in bed. I felt sorry for my room mate Alex Stepney, but even sorrier for myself.

On the morning of the game my condition improved somewhat. I was slightly cheered at the thought that my body had seemingly purged itself of all the poison and rubbish that had been making me feel so ill. I couldn't face a normal breakfast, but I did manage to keep down two slices of dry toast and some bottled water.

Alf asked how I was feeling.

'A bit better,' I said.

'Fit enough to play?'

'I'll give it a go,' I said doubtfully.

Alf suggested I go back to my room and change into my training gear ready for a fitness test. I'd seen Alf's fitness tests before; they were quite rigorous workouts and I knew that if I passed the test in reasonable shape, I'd be fine for the game against West Germany.

There was no practice pitch at the hotel, but on one side of the building was a strip of lawn dotted with acacia trees and that's where Alf and Harold Shepherdson took me. My stomach was still delicate and to be truthful I was also feeling weak, but with over three hours to go before the game I felt that, if my improvement continued, I might be OK.

'Gordon, will you jog over to the far tree and back again, please?' said Alf.

I jogged in a leisurely manner to an acacia tree some twelve yards away and returned.

'How do you feel?' Alf asked.

'OK.'

'Will you do that again for me, please?' asked Alf.

I slowly jogged over to the same tree and back again.

'How are you now?'

'Still OK.'

'Excellent! Excellent!' said Alf, a beaming smile appearing on his face.

I didn't share Alf's great optimism. Two leisurely jogs to a tree twelve yards away and back again hardly constituted a fitness test in my book.

'Harold will now give you some ball work,' announced Alf. This was more like it, I thought to myself, this would really test me.

Alf asked me to walk to a point some eight yards away. As best I could, I bounced up and down on my toes. I did some arm stretching and then spat into the palms of my hands ready for the expected shooting practice.

Harold Shepherdson rolled a ball underarm across the lawn, like a father to a toddler. There was so little power behind the ball it only just reached me. I bent down and picked the ball up and threw it back to Alf.

'Good. Very good,' Alf said. 'And again Harold, if you please.'

Harold rolled another ball underarm in my direction, if anything, with even less momentum than before. It had all but stopped rolling when I bent down and picked it up.

'How d'you feel?' asked Alf.

'OK, I think,' I replied, wondering when the fitness test was going to begin.

'Splendid!' said Alf. 'You're playing.'

I couldn't believe it. What I had been subjected to was a fitness test designed for an 80-year-old. I returned to my room unconvinced of my fitness but hopeful that Alf knew what he was doing. I lay down on my bed hoping to get an hour's sleep but after only ten minutes the sickness gripped me again. I hoped this latest bout would be the final fling of the bug that had laid me so low. But it wasn't to be.

There was no lounge or conference room in the hotel available to Alf, so he summoned us all to his room for a team meeting. We all crammed in and I sat down on the floor by the door. As Alf began speaking, I began groaning. The stomach cramps had returned and with a vengeance. I'd hardly eaten a thing and there can't have been anything more to come. I felt dreadfully sick, my shirt clung to my body with my own perspiration, great beads of sweat formed on my brow then ran in rivulets down my face. As Alf talked to the squad he kept glancing over in my direction. Eventually he addressed me in person.

'Well?' Alf enquired.

I shook my head. 'Not well,' I replied.

Alex Stepney and Nobby Stiles helped me to my feet. I heard Alf tell Peter Bonetti that he was playing in place of me, and I walked out of the team meeting and out of the World Cup.

Once again we were handed a noon kick-off time to accommodate TV audiences in Europe who were watching it in the early evening. To play in the heat of midday is unwise at the best of times; for me it would have been suicidal. It was also broadcast on Mexican television, but with a time delay of fifty minutes, presumably to maximize ticket sales. Thus, when the game kicked off on the television in my hotel room the teams at the stadium were about to come out for the second half.

I was feeling dreadful but my spirits soared as I watched Alan

Mullery, with his first goal for England, give us a 1–0 lead at half time. Five minutes into my televised broadcast of the second half, my joy turned into euphoria as I watched a low cross from Keith Newton converted at the far post by Martin Peters. I rubbed my hands with glee: 2–0! The lads were doing England and me proud.

About twenty-five minutes from time the door of my room opened and in shuffled Bobby Moore, Brian Labone, Alan Mullery and Alan Ball. Their faces were grim, but I wasn't falling for another of their practical jokes. After all, on the telly we were still two up . . .

'How'd we get on?' I asked.

'Lost 3–2, after extra time,' said Bobby glumly.

'You're having me on, how'd we really do?' I asked.

'We're out, Banksy. We're going home,' said Bally.

'Pack it in, lads,' I said, 'I'm not in the mood.'

Then Bobby Charlton came into my room and I froze. Tears were streaming down his face – and at last the penny dropped. This was no wind-up.

I swung my legs out of bed, tottered across the room and turned off the television with us still leading 2–0. That's how I remember our game against West Germany. We are still leading 2–0. I didn't watch the remainder of the broadcast, nor the edited highlights that were shown later in the day. I just couldn't bring myself to sit and watch it and endure the pain. To this day I still haven't seen the match in its entirety.

A lot has been said about Alf's tactics and substitutions that day, and about the performance of Peter that day. Since, as I say, I've not seen the whole game, it would be wrong of me to comment. In his defence I can say that Peter was a first-class goalkeeper and that both Alf and I had every confidence in his ability. As my deputy since 1966, Peter had played just six times in four years for England when Alf told him, at the last minute, that he was to play against West Germany. Perhaps Peter felt deep down that, though a regular member of the England squad, he would never get his chance, that he might always be 'number two'. In not expecting to play there is a case for saying that he was given no time to prepare mentally for what was the biggest game of his life. Only Peter himself can say with any degree of certainty whether his performance suffered as a result.

What I do know for certain is that Alf was desperate for me to play against West Germany. The ridiculous fitness test apart, Alf is on record as saying, 'The one player I could not do without against West Germany was Gordon Banks.' If he couldn't envisage losing me, then he clearly couldn't bring himself to tip Peter the wink that he might be needed in the quarter-final, so providing him with some vital extra time to focus on deputizing for me.

After the game the football writer Ken Jones, then of the *Mirror*, went looking for Alf. (Ken Jones was held in high regard by the players because he wrote objectively about our games and, though he didn't pull his punches, was sensitive to the feelings of managers and players in defeat.) Ken found Alf in his room, very morose and with a few drinks inside him – both quite out of character for him.

'I don't know what to say to you, Alf,' said Jones. 'Me, the rest of the press lads . . . we feel for you.'

Alf told him to pour himself a drink. 'It had to be *him*,' said Alf to the bottom of his glass. 'Of all the players to lose, Ken, it had to be him!'

I am flattered that Alf seemed to think so highly of me, though whether my presence would have made any difference to the result of that game is impossible to say.

Likewise, I can't say for sure that the bottle of beer, suspected to have been the source of my illness, had indeed been tampered with.

It irks me when some people resort to conspiracy theories to explain a bad result. Following England's 1–0 defeat of Argentina in the 2002 World Cup some Argentinian supporters alleged that England, FIFA and the referee had conspired and contrived to produce an English victory as compensation for Maradona's 'Hand Of God' goal in 1986. That, of course, is absolute rubbish, the sort of theory that belongs to a fifth-rate thriller movie.

Similarly, I can't bring myself to believe that anyone could have been so determined to prevent me playing for England against West Germany in 1970 that they resorted to poisoning me, even though I had eaten the same food as my team mates and drunk from the same case of beer. Still, stranger things have happened – and I was the only player to be taken ill. Concrete proof simply won't be produced after this length of time.

Everyone was devastated after the Germany game, no one more so than Peter Bonetti. Peter believed he had let everyone down, though we all tried to persuade him otherwise. No one blamed him for what had happened. For six years the England players had adhered to a philosophy of collective responsibility: 'We'll all work together and battle together, and come what may, we'll either celebrate or die together.' Or, to put it more succinctly, 'All for one and one for all' – precisely the quality that continental teams say they fear and admire about English football. Rather than placing blame at the door of individuals, the spirit and great camaraderie among the players ensured we accepted defeat as a team. Though that didn't make our defeat any easier to swallow as we packed our bags to return 'Back Home'.

In their semi-final West Germany lost 4–3 to Italy who, in turn, lost 4–1 to Brazil in the final. Brazil's performance in the World Cup final of 1970 was a master class. On that day Brazil firmly planted their flag on the summit of world football, a peak to which all other teams must aspire. Their success was a triumph for adventurous football of the most sublime quality. The day when the most attack-minded team came up against arguably the best defence in the world. Samba soccer took on *catenaccio* and effortlessly swept it aside.

Brazil's triumph was also that of Pelé and of football in general.

Following his bitter disappointment of 1966, Pelé had a World Cup swansong to remember. The 'beautiful game' had a beautiful final in which we witnessed what is probably the most complete performance by the most complete team in the history of international football.

It would be twelve years before England were to compete at another World Cup finals. As far as the international team was concerned, England were about to enter a prolonged decline. At the time, if anyone had told me that England were to spend the seventies and beyond watching from the wings and sliding down FIFA's international rankings, I would have laughed, believing it to be nonsense. As a new decade was finding its feet we had not only very good international players, but a number who were world class. No one could foresee how our fortunes would plummet.

When we arrived home, Alf gathered us together for one last chat.

'You've all done me proud and you've done yourselves proud,' he said. 'You didn't deserve what happened in León. Let me tell you all, I am so very, very proud of you. As England manager, it has been an honour and a privilege to have you in my charge.'

He then shook every one of us by the hand and thanked us for our efforts, before slipping quietly away.

Some of the older players such as Jack and Bobby Charlton and Nobby Stiles saw this gesture as an epitaph to their international careers. Looking back now, perhaps Alf could see dark clouds on the horizon, and intended it as his own.

17. The Agony and the Ecstasy

It was the belief of Sir Stanley Matthews that Stoke City, although never fielding what he classed as a great team, had two that he judged to be 'very good'. Those were the team that was pipped for the League Championship on the last day of the season in 1947, and Tony Waddington's side of the early seventies.

I was lucky enough to be a member of the latter when Stoke City suffered agonizing defeats in two FA Cup semi-finals and won the League Cup. Cruelly, I was to be denied a place in the side that went so very close to winning the First Division title in 1974 for the first time in the club's history, but more of that later.

At the time I joined Stoke City it was because I believed they were a good side with the potential to be even better. By 1970–71 that potential had been realized under Tony Waddington and Stoke were competing for honours with the best.

We began the 1970–71 term modestly enough. A goalless draw on the opening day of the season against Ipswich Town was followed by two victories and three draws in our next eight league matches. On 26 September, however, we started to believe in our own ability. Arsenal, who boasted the meanest defensive record in the First Division, came to the Victoria Ground and we took them apart. Arsenal had made a habit of winning games 1–0, earning their 'boring Arsenal' tag to go with the 'lucky Arsenal' that they had been saddled with since way back in the thirties. While they may have lacked the flamboyance of Manchester United, the flair of Liverpool and the zest of Leeds United, in truth this Arsenal team, containing players such as my old Leicester City team mate Frank McLintock, John Radford, Ray Kennedy, George Graham and Charlie George, were a great side (as they were to prove by going on to win the League and Cup double that season). And on that day we thrashed them.

Stoke City were absolutely humming and the normally resolute Gunners defence had no answer. Two goals from John Ritchie and one each from Terry Conroy, Jimmy Greenhoff and Alan Bloor gave us a convincing 5–0 victory and sent the statisticians searching their records for the last time Arsenal had conceded so many goals in the course of a game.

Terry Conroy's was a marvellous goal. His stinging drive from all of twenty-five yards followed a six-man passing movement and was voted *Match of the Day*'s Goal of the Season. (By coincidence the Arsenal goalkeeper Bob Wilson was being sounded out as a potential presenter by the BBC and had been invited on to the programme that evening to talk about the game. On his TV debut poor Bob had to sit and pass comment on the five goals he had just conceded!)

Our fine victory over Arsenal gave the team an immense boost in confidence, though it was to be in the FA Cup rather than the League where our self-belief was to have an impact on our performances that season.

Stoke finished the campaign in mid-table, though we did enjoy some memorable results. Leeds United arrived at the Victoria Ground as leaders of the First Division, and in front of Alf Ramsey we sent them away with their tails between their legs, two goals from John Ritchie and one from Harry Burrows giving us a 3–0 victory. We also earned a fine goalless draw at Fortress Anfield at a time when few sides ever left with anything more than a cup of tea. I was pleased with my own performance in this Boxing Day game. Liverpool put us under almost constant pressure and I had to be at my best to deny John Toshack, Phil Boersma and Steve Heighway, all three of whom had me at full stretch.

The Kop gave me a terrific reception as I ran into the penalty area for the pre-match kickabout. When I acknowledged their applause with a wave they applauded even more. I found the

Kop's sporting reception very gratifying, though by no means unique. At most grounds I was given a rousing welcome by the home fans, which never failed to leave me feeling humble. Bobby Moore, Bobby Charlton and Geoff Hurst told me they too received similar approbation from the opposition's fans. That's how it was in 1970. Supporters of opposing teams, appeared to me, to appreciate the efforts of top players, in particular those who had excelled for England.

It narks me no end to hear someone like David Beckham being booed every time he touches the ball at grounds all over England. Though these boo boys are in the minority of all football fans, there have been occasions when the reception David Beckham has received has bordered on hatred. Not only is that unjust, it is also unwarranted. To his credit, David had risen above it all with dignity, and is all the more appreciated by true lovers of the game as a result.

Supporters were no less fanatical followers of their team in the sixties and early seventies. Arguably, given the spartan conditions in which they watched matches, their support was even more committed. However, these bedrock supporters of clubs were also lovers of football as a sport, and quick to acknowledge good play on the part of the opposition and the achievements of visiting players. Sadly, all that was to change as the seventies unfolded and moronic tribalism infested a great many of our football grounds to the great detriment of the game. The discerning fan has always appreciated the efforts of a player, irrespective of what colours he wears. Happily, in recent years, as football has reverted once again to being a family game, I've seen ample evidence of supporters appreciating the efforts of players of opposing sides. Long may that attitude prevail throughout the country.

In March 1971 Stoke City entertained Manchester United at the Victoria Ground. For all my efforts and those of my team mates, there was no stopping George Best. In this game George was simply scintillating and his wizardry on the ball caused us all manner of problems from start to finish. Wilf McGuinness had just been sacked as United manager and Sir Matt Busby had returned to take temporary charge of the team. Perhaps this inspired George, for the Victoria Ground lit up like a Catherine wheel as George displayed his staggering array of skills to the full, culminating in what I believe to be the best ever goal scored against me.

We were defending the Boothen End. George received the ball just outside our penalty area and junked along our defensive line in search of an opening. Faced with Jackie Marsh and Alan Bloor, George dropped his left shoulder and made as if he was about to sprint off to his left, only to drag the ball back with the sole of his boot and move to his right. It was as if someone had just played Chubby Checker on the Tannoy. Jackie and Alan twisted their bodies this way and that as they frantically sought to block his way.

George appeared to be showing too much of the ball. Eric Skeels came charging in for the tackle, his left boot extended ready to sweep the ball away, while George danced joyously on his toes before making the ball do a disappearing act, once again pulling it back with the sole of his boot. Denis Smith and Mike Pejic then presented themselves for a dose of humiliation. George duly obliged, motioning towards them before curling his foot around the ball and dragging away to his left. A three-yard burst of speed and he was free. That left just yours truly between him and the goal.

I came rushing out to cut down the angle. A goalkeeper faced with a one-on-one situation has to keep his eyes on the ball, not on the body of the opponent. George's left boot flashed over the ball. I was on the point of going down to my right when his right boot took the ball the opposite way. I immediately adjusted my position. All my weight fell on my left leg as I prepared to spreadeagle myself at his feet. But with another drop of his shoulder, George veered away to my right. Unbalanced I rocked on the heels of my boots before flopping down unceremoniously on my backside in the muddy goalmouth. George, as if out for a stroll in the park, carried on before leisurely rolling the ball into the empty net. For a brief moment there was silence. Then the whole of the Victoria Ground burst into appreciative applause.

George didn't sprint over to the United supporters and strut like a peacock before them; didn't run to his team mates for a schoolgirl embrace, then push them aside and make them play kiss-chase. He simply walked back to the centre line, his right arm half-raised in acknowledgement of the applause he so richly deserved.

I wouldn't have thought it possible for any player to bamboozle so many would-be custodians in such a confined space. That George did was a truly remarkable demonstration of his skills. He shook off five quality defenders the way a dog shakes water off its back, before dumping me on my arse in the mud. Such golden memories are treasured for ever, even by those on the receiving end.

Stanley Matthews, who was at the game, always left the ground a few minutes before the final whistle to avoid the crowds. Stoke employed a commissionaire in those days, who because his job was to remain in the foyer entrance, never saw a game. As Stan made his way through the foyer, the commissionaire asked him the score. He summed it up perfectly in five words: 'Stoke one, George Best two.'

Among the many photographs hanging in my study is a set which shows George's goal in sequence. I often look at them and wonder how he managed to do it and I still haven't worked it out. I display them as a constant reminder to me of how privileged I am to have played against a man of such breathtaking brilliance.

As is well known, for much of his career and since George lived a lifestyle that many people may view as being at odds with mine as a family man. I never think like that. I have never passed judgement on George on anything but his ability as a footballer and, as footballers go, he was a true genius. In May 1971, just two months after the wonder goal at Stoke, I was confronted with George's genius yet again when playing for England against Northern Ireland at Windsor Park, Belfast. The first half was a very tight affair, with neither side able to break the deadlock. I had just made a save from Middlesbrough's Eric McMordie and was preparing to kick the ball upfield.

George positioned himself in front of me, presumably in an effort to disrupt my clearance kick. I veered around him and threw the ball in the air ready to kick it upfield. As I tossed it, George struck like a viper. He suddenly raised a boot and managed to flick the ball away from me. The ball, still airborne, headed for the goalmouth and we jostled each other like two schoolboys on sports day as we raced to reach it first. George leaned forward, extended his neck and managed to head the ball into the net. Windsor Park erupted, first with cheers and then with catcalls as the referee rightly awarded a free kick against George. He was furious and argued with the referee, saying his goal should be allowed because the ball had not been in my hand when he kicked it away. The referee was having none of his protests, however, and ruled he had been guilty of dangerous kicking.

For days this audacious piece of opportunism fuelled much debate on television and in the newspapers, but the consensus of opinion was that the referee was right to disallow the goal. In the end England won the match with a goal from Allan Clarke, but all anyone ever remembers of that game is George's lightning reaction to a ball tossed eighteen inches in the air. Whenever I meet George nowadays, usually at sporting dinners, I often have cause to remind him of the perfect timing he used to demonstrate on the field, particularly in that game at Windsor Park – now he's a hopeless timekeeper and invariably turns up late!

The 1970–71 season saw Stoke City embark upon a thrilling FA Cup run that was to end in heartache and controversy.

We began our FA Cup trail with a 2–1 success over Millwall.

We then dispatched Huddersfield Town, though only after two replays. In round five we beat Ipswich Town after a replay, and then met Hull City at snowswept Boothferry Park where the home side gave us one almighty scare.

A crowd of 42,000 packed into the Second Division side's ground to see Hull race into a two-goal lead, both goals coming from Ken Wagstaff. Terry Conroy gave us hope when scoring right on half time and two second-half goals from John Ritchie crowned a remarkable comeback for us. But Hull just wouldn't lie down. In the last ten minutes they piled on the pressure. It was backs-to-the-wall stuff and I had to be at my best to deny Chris Chilton and Ken Houghton. When the referee finally blew his whistle after six minutes of injury time, it came as a blessed relief to us all.

The semi-finals pitched us against Arsenal at Hillsborough. The Stoke fans were gripped by cup fever and our allocation of 27,500 tickets was sold out within four hours of going on sale. Arsenal were on course for a league and cup double and came into the match on the back of a run that had seen them win fourteen of their last sixteen games.

But we didn't fear them. After all, we'd beaten them 5–0 back in September. Tony Waddington told us to take the game to Arsenal from the start, to hustle and harass in midfield and so disrupt their rhythm. That was the way we liked to play it. The cavalier football we were known for quickly produced dividends. Denis Smith gave us the lead in somewhat fortunate circumstances when he blocked an attempted clearance from Peter Storey and the ball ricocheted off his body and into the Arsenal net. After half an hour we doubled our lead. Charlie George attempted to pass the ball back to Bob Wilson, didn't get enough weight on it and John Ritchie nipped in.

Though Arsenal were a team never beaten until the final whistle, I really did think we were going to do it. Then, just after half time, Peter Storey pulled a goal back for the Gunners and the jitters set in. Perhaps owing to the inexperience of many of the Stoke players of the big-match occasion, a nervous edginess entered our play. We didn't display the calm authority required to play ourselves out of defence. We conceded possession too often and Arsenal were not the sort of side to give it back again without a struggle.

None the less we weathered the storm and with the game deep into injury time it looked as if we were Wembley bound. With a last throw of the dice, George Armstrong played the ball into my penalty area. In jumping up to collect it, I found myself being bundled over by a marauding yellow shirt. I thought the referee, Pat Partridge from Middlesbrough, would award us a free kick for the foul on me. But to my shock I saw him point to indicate a corner for Arsenal. I and several team mates gathered round the official to protest, but referees never change their minds once they've made their decision, do they?

When the corner came across, it was, typically, my old Filbert Street mate Frank McLintock who headed it goalwards. I was left stranded. John Mahoney did a passable impression of me by diving full-length and tipping the ball to safety with his hand. It was all John could do. If he had tried to intercept the ball legitimately with his head, or, boot, it would have been a certain goal – and you weren't sent off for deliberate handball to prevent a certain goal in those days. Peter Storey stepped up to take the penalty for Arsenal and scuffed the ground with his studs as his boot made contact with the ball. His scuffed kick deceived me, and 'lucky Arsenal' had their draw. I still think I was unjustly denied a free kick and that that mistake by Mr Partridge cost Stoke a trip to Wembley.

Again, I think the inexperience of many of the Stoke players in handling the pressure of a big match had a lot to do with the result of the replay. Only Jimmy Greenhoff and I had played in an FA Cup final, and at the time I was the only current England international at the club, though Terry Conroy was a regular with the Republic of Ireland. Many of my team mates were devastated to concede an equalizing goal as a result of a controversial refereeing decision so deep into injury time. Arsenal, meanwhile, had been thrown an unexpected lifeline, which they grasped with both hands like a drowning man.

I suppose some of us felt our best chance of reaching the FA Cup final had gone. The mental strength and fortitude a team must show to come so close, and then to have victory snatched away at the last minute, was not to be forthcoming in the replay. That tremendous letdown – however well we play, how much we deserve to win, how close we are to Wembley, it's still not enough – must explain our poor performance at Villa Park. We never came anywhere near to repeating the sterling performance we had given at Hillsborough. Arsenal won 2–0 and were, in truth, comfortable winners.

The following season we reached the FA Cup semi-final for a second time. Again our opponents were Arsenal. Again the match went to a replay and, incredibly, once more a terrible mistake on the part of an official was to rob us of glory.

Having disposed of my old club Chesterfield in round three of the FA Cup, we then beat Tranmere Rovers (after a replay) and, for the second year running, Hull City, before being drawn away to Manchester United in the sixth round.

A crowd of 54,000 was at Old Trafford to see a United team that included George Best, Denis Law, Willie Morgan, Brian Kidd and three members of the England squad of 1970, Bobby Charlton, Alex Stepney and David Sadler. Jimmy Greenhoff put us in front and for a time I thought we would resist the resultant United pressure. Minutes from time, however, a piece of magic from George Best (who else?) gave United a replay.

A capacity crowd of 49,097 at the Victoria Ground witnessed a thrilling second encounter between the sides. That man Best (again) gave United the lead on seventy minutes that our centre half Denis Smith cancelled out only four minutes later.

This was a personal triumph for Denis, who is listed in the *Guinness Book of Records* as being Britain's most-injured professional footballer. Denis was a one-club man and in seventeen

years as a player at Stoke City broke his leg five times, his nose
on four occasions and his ankle and collar bones once. He also
sustained a chipped spine, six broken fingers and over a hundred
facial stitches. When Denis finally hung up his boots in 1982,
Terry Conroy – who nicknamed Denis 'Lucky' – said, 'If Lucky
had carried on playing for another season, BUPA would have
gone bust.'

It says much for Denis's character, fortitude and combative
spirit that, when he wasn't in A&E, he was a super centre half,
one who never held back in a tackle. He was a rock in that Stoke
City defence and is unfortunate not to have a few England caps
to display in his cabinet alongside his plaster casts.

Just before our replay against Manchester United, the injury-
prone Denis ricked his back in training. It was so painful and
debilitating that he was immediately declared unfit for the return
tie. Like the trooper he was, however, Denis still wanted to come
along and cheer us on. As he was getting out of his car on the
evening of the game, he bent forward and, amazingly, his spine
righted itself. Denis suddenly marched straight into Tony
Waddington's office and declared himself fit to face United!

Denis's equalizer took the game into extra time. I somehow
managed to keep out efforts from George Best and Bobby Charlton before Terry Conroy sealed what had been an amazing night
for Stoke, and Denis Smith in particular, by hitting a great
half-volley past Alex Stepney to take us into the last four of
the Cup.

The FA Cup semi-final again. A packed Hillsborough again.
Arsenal again . . . George Armstrong gave the Londoners the
lead two minutes after half time. On this occasion, however, we
didn't capitulate as we had at Villa Park the previous season and
concerted pressure on the Arsenal goal produced a deserved
equalizer on sixty-five minutes.

Bob Wilson had earlier been injured when collecting a cross
and the forward John Radford had replaced him in goal. As I

have previously said, there is little room for sentiment in football. Knowing John Radford would be nervous and uneasy about taking over in goal, we immediately put him under severe pressure. Our ploy was to test him with high balls into the box and our second such effort produced the equalizer. Peter Dobing drove a centre into the Arsenal penalty area and Radford was seemingly undecided about whether or not to come for the ball. He left it to Peter Simpson who, under pressure from Denis Smith, headed into his own net. The goal was just what we needed. We took the game to Arsenal and only some desperate defending on their part, and the width of a post, denied us the winner.

'History repeats itself,' said the eminent historian A. J. P. Taylor, 'and that's its biggest failing.' Having been denied victory over Arsenal in controversial circumstances in the previous year's semi-final, no one thought it possible that another error of judgement by a match official would once again wreck our chances of reaching Wembley. That, however, is exactly what happened in the replay at Old Trafford.

Geoff Barnett in goal for the injured Bob Wilson was the only team change that night. In the opening exchanges Alan Ball fizzed for Arsenal. George Graham also posed problems but Denis Smith and Alan Bloor kept a tight rein on John Radford (much happier without those goalkeeper's gloves) and Charlie George, and we rode out Arsenal's initial pressure and began to exert a little of our own.

On twenty minutes Jimmy Greenhoff burst into the Arsenal penalty area and was sent sprawling by the outstretched leg of Frank McLintock. Jimmy picked himself up, dusted himself down, took the penalty and nearly ripped the net off its hooks.

Arsenal had a reputation for coming back more times than the postman, and they got back into this game in dubious circumstances. After fifty-five minutes George Armstrong cut in from the left with Peter Dobing at his side. Both players were jostling one another for possession of the ball. Arms were flailing, shoulders leaning in. Suddenly, Armstrong took a tumble and I was horrified to see the referee, Keith Walker, point to the penalty spot. To my mind, it had been six of one and half a dozen of the other. It was a highly contentious penalty award, but a penalty it was. Charlie George stepped up to take the kick and pinged the ball into my left hand corner. Arsenal were level.

We thought ourselves hard done by, but ten minutes later worse was to follow. Following a spell of pressure from Stoke, Frank McLintock played a long ball out of defence. John Radford was offside when Frank played the ball but, hearing no whistle from the referee, John did the professional thing and ran towards my goal with the ball at his feet. I came out to narrow his angle, John swept away to my left and planted the ball firmly into the back of the net. We were furious. Radford had been clearly offside yet was allowed to continue. The referee had been caught out by the swiftness of the Arsenal counter-attack and, like most of the Stoke team, had not been up with play when Radford received the ball.

Well, that's what linesmen are supposed to be there for and, after our vehement protests on the matter, Mr Walker decided to consult his man with the flag, Bob Matthewson. Matthewson had been well placed to judge on Radford, and I was confident that, after consulting his linesman, Mr Walker would disallow the goal for offside. The pair exchanged a few words and I was stunned when the referee then turned and pointed to the centre circle. Goal to Arsenal.

If we were angry before, we were livid now. I sprinted up to the referee to challenge his decision, while Jackie Marsh and a posse of Stoke players besieged Bob Matthewson. For a moment there was chaos. The Stoke supporters were incensed, the Arsenal fans ecstatic. Press cameras popped and flashed, and Jackie Marsh subjected the beleaguered official to a verbal tirade that would have made a navvy blush. It was all to no avail. The goal stood and we exited from the FA Cup in cruel circumstances for the second successive season.

Our dressing room was like a morgue. Jackie summed it up for everyone when he said, 'I'd rather be beaten 4–0 and know we had lost fair and square than go out like that.'

The TV highlights of the game conclusively proved that John Radford had been offside when receiving the ball. The programme also explained why his goal had not been disallowed.

To avoid a colour clash, both teams had worn their second strips. Arsenal wore yellow shirts and blue shorts, while Stoke played in all white. When the ball had been played up to Radford, the linesman had apparently mistaken an Everton programme seller wearing a white overall-type coat on the far side of the pitch for a Stoke City player. Matthewson had waved Radford onside.

It's easy to say that it was just one of those things, simple human error. But it proved to be a very costly mistake for Stoke City, one that generated not only bitter disappointment but bitter feelings. After the match the football reporter John Bean asked Jackie Marsh when had been the turning point of the game. 'When the linesman turned up,' replied Jackie.

Consolation for the Potters and their marvellous, long-suffering supporters came in the League Cup. Not only was this the first major trophy in the club's history, but it was the first time Stoke had appeared in a Wembley final and, believe me, we really made the most of it. But our route to Wembley glory was far from easy. Including the final against Chelsea, it took us twelve matches to achieve success, a record for the competition. Our semi-final against West Ham United remains the longest League Cup tie in duration. It involved four matches, the first on 8 December, with the tie not reaching a conclusion until 26 January.

Our League Cup campaign began modestly with a 2–1 win over Southport, a game I missed through injury. No team wins a trophy without enjoying a slice of luck and we had ours in the following round at Oxford United. We could have easily gone out of the League Cup that night. Oxford dominated the match for long periods but we managed to come away with a 1–1 draw and comfortably won the replay at the Victoria Ground.

There then followed three epic ties against Manchester United. Having drawn at both Old Trafford and Stoke, we faced United for a third time. United arrived at the Victoria Ground as leaders of the First Division and struck the first blow after thirty-seven minutes when George Best hit a screaming right-foot drive into the top left-hand corner of my net. United, and George Best in particular, were rampant, but in the second half the experienced George Eastham proved his worth to Stoke by taking control of the midfield.

At times United had been running us ragged, but George started to put his foot on the ball and slow the pace of the game. With George setting his own tempo and orchestrating matters from the middle of the park we slowly took control of affairs. Peter Dobing returned the scores to parity on seventy minutes. Then, with only two minutes remaining, John Ritchie leapt above every United defender to head home a corner from George Eastham.

Over 33,000 turned up at Eastville to see us beat Bristol Rovers 4–2 in the fifth round, which set up a tasty semi-final clash against West Ham United and my good pals Bobby Moore and Geoff Hurst.

Things didn't go to plan in the first leg at Stoke. A penalty from Geoff Hurst and a second West Ham goal from Clyde Best cancelled out the lead Peter Dobing had given us. We believed we could turn the tie around at Upton Park though, and our implicit belief in our own ability was not misplaced.

West Ham were a superb footballing side but we felt we had the measure of them. The second leg was an epic cup tie. John Ritchie scored deep into the second half to send the match into extra time on the aggregate score of 2–2. There wasn't a cigarette paper's width between the two teams and, with three minutes of extra time remaining, a replay looked a certainty. It was then that my heart almost jumped into my mouth.

I managed to parry a shot from Geoff Hurst. When the ball ran loose an almighty goalmouth scramble ensued resembling a pinball machine as the West Ham players fired one shot after another only to see the ball cannon back repeatedly from a thicket of legs. I decided to seize the initiative.

I had drummed into my defenders that, if I shouted 'keeper's', they would leave the ball regardless. The ball skidded across the mud towards Mike Pejic, who was standing in front of me. 'Keeper's!' I shouted. Mike seemed not to have heard me, for he shaped to clear. I relaxed, only to find that Mike had let the ball go. I then had to scramble again to get near the ball, fumbled it, snatched at it and watched it squirm away from me. Harry Redknapp half-collided with me as he came across in front. I thought he was trying to prevent me from reaching the ball, so I put my hand around his midriff and yanked him to one side. Harry was actually obstructing me, but the referee, Keith Walker (yes, him again), didn't see it my way and awarded West Ham a penalty. I was furious, not with the ref but with Mike Pejic. It was his indecision that caused the mayhem in the first place.

Up stepped my old mate Geoff Hurst. As he ran up to take the kick, an eerie silence descended on Upton Park. Geoff always relied on sheer power when taking penalties and it looked as though he was really going to tank this one. When he had scored from the spot in the first leg, he'd taken a big run-up and hit the ball to my right. I got a hand to it, but couldn't stop it going just inside the post. Now Geoff was setting himself to take the same sort of run-up.

I thought, 'He's not going to change here. I'll gamble,' and hurled myself to the right as he thumped it at shoulder height to that side.

I was flying through the air with both my arms pointing skywards. Geoff had hit the ball so hard that when my left hand made contact with it, I had to tense the muscles in my arm and wrist. Otherwise the ball would have knocked my hand aside.

To my great relief, the ball ricocheted up into the murky gloom of the East End night and over the bar.

My team mates could hardly believe their eyes. They ran up to me en masse to shower me with their congratulations. We were still in the League Cup.

A press photographer standing behind the goal captured me executing the save from Geoff's penalty. It's one of my favourite photographs, it often turns up in books about football (including this one – see the frontispiece), though I haven't got a copy myself. It's very atmospheric, with the floodlight piercing the gloom above our heads. In contrast to the animated action of penalty-taker and goalkeeper, three Stoke defenders stand with their hands on their hips, presumably resigned to an inevitable goal. The Upton Park pitch looks like a ploughed field and my jersey is caked in mud. I like the photograph, not only because it exemplifies how British football used to be, but also because it captures both the drama and the atmosphere of the occasion. As I study the photograph, the save ceases to command my attention. I pick up the incidental but evocative detail in the image: the players are not dressed like advertising hoardings for their club sponsors; in the background the packed terraces where not a single replica shirt can be seen, and the half-time number board – it is this detail that conjures up the flavour of football of that era. Football as a central force in people's lives.

Over the years football photography has changed almost as much as the sport itself. Most of today's press reports are accompanied by a shot of two players in competition with each other for the ball in pin-sharp detail. Telephoto lenses are wonderful, but what they have done is to take all the atmosphere and sense of occasion out of football photography. The telephoto lens limits the photographer's field of vision to a very small area, so that what we often see now is a close-cropped image of two players challenging for the ball in a combative tangle of limbs. The bigger picture – the context of crowd, weather and so on – is excluded, precisely the details that are so evocative in that shot of me saving Geoff Hurst's penalty. This narrow focus on the individual at the expense of the panoramic view (or, if you like, the social context) is an apt symbol of the way the game is today.

It took another two games before Stoke City eventually got the better of West Ham, and so progress to that history-making first appearance at Wembley. First, at Hillsborough, ninety minutes plus half an hour of extra time failed to produce a goal. In the second replay, at Old Trafford, Bobby Moore deputized in goal for a spell while West Ham's keeper Bobby Ferguson was receiving treatment for concussion. After goals from Mike Bernard, Peter Dobing and Terry Conroy finally secured a thrilling and hard-fought 3–2 victory, we could begin to look forward to our day in London.

Our opponents there were Chelsea. They were the bookies' favourites to win the League Cup, but our confidence was sky high. Chelsea were stylish and swaggering. In Alan Hudson, Charlie Cooke, Peter Houseman and Peter Osgood they could boast players with as much flair as their flared trousers. Dave Sexton's side were far from being simply a collection of football artists and King's Road poseurs, however. David Webb, Paddy Mulligan and Ron Harris provided Chelsea with steel and backbone. They were a formidable team, but on the big day they were not quite formidable enough.

Terry Conroy gave us the lead with a choice header following a cross from George Eastham. Following his goal, Terry appeared to go off into a dream. I'd seen this sort of thing before – a good player gets a few nice early touches on the ball, scores a goal and then thinks his day's work is done. How easy it is to lose momentum and a superior position thrown away when one player reacts like this.

Seeing Terry start to coast, I shouted to Jackie Marsh to get upfield and snap him out of his stupor. A few well-chosen words from Jackie did the trick and moments later Terry was back to his old self, hustling and harassing the Chelsea defence, making darting runs across our front line and tracking back with John Dempsey when Chelsea pushed forward.

With the half-time interval approaching, Chelsea put themselves back into the game. Alan Bloor, who up to this point had been having a fine game, failed to clear his lines and the ball found its way to the feet of Peter Osgood. As he was about to get in a shot on goal, Ossy lost his footing on a divot. His tumble made me hesitate for a moment in coming out, and Peter, lying prostrate on the ground, hooked the ball past me. We went into half time level.

Both sides battled to gain the upper hand in the second half. We were two evenly balanced sides but the deadlock was broken after seventy-three minutes and, thankfully, it was Stoke who achieved what proved to be the decisive breakthrough. Terry Conroy beat Ron Harris and his far-post cross found John Ritchie, who cushioned the ball back into the path of the oncoming Jimmy Greenhoff. Jimmy hit one of his trademark volleys, Peter Bonetti parried and there was the oldest player on the pitch, George Eastham, to prod the ball home to secure a 2–1 win.

George, at 35 years and 161 days, became the oldest recipient of a League Cup winner's medal, while Stoke City's victory over Chelsea gave me my second such gong and not a little satisfaction. My conviction on joining Stoke that they had the potential to win honours had now proved well founded. Happily I joined my team mates and the population of Stoke in celebrating our success to the full.

When a team from the provinces with no history of success wins a major trophy, the players and supporters go overboard. For days the city of Stoke took on a carnival atmosphere. It was reported that productivity in the potteries and coal mines of North Staffordshire suddenly rose dramatically. The city council gave us a civic banquet and over a quarter of a million people thronged the streets to see us parade the League Cup. The Lord Mayor, Arthur Cholerton, was in the process of arranging for

Stoke to be twinned with a town in Germany. At the civic banquet Mr Cholerton told us that his German counterpart had asked him, 'Where is Stoke?' 'It's where the League Cup is,' replied Cholerton.

Our success in the League Cup was the highlight of what had been a marathon season for Stoke City. The records show that we played a total of sixty-seven matches in 1971–72, not to mention a number of friendlies. On top of my club commitments I was also involved with England. Our full back Jackie Marsh played sixty-five games that season, sixty-nine if you include the friendlies. Did I mention our rotation system? When you collapsed from exhaustion, you got a game off!

To cap what had been a great season for me, I had the honour of being voted the football writers' Footballer of the Year. I was very proud to be the first goalkeeper to receive this prestigious title since my boyhood hero, Bert Trautmann, in 1956. I was delighted not just from a personal point of view, but also because the award acknowledged the importance of goalkeeping in general. As if to emphasize the point, Tottenham Hotspur's Pat Jennings won it the following year.

When we were together in the England squad I was forever 'selling' Stoke City to Geoff Hurst. I firmly believed Stoke had a team good enough to win the First Division title. I kept telling Geoff that if he wanted to top up his collection of trophies with a League Championship medal he could do worse than take a trip to the Potteries. When West Ham decided to sell Geoff, I had a word with Tony Waddington, to the effect that Geoff would be a super acquisition for the club, and that he might be inclined to listen to an offer from Stoke.

Geoff duly signed for Stoke City in August 1972 and immediately made his presence felt in a team with high hopes of making a concerted challenge for the title. By October Stoke were established as a top ten team and had a good chance of catching the pacesetters Liverpool, Leeds and Arsenal. On 21 October we travelled to Anfield, where we lost 2–1. Just another game, I thought. Little did I know, however, that this match was to be my last in English football.

The following day I reported to the Victoria Ground for treatment on a minor injury sustained against Liverpool. I was driving home to Madeley Heath, when I approached a part of the country road flanked by trees where it dipped before taking a sharp turn to the right. A car was idling along in front of me. Not a great place to overtake, but I was keen to be home with Ursula and her Sunday dinner. I swung my Ford Consul on to the other side of the road ready to pass the slower vehicle. Suddenly, I saw another vehicle approaching. I slammed my foot hard on the brake as a prickle of adrenalin rushed across my forehead. There was an almighty bang. There was the sound of glass shattering. Then nothing.

I've never liked the smell of hospitals. The stuffy, clinical fug was the first thing I sensed when I awoke from a deep, drug-induced sleep. I tried to open my eyes but nothing happened. It was as if someone had glued down my eyelids. I broke out in a cold sweat. I started to panic. A cool, clean, gentle hand held mine. Another hand eased me forward, then guided me back on to a tower of crisp pillows.

The nurse gave me a welcome cup of tea. She told me I had been in the operating theatre. That I'd had surgery on my eyes.

'How bad?' I asked.

'You can't see out of your left eye because it's so swollen. But that should clear up in a day or two,' she said.

'And what about my other eye?'

'I'm afraid you will have to wait until the surgeon pays you a visit,' she said. 'You've had a very delicate operation.'

It seemed an eternity before the surgeon eventually arrived at my bedside.

'The operation went smoothly, Gordon,' he said. 'It lasted three hours. I had to do a lot of repair work. Fragments of the windscreen perforated your right eye. I have to tell you, there has been damage to the retina.'

I summoned every ounce of courage I had to ask him the inevitable question. 'How bad?'

'It will be a couple of weeks before I know for sure. With damage of this nature there can be all manner of complications. You have a deep wound extending from your scalp to your forehead, but that will heal in time. A colleague of mine is an excellent skin surgeon, he'll see to it that the scars will not be too obtrusive.'

'How bad?' I asked again, trying to pin him down.

'Your right eye?'

I nodded. At last he committed himself. 'I'm afraid I couldn't put the chances at better than evens.'

Three days later the swelling on my left eye had subsided sufficiently to allow me to see. I asked for a mirror. I wasn't a pretty sight. When a nurse arrived to change my dressing, the full extent of my injuries was brought home to me. I had more than two hundred stitches running from my face to my scalp. I was later to discover that this was only the half of it. The surgeon had also inserted over a hundred micro-stitches inside the socket of my right eye and around the periphery of the retina. I hadn't a clue how much that surgeon was paid for his skills and care. But whatever it was, in my book, it could never be enough.

I can't put into words the extent to which the love and support of Ursula, our children and the rest of our family helped me through the most harrowing and desperate time of my life. Nor can I ever truly express my gratitude to the surgeon, doctors, nurses and other members of the North Staffordshire Hospital who gave me such tender care and attention. Even now, all these years later, remembering the kindness and love I felt from everybody brings a lump to my throat.

As the days passed I made a concerted effort, both mentally and physically, to come to terms with my disability. At first I thought I could simply carry on as if enjoying sight in both eyes. Then one day I leaned over to pick up a cup of tea that was standing on my bedside table and was shocked to grasp thin air. That's when the reality of my situation really hit home. I prayed that when the dressing was removed once and for all, the sight in my right eye would return. I remember thinking, If I can't even get the angle right to pick up a cup of tea, how will I ever judge the flight and speed of a football again? Perhaps I shouldn't have been thinking about it, but football was all I knew. How could I provide for my family if I couldn't play again?

My accident made national news. Tony Waddington held numerous press conferences to update the media on my situation. But that wasn't enough for some. Every day Ursula opened the curtains of our home in Madeley Heath to see a knot of photographers camped at the end of the drive.

Tony paid me regular visits in hospital, but also came over to see Ursula and the children. One afternoon, after training, Tony turned up at our home to find thirty reporters and photographers blocking his way. Inside, he was shocked to discover Ursula in tears. The pressure was getting too much for her. Tony went outside and pleaded with them to give Ursula and the children a break. He offered to act as spokesman for the family and give the media regular bulletins on my progress. Most understood, although one photographer was to overstep the mark.

The doctors at the North Staffs decided my left eye had recovered sufficiently for me to watch a little television. I was in a private room with no TV, so a set was sent for. It duly arrived, carried by a man wearing a doctor's long white coat. He placed the television on a table and then, to my utter astonishment, produced a camera from under his coat.

'It's like trying to get into Fort Knox trying to get in here,' he said cheerfully. 'I had to slip the TV engineer a tenner. Just one shot of you, Gordon? We'll make it worth your while.'

I'm not a man given to swearing as a rule, but rules are made to be broken and I told that photographer in no uncertain terms what he could do with his camera and his money.

I was so incensed that the startled photographer lowered his camera to his side before backing out of the room in double quick time. When the real TV engineer arrived I was ready to dish out another tongue-lashing, but it transpired that the photographer hadn't slipped the engineer any money at all, just conned him into believing that he was a close personal friend of mine, and that his visit would raise my spirits.

When the surgeon eventually removed the dressing I thought my prayers had been answered. In fact they had, in a way. I could see out of my right eye, even though everything was a blur and when people were close to me they became shadowy dark shapes. My hopes and spirits soared, especially when the surgeon told me there was an even chance that my vision would continue to improve with time. On the downside, there was an equal chance of this partial sight deteriorating. But I didn't want to think about that.

I was discharged from hospital and ordered to wear an eyepatch for the duration of my convalescence to minimize possible infection. I took things easy and thanked God that I had survived the crash to be with my family. After six weeks of rest and love at home I was feeling good, and told Tony Waddington my recovery was such that I was ready to come down to the ground for a little light training.

Just to be back at the ground and among the lads gave me a tremendous lift. I was very hopeful of gradually recovering full sight in my right eye and then embarking on a fitness schedule that would lead to my comeback.

At first everything went well. On my previous visit to the eye surgeon he had been impressed and pleased with the progress I had made. The sight in my right eye had improved sufficiently for me to read the calendar hanging on his wall and count the bulbs in his chandelier, though I still had to guard against infection with my Captain Pugwash eyepatch.

I was sitting in our living room and looking out at the garden when I decided to lift my patch to see whether the improvement was continuing. My body was immediately gripped by fear. Something was very wrong. I could see nothing out of my right eye. I closed my left, and saw total blackness.

The surgeon informed me that there was nothing more he could do. The edifice of hope I'd erected during the weeks since the crash came tumbling around my ears. Once again I struggled to come to terms with my predicament. I had overcome some enormous obstacles during my career in football, but now I was about to face the biggest and most difficult challenge of my life. I called on every drop of strength, fortitude and resolve I could muster, and told Ursula that I wasn't going to wallow in a trough of self-pity. Not only was I going to come to terms with this situation, I was going to fight it.

'God's been good,' I said to her. 'I'm still here, and so are you, Robert, Wendy and Julia. That's the most important thing. As for the football – I'm going to play again.'

18. Striking Back

I received literally thousands of letters from well-wishers. Many were from people who had readjusted to life following the loss of an eye; one, from a little girl who sent me a wonderful drawing of herself which I still have, was especially touching. Every single letter moved me, but owing to their sheer number – one day twelve sackloads arrived – I simply couldn't reply to each one in person. I know that three decades have passed, but I'd like to take this opportunity of thanking everyone who sent me messages of sympathy and good wishes for my recovery. Your letters and cards were a great source of strength both to me and my family, and I will be forever grateful to you all for your heartfelt words of encouragement.

Tony Waddington allowed me a six-month period of adjustment. I began with light training and gradually built up my programme over the months. My eyesight was examined periodically and I underwent numerous tests to see how I coped with the speed, flight and direction of the ball. After the six months were up, Tony called me into his office and asked the $64,000 question: 'Can you play on?'

It was what I'd been asking myself for weeks. It had lain there at the forefront of my thoughts, ticking away like a time-bomb.

'Tony, you've been a great boss,' I told him. 'You've always been honest with me and I want to be honest with you. I think you know as well as I do what the answer to your question is.'

Tony slowly nodded his head. 'I've seen you in training. Personally speaking, I think you could still do us a job,' he said.

'I could,' I told him, 'but not the job that I used to do. I don't want that, Tony. I have to be honest with you, with the club, and myself. If I can't meet the standards I set for myself, I'm going to have to call it a day.'

It was the summer of 1973. My career as a goalkeeper in league football was over. Tony Waddington gave me a job as coach to the Stoke City youth team, with a brief to offer specialist coaching to young goalkeepers.

The first day I gathered my young charges together, I was dumbfounded. Of all the apprentices on the club's books, there was not a single goalkeeper! The lad who kept goal for the Stoke youth team was an amateur who had a day job and only trained at Stoke two evenings a week.

The club were very supportive and granted me a testimonial. It was a great night. All my former England colleagues turned up to play, along with several stars from around the world. I was treated to the unique sight of Bobby Charlton running out of the tunnel alongside Eusebio, both wearing the red and white stripes of Stoke City.

Seeing Bobby Charlton and Eusebio playing for Stoke was not the only surprise I had that year. I travelled to London thinking I was about to do some promotional work for a company. The meeting was to take place in the lounge bar of a well-known hotel. For some minutes I hung about wondering where the representatives of the company were. I was suddenly aware of a man at my shoulder. I turned and was surprised to see Eamonn Andrews holding the Big Red Book in his hand.

'Tonight, Gordon Banks,' he said, 'this is your life!'

I had had no inkling about this at all. I was whisked away in a daze to a television studio where Ursula, Robert, Wendy, Julia, my mum and other members of my family were waiting to spill the beans.

One by one their disembodied voices sounded behind the scenes before revealing themselves to me and the nation. Members of my immediate family were followed by close friends, staff from the North Staffs Hospital, Tony Waddington, my former Stoke City team mates, Alf Ramsey, ex-England colleagues, old school chums and two guys I didn't know from Adam and still don't. Just when I thought one of my best pals had more important things to do, a voice from behind the screen said, 'You're getting old, Banksy. You used to hold on to them.'

Good old Bobby. I should have known he'd never let me down.

I was happy coaching, but gnawing away at me was a desire to get back to playing. In 1976 the opportunity came. I received a call from a representative of Ford Lauderdale Strikers asking if I would like to play for them in the NASL, the recently formed North American Soccer League. Although itching to get back between the sticks, I asked to be given some time to think about it, but as I discussed the matter with my family and Tony Waddington it became increasingly clear that there was only one answer: I was going to make a comeback. Tony, who was right behind my decision, even promised me that there would always be a job for me at Stoke as a coach as long as he was manager.

The NASL was founded in 1968 when the United Soccer Association and the National Professional Soccer League of America merged. The NASL sold franchises throughout the USA and Canada which gave rise to such teams as Atlanta Chiefs, Vancouver Whitecaps, Tulsa Roughnecks, Kansas City Spurs, Chicago Sting, Tampa Bay Rowdies, New York Cosmos, Los Angeles Aztecs and, of course, Fort Lauderdale Strikers.

What the Americans call soccer was a minor sport in the United States, played in the main by children and college students. It received very little if any coverage on TV or in the newspapers, which were dominated by baseball, American football, basketball and ice hockey. In order for the NASL to establish a good level of football from the outset, the teams, with their smattering of homegrown players, were bolstered by major stars from Europe and South America who were coming toward the end of their careers, along with good honest journeyman professionals from the lower leagues of many nations.

The money was good, the level of football, though not up to the standard I was used to, was reasonable and the lifestyle was amazing. It was these working conditions that attracted the likes of Pelé and Carlos Alberto (Brazil), Luigi Riva, Dino Zoff, Gianni Rivera and Giacinto Facchetti (Italy), Eusebio (Portugal), Gerd Muller, Franz Beckenbauer and Uwe Seller (Germany), Johann Cruyff (Holland) and Teofilo Cubillas (Peru). The sizeable British contingent included at various times Bobby Moore, George Best, George Graham, Rodney Marsh, Tony Waiters, Trevor Hockey and Charlie Cooke.

The NASL boasted some world-class players, but I'd been led to believe that many of the games were little more than keenly contested exhibition matches. Though I knew I had no place in the competitive maelstrom of English league football, I thought the comparatively relaxed nature of the American version would be ideal for me. In truth the standard of football in the NASL was higher than I had been led to believe. I would say it was on a par with the upper reaches of what is now the First Division in England. A good standard indeed.

I flew out to Fort Lauderdale but, before putting pen to paper for the Strikers, the club insisted I undergo a medical. I reported to a clinic, where a white-coated doctor took a series of X-rays of various parts of my body, before giving me a thorough medical examination. When that was completed a nurse brought in the developed X-rays. The doctor slotted them into a wall-mounted lightbox and tutted.

'Mr Banks, I see evidence of something in your right knee,' he said.

'Yes. That's a metal pin I had inserted during my career in England,' I informed him.

He ummed and ah'd.

'Uh-huh. Right. I see . . . Er, there also appears to be some sort of plate in your right elbow.'

'Yes. When I was a young player I shattered my elbow.

The metal plate was put in to strengthen that elbow and aid movement.'

More umming and ah-ing to himself. He seemed to reach a decision.

'Mr Banks, could you stand upright, then bend and touch your toes for me?'

'I'm afraid I can't. I get a lot of stiffness in my knees. Although I can get down to a ball OK, I can't bend and touch my toes.'

The doctor gave me a funny look and made a note on his pad.

'OK, Mr Banks,' he said, 'take a seat over there. Place your left hand over your right eye. Now, can you read the top and second line on that eyechart for me?'

'Read it? I know him. He played for Czechoslovakia.'

Not a flicker. 'Just read the top and second line, please,' he repeated, a frown now enveloping his face.

I did as I was asked. To his delight, at last he'd found something I could do.

'Good! Now can you place your right hand over your left eye and read the same two lines.'

'Ah, well, there we have a problem,' I told him. 'I have no sight whatsoever in my right eye.'

The doctor looked at me sternly. 'Mr Banks, did I hear you correctly? You're telling me that you can only see out of one eye?'

'Yes.' He had stopped making notes after 'bad knees, bad elbow, half-blind . . .'

'Sir, what position do you play for the Strikers?' he asked.

'Er, I'm the goalkeeper,' I said sheepishly.

I took to life in Florida, and American soccer, straight away. In England I had been used to playing on Christmas-pudding pitches. Every pitch in the NASL was like a bowling green. Though I loved North Staffordshire (and still do), my route to work there took me past pottery banks, a murky canal and grimy factories, more often than not under a sky the colour of a non-stick frying pan. When I drove to the Strikers stadium, I did so down avenues of trees like candelabra and past delis where the Danish pastries in the windows were displayed like works of art. The sun, which always seemed to be shining, had the intensity of gold leaf and felt like a warm hand caressing your face all day and night.

I've never been a great fan of motoring simply for the sake of motoring, but I did enjoy cruising around Fort Lauderdale. It was fun just driving around the downtown district, past the myriad parks and promenades, then along the north shore of the New River that snakes through the city. I'd take in the shops, galleries and sidewalk cafés on Las Olas Boulevard, then drive over the arching intracoastal bridge that leads to the ocean.

My apartment was spacious, light and airy. My building fronted a billiard-table lawn that drifted down to the sidewalk, passing on the way a large eucalyptus tree around which it flowed like a cool green tide around a rock. It looked as if Jackson Pollock's palette had been tipped over the flower beds, so diverse were their colours. All the time I was there I never saw litter on the street where I lived. The service in the shops, restaurants and cafés was faultless and the amenities of the city first class. The quality of life in Fort Lauderdale was better than I had ever experienced. I absolutely loved it.

I also took to the football, though it was a world away from what I had been used to. There were six points for a win, for a start. Should a match end level, it was decided by a series of one-on-one confrontations between striker and goalkeeper, the winners of which were awarded four points. Teams also received a bonus point for every goal scored, up to a maximum of three. Owing to the sheer size of the USA, teams did not play alternately on a home and away basis. We went 'on the road' for three games, then played three matches at home.

The mechanics of the NASL took no getting used to, but the pomp and circumstance that preceded each game was something else. The phrase 'over the top' doesn't do justice to the pre-match hoopla.

At one end of the Fort Lauderdale stadium stood a set of metal gates that would have done justice to Solomon's temple. They led to a compound not unlike a car park, at the rear of which towered mock-Corinthian columns. Before a home game began the team assembled in this compound prior to being introduced individually to the crowd. The match announcer made every player sound as if he were a gladiator. He hyped up each and every one of us to the limit, stringing out his vowels as if he were the master of ceremonies at a world heavyweight boxing match.

'Laaaaaay-deeeeeees an' genel-merrrrrrrn. Let's hear it fooooooor, the he-row of the Stri-kuuuuuuurs deeeee-fey-yance, the worn 'n' ownleeeeeeea – Go-or-or-dain Bang-kssssss!'

That was my cue to leave the compound and sprint through the gates on to the pitch to acknowledge the adulation of the masses.

The protracted nature of each introduction meant that I had a couple of minutes to kill even before our right back took to the field. I felt a bit of a spare part standing out there all on my own (the keeper was always introduced first, the star striker last), so I'd embark on a series of stretching and bending exercises followed by some short sprints, making out that I was finely tuning my body for the battle ahead. What a warrior!

The introduction of the home team lasted about twenty minutes, during which, our opponents were already out there kicking their heels. But all this was as nothing compared with the hullabaloo that every NASL team made when a new signing was introduced. I remember one away game against the Las Vegas Cannons, who included Eusebio in their ranks. As we took the field the home side were introducing their latest signing, the former Birmingham City and Sheffield United midfield player Trevor Hockey. As I ran out I couldn't help laughing. Trevor rolled past me in a tank saluting to the crowd, wearing army fatigues and sporting a military helmet. As the tank rumbled by I said, 'You look a right plonker, Trev.'

My smile was soon wiped off my face, however, when the tank turned round and passed me again as I walked towards my penalty area. With no warning, it fired its cannon. It was as if a bomb had gone off three yards away from me. I wasn't ready for that and instinctively hunched my shoulders and ducked. I glanced up to see Trevor turn around and look in my direction, a wide-eyed look of surprise on his face.

'I think I may have embarrassed myself, Gordon,' said Trevor.

To this day I am not sure to which context he was referring.

We had a decent side at Fort Lauderdale. It included Norman Piper, who had given sterling service to Portsmouth and Plymouth Argyle. Norman played wide on the wing and was a really good player. He got through a lot of work in a game, which was no mean feat in the conditions. Although all our home games were played in the cooler evenings, the biggest problem we had was adjusting to the humidity. That could be really debilitating, especially in the last twenty minutes of a game. Norman, however, just kept on going. He liked to run at opponents and, as they tired in the latter stages, not only scored but created a lot of late goals for us.

Unless you want to include me, the Strikers didn't boast any real stars until the arrival of George Best. In the main the team comprised good solid pros from clubs in the lower divisions of the English Football League. Maurice Whittle joined us from Rochdale, where he had been used to playing in front of crowds of around 3,000. I remember Maurice standing open-mouthed before a game at New York Cosmos, where a crowd of almost 70,000 had turned up to see Pelé and Franz Beckenbauer display their skills. Not only did the NASL offer the likes of Maurice an opportunity to make some decent money from the game, it also offered the experience of playing against some of the giants of world football – World Cup winners Pelé and Carlos Alberto to name but two. You wouldn't find them lining up against you on a wet Wednesday at Spotland.

The team spirit was first class and, as in football dressing rooms the world over, practical jokes were rife. We had a young player called Tony Whelan, who had played for Manchester United reserves. Following a home friendly match against the Italian club Torino, the team assembled at the airport with our manager, Ron Newman, ready to go on the road again. A bunch of us were sitting playing cards when I noticed Tony walking towards us. I nudged some of the other lads.

'They were terrific watches Torino gave us as keepsakes, weren't they?' I said to Norman Piper as Tony approached.

The lads all agreed enthusiastically.

Tony pricked up his ears. 'What watches are these?' he asked.

'Cartier,' I said. 'We all got one. From the Torino manager.'

'He never gave me one,' said Tony, obviously miffed.

'Then you'd better have a word with Ron Newman,' I suggested, 'he's obviously pocketed yours.'

We doubled up with laughter as we watched Tony taking Ron to task about the 'missing' watch, and a bemused Ron protesting with increasing vehemence that he didn't have a clue what Tony was on about. They argued for fully five minutes before the penny finally dropped and they turned as one to see our card school rolling on the floor in disarray.

Ron Newman had played the majority of his football in the lower divisions of the Football League. He was a good manager for the NASL, not least because he lapped up the hype of the American game. The NASL was at that time divided into two conferences – Pacific and Atlantic – each of which had two divisions. The top teams from each division met each other in end-of-season play-offs. We were leading the Eastern Division of the Atlantic Conference as we took to the road for three away matches. We won one and lost two, though we did pick up some bonus points in the third game, which was decided on a shoot-out.

Those two defeats saw the Strikers slip to third and the local media believed our chance of winning the title had gone. As we took to the pitch for our next home game, against Tampa Bay

Rowdies, I was surprised to see a table in the centre of the pitch with a coffin on it. I had no idea why it was there. Once the formalities of introducing the team were over, a man with a microphone walked on to the field and headed for the coffin. We all watched agog, wondering what on earth was going on. This man made a short speech about how, according to reports in the media, our chances of winning the title were dead and buried. Suddenly the lid of the coffin was flung open and up popped Ron Newman like a jack-in-the-box. He grabbed the microphone and announced loudly, 'But, as you can see, the Strikers ain't dead yet, folks!'

The stadium erupted as the Strikers fans lapped up Ron's piece of showmanship. I can understand why they did. I mean, who wouldn't pay good money to see Sir Alex Ferguson do that at Old Trafford?

My decision to resume playing had been a massive one for me. I was confident I could do a good job for the Strikers, but at the back of my mind was the fear that I would make a fool of myself. After all, how many one-eyed goalkeepers have *you* come across? Thankfully, nothing could have been further from the truth. I coped well with the flight and speed of the ball. My reactions were good and I was pleased with my general level of fitness. The only problem I had was in the drastic reduction of my peripheral vision. I found I had to make a half-turn to bring players on my right-hand side into my field of view. This did not hamper my performance, though. On the contrary, I think I did pretty well. In 26 games that season the Strikers conceded 29 goals – the fewest in the NASL. Not only did this help us to win matches, it also denied our opponents bonus points for goals scored.

To my great delight, the Fort Lauderdale Strikers won our division, though we were beaten by the New York Cosmos in the final play-offs. To cap what for me had been a great comeback and a marvellous swansong to my career, I was voted NASL

Goalkeeper Of The Year. That award gave me as much if not more satisfaction than many I had picked up in England.

Having had a great time with the Strikers I decided to hang up my boots for good. I had overcome what had undoubtedly been the greatest challenge of my life. I had played football again and at a very good standard. My disability had not beaten me.

I returned to England in 1979 to discover that I was unemployed. Tony Waddington, who had told me I would always have a coaching job at Stoke City as long as he was in charge, had resigned in 1977 after seventeen years as manager. I wasn't out of work for long, however. The Port Vale manager, Dennis Butler, offered me a coaching role at Vale Park. When Dennis resigned only months after I had taken up my duties, my old Stoke City team mate Alan Bloor took over. So I was back in harness with Alan, who took on as his assistant the former Preston and Blackburn player Graham Hawkins.

At first everything went well. But one thing I was beginning to understand about coaching is that you can only teach those who are willing to learn. One day I gathered the first-team squad together to make a point on attacking play. The Port Vale centre forward was Bernie Wright, a burly and somewhat surly striker who had been at Walsall (twice), Everton and Bradford City before joining Vale for £9,000 in 1978.

Having watched Bernie play for the first team on a number of occasions, I'd noticed he wasn't helping his midfield the way he should. Bernie tended to stay too close to his marker, instead of dropping off into space to receive the ball, hold it up and allow support to arrive from midfield. I pointed this out to him, but he was having none of it.

'I'm not doing that. Can't see the point,' he informed me. We discussed the issue, but still Bernie wouldn't follow my instructions. He was intransigent, belligerent, and in the end, quite rude.

I was very annoyed. I had been employed as the coach, yet here was a player who didn't value my ideas and what I had to say about the game. I suppose that sort of attitude is something a coach is paid to sort out, but it certainly wasn't my idea of job satisfaction. I spoke to Alan Bloor, who said he'd have a word with Bernie. Whether he ever did, I don't know. A few days later Alan resigned and I left Port Vale with him.

On the whole I enjoyed coaching, but I was hankering to be a manager. I applied for two vacant jobs, at Lincoln City and Rotherham United and was interviewed for both. In the meantime I received a telephone call from the chairman of Telford United of the Alliance Premier League, the equivalent of the Vauxhall Conference today. The Telford chairman invited me to take over as club manager. I politely declined, telling him that my aim was to manage a Football League club, for which I had two forthcoming interviews.

Big mistake. The Lincoln job went to Colin Murphy and Rotherham United appointed Ian Porterfield as their new team boss. A few days later, however, the Telford chairman was back on the phone. With about ten games to go to the end of the season, Telford were in danger of relegation to the Southern League. Obviously, he added, he didn't want that to happen. All he wanted me to do was come along and do what I had to do to keep them up. This time I accepted his offer.

Telford United were a team of part-time professionals who trained two evenings a week. Before signing the contract that had been offered I watched the players train in midweek and play on the following Saturday. It was obvious to me that Telford were not a good side, even for the Alliance Premier League. I knew I would have my work cut out, but I accepted the challenge. Telford may not have had a good team, but I knew a man who did.

Bangor City had previously won the Alliance, but at the time were experiencing financial difficulties. My thinking was simple: if Bangor had won this league, then they must have good players.

And if they're strapped for cash, they might be willing to sell some.

I drove to Bangor's Ferrar Road ground to watch them in action and was impressed by their goalkeeper and centre half. Having been given a budget to work to, I approached the Bangor chairman, Mr Roberts, and asked him how much he wanted for the pair.

'Fifteen hundred pounds . . .' said Mr Roberts.

'It's a deal,' I said.

'. . . But you're going to have to take our centre forward as well.'

I had seen the Bangor centre forward in action and, with the best will in the world, he just didn't look good enough.

'I'm not so keen on him,' I said.

'If you don't take our centre forward, you won't get the other two,' said Mr Roberts. 'They travel down from Cheshire together for games, and he has the car!'

What else could I do? I signed the centre forward as well. The goalkeeper and centre half did a great job for Telford United and, as luck would have it, so too did the centre forward. (Either I'm a poor judge of a striker, or he'd been having an off day when I first watched him.) He scored a hatful of goals for us and by the end of the season Telford United were comfortably clear of relegation.

The following year, 1980–81, we enjoyed a good pre-season. I signed John Ruggerio from Stoke City, organized friendlies against Stoke and Wolves and followed up with a satisfactory if unspectacular start to the season.

We were in mid-table in November when I took a sabbatical in order to undergo an operation. I asked the former Blackpool and Stoke City player Jackie Mudie to take temporary charge of team affairs while I was absent, satisfied that the team would be in good hands.

Unfortunately, during Jackie's temporary period holding the reins, Telford lost an FA Trophy match to a team from a lower league. I returned to work in December and was asked by the chairman to attend a meeting at the offices of the travel agents he owned.

'I'm sorry, but we are relieving you of your duties as manager of this club,' he informed me.

I was shocked. My sacking hit me hard. For a time it knocked for six all the passion and enthusiasm I had for the game. I had high hopes of taking Telford United on to bigger and better things, but felt I hadn't been given sufficient time to achieve my aim. Time is the most important asset a manager can be given and, to my mind, I had been denied that.

I was still under contract, but the club were in no position to pay me off. I was rather naive about such matters at the time, and had no idea what my legal position was. A few days later the Telford chairman called me at home. He confirmed the fact that, such was the club's financial position, the only way they could pay up the remainder of my contract was if I were to take up another position on the staff. I was gullible enough to believe him. My new role at the club was to stand in a small kiosk outside a supermarket and sell Telford United raffle tickets! Furthermore, he banned me from attending Telford games. I think the chairman expected me to reject my new role outright, which would have suited him fine. But out of sheer bloody mindedness I accepted his ridiculous offer and reported for duty at the kiosk the following Monday.

I sold draw tickets from that little kiosk outside the supermarket for nigh on six weeks, as much as anything so that the locals could see just how shabbily their football club had treated me. Talk about hero to zero! Many ex-supporters agreed:

'A member of the England team that won the World Cup, the greatest goalkeeper there has ever been, selling draw tickets from this hovel? It's a bloody disgrace, the way you've been treated.'

The groundswell of dissent grew, and gave me the strength not to walk away from the money I was entitled to. Eventually public opinion in Telford swayed matters my way; well, half way at least. The chairman called me into his office and pushed a cheque across the desktop. The amount was about 50 per cent of what I was entitled to, but I had made my point. I accepted it and walked out of his office and out of football management. Ironically, the team I had largely assembled at Telford went on to enjoy considerable success, not only in non-league football, but also in the FA Cup where they performed a number of giantkilling acts.

With a short and not so sweet career in football management behind me, I turned to the world of business. A Leicester businessman with a motor dealership in the city telephoned me to discuss his plans to open a corporate hospitality company and asked if I would run it for him. We had a number of meetings and he seemed genuine enough, so I accepted his offer, which necessitated Ursula and I moving back to the Leicester area. We bought a house in Quorn and I settled down to running a business. The business wasn't mine, but it traded off my name. I fronted the company for ten years and enjoyed it, though it wasn't all plain sailing.

The business provided hospitality packages to almost all the major British sporting events. In the main our clients were companies, but on occasions we dealt with individual customers as well. One day one of the girls in my office received a telephone call asking for Centre Court tickets for Wimbledon. This was not a problem, but then the caller asked for something else. He said that his clients were two very rich businessmen from Saudi Arabia and, as part of the package, could we supply a couple of escort girls?

'Er, I'll have to get back to you on that,' my secretary said in a fluster.

I advised her not to do anything for half an hour, then return the call and tell the mystery man that we don't supply the sort of hospitality he had in mind.

'If a company receptionist answers, we at least know this

unusual request has come from a potential client,' I told her. 'If he answers the phone himself, just hang up. Give it another half an hour, then ring him back. Tell him that Mr Banks says that this company is not an escort agency.'

She made the call. The same voice answered, so she put the phone down. After half an hour she rang again. The same man answered and she carried out my instructions to the letter.

The following Sunday, a well-known red-top newspaper carried a sensational story under a banner headline. I don't remember the exact wording, but you know the sort of thing: 'Strawberries and Sex on Centre Court'. I do remember the accompanying photograph, though – a telephoto-lens shot of the manager of a rival company walking down one of the aisles at the main arena at Wimbledon with two escort girls in tow, presumably searching for two non-existent Saudi clients.

I have no doubt that the whole thing had been a set-up. Fortunately, the sound principles by which we ran the business saved the company from acute embarrassment that time, but on another occasion I wasn't so lucky.

As everyone knows, tickets for an FA Cup final are like gold dust. There are never enough to satisfy the needs of genuine supporters, and corporate hospitality companies have equal difficulty in meeting demand. So when I was offered a bunch of tickets for the 1987 Cup final by a tout, I snapped them up.

A few weeks after the match the Football Association had me up before them to explain how tickets allocated to players from a leading club had found their way into the hands of my clients. I told the hearing that I hadn't bought the tickets direct from players, but had acquired them from a third party for the purposes of corporate hospitality. To my mind, the players who had sold their ticket allocation to the tout in the first place should also have been brought to book. The FA decreed that what I had done was a gross infringement of their rules and that I would have to accept the consequences.

I admit that I was silly to buy those tickets. I didn't really have a leg to stand on. All I could hope for was that the FA would give me credit for my honesty and immediate admission in deciding my punishment. I was given a seven-year ban from receiving Cup final tickets. I accepted the ban with good grace, though at the time I believed it to be somewhat harsh, with more than an element of giving me an exemplary punishment as a warning to others.

I was, by this time, working on the pools panel, a job I still do. Following the news of my ticket ban I turned up one Friday evening at the London hotel that served as our base to find that two other members of the panel, Roger Hunt and Tony Green, had mounted and framed two old Cup final tickets which they presented to me with great relish.

When the motor dealership that was the parent company of Gordon Banks Corporate Hospitality went down the pan shortly afterwards, it took a lot of my savings with it. The hospitality business ceased trading. I had invested in the finance arm of the motor dealership and lost the lot. To my eternal gratitude, Leicester City offered me a testimonial game to help me out. It was a wonderful gesture on the part of the club, and one that touched me greatly. I had a great night and it was fantastic to see so many familiar faces again. We talked about the old days and I was amazed to find that, although we had all given up the game long ago, in the ensuing years we had all become better players!

I have now worked for the pools panel for some sixteen years. The panel currently comprises my England team mate Roger Hunt, the former Blackpool and Newcastle United midfield player Tony Green and myself, together with an adjudicator. In my early days the panel also included the former referee Arthur Ellis and the former Scotland goalkeeper Ronnie Simpson. When I first joined the panel we used to meet in the Waldorf Hotel in London. The food at the Waldorf was excellent and I remember being particularly impressed by the variety of the cheeseboard – although not quite as impressed as Arthur. We had all sampled a little cheese, but large portions of Red Leicester, Cheshire,

Cheddar, Caerphilly, Lancashire and Brie remained. Suddenly Arthur Ellis asked, 'Will anyone be wanting more cheese?'

We all politely declined. Arthur clapped his hands with delight, then produced a large plastic bag from his briefcase and proceeded to fill it with large chunks of cheese.

'You lads don't know what you're missing – this is first-rate cheese. It's all been paid for. Be a shame to leave it,' said Arthur, oblivious to our embarrassment.

'Waste not, want not' was definitely Arthur's philosophy and, judging by the size of his waist, he didn't want for much. Whatever food remained, Arthur had it. He'd leave the Waldorf with his briefcase full of beef, chicken pieces, pork pies, tomatoes, grapes, you name it. He even wore a jacket with a deep inside pocket which he filled with slices of ham or turkey wrapped in tin foil. 'He's a walking Fortnum and Mason,' said Roger Hunt one Saturday.

The jokes and leg-pulling were integral to the atmosphere of these meetings of the pools panel. During one session, Arthur Ellis announced that he was thinking of buying a grandfather clock. 'You'll be having the pendulum taken out, then, Arthur,' I suggested. 'You'll not want the shadow it casts wearing a hole in your wallpaper!'

For a time the adjudicator of the pools panel was Lord Bath. He was a very friendly man who took his responsibilities as seriously as we did. We all became very good friends, and when Arthur Ellis's wife died Lord Bath attended the funeral in Yorkshire with the rest of us. After the service Arthur laid on a buffet at his home. After a suitable time had elapsed to pay his respects, Lord Bath, who had travelled up north by train, asked Arthur if he could telephone for a taxi to take him to the station.

'I'm not having you travelling in a taxi, Lord Bath,' said Arthur. 'I'll sort you out for transport.'

Lord Bath thanked Arthur for his kindness. Ten minutes later Arthur was back.

'When you're ready, sir,' said Arthur, and led his lordship outside to the Co-op's hearse idling at the kerbside.

'It's all paid for. The driver has to pass the station, so he might as well drop you off on the way,' said Arthur to the speechless lord.

I really enjoy my work with the pools panel. We sit every weekend to pass judgement on what we believe will be the outcome of games both here and in Australia. To accommodate the needs of television, quite a number of games are switched late from their original Saturday date to Sunday or Monday. If they were originally on the pools coupons, we must pass judgement on what we believe would have been the result. So there's usually something for us to do even when the weather doesn't disrupt the fixture list.

On occasions the conclusions we arrive at seemingly have repercussions far beyond their pools-points value. In 1993 we declared the outcome of a postponed game between Tranmere Rovers and Sunderland. In the end our verdict was a win for Tranmere. The following day the Sunderland manager, Malcolm Crosby, was sacked! Pure coincidence, of course, but the newspapers couldn't resist saying that Crosby had become the only manager ever to be dismissed for losing a postponed game.

In addition to my work with the pools panel, I am still involved with the 1966 World Cup team. We often reunite to promote charitable projects, and also work together on cruise ships where we regale the holidaymakers with tales of the old days and offer our opinions on the current game. I do a little after-dinner speaking and I have become involved with a number of charities. One of these is the children's hospice at the North Staffordshire Hospital, a cause very dear to my heart. I've been very lucky myself, and feel a strong need to try and give something back. It's important to help those who are less able to help themselves.

Not only do I have a wonderful family and a fantastic career, but I've also survived a number of threats to my health. I've had two tumours removed, the first and most serious some fifteen years ago. I had become aware of a lump in my stomach, but as it caused me no pain or discomfort I thought little of it. Ursula, however, suggested that I should see a consultant 'just to be on the safe side'. I'm glad I did.

The consultant examined my X-rays and told me I had a large tumour that would have to be removed. Even then the serious nature of my condition didn't register with me. As the consultant described what the operation involved, I took out my diary and began looking for some free dates.

'What on earth are you doing, Mr Banks?' asked the consultant. I told him I was checking in my diary to see when I would be available to come in for the operation.

'Good God, man, this is so serious I'm going to operate straight away,' he said. 'Go straight home, pack a bag and get back here.' I quietly put away my diary.

The surgeon removed a tumour the size of a melon from my stomach. Apparently, it was one of the largest he'd ever seen.

'It's a beauty! Throughout Britain and the USA, only thirty-two have been found bigger than this,' he informed me with some pride.

I have to admit, I didn't share his enthusiasm. Obviously I was very relieved to be rid of it and didn't want to see it, let alone discuss its dubious merits. When the time came for me to leave hospital, the consultant presented me with a photograph of the tumour 'as a keepsake'. Needless to say, that's one snap we don't get out of the drawer when relatives or friends come round for dinner.

My sudden exit from the Leicester business community wasn't without its compensations. Our children had grown up and settled in North Staffordshire and Warrington. In order to be nearer to them, Ursula and I moved back to Cheshire. We now live in a village just over the Staffordshire border, some ten miles from Stoke. We're much closer as a family and we're very happy.

In recognition of the efforts of the Stoke team of 1972 in winning the League Cup, in 2002 the club gave every member of the side a ticket for life at Stoke City and I was made president of the club in succession to the late Sir Stanley Matthews. I regularly attend matches at the Britannia Stadium, but also travel with my son Robert to watch Leicester City whenever we can. I also make the occasional nostalgic trip to Chesterfield – I'm not the sort of guy who will ever forget his roots and Chesterfield were, after all, the club that gave me my chance in league football.

In addition to attending a lot of games, I watch as many televised matches as I can. As you've probably gathered, I have plenty of views on the state of the game today, particularly where goalkeeping is concerned. Though before I air those views, let me say this: the standard of football today is no better or worse than when I played. But, my word, it's certainly different . . .

19. The Changing Game

Football has indeed changed. Many of these well-documented and widely debated changes have been to the great benefit of the game, though we have seen a number of developments in recent years that I believe have been detrimental to the game. Compared to my days, the game today is quicker, players are fitter and teams better organized, irrespective of the level at which they play.

There is one change, however, that has received little attention, despite having a key role in changing the way football is played – the ball itself.

When I started my career at Chesterfield, the ball most often used was a Webber Premier. This was a leather-panelled caseball, an improvement on the lace-up Tomlinson 'T' and Tugite balls used in the thirties, forties and early fifties. The Webber Premier had more leather panels, so kept its shape irrespective of how wet conditions were. It was advertised as being waterproof, but had to be rubbed with Chelsea dubbin to make it so, and even then would soak up some moisture on rainy days. Inside the leather casing the ball contained a valve bladder, which also added to the weight. The official weight of a football in the fifties was set at 16 ounces (454g). On very wet days, however, this type of ball was often considerably heavier due to the moisture and mud it collected.

The Webber made life for a goalkeeper relatively easy owing to the simple fact that, when struck, it travelled true. The Webber never deviated in the air; consequently when diving to make a save, especially from a shot hit from some distance, if I had anticipated correctly, more often than not I would make the save.

In the sixties the Webber was replaced by the Mitre Perma-white Super, an altogether lighter (and whiter) ball. The white panels of this ball were laminated leather, which did away with the need to dubbin. The Mitre and its competitor made by Stuart Surridge were very good balls but the big difference from a goalkeeper's point of view was that both deviated slightly in the air. Not a lot, but by enough to increase the uncertainty when executing a save.

The ball in general use as I write is much lighter than its predecessor; the type used in the 2002 World Cup is lighter still. When struck with force it deviates in flight, both swerving and dipping. This is a nightmare for goalkeepers, and often they cannot anticipate the exact height a shot will be when it reaches the goal. It is little surprise, then, that goalkeepers can be made to seem incompetent, even foolish, when attempting to make a save.

When Rivelino swerved a Brazilian free kick round the defensive wall in the altitude of Mexico '70, the world gasped. Goals like that are knocked in every week up and down the country these days, and not because all those players possess the skill of Rivelino. Today's ball may well make for more spectacular football and enables David Beckham to hit superb forty-yard crosses into the penalty area and sublime crossfield passes, but it stacks the odds against the poor goalkeeper.

The ball used in Japan and Korea in 2002 was so light that at times it was impossible for goalkeepers. When England secured their place in the quarter-finals by beating Denmark, many commentators rightly praised England but also made a point of mentioning how poor the performance of the Danish goalkeeper, Thomas Sorensen, had been. True, he didn't have the best of matches, but the light ball and wet conditions played their part in that. England's opening goal came when Rio Ferdinand headed the ball at him in a downpour and Sorensen fumbled the ball over the line. That lightweight laminated ball in such wet conditions must have been like a bar of soap. Despite three attempts to grasp the ball, he just couldn't get a firm hold. When Emile Heskey's first-time shot on the run from twenty yards gave England their third goal one commentator remarked, 'You have to ask questions of the goalkeeper.' Heskey hit his shot low and hard. The ball swerved one way then the other before bouncing on the sodden turf just in front of the diving Sorensen. Then, instead of rising a few inches, it skidded low under his body. What may have looked like a straightforward save to that commentator was anything but.

In the same match a Danish player cut in from the right and hit a stinging shot towards David Seaman's left-hand post. David does not have the nickname 'Safe Hands' for nothing. He had got his angles and positioning spot on, which made it appear as if the Danish player had shot straight at him and it would be perfectly straightforward for David simply to gather the ball into his midriff. But he beat it out with both hands. Why did he do that? Because he couldn't be confident of taking the ball cleanly.

Seaman did exactly right. The ball was travelling at considerable speed and he was obviously wary of the fact that it could deviate in the air at the last moment. The conditions were very wet, so rather than risk fumbling the ball and presenting an oncoming Danish player with the chance of a goal, Seaman made a blocking save. The TV commentator said, 'A great save from Seaman.' It was, but he never picked up on the fact that the England keeper had decided to block rather than attempt to hold the shot.

After the game a reporter asked Seaman about the quality of his opposite number's performance, particularly on two of England's goals. He refused to be drawn, simply replying, 'Well, conditions were very difficult out there.' They were and he knew it. Apart from the fact Seaman would not want to criticize a fellow professional, his guarded reply to the question had more than an element of 'the goalkeepers' union' about it. Given the lightweight ball and the extremely wet conditions, I should imagine that at the back of Seaman's mind was a large dose of 'There but for the grace of God . . .'

The innovatory light ball also played a role in the downfall of

England in the 2002 World Cup. David Seaman cannot be blamed for conceding what proved to be Brazil's winning goal in the quarter-final. Video footage from behind Ronaldinho clearly showed the ball heading beyond the left-hand post before curving so much that it ended up in the right-hand corner of the goal.

When defending an angled free kick from thirty yards out a goalkeeper has to anticipate the ball's trajectory. A free kick flighted from that distance is usually aimed at a point just beyond the six-yard box, where opposing forwards can run on to it. When the ball was struck David Seaman had to come off his line and gamble that he would reach the ball before the Brazilian forwards. Consequently he took three paces forward, which was the correct thing to do. He was simply caught out by the way the ball arced so severely in the air. As soon as the ball left Ronaldinho's boot, Seaman was sunk. He had played the percentages and lost.

To add to Seaman's problems, Paul Scholes had, quite rightly, positioned himself in front of Ronaldinho as he ran to take the kick. However, as the Brazilian struck the ball Scholes moved just a little, perhaps blocking Seaman's view for a vital split second. A goalkeeper must be able to judge the pace of the ball in order to determine its probable flight, and I don't think David could see it at the point of contact. He may have been unsighted for a split second only, but, as he and England found to their cost, such margins can be crucial.

Both Seaman and Scholes were blameless: it was just one of those things. A goalkeeper has only brief moments to weigh up his options and act, and circumstances conspired to make Seaman's usually solid judgement go awry. That can happen even to the best goalkeepers, of which he is undoubtedly one.

Following the game Seaman was inconsolable, but his performance after conceding that goal was an object lesson for any would-be goalkeeper. If you feel you have made an error, you have to push it to the back of your mind for the rest of the game.

A lesser player might have let that goal play on his mind, and could have let in two or three more as a result. Not Seaman. He contained his emotions until the final whistle. Such an attitude is the mark of a top-class keeper.

When asked to define a great player Sir Matt Busby said, 'The great players have great games in the great games. When it really matters, they perform.' And that sums it up. It's no good saying, 'If we played them again tomorrow we could beat them.' It's today that counts. Perhaps England didn't have enough players who fulfilled Sir Matt's definition of greatness in the 2002 World Cup.

In May 1966 the top five teams in the FIFA rankings were Portugal, Brazil, England, West Germany and Argentina. In July England beat three of them in the space of seven days to win the World Cup. We didn't have it easy. As both Pelé and Gerd Muller have said, winning the World Cup is the hardest thing to do in football. With FIFA's top-ranked teams (France, Argentina and Italy) out of the competition, England had a great chance to do just that in 2002. That they didn't take that chance might haunt those players for the rest of their lives. Football is a team sport, and it was the team that failed against Brazil, not David Seaman.

Nevertheless, I remain very hopeful for the future. We have some excellent young players who should be even better, more experienced internationals by 2006. The nucleus of the 2002 squad will remain part of the England set-up for some time to come. So long as they maintain their development and, just as important, their desire to land the biggest prize in the game, England can go all the way in Germany in 2006. Should that happen, no one will be more delighted than the Class of '66.

I think the decision to introduce a very light ball for the 2002 World Cup was crazy. The new ball would obviously have been subjected to many tests, but it was a completely new phenomenon for the players, all of whom had to spend time adjusting their game. But it was the goalkeepers I really felt for as time and again I watched the ball deviate two or even three times in the air.

Of course we all want to see more goals, but spare a thought for the man between the posts who has put in years of specialist training only to find that a hard job has become even harder overnight.

If FIFA want to create more goals, rather than introducing a balloon for a ball they should have concentrated on other areas. On shirt pulling, for example. I've lost count of the number of times I have seen a player bearing down on goal with the ball at his feet, or running into the penalty area to meet a cross, who has been pulled back by his shirt. Such fouls are intended to prevent a certain goal. Clamp down on foul play and gamesmanship and there would be no need to manufacture goals by 'doctoring' the ball. Like everyone else, I want to see more goals, but not by making goalkeepers look foolish.

At a time when managers and coaches have finally realized the importance and value of having a good goalkeeper in their team, FIFA are turning the art of great goalkeeping into a lottery.

I've said it before and I'll say it again – few sides win the Premiership in England unless their goalkeeper has enjoyed an exceptional season. When Blackburn Rovers won the title in 1995, their goalkeeper Tim Flowers had a super campaign. Likewise, Manchester United in the nineties had the outstanding Peter Schmeichel, and the well-documented errors of Fabien Barthez were at least part of the reason for their defensive frailty and consequent failure to retain their title in 2001–02. In contrast, David Seaman's return to top form underpinned their usurpation by an excellent Arsenal side.

Another major difference in today's game is the quality of the pitches. Today's pitches are used almost exclusively for first team games. Rarely these days does the reserve team of a Premiership club play on the home pitch – most have arrangements with clubs in lower leagues to use their grounds for second-team games. Along with the reduced wear and tear, drainage is also far more efficient today. When I played, midwinter pitches often resembled quagmires and the ball picked up mud as well as moisture, making it very heavy to kick and well-nigh impossible to swerve and bend. I'm a great admirer of David Beckham but today's true playing pitches and the lightweight ball do give him an advantage. When pinging a cross into the goalmouth with the inside of his right boot, the ball curls away from the goalkeeper. This is very difficult to defend, although, credit to Beckham, he has practised his art to near perfection. A cross played into this 'zone of uncertainty' between the goalkeeper and his central defenders, because it swerves away from the goalkeeper at the last moment, is a particularly fruitful attacking option and Manchester United have scored a good many goals as a result of this.

David is a great player, but he is fortunate to be playing at a time when conditions are so complementary to his undoubted talents. On pudding-like pitches and with a heavy ball he might have been merely a good one. As I said, football today is no better or no worse than when I played – simply different.

I love the modern game. I like the way it is played, more often than not, in a cavalier and entertaining manner. Foreign players have exerted a positive influence, especially in the Premiership, but I do worry that their sheer number is impeding the development of home-grown players. Cream will always rise to the top – young players like Danny Mills, Ashley Cole, Joe Cole, Steven Gerrard and Michael Owen are living proof of that – but it is the influx of foreign imports in the lower divisions of English football that gives me real cause for concern. Often a Nationwide League club will buy a player from Eastern Europe simply because he is happy to settle for wages below that of a domestic player. Such journeymen do a job, but are invariably a short-term solution. Wages apart, many managers know they have only two, maybe three years to bring success to a club. Once again, the short-term solution is to buy a foreign player since it can take anything up to four years before an exciting academy player makes the first team. That is, four years of investment in time, expertise and money. What is the point, so the pragmatists argue, when a manager can buy a player for £400,000 who will do the job straight away? Or, as if often the case, there isn't even a fee to pay, as he will arrive free on a 'Bosman'.

We don't have football grounds any more – they're all stadiums. The Taylor Report was long overdue, and it took the human tragedies of Heysel, Valley Parade and Hillsborough before football took a long hard look at how it treated its paying customers. Facilities offered to spectators are much improved, and I'm all for that. The new or redesigned stadiums have also helped to rid the game of the criminal element, often erroneously referred to as 'football' hooligans, who besmirched its name in the past. There are real signs that football is once again becoming a family game.

'A little is lost and a little is gained in every day', to quote William Wordsworth. The same can be said of developments in football. Let me say now, though, I wouldn't go back to how it was. Having been cannon fodder in a world war, many people in the late forties were treated as little more than terrace fodder by those who ran the game at the time. That attitude largely prevailed until the terrible tragedy of Hillsborough.

Having said that, I can't help grieving for what we have lost with the advent of the new stadiums. On the terraces everyone had their favourite spot and stood there season in, season out, for years, as did other supporters who stood near them. Going to a match was a social occasion; football was the glue that cemented a sense of community. Now, if you are not a season-ticket holder, you have to buy your ticket every time and you end up sitting in a different position for every match, among faces you don't recognize.

At many of the spacious stadiums today, whether new or redeveloped, the fans are so far from the action that they can't feel the intimate atmosphere of the grounds of the past. Both as a player and spectator I loved the atmosphere of the old grounds – the Victoria Ground at Stoke City was typical – where the supporters were only yards from the action. Though at either end it boasted alp-like terracing, it guaranteed physical and emotional enclosure. Very little that happened on the pitch escaped the attention of the supporters. They felt very close to the players and vice versa. Someone standing by the tunnel entrance could sniff the liniment wafting up from the legs of the players as they ran out; they could hear me calling to my full backs; the grunts of two players tussling for the ball. The old grounds did not boast the architecture of the Reebok, the Stadium of Light or the redeveloped Elland Road – they were simply bear-pits where attention was focused on the action taking place a few yards away.

There is still brilliance, drama and excitement on the pitch, of course, but fans have been physically distanced from the action. The clubs and authorities appear to have compensated by encouraging supporters to become part of something bigger than just the match. Going to a game has been turned into an 'experience' in which the marketing of the footballer and his club as a brand can be deployed. With the word 'profit' being the first to be uttered by most club chairmen, the football 'experience' inevitably involves parting a lot of supporters from a lot of cash. If you have shelled out £50 for a replica shirt, have the club's credit card and have paid extra simply to have a concourse that offers you exclusive use of a bar, the stadium needs to look something special!

When I played there was a close connection between players and fans that is absent today. On Saturdays they would be less than five yards from my back. When I extended a hand to block the ball they heard the impact. When Terry Conroy or Mike Stringfellow took off at speed, many supporters saw the soil kick up from the pitch. We shopped in the same supermarkets, drank in the same pubs. Before every match we were besieged by autograph hunters and were happy to sign their books. When the Premiership players of today arrive at a stadium, the supporters are kept well back, often behind metal crush barriers. Superstardom has its benefits, but also has its price, and an important aspect of contact between player and supporter is now gone for ever.

I may be in my mid-sixties, but that's not where I'm living. I don't yearn for a return to the so-called 'good old days'. But there are times when I miss the simplicity of how football used to be. The game we played was simple. I remember Matt Busby once being asked whether the game-plan approach of Manchester United in 1968 was a sign that football was becoming too complicated. 'Our game plan is this,' said Matt. 'When we have the ball we are all attackers. When the opposition has the ball, we are all defenders. Now what's complicated about that?'

Life was less sophisticated, and so was football; but I miss the little things we have lost. Young fans today haven't felt the frisson of anticipation at half time as the stewards hung up the scores from the other matches around the country, for example. You had to match the scores with the letters in a table printed in the programme. Slower than electronic scoreboards and SMS messages, perhaps, but I know which I preferred. Believe me, from a player's point of view it's better not to know how your rivals are getting on elsewhere. Ignore the electronic scoreboard, concentrate on your own game and discover your fate at the final whistle. It's much simpler that way.

After the TV-induced boom of the nineties, many clubs are now experiencing the bust. The collapse of ITV Digital has affected many Nationwide League clubs. The Premiership is comparatively healthy, but the Nationwide League is looking more and more like the symptoms on a medicine bottle.

I believe the collapse of the digital deal was a symptom of changing fashion. In the nineties football fell into the hands of passive supporters, people who couldn't really care less about the game. Football, as one person put it, became 'sexy', the new rock 'n' roll. Many professional people became interested in the game not only because it was perceived to be trendy, but because they realized that to support a club offered social advantages. There's nothing wrong in that, but, in a similar way to the dotcom bubble, people stopped discriminating in the scramble to climb aboard the bandwagon. Or perhaps they knew nothing about football in the first place.

I say that because I can't imagine that anyone who knows anything at all about the game would ever believe that live TV coverage of, with all due respect, Bradford City versus Barnsley, might attract a large subscription audience to television. The notion that ITV Digital would attract subscribers in sufficient numbers to make its Nationwide League deal financially viable was flawed from the start, as any genuine football fan could have told them.

Arguably, the advent of the transfer window will have an even greater impact on the finances of clubs than the collapse of ITV Digital. UEFA introduced two transfer windows, one in the summer and the other at Christmas, which means that clubs can buy or sell players only within those windows. Such a system would prevent smaller clubs selling a promising player at short notice to a larger club to offset a cashflow crisis. Clubs such as Crewe Alexandra are very adept at unearthing talented young-sters, developing them and selling them on to top sides. If this source of revenue is limited to two short periods a year, the cashflow implications could be extremely serious.

Nationwide League clubs need to be allowed to develop young talent and given the opportunity for that emerging talent to filter up the pyramid system. Surely it would be far better for English football, and European football in general, if we had an international transfer window, but not a domestic one. This would help the finances of our game because our top clubs would be able to buy players from smaller clubs at any time, but foreign players only during the two window periods. Such a system would allow young home-grown players to move up the league ladder towards the Premiership, which has to be good for English football. We would still have the interest and skill that foreign imports bring to the domestic game, and money would continue to circulate throughout the year. At the same time, young British talent would have the chance to shine. If some of the ninety-two league clubs fold we will lose not only some of the unique flavour and truly nationwide spread of English football, but also its strength in depth. If all the power and talent are concentrated in too few hands, the entire system could become top-heavy and be in danger of collapse.

If I had but one wish for football, it would be that the success of the Premiership and the national team could be shared among every English football club. The almost daily news of another club going into receivership or administration saddens me greatly. Should the Carlisle Uniteds, York Citys and Port Vales of English football disappear, it would be tragic. Not only would we be losing a club, a business and careers, but also a small but important part of the fabric of our society would be lost. Those who administer our game must do all they can to prevent that happening. The working man and woman must continue to have their ballet.

I have been especially pleased to see the England team emerge once again as a power in world football. We have some fine young players of true international quality and, in David Beckham, Michael Owen, Paul Scholes and Rio Ferdinand, players of world class. Under the careful and objective manager-ship of Sven-Göran Eriksson I am very optimistic for the future of both the national side and English football in general.

I have been involved in football as a player, coach, manager, raffle-ticket seller and supporter for over fifty years. I've seen a lot of changes and will, no doubt, see many more. The game has changed irrevocably, but in essence it remains the same. Football, as Danny Blanchflower once said, is about the pursuit of glory. That is true, but it is also about human endeavour, about passion, courage and emotion. Occasionally it is about pride and honour, and sometimes even humour. When played at its best and in a spirit of true sportsmanship, a football match becomes much more than a mere sporting contest. The truly beautiful game is a miracle of man's physical and mental capabilities. When that happens, the pitch becomes a nirvana.

I have been so very lucky. I have a loving and caring family who have been the hub around which my life has revolved. Robert is a sales executive for a timber merchant. Wendy is also in sales, for a shoe company, and in what spare time she has, is also a dressmaker to the entertainment industry. Julia is a solicitor in Cheshire. Ursula and I are keen gardeners and you'll find us outside most days attending to the beds and borders or mowing the grass. I always ensure the lawns are not too lush and that they'll take a short stud! We all enjoy watching movies. I often take my grandchildren to the cinema and consequently have become something of an expert on *Star Wars* and *Spiderman*.

Ursula and I love having the family over for a meal. I haven't inherited my mam's talent for cooking, nor have I learned from Ursula, who likes the kitchen to herself when she's cooking and packs me off to the lounge in order to avert a culinary disaster. I miss Mam. She died nearly twenty years since, but the legacy she left was one of love.

I have also been fortunate enough to have made a career in what I believe is the greatest sport on earth. Football is a serious business, but the key to enjoying it to the full, and to surviving in the game, is not always to take it too seriously. That has been my philosophy in both football and life. Of course, seriousness has its place – any waiter will tell you that – but in life, as in football, to everything there is a season.

Football has given me an awful lot. I have played alongside and against some of the greatest names ever to have graced the game. No amount of money could buy that wonderful experience and its store of golden memories that I will cherish forever. It remains only to say thank you to all those players, managers, club officials and supporters whose lives I have touched and who,

37. Doing some pre-season training of my own around the lanes of Cheshire in 1972.

38. My favourite photograph. Saving Geoff Hurst's penalty in the 1972 League Cup semi-final second leg at a very atmospheric Upton Park. The poses struck by my Stoke team-mates suggest they were expecting Geoff to score!

39. I celebrate Stoke City's victory over West Ham in the semi-final of the League Cup in 1972. This was our fourth meeting, at Old Trafford, and the longest League Cup tie ever.

40. I check that the laces of John Dempsey's boots are correctly tied during the League Cup final of 1972 between Stoke City and Chelsea.

41. A great day for Stoke City and George Eastham. After our epic win against Chelsea in 1972 I congratulate the scorer of Stoke's winning goal. At 35 years and 161 days old, George remains the oldest recipient of a League Cup winner's medal.

42. My son Robert puts me through my paces at our home in Madeley Heath. I even worked out the angle and my positioning for this one.

43. A great moment for me. Receiving my Footballer of the Year award in 1972. I was the first goalkeeper to win it since my boyhood hero Bert Trautmann in 1956. The following year, Pat Jennings won.

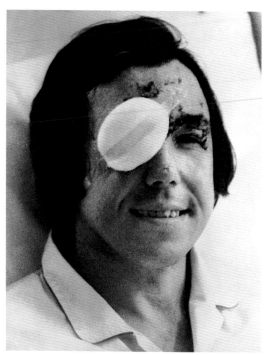

44. Still managing a smile after my near-fatal car crash in 1972. I wouldn't let my disability beat me. Encouraged by my family and literally thousands of well-wishers, I was to make a comeback in America.

45. My Ford Consul after the crash in October 1972 which resulted in me losing the sight in my right eye.

46. Ursula and Wendy sift through thousands of letters from well-wishers received after my accident.

47. *This is Your Life*. Left to right, front: my brothers Michael and David, Ursula, Wendy, Julia, me, Tony Waddington (on my left shoulder), Robert, Geoff Hurst and Bobby Moore.

48. In action for Fort Lauderdale Strikers. Following the loss of my eye, the decision to play again had been the most difficult of my life. Here, George Graham (8) decides to test out the strength of my ribcage.

49. *Below*: With my good friend George Best in the colours of the Strikers. George scored what I believe to be the best-ever goal against me. Quite simply, he was a football genius.

50. Pelé visits Wembley prior to England's last game there against Germany in the qualifying group for the 2002 World Cup. I was coaching some youngsters when my old friend turned up. I think the love and respect Pelé and I have for one another are obvious.

51. Working on the book with friend and collaborator Les Scott.

in turn, have touched mine. Collectively, you have given me so much more than a lad from Tinsley could ever have expected. Words could never express my true gratitude. Some people think there's no place for sentiment in football – there is now.

Career Record

Football League

CHESTERFIELD

1958–59

29 Nov	Colchester United	(h) 2–2	
6 Dec	Carlisle United	(a) 0–0	FA Cup
10 Dec	Carlisle United	(h) 1–0	FA Cup (replay)
13 Dec	Norwich City	(h) 1–1	
20 Dec	Halifax Town	(a) 2–3	
26 Dec	Wrexham	(h) 1–1	
27 Dec	Wrexham	(a) 4–3	
1 Jan	Hull City	(h) 2–1	
3 Jan	Newport County	(h) 3–1	
10 Jan	Colchester United	(a) 0–2	FA Cup
17 Jan	Southend United	(a) 5–2	
24 Jan	Reading	(a) 2–1	
31 Jan	Notts County	(a) 1–3	
7 Feb	Mansfield Town	(h) 3–1	
14 Feb	Swindon Town	(a) 2–1	
21 Feb	Brentford	(h) 1–2	
28 Feb	QPR	(h) 2–3	
7 Mar	Rochdale	(a) 0–0	
14 Mar	Doncaster Rovers	(a) 1–2	
21 Mar	Plymouth Argyle	(a) 0–2	
27 Mar	Bury	(h) 3–0	
11 Apr	Bournemouth	(h) 1–0	
13 Apr	Stockport County	(h) 1–0	
18 Apr	Colchester United	(a) 0–1	

| 25 Apr | Reading | (h) 1–0 |
| 29 Apr | Norwich City | (a) 1–2 |

Summary: League 23; FA Cup 3; Total 26.

LEICESTER CITY

1959–60

9 Sep	Blackpool	(h) 1–1	
12 Sep	Newcastle United	(a) 0–2	
17 Oct	Manchester City	(a) 2–3	
24 Oct	Arsenal	(h) 2–2	
31 Oct	Everton	(a) 1–6	
7 Nov	Sheffield Wednesday	(h) 2–0	
14 Nov	Nottingham Forest	(a) 0–1	
21 Nov	Fulham	(h) 0–1	
28 Nov	Bolton Wanderers	(a) 1–3	
5 Dec	Luton Town	(h) 3–3	
12 Dec	Wolves	(a) 3–0	
19 Dec	West Ham United	(h) 2–1	
26 Dec	Preston North End	(h) 2–2	
28 Dec	Preston North End	(a) 1–1	
2 Jan	Chelsea	(a) 2–2	
9 Jan	Wrexham	(a) 2–1	FA Cup
16 Jan	West Bromwich Albion	(h) 0–1	
23 Jan	Newcastle United	(a) 2–0	
30 Jan	Fulham	(h) 2–1	FA Cup
6 Feb	Birmingham City	(h) 1–3	
13 Feb	Tottenham Hotspur	(a) 2–1	
20 Feb	West Bromwich Albion	(h) 2–1	FA Cup
24 Feb	Manchester United	(h) 3–1	
27 Feb	Luton Town	(a) 0–2	
5 Mar	Manchester City	(h) 5–0	
12 Mar	Wolves	(h) 1–2	FA Cup

15 Mar	Arsenal	(a) 1–1
19 Mar	Wolves	(h) 2–1
2 Apr	Nottingham Forest	(h) 0–1
6 Apr	Sheffield Wednesday	(a) 2–2
9 Apr	Fulham	(a) 1–1
15 Apr	Burnley	(a) 0–1
16 Apr	Everton	(h) 3–3
18 Apr	Burnley	(h) 2–1
23 Apr	Blackburn Rovers	(a) 1–0
30 Apr	Bolton Wanderers	(h) 1–2

1960–61

20 Aug	Blackpool	(h) 1–1
24 Aug	Chelsea	(a) 3–1
27 Aug	Everton	(a) 1–3
31 Aug	Chelsea	(h) 1–3
3 Sep	Blackburn Rovers	(h) 2–4
7 Sep	Wolves	(a) 2–3
10 Sep	Manchester United	(a) 1–1
14 Sep	Wolves	(h) 2–0
17 Sep	Tottenham Hotspur	(h) 1–2
24 Sep	Newcastle United	(a) 3–1
1 Oct	Aston Villa	(a) 3–1
8 Oct	Arsenal	(h) 2–1
15 Oct	Manchester City	(a) 1–3
22 Oct	West Bromwich Albion	(h) 2–2
26 Oct	Rotherham United	(h) 1–2 League Cup
28 Oct	Cardiff City	(a) 1–2
4 Nov	Preston North End	(h) 5–2
12 Nov	Fulham	(a) 2–4
19 Nov	Sheffield Wednesday	(h) 2–1
26 Nov	Birmingham City	(a) 2–0
3 Dec	Nottingham Forest	(h) 1–1
10 Dec	Burnley	(a) 2–3

17 Dec	Blackpool	(a) 1–5	
24 Dec	Bolton Wanderers	(a) 0–2	
26 Dec	Bolton Wanderers	(h) 2–0	
31 Dec	Everton	(h) 4–1	
7 Jan	Oxford United	(h) 3–1	FA Cup
14 Jan	Blackburn Rovers	(a) 1–1	
21 Jan	Manchester United	(h) 6–0	
31 Jan	Bristol City	(h) 5–1	FA Cup
4 Feb	Tottenham Hotspur	(a) 3–2	
11 Feb	Newcastle United	(h) 5–3	
18 Feb	Birmingham City	(a) 1–1	FA Cup
22 Feb	Birmingham City	(h) 2–1	FA Cup (replay)
25 Feb	Arsenal	(a) 3–1	
4 Mar	Barnsley	(h) 0–0	FA Cup
8 Mar	Barnsley	(a) 2–1	FA Cup (replay) (aet)
18 Mar	Sheffield United	(n) 0–0	FA Cup semi-final
23 Mar	Sheffield United	(n) 0–0	FA Cup (replay) (aet)
25 Mar	Preston North End	(a) 0–0	
27 Mar	Sheffield United	(n) 2–0	FA Cup (2nd replay)
31 Mar	West Ham United	(a) 0–1	
1 Apr	Burnley	(h) 2–2	
3 Apr	West Ham United	(h) 5–1	
8 Apr	Sheffield Wednesday	(a) 2–2	
10 Apr	Cardiff City	(h) 3–0	
15 Apr	Fulham	(h) 1–2	
19 Apr	Aston Villa	(h) 3–1	
22 Apr	Nottingham Forest	(a) 2–2	
26 Apr	Manchester City	(h) 1–2	
29 Apr	Birmingham City	(h) 3–2	
6 May	Tottenham Hotspur	(n) 0–2	FA Cup final

1961–62

| 19 Aug | Manchester City | (a) 1–3 | |
| 23 Aug | Arsenal | (h) 0–1 | |

26 Aug	West Bromwich Albion	(h)	1–0	
29 Aug	Arsenal	(a)	4–4	
2 Sep	Birmingham City	(a)	5–1	
5 Sep	Burnley	(a)	0–2	
9 Sep	Everton	(h)	2–0	
13 Sep	Glenavon	(a)	4–1	ECWC (1)
16 Sep	Fulham	(a)	1–2	
20 Sep	Burnley	(h)	2–6	
23 Sep	Sheffield Wednesday	(h)	1–0	
27 Sep	Glenavon	(h)	3–1	ECWC (2)
30 Sep	West Ham United	(a)	1–4	
7 Oct	Sheffield United	(h)	4–1	
9 Oct	York City	(a)	1–2	League Cup
14 Oct	Chelsea	(a)	3–1	
21 Oct	Blackpool	(h)	0–2	
25 Oct	Atletico Madrid	(h)	1–1	ECWC (1)
28 Oct	Blackburn Rovers	(a)	1–2	
4 Nov	Wolves	(h)	3–0	
11 Nov	Manchester United	(a)	2–2	
15 Nov	Atletico Madrid	(a)	0–2	ECWC (2)
18 Nov	Cardiff City	(h)	3–0	
2 Dec	Aston Villa	(h)	0–2	
9 Dec	Nottingham Forest	(a)	0–0	
16 Dec	Manchester City	(h)	2–0	
23 Dec	West Bromwich Albion	(a)	0–2	
26 Dec	Ipswich Town	(a)	0–1	
10 Jan	Stoke City	(h)	1–1	FA Cup
13 Jan	Birmingham City	(h)	1–2	
15 Jan	Stoke City	(a)	2–5	FA Cup (replay)
20 Jan	Everton	(a)	2–3	
3 Feb	Fulham	(h)	4–1	
10 Feb	Sheffield Wednesday	(a)	2–1	
17 Feb	West Ham United	(h)	2–2	
24 Feb	Sheffield United	(a)	1–3	
10 Mar	Blackpool	(a)	1–2	

17 Mar	Blackburn Rovers	(h) 2–0
24 Mar	Wolves	(a) 1–1
28 Mar	Ipswich Town	(h) 0–2
4 Apr	Manchester United	(h) 4–3
7 Apr	Cardiff City	(a) 4–0
11 Apr	Chelsea	(h) 2–0
21 Apr	Aston Villa	(a) 3–8
23 Apr	Bolton Wanderers	(a) 0–1
24 Apr	Bolton Wanderers	(h) 1–1
28 Apr	Nottingham Forest	(h) 2–1
30 Apr	Tottenham Hotspur	(h) 2–3

1962–63

18 Aug	Fulham	(a) 1–2	
22 Aug	Sheffield Wednesday	(h) 3–3	
25 Aug	Nottingham Forest	(h) 2–1	
29 Aug	Sheffield Wednesday	(a) 3–0	
1 Sep	Bolton Wanderers	(h) 4–1	
4 Sep	Burnley	(a) 1–1	
8 Sep	Everton	(a) 2–3	
15 Sep	West Bromwich Albion	(h) 1–0	
19 Sep	Burnley	(h) 3–3	
22 Sep	Arsenal	(a) 1–1	
26 Sep	Charlton Athletic	(h) 4–4	League Cup
29 Sep	Birmingham City	(h) 3–0	
2 Oct	Charlton Athletic	(a) 1–2	League Cup (replay)
6 Oct	Ipswich Town	(a) 1–0	
13 Oct	Liverpool	(h) 3–0	
20 Oct	Blackburn Rovers	(a) 0–2	
27 Oct	Sheffield United	(h) 3–1	
3 Nov	Tottenham Hotspur	(a) 0–4	
10 Nov	West Ham United	(h) 2–0	
17 Nov	Manchester City	(a) 1–1	
24 Nov	Blackpool	(h) 0–0	

1 Dec	Wolves	(a)	3–1	
8 Dec	Aston Villa	(h)	3–3	
15 Dec	Fulham	(h)	2–3	
26 Dec	Leyton Orient	(h)	5–1	
8 Jan	Grimsby Town	(a)	3–1	FA Cup
30 Jan	Ipswich Town	(h)	3–1	FA Cup
9 Feb	Arsenal	(h)	2–0	
12 Feb	Everton	(h)	3–1	
19 Feb	Nottingham Forest	(a)	2–0	
23 Feb	Ipswich Town	(h)	3–0	
2 Mar	Liverpool	(a)	2–0	
9 Mar	Blackburn Rovers	(h)	2–0	
16 Mar	Leyton Orient	(a)	1–0	FA Cup
23 Mar	Tottenham Hotspur	(h)	2–2	
26 Mar	Sheffield United	(a)	0–0	
30 Mar	Norwich City	(a)	2–0	FA Cup
3 Apr	Leyton Orient	(a)	2–0	
8 Apr	Blackpool	(a)	1–1	
13 Apr	West Ham United	(a)	0–2	
15 Apr	Manchester United	(a)	2–2	
16 Apr	Manchester United	(h)	4–3	
20 Apr	Wolves	(h)	1–1	
27 Apr	Liverpool	(n)	1–0	FA Cup semi-final
4 May	West Bromwich Albion	(a)	1–2	
25 May	Manchester United	(n)	1–3	FA Cup final

1963–64

24 Aug	West Bromwich Albion	(a)	1–1
28 Aug	Birmingham City	(h)	3–0
31 Aug	Arsenal	(h)	7–2
4 Sep	Birmingham City	(a)	0–2
7 Sep	Stoke City	(a)	3–3
11 Sep	Sheffield Wednesday	(h)	2–0
14 Sep	Bolton Wanderers	(a)	0–0

21 Sep	Fulham	(h)	0–1	
25 Sep	Aldershot	(h)	2–0	League Cup
28 Sep	Manchester United	(a)	1–3	
2 Oct	Sheffield Wednesday	(a)	2–1	
5 Oct	Burnley	(h)	0–0	
8 Oct	Nottingham Forest	(a)	0–2	
14 Oct	Wolves	(h)	0–1	
16 Oct	Tranmere Rovers	(a)	2–1	League Cup
19 Oct	Tottenham Hotspur	(a)	1–1	
26 Oct	Blackburn Rovers	(h)	4–3	
2 Nov	Liverpool	(a)	1–0	
9 Nov	Sheffield United	(h)	0–1	
16 Nov	West Ham United	(a)	2–2	
23 Nov	Chelsea	(h)	2–4	
27 Nov	Gillingham	(h)	3–1	League Cup
30 Nov	Blackpool	(a)	3–3	
7 Dec	Aston Villa	(h)	0–0	
14 Dec	West Bromwich Albion	(h)	0–2	
21 Dec	Arsenal	(a)	1–0	
26 Dec	Everton	(h)	2–0	
28 Dec	Everton	(a)	3–0	
4 Jan	Leyton Orient	(h)	2–3	FA Cup
11 Jan	Stoke City	(h)	2–1	
15 Jan	Norwich City	(h)	2–1	League Cup (replay) (aet)
18 Jan	Bolton Wanderers	(h)	1–0	
1 Feb	Fulham	(a)	1–2	
5 Feb	West Ham United	(h)	4–3	League Cup semi-final (1)
8 Feb	Manchester United	(h)	3–2	
22 Feb	Wolves	(a)	2–1	
29 Feb	Nottingham Forest	(h)	1–1	
23 Mar	West Ham United	(a)	2–0	League Cup semi-final (2)
28 Mar	Liverpool	(h)	0–2	
30 Mar	Ipswich Town	(a)	1–1	
31 Mar	Ipswich Town	(h)	2–1	
6 Apr	Chelsea	(a)	0–1	

15 Apr	Stoke City	(a) 1–1 League Cup final (1)
18 Apr	Aston Villa	(a) 3–1
22 Apr	Stoke City	(h) 3–2 League Cup final (2)
25 Apr	Tottenham Hotspur	(h) 0–1

1964–65

22 Aug	Sunderland	(a) 3–3
26 Aug	Wolves	(h) 3–2
29 Aug	Manchester United	(h) 2–2
2 Sep	Wolves	(a) 1–1
5 Sep	Chelsea	(h) 1–1
9 Sep	Liverpool	(h) 2–0
12 Sep	Leeds United	(a) 2–3
19 Sep	Arsenal	(h) 2–3
23 Sep	Peterborough United	(h) 0–0 League Cup
26 Sep	Blackburn Rovers	(a) 1–3
30 Sep	West Bromwich Albion	(h) 4–2
5 Oct	Blackpool	(h) 3–2
8 Oct	Peterborough United	(a) 2–0 League Cup (replay)
10 Oct	Fulham	(a) 2–5
17 Oct	Nottingham Forest	(h) 3–2
31 Oct	Tottenham Hotspur	(h) 4–2
4 Nov	Crystal Palace	(h) 0–0 League Cup
7 Nov	Burnley	(a) 1–2
11 Nov	Crystal Palace	(a) 2–1 League Cup (replay)
14 Nov	Sheffield United	(h) 0–2
21 Nov	Everton	(a) 2–2
28 Nov	Birmingham City	(h) 4–4
1 Dec	Coventry City	(a) 8–1 League Cup
5 Dec	West Ham United	(a) 0–0
12 Dec	Sunderland	(h) 0–1
26 Dec	Sheffield Wednesday	(h) 2–2
28 Dec	Sheffield Wednesday	(a) 0–0
2 Jan	Chelsea	(a) 1–4

9 Jan	Blackburn Rovers	(h) 2–2	FA Cup
14 Jan	Blackburn Rovers	(a) 2–1	FA Cup (replay)
16 Jan	Leeds United	(h) 2–2	
20 Jan	Plymouth Argyle	(h) 3–2	League Cup semi-final (1)
23 Jan	Arsenal	(a) 3–4	
30 Jan	Plymouth Argyle	(h) 5–0	FA Cup
6 Feb	Blackburn Rovers	(h) 2–3	
10 Feb	Plymouth Argyle	(a) 1–0	League Cup semi-final (2)
13 Feb	Blackpool	(a) 1–1	
20 Feb	Middlesbrough	(a) 3–0	FA Cup
24 Feb	Fulham	(h) 5–1	
27 Feb	Nottingham Forest	(a) 1–2	
6 Mar	Liverpool	(h) 0–0	FA Cup
10 Mar	Liverpool	(a) 0–1	FA Cup (replay)
13 Mar	West Bromwich Albion	(a) 0–6	
15 Mar	Chelsea	(a) 2–3	League Cup final (1)
26 Mar	Sheffield United	(a) 2–0	
3 Apr	Everton	(h) 2–1	
5 Apr	Chelsea	(h) 0–0	League Cup final (2)
12 Apr	Manchester United	(a) 0–1	
17 Apr	West Ham United	(h) 1–0	
19 Apr	Aston Villa	(h) 1–1	
20 Apr	Aston Villa	(a) 0–1	
24 Apr	Tottenham Hotspur	(a) 6–2	

1965–66

22 Sep	Manchester City	(a) 1–3	League Cup
25 Sep	Sheffield United	(a) 2–2	
2 Oct	Northampton Town	(h) 1–1	
9 Oct	Stoke City	(a) 0–1	
16 Oct	Burnley	(h) 0–1	
23 Oct	Chelsea	(a) 2–0	
30 Oct	Arsenal	(h) 3–1	
6 Nov	Everton	(a) 2–1	

13 Nov	Manchester United	(h)	0–5
20 Nov	Newcastle United	(a)	5–1
27 Nov	West Bromwich Albion	(h)	2–1
4 Dec	Nottingham Forest	(a)	0–2
11 Dec	Sheffield Wednesday	(h)	4–1
18 Dec	Burnley	(a)	2–4
28 Dec	Fulham	(h)	5–0
1 Jan	Stoke City	(h)	1–0
8 Jan	Sheffield Wednesday	(a)	2–1
22 Jan	Aston Villa	(a)	2–1 FA Cup
29 Jan	Liverpool	(a)	0–1
5 Feb	Aston Villa	(h)	2–1
12 Feb	Birmingham City	(a)	2–1 FA Cup
19 Feb	Sunderland	(a)	3–0
5 Mar	Manchester City	(a)	2–2 FA Cup
9 Mar	Manchester City	(h)	0–1 FA Cup (replay)
12 Mar	Leeds United	(a)	2–3
19 Mar	Sheffield United	(h)	1–0
21 Mar	Chelsea	(h)	1–1
26 Mar	Northampton Town	(a)	2–2
8 Apr	Blackburn Rovers	(a)	2–0
9 Apr	Manchester United	(a)	2–1
12 Apr	Blackburn Rovers	(h)	2–0
16 Apr	Newcastle United	(h)	1–2
18 Apr	Fulham	(a)	4–0
22 Apr	West Bromwich Albion	(a)	1–5
30 Apr	Nottingham Forest	(h)	2–1
7 May	Arsenal	(a)	0–1
9 May	West Ham United	(h)	2–1

1966–67

20 Aug	Liverpool	(a)	2–3
22 Aug	Blackpool	(a)	1–1
27 Aug	West Ham United	(h)	5–4

30 Aug	Blackpool	(h) 3–0	
3 Sep	Sheffield Wednesday	(a) 1–1	
7 Sep	Chelsea	(a) 2–2	
10 Sep	Southampton	(h) 1–1	
14 Sep	Reading	(h) 5–0	League Cup
17 Sep	Sunderland	(a) 3–2	
24 Sep	Aston Villa	(h) 5–0	
1 Oct	Arsenal	(a) 4–2	
5 Oct	Lincoln City	(h) 5–0	
8 Oct	Nottingham Forest	(h) 3–0	
15 Oct	Burnley	(a) 2–5	
25 Oct	QPR	(a) 2–4	League Cup
29 Oct	Everton	(a) 0–2	
5 Nov	Burnley	(h) 5–1	
12 Nov	Leeds United	(a) 1–3	
19 Nov	West Bromwich Albion	(h) 2–1	
26 Nov	Sheffield United	(a) 1–0	
30 Nov	Manchester United	(h) 1–2	
3 Dec	Stoke City	(h) 4–2	
10 Dec	Tottenham Hotspur	(a) 0–2	
26 Dec	Fulham	(h) 0–2	
27 Dec	Fulham	(a) 2–4	
31 Dec	West Ham United	(a) 1–0	
7 Jan	Sheffield Wednesday	(h) 0–1	
14 Jan	Southampton	(a) 4–4	
18 Jan	Liverpool	(h) 2–1	
21 Jan	Sunderland	(h) 1–2	
28 Jan	Manchester City	(a) 1–2	FA Cup
4 Feb	Aston Villa	(a) 1–0	
11 Feb	Arsenal	(h) 2–1	
25 Feb	Nottingham Forest	(a) 0–1	
4 Mar	Everton	(h) 2–2	
18 Mar	Manchester United	(a) 2–5	
24 Mar	Manchester City	(a) 3–1	
25 Mar	Tottenham Hotspur	(h) 0–1	

28 Mar	Manchester City	(h) 3–1
1 Apr	Newcastle United	(a) 0–1
10 Apr	Leeds United	(h) 0–0

Summary: League 293; FA Cup 34; League Cup 25; European Cup-Winners Cup 4; Total 356.

STOKE CITY

1966–67

22 Apr	Chelsea	(a) 0–1
29 Apr	Leicester City	(h) 3–1
6 May	Arsenal	(a) 1–3
13 May	Manchester United	(a) 0–0

1967–68

19 Aug	Arsenal	(a) 0–2	
23 Aug	Sheffield United	(h) 1–1	
26 Aug	Manchester City	(h) 3–0	
29 Aug	Sheffield United	(a) 0–1	
2 Sep	Newcastle United	(a) 1–1	
6 Sep	Leicester City	(h) 3–2	
9 Sep	West Bromwich Albion	(h) 0–0	
13 Sep	Watford	(h) 2–0	League Cup
16 Sep	Chelsea	(a) 2–2	
23 Sep	Southampton	(h) 3–2	
30 Sep	Liverpool	(a) 1–2	
7 Oct	West Ham United	(a) 4–3	
11 Oct	Ipswich Town	(h) 2–1	League Cup
14 Oct	Burnley	(h) 0–2	
23 Oct	Sheffield Wednesday	(a) 1–1	
28 Oct	Tottenham Hotspur	(h) 2–1	
1 Nov	Sheffield Wednesday	(a) 0–0	League Cup

4 Nov	Manchester United	(a) 0–1	
18 Nov	Wolves	(a) 4–3	
25 Nov	Fulham	(h) 0–1	
2 Dec	Leeds United	(a) 0–2	
9 Dec	Everton	(h) 1–0	
13 Dec	Leeds United	(a) 0–2	League Cup
16 Dec	Arsenal	(h) 0–1	
23 Dec	Manchester City	(a) 2–4	
26 Dec	Nottingham Forest	(a) 0–3	
6 Jan	Newcastle United	(h) 2–1	
20 Jan	Chelsea	(h) 0–1	
27 Jan	Cardiff City	(h) 4–1	FA Cup
3 Feb	Southampton	(a) 2–1	
17 Feb	West Ham United	(h) 0–3	FA Cup
26 Feb	West Ham United	(h) 2–0	
13 Mar	West Bromwich Albion	(a) 0–3	
16 Mar	Sheffield Wednesday	(h) 0–1	
23 Mar	Tottenham Hotspur	(a) 0–3	
30 Mar	Manchester United	(h) 2–4	
6 Apr	Sunderland	(a) 1–3	
13 Apr	Wolves	(h) 0–2	
15 Apr	Coventry City	(a) 0–2	
16 Apr	Coventry City	(h) 3–3	
20 Apr	Burnley	(a) 0–4	
23 Apr	Leeds United	(h) 3–2	
1 May	Fulham	(a) 2–0	
11 May	Leicester City	(a) 0–0	
15 May	Liverpool	(h) 2–1	

1968–69

10 Aug	Sunderland	(h) 2–1
14 Aug	West Ham United	(h) 0–2
17 Aug	Leeds United	(a) 0–2
28 Sep	Ipswich Town	(a) 1–3

5 Oct	Nottingham Forest	(a) 3–3	
12 Oct	Burnley	(h) 1–3	
19 Oct	Everton	(a) 1–2	
26 Oct	Chelsea	(h) 2–0	
2 Nov	Tottenham Hotspur	(a) 1–1	
9 Nov	Coventry City	(h) 0–3	
16 Nov	West Bromwich Albion	(a) 1–2	
23 Nov	Manchester United	(h) 0–0	
30 Nov	Sheffield Wednesday	(a) 1–2	
7 Dec	Newcastle United	(h) 1–0	
14 Dec	Burnley	(a) 1–1	
21 Dec	Everton	(h) 0–0	
26 Dec	Nottingham Forest	(h) 3–1	
4 Jan	York City	(a) 2–0	FA Cup
11 Jan	Tottenham Hotspur	(h) 1–1	
25 Jan	Halifax Town	(h) 1–1	FA Cup
28 Jan	Halifax Town	(a) 3–0	FA Cup (replay)
1 Feb	West Bromwich Albion	(h) 1–1	
12 Feb	Chelsea	(a) 2–3	FA Cup
1 Mar	Sunderland	(a) 1–4	
15 Mar	Leicester City	(a) 0–0	
18 Mar	Coventry City	(a) 1–1	
22 Mar	Wolves	(h) 4–1	
24 Mar	Manchester United	(a) 1–1	
29 Mar	Manchester City	(a) 1–3	
5 Apr	Ipswich Town	(h) 2–1	
7 Apr	Liverpool	(a) 0–0	
8 Apr	West Ham United	(a) 0–0	
12 Apr	QPR	(a) 1–2	
19 Apr	Arsenal	(h) 1–3	
22 Apr	Sheffield Wednesday	(h) 1–1	

1969–70

9 Aug	Wolves	(a) 1–3	

12 Aug	Nottingham Forest	(a) 0–0	
16 Aug	West Ham United	(h) 2–1	
20 Aug	Nottingham Forest	(h) 1–1	
23 Aug	Derby County	(a) 0–0	
27 Aug	Coventry City	(h) 2–0	
30 Aug	Southampton	(h) 2–1	
3 Sep	Burnley	(h) 0–2	League Cup
6 Sep	Crystal Palace	(a) 1–3	
13 Sep	Sunderland	(h) 4–2	
17 Sep	West Bromwich Albion	(a) 3–1	
20 Sep	Liverpool	(a) 1–3	
27 Sep	Manchester City	(h) 2–0	
4 Oct	Leeds United	(a) 1–2	
6 Oct	West Ham United	(a) 3–3	
11 Oct	Arsenal	(h) 0–0	
15 Nov	Sheffield Wednesday	(a) 2–0	
22 Nov	Ipswich Town	(h) 3–3	
6 Dec	Newcastle United	(h) 0–1	
13 Dec	Sunderland	(a) 3–0	
20 Dec	Crystal Palace	(h) 1–0	
26 Dec	Derby County	(h) 1–0	
27 Dec	Southampton	(a) 0–0	
3 Jan	Oxford United	(a) 0–0	FA Cup
7 Jan	Oxford United	(h) 3–2	FA Cup (replay)
10 Jan	Liverpool	(h) 0–2	
17 Jan	Manchester City	(a) 1–0	
24 Jan	Watford	(a) 0–1	FA Cup
31 Jan	Leeds United	(h) 1–1	
7 Feb	Arsenal	(a) 0–0	
14 Feb	Wolves	(h) 1–1	
21 Feb	Tottenham Hotspur	(a) 0–1	
28 Feb	Manchester United	(h) 2–2	
7 Mar	Ipswich Town	(a) 1–1	
17 Mar	Chelsea	(a) 0–1	
20 Mar	Newcastle United	(a) 1–3	

27 Mar	Burnley	(a)	1–1
28 Mar	Sheffield Wednesday	(h)	2–1
30 Mar	Everton	(h)	0–1
4 Apr	Coventry City	(a)	3–0
13 Apr	Chelsea	(h)	2–1
15 Apr	West Bromwich Albion	(h)	3–2

1970–71

15 Aug	Ipswich Town	(h)	0–0	
19 Aug	Newcastle United	(h)	3–0	
22 Aug	Derby County	(a)	0–2	
26 Aug	West Bromwich Albion	(a)	2–5	
29 Aug	Crystal Palace	(h)	0–0	
2 Sep	Nottingham Forest	(h)	0–0	
5 Sep	Wolves	(a)	1–1	
9 Sep	Millwall	(h)	0–0	League Cup
12 Sep	Leeds United	(h)	3–0	
19 Sep	Manchester City	(a)	1–4	
3 Oct	Blackpool	(a)	1–1	
10 Oct	West Ham United	(h)	2–1	
17 Oct	Ipswich Town	(a)	0–2	
24 Oct	Tottenham Hotspur	(a)	0–3	
31 Oct	Huddersfield Town	(h)	3–1	
7 Nov	Manchester United	(a)	2–2	
14 Nov	Everton	(h)	1–1	
18 Nov	Leeds United	(a)	1–4	
21 Nov	Chelsea	(a)	1–2	
28 Nov	Southampton	(h)	0–0	
5 Dec	Coventry City	(a)	0–1	
12 Dec	Burnley	(h)	0–0	
19 Dec	Derby County	(h)	1–0	
26 Dec	Liverpool	(a)	0–0	
2 Jan	Millwall	(h)	2–1	FA Cup
9 Jan	Newcastle United	(a)	2–0	

16 Jan	West Bromwich Albion	(h) 2–0	
23 Jan	Huddersfield Town	(h) 3–3	FA Cup
26 Jan	Huddersfield Town	(a) 0–0	FA Cup (replay) (aet)
30 Jan	Southampton	(a) 1–2	
8 Feb	Huddersfield Town	(n) 1–0	FA Cup (2nd replay)
13 Feb	Ipswich Town	(h) 0–0	FA Cup
16 Feb	Ipswich Town	(a) 1–0	FA Cup (replay)
20 Feb	Chelsea	(h) 1–2	
23 Feb	Burnley	(a) 1–1	
27 Feb	Huddersfield Town	(a) 1–0	
6 Mar	Hull City	(a) 3–2	FA Cup
13 Mar	Everton	(a) 0–2	
20 Mar	Manchester United	(h) 1–2	
27 Mar	Arsenal	(n) 2–2	FA Cup semi-final
31 Mar	Arsenal	(n) 0–2	FA Cup (replay)
4 Apr	Crystal Palace	(a) 2–3	
7 Apr	Wolves	(h) 1–0	
10 Apr	Liverpool	(h) 0–1	
13 Apr	Blackpool	(h) 1–1	
17 Apr	West Ham United	(a) 0–1	
24 Apr	Manchester City	(h) 2–0	
27 Apr	Nottingham Forest	(a) 0–0	
1 May	Arsenal	(a) 0–1	
5 May	Tottenham Hotspur	(h) 0–1	
7 May	Everton	(n) 3–2	FA Cup 3rd place match

1971–72

14 Aug	Coventry City	(a) 1–1
17 Aug	Southampton	(a) 1–3
21 Aug	Crystal Palace	(h) 3–1
25 Aug	Leicester City	(h) 3–1
28 Aug	Arsenal	(a) 1–0
31 Aug	Nottingham Forest	(a) 0–0
4 Sep	Wolves	(h) 0–1

11 Sep	Derby County	(a)	0–4	
18 Sep	Huddersfield Town	(h)	1–0	
26 Sep	West Ham United	(a)	1–2	
2 Oct	Liverpool	(h)	0–0	
6 Oct	Oxford United	(a)	1–1	League Cup
9 Oct	Sheffield United	(a)	3–2	
16 Oct	Coventry City	(h)	1–0	
18 Oct	Oxford United	(h)	2–0	League Cup (replay)
23 Oct	Ipswich Town	(a)	1–2	
26 Oct	Manchester United	(a)	1–1	League Cup
30 Oct	Tottenham Hotspur	(h)	2–0	
6 Nov	West Bromwich Albion	(a)	1–0	
8 Nov	Manchester United	(h)	0–0	League Cup (replay) (aet)
13 Nov	Chelsea	(h)	0–1	
15 Nov	Manchester United	(h)	2–1	League Cup (2nd replay)
20 Nov	Leeds United	(a)	0–1	
23 Nov	Bristol Rovers	(a)	4–2	League Cup
27 Nov	Newcastle United	(h)	3–3	
4 Dec	Everton	(a)	0–0	
8 Dec	West Ham United	(h)	1–2	League Cup semi-final (1)
11 Dec	Manchester United	(h)	1–1	
15 Dec	West Ham United	(a)	1–0	League Cup semi-final (2)
18 Dec	Wolves	(a)	0–2	
27 Dec	Manchester City	(h)	1–3	
1 Jan	Huddersfield Town	(a)	0–0	
5 Jan	West Ham United	(n)	0–0	League Cup (replay)
8 Jan	Arsenal	(h)	0–0	
15 Jan	Chesterfield	(h)	2–1	FA Cup
22 Jan	Southampton	(h)	3–1	
26 Jan	West Ham United	(n)	3–2	League Cup (2nd replay)
29 Jan	Leicester City	(a)	1–2	
5 Feb	Tranmere Rovers	(a)	2–2	FA Cup
9 Feb	Tranmere Rovers	(h)	2–0	FA Cup (replay)
12 Feb	Ipswich Town	(h)	3–3	
19 Feb	Tottenham Hotspur	(a)	0–2	

26 Feb	Hull City	(h) 4–1	FA Cup
3 Mar	Chelsea	(n) 2–1	League Cup final
18 Mar	Manchester United	(a) 1–1	FA Cup
22 Mar	Manchester United	(h) 2–1	FA Cup (replay) (aet)
25 Mar	Derby County	(h) 1–1	
28 Mar	Liverpool	(a) 1–2	
1 Apr	Manchester City	(a) 2–1	
4 Apr	West Ham United	(h) 0–0	
8 Apr	Leeds United	(h) 3–0	
15 Apr	Arsenal	(n) 1–1	FA Cup semi-final
19 Apr	Arsenal	(n) 1–2	FA Cup (replay)
22 Apr	Everton	(h) 1–1	
5 May	West Bromwich Albion	(h) 1–1	
8 May	Newcastle United	(a) 0–0	

1972–73

26 Aug	Everton	(h) 1–1	
30 Aug	Norwich City	(a) 0–2	
2 Sep	Coventry City	(a) 1–2	
6 Sep	Sunderland	(h) 3–0	League Cup
9 Sep	Leeds United	(h) 2–2	
13 Sep	Kaiserslautern	(h) 3–1	UEFA Cup
16 Sep	Ipswich Town	(a) 0–2	
3 Oct	Ipswich Town	(a) 2–1	League Cup
7 Oct	Tottenham Hotspur	(a) 3–4	
14 Oct	Newcastle United	(h) 2–0	
21 Oct	Liverpool	(a) 1–2	

Summary: League 194; FA Cup 27; League Cup 19; UEFA Cup 1; other sponsored cup competitions (not shown) 5; Total 246.

International Matches

1963

6 Apr	Scotland	Wembley	1–2
8 May	Brazil	Wembley	1–1
20 May	Czechoslovakia	Bratislava	4–2
20 June	East Germany	Leipzig	2–1
12 Oct	Wales	Cardiff	4–0
23 Oct	Rest of the World	Wembley	2–1
20 Nov	Northern Ireland	Wembley	8–3

1964

11 Apr	Scotland	Glasgow	0–1
6 May	Uruguay	Wembley	2–1
17 May	Portugal	Lisbon	4–3
27 May	USA	New York	10–0
4 June	Portugal	São Paulo	1–1
6 June	Argentina	Rio de Janeiro	0–1
3 Oct	Northern Ireland	Belfast	4–3

1965

10 Apr	Scotland	Wembley	2–2
5 May	Hungary	Wembley	1–0
9 May	Yugoslavia	Belgrade	1–1
12 May	West Germany	Nuremberg	1–0
16 May	Sweden	Gothenburg	2–1
10 Nov	Northern Ireland	Wembley	2–1
8 Dec	Spain	Madrid	2–0

1966

5 Jan	Poland	Liverpool	1–1
23 Feb	West Germany	Wembley	1–0
2 Apr	Scotland	Glasgow	4–3
4 May	Yugoslavia	Wembley	2–0
26 June	Finland	Helsinki	3–0
5 July	Poland	Chorzow	1–0
11 July	Uruguay (WC)	Wembley	0–0
16 July	Mexico (WC)	Wembley	2–0
20 July	France (WC)	Wembley	2–0
23 July	Argentina (WC)	Wembley	1–0
26 July	Portugal (WC)	Wembley	2–1
30 July	West Germany (WCF)	Wembley	4–2 (aet)
22 Oct	Northern Ireland (ECQ)	Belfast	2–0
2 Nov	Czechoslovakia	Wembley	0–0
16 Nov	Wales (ECQ)	Wembley	5–1

1967

15 Apr	Scotland (ECQ)	Wembley	2–3
21 Oct	Wales (ECQ)	Cardiff	3–0
22 Nov	Northern Ireland (ECQ)	Wembley	2–0
6 Dec	USSR	Wembley	2–2

1968

24 Feb	Scotland (ECQ)	Glasgow	1–1
3 Apr	Spain (ECQ)	Wembley	1–0
1 June	West Germany	Hanover	0–1
5 June	Yugoslavia (ECF)	Florence	0–1
8 June	USSR (ECF)	Rome	2–0
6 Nov	Romania	Bucharest	0–0

1969

15 Jan	Romania	Wembley	1–1
12 Mar	France	Wembley	5–0
3 May	Northern Ireland	Belfast	3–1
10 May	Scotland	Wembley	4–1
8 June	Uruguay	Montevideo	2–1
12 June	Brazil	Rio de Janeiro	1–2

1970

14 Jan	Holland	Wembley	0–0
25 Feb	Belgium	Brussels	3–1
18 Apr	Wales	Cardiff	1–1
21 Apr	Northern Ireland	Wembley	3–1
25 Apr	Scotland	Glasgow	0–0
20 May	Colombia	Bogotá	4–0
24 May	Ecuador	Quito	2–0
2 June	Romania (WC)	Guadalajara	1–0
7 June	Brazil (WC)	Guadalajara	0–1
11 June	Czechoslovakia (WC)	Guadalajara	1–0

1971

3 Feb	Malta (ECQ)	Valletta	1–0
21 Apr	Greece (ECQ)	Wembley	3–0
12 May	Malta (ECQ)	Wembley	5–0
15 May	Northern Ireland	Belfast	1–0
22 May	Scotland	Wembley	3–1
13 Oct	Switzerland (ECQ)	Basle	3–2
1 Dec	Greece (ECQ)	Athens	2–0

1972

29 Apr	West Germany (ECQ)	Wembley	1–3
13 May	West Germany (ECQ)	Berlin	0–0
20 May	Wales	Cardiff	3–0
27 May	Scotland	Glasgow	1–0

Total caps: 73.

Overall

	League	FA Cup	League Cup	Other	Total
Chesterfield	23	3			26
Leicester City	293	34	25	4	356
Stoke City	194	27	19	6	246
England					73
England Under-23s					2
TOTAL	510	64	44	10	703

Miscellaneous Statistics

Kept 162 clean sheets in 628 first-class matches in English domestic football.

Kept 35 clean sheets in 73 appearances for England and was on the losing side on only nine occasions.

Conceded 57 goals in 73 matches for England – an average of 0.78 per game.

Played in 23 consecutive matches for England between 1964 and 1967 without defeat.

Honours

OBE 1970
World Cup Winner 1966
League Cup Winner 1964, 1972
FA Cup runner-up 1961, 1963
League Cup runner-up 1965
English Football Writers' Association Player of the Year 1972
FIFA Goalkeeper of the Year 1966, 1967, 1968, 1969, 1970, 1971
NASL Goalkeeper of the Year 1977
Daily Express Sportsman of the Year 1971, 1972

Index

He just wanted a decent book to read ...

Not too much to ask, is it? It was in 1935 when Allen Lane, Managing Director of Bodley Head Publishers, stood on a platform at Exeter railway station looking for something good to read on his journey back to London. His choice was limited to popular magazines and poor-quality paperbacks – the same choice faced every day by the vast majority of readers, few of whom could afford hardbacks. Lane's disappointment and subsequent anger at the range of books generally available led him to found a company – and change the world.

'We believed in the existence in this country of a vast reading public for intelligent books at a low price, and staked everything on it'
Sir Allen Lane, 1902–1970, founder of Penguin Books

The quality paperback had arrived – and not just in bookshops. Lane was adamant that his Penguins should appear in chain stores and tobacconists, and should cost no more than a packet of cigarettes.

Reading habits (and cigarette prices) have changed since 1935, but Penguin still believes in publishing the best books for everybody to enjoy. We still believe that good design costs no more than bad design, and we still believe that quality books published passionately and responsibly make the world a better place.

So wherever you see the little bird – whether it's on a piece of prize-winning literary fiction or a celebrity autobiography, political tour de force or historical masterpiece, a serial-killer thriller, reference book, world classic or a piece of pure escapism – you can bet that it represents the very best that the genre has to offer.

Whatever you like to read – trust Penguin.